YEMEN

Revolution, Civil War and Unification

Uzi Rabi

I.B. TAURIS
LONDON · NEW YORK

Published in 2015 by I.B.Tauris & Co Ltd
6 Salem Road, London W2 4BU
175 Fifth Avenue, New York NY 10010
www.ibtauris.com

Distributed in the United States and Canada
Exclusively by Palgrave Macmillan
175 Fifth Avenue, New York NY 10010

References to websites were correct at the time of writing.

Library of Modern Middle East Studies 160

ISBN 978 1 78076 946 2
eISBN 978 0 85773 771 7

A full CIP record for this book is available from the British Library
A full CIP record for this book is available from the Library of Congress

Library of Congress catalog card: available

Typeset by Newgen Publishers, Chennai
Printed and bound by CPI Group (UK) Ltd, Croydon, CR0 4YY

MIX
Paper from responsible sources
FSC www.fsc.org FSC® C013604

Uzi Rabi is Director of the Moshe Dayan Center for Middle Eastern Studies at Tel Aviv University. He is the author of *The Emergence of States in a Tribal Society: Oman Under Sa'id bin Taymur, 1932–1970* (2006), and the editor of *International Intervention in Local Conflicts: Crisis Management and Conflict Resolution Since the Cold War* (I.B.Tauris, 2010).

CONTENTS

List of Maps viii
Acknowledgements ix
Abbreviations x
A Note on Transliteration xi
Preface xii

1. **Ecological, Cultural and Historical Structures** 1
   Topography, Geography and Socio-Demographic Features 1
   Religious Characteristics 4
   Tribal Structures 7
   External Powers 9
      The Ottoman Presence 9
      The British Occupation 11
   The Imamate of Yemen in the Twentieth Century 13
   The Transitory Period: The Road to Revolution, 1948–1962 26
   British Policy in the South: Federalism, Over-Involvement and War in Yemen 29

2. **The Age of Revolutions: 1962–1978** 41
   Revolution in the North: from Imamate to Republic 41

Sallal's Republic, 1962–1967 50
The Path to Revolution in the South:
The End of the British Era 59
The Two Yemens: the Republican North and the
Socialist South 66
North Yemen under the Rule of al-Iryani, al-Hamdi
and al-Ghashmi, A Transition Period: 1970–1978 67
Al-Iryani's Presidency: September 1971–June 1974 69
Ibrahim al-Hamdi's Presidency: 1974–1977 72
Al-Ghashmi's Presidency: October 1977–April 1978 80
Socialism in South Yemen: 1970–1978 82
Salim Rubay' 'Ali's Presidency: June 1969–June 1978 84
The Two Yemens: A Futile Dialogue and
Civil War, 1970–1978 87
The Unification Initiative of June 1972 and the
Causes of its Failure 89
Education and Popular Culture in the 1970s 92

3. The Decline of the Socialist and Arab Nationalist Revolutions: 1978–1990 97

Civil War: February 1979 98
The Inter-Elitist Rivalries within Aden: 1986 103
'Ali 'Abdallah Salih: The Victorious Leader 107
The Ascendance of the Islamists in North Yemen 111

4. United Yemen 115

The Path to Unification 115
The Act of Unification 118
Civil War Returns: May 1994 128
Unification through Coercion 130

5. Heading Toward a "Failed State" 136

Tribe and State: Between Confrontation and
Accommodation 136
The Socio-Economic Crisis 139
The Free South (*al-Janub al-Hurr*) 141
The Shi'i revolt in Sa'da 154
The Challenge of Radical Islam: al-Qa'ida 172

6. The Arab Spring: New Challenges Exacerbate the Old **193**
The Early Days 194
The March 18 Turning Point 195
The Gulf Initiative 198
The Violence Escalates 199
The Retreat of Central Authority 202
June 3, 2011 203

Conclusion **204**

Notes 209
Bibliography 251
Index 268

LIST OF MAPS

Map of Yemen	3
Distribution of Ethnoreligious Groups and Key Tribal Areas	8
Yemen's Administrative Divisions	12
The Power Centres in Yemen	191

ACKNOWLEDGEMENTS

This book has been completed with deep sorrow, with the passing of my dear colleague, Joseph Kostiner. Joseph Kostiner, one of the world's leading scholars in his field of expertise, was a central pillar in teaching and research on the Gulf and the Arabian Peninsula. He was a true gentleman, a very sensitive man and an admirable person, loved by his colleagues and students alike. I am indebted to him for having led me through the dynamics of states and societies in the Arabian Peninsula and the Persian Gulf. His wise comments and useful insights were instrumental to the completion of this book. Needless to say, any errors that remain are my own.

I also valued my conversations on Yemen with my colleagues from the Gulf and Yemen. I honor their requests for anonymity but wish to thank them for providing me their insights and for their generosity and helping me to understand the complex social and historical structures of Yemen.

Thanks are due to Rachel Kanz for her fine translation from the Hebrew. Special thanks go to my research assistants Chelsi Mueller, Brian Albert and Jordan Sokolic, who provided editorial assistance. Last but certainly not least, I owe my gratitude to my wife, Aviva and to our daughter and son, Gali and Guy, who have supported and inspired me throughout the research and writing of this book.

ABBREVIATIONS

AQAP	Al-Qa'ida in the Arabian Peninsula
ATUC	Aden Trade Union Congress
FLOSY	Front for the Liberation of Occupied Southern Yemen
GCC	Gulf Cooperation Council
GPC	General People's Congress
JMP	Joint Meeting Parties
NDF	National Democratic Front
NLF	National Liberation Front
SNACC	Supreme National Anti-Corruption Committee
YSP	The Yemeni Socialist Party

A NOTE ON TRANSLITERATION

Diacritical marks for long vowels have been left out; the *ta marbuta* is not shown; the *shadda* is indicated by doubling the consonant containing it; both the *dal* and the *dhad* are transliterated with a 'd' and the *dhal* is transliterated with a 'dh'. I also used the common English of the names of known individuals and countries, as well as words that have gained common usage in English. For example, 'Gamal 'Abd al-Nasser' instead of 'Nasir', 'Sanaa' instead of 'San'a' and *mujahideen* instead of *mujahidin.* The plural of transliterated terms is formed with an '-s'.

PREFACE

Although Yemen's history is unique, it has been relegated to the sidelines of research on the modern history of the Arab Middle East. Yemen, located in the south-western corner of the Arabian Peninsula, has been far from the purview of regional and international attention. The aim of this book is to expose the reader to the history of Yemen in the modern era and provide some insights into the dynamics of state and society in Yemen throughout the twentieth century.

In its glorious past, Yemen served as a crossroads for the great civilizations in Egypt, Mesopotamia, East Africa, the Indian sub continent and the Far East. Valuable goods were exported from Yemen's south, in particular aromatics such as frankincense and myrrh. This civilization reached its zenith under the kingdoms of Saba and Himyar, which developed in the territorial region of *Yaman*, a region smaller than that of modern Yemen.[1] The incense trade route served as the basis for the emergence of trade in the kingdoms of Saba and Himyar. These kingdoms played a pivotal role as transition points in the trade routes between the Middle East and India. Through their control over the trade route for valuable goods, these kingdoms flourished, and the entire region was known as Arabia Felix (*al-'Arabiyya al-Sa'ida*) in ancient times. The disappearance of these trade kingdoms marked the decline of *Yaman*'s greatness. The impressive archaeological remnants that were left behind testify to the story of a glorious civilization.

With the emergence of Islam, Yemen became an inseparable part of the Muslim world. Beginning in the tenth century, the territory became detached from the large Islamic empires and was ruled by various dynasties. In the early sixteenth century, Yemen fell to foreign occupiers and domination, beginning with the Dutch and Portuguese and followed by the Ottomans. Later in the nineteenth century, Yemen's territory was further divided by the Ottomans and the British.

Throughout history, Yemen was rarely ruled as a single entity. The topography of the country rendered this a complicated mission. The scanty base of resources and limited economic surpluses made the establishment of strong and efficient central rule a formidable task. Moreover, the society's religious characteristics – a Shi'i Zaydi population in the northern highlands and Sunni Shafi'i populations in the south and south-west – complicated the development of an ideological and legitimate basis from which to rule the entire country. Above all, Yemen remained a predominantly tribal society, which is perhaps one of the country's most influential legacies.

Yemen witnessed two Ottoman occupations. The Ottomans ruled the Arabic-speaking lands of the Middle East, including Yemen, beginning in the second decade of the sixteenth century. The first period of Ottoman rule in Yemen lasted from 1539 until 1636. The Ottomans returned in 1849, this time in the north of the country. Just ten years earlier the British had established a foothold in the south of the country, turning Aden into their port and colony. Throughout the nineteenth century, the British and the Ottomans divided the country into two spheres of influence.

With the waning of Ottoman power, the Zaydi Imamate began to entrench its control in the north of the country, and under the leadership of the Hamid al-Din dynasty, it re-staked its claim over Yemen. Imam Yahya bin Husayn bin Muhammad (r. 1905–1948) demonstrated an impressive ability to unite the country under his rule, whereas geographical conditions had caused many of his predecessors to fail. Though in his career Yahya would bring large areas of north Yemen under his control, the south remained under British control despite his moral claim to rule all of Yemen. Throughout his reign, Yahya zealously maintained divisive policies and administered his state according to tribal patterns, but he nevertheless ensured his state's relative stability. This strategy ran its course during the rule of his son Ahmad, as Yemen was exposed to the winds of change from the outside world and the forces of reform from within.

The revolutionary winds that were awash in the middle of the twentieth century in the Middle East did not spare Yemen. Yahya and Ahmad's Imamate could not withstand this pressure and it eventually collapsed in 1962. Henceforth, Yemen was a battleground for various revolutionary forces. In the turbulence that beset the country, Yemen's pre-existing division into Ottoman and British spheres of influence continued as two states with two different orientations – republican North Yemen (formerly known as the Yemeni Arab Republic) and socialist South Yemen (formerly known as the People's Democratic Republic of Yemen). This book tells the story of twentieth-century Yemen – a state that went through a transition from a traditional society to a melting-pot of revolutions accompanied by foreign intervention. To a large extent, Yemen was a microcosm of the political and ideological currents of the twentieth-century Middle East.

Toward the end of the century, the two Yemens were reunited in the framework of the "Republic of Yemen". The idea of unification, which was promoted intermittently by Yemen's leaders throughout its history, was in line with the millennium-old ideal of one united Yemeni nation, but it did not herald a calm chapter in Yemen's story.[2]

The first chapter is introductory and presents the ecological, cultural and historical structures of the country. Geographical and topographical diversity had a compelling impact on the development of Yemen and its cultural and societal patterns. The chapter highlights the unique characteristics of the country and the benchmarks in its past: the centrality of tribes in the political, religious and social mosaic of Yemen; ideological and geographical aspects of the division between the Zaydiyya and Shafi'iyya, the two largest religious groups in Yemen; and the involvement of foreign powers in Yemen's affairs and its repercussions on the process of the state's development in the twentieth century.

This chapter discusses the Imamate, its attributes and its landmark events in the first half of the twentieth century. Coercion, cultivation of religious affinity, hostage-taking and bribery were all methods of control used by Imam Yahya to ensure the Imamate's survival. The Imamate's direct authority was most discernible amongst the settled tribes of Sanaa and its environs. In the more distant regions, the imam enjoyed only nominal control, and in most cases, he arrived at an understanding with the tribesmen and did not infringe upon their autonomy. Finally, Yemen was thrust into a struggle between tradition and modernization, and at the end of a period of consecutive upheavals, the Imamate eventually collapsed under the pressure of the 1962 revolution. Imam Yahya (r. 1905–1948), his son Ahmad bin Yahya (r. 1948–1962) and Ahmad's son Mansur Muhammad al-Badr were the last imams in Yemen. Mansur would only rule for one week between the death of Ahmad and the September 26 coup in 1962. The end of their rule signified the demise of the Imamate – a time-honoured institution in Yemen's history.

Chapter Two, focuses on the revolutionary dynamics that swept the country throughout the 1960s. The states of the Arabian Peninsula are traditional monarchical regimes whose survival, many claim, is owed to the unique characteristics of the peninsula: tribalism and conservative Islam. However, the Yemeni Imamate – no less tribal than its neighbours and no less Islamic or conservative – did not survive.

During the 1960s, the traces of the Zaydi Imamate were eliminated, giving way to revolutionary regimes. Gamal 'Abd al-Nasser's banner of Arab unity was rife with appealing messages for Yemeni society. On one hand, there was the struggle against the "reactionary" regime of the tyrannical Imamate in the north; on the other, an uncompromising battle against British colonialism in the south. The ousting of the imam in the 1962 Revolution paved the way for the establishment of the first republic in North Yemen. In its first five years of existence (1962–1967), this republic experienced a bloody civil war. Egyptian influence, Saudi involvement and the intense struggle between the Royalists and the Republicans turned North Yemen into an additional arena of the "Arab Cold War". The dimensions of the conflict broadened even further: the Soviet Union aligned itself with Egypt and the United States and Britain backed the Saudis. Hence, at its peak, the struggle also represented the competition between the Soviet Union and the socialist bloc, and the United States and its allies. Simultaneously, in the south of the country, events set the stage for a new variety of revolution. The defeat of Britain and its allies in November 1967 paved the way for the formation of an entirely different regime in South Yemen: the only declared Marxist regime in the Arab world, the Popular Republic of South Yemen.

The chapter continues by analysing the Yemeni political duality that ensued. The evacuation of Egyptian and British forces from Yemen left two states with two different orientations: the republican North Yemen and the socialist South Yemen. It seemed as though unification was an attainable goal, because the two forces that opposed the revolution and also put the brakes on Yemen's unification – the tyrannical Imamate in the North and British colonialism in the South – were eliminated. However, the unification did not occur as easily as many Yemenis thought it would. Intense ideological differences divided the leaderships in the North and the South, and each of them toiled to consolidate its power and to plan its future path. The two Yemens teetered on the brink of conflict; for the next 20 years the two treated each other suspiciously, and in the words of a local political sociologist, "North Yemen turned into an internal problem for South Yemen and vice versa".[3]

Chapter Three, describes how in both North and South Yemen, the needs of the state collided with the ideologies of their respective revolutions. In North Yemen, the grandiose vision of the creation of a new Arab state on the ruins of the one-time tribal, patrimonial system lost appeal and the regime re-introduced dimensions of "family rule" and a patriarchal system of governance. In the South, the Yemeni Socialist Party (YSP) was established and assumed a stronger doctrinal orientation than ever before. Internal strife soon ensued amongst the leadership in South Yemen; the pragmatists sought to modify the revolutionary example for the needs of the state, and the dogmatists sought to cling to the principles of the revolution. The bloody civil war that occurred in January 1986 brought South Yemen close to collapse.

The chapter goes on to explain how at this stage in the crisis, unification of the two Yemens, a long-standing vision, came to fruition just when no one expected it. Unification occurred in May 1990. The chapter takes into account economic and political, both regional and international, factors while offering a multifaceted explanation for the unification of Yemen.

Chapter Four, elucidates the root problems that accompanied unification. The unification between the two Yemens seemed most natural and, in contrast to other unifications that the Arab world witnessed, Yemenis in North and South Yemen had a lot in common, and therefore the unification abounded with hope for future prosperity. However, the cautious optimism soon gave way to more gloomy assessments, and the fragility of the unification agreement was exposed.

The chapter inquires into the governing mechanism of the unified state in order to better explain how the practice of power-sharing became ineffective. The explanation for the failure of unification draws upon the historical experience of both Yemens. The two different types of colonial rule and different socio-religious attributes that distinguished the North from the South indicated that the disparity was so extensive that it was difficult to bridge the gaps between their world views and political aspirations. The renewal of bloodshed in 1994 put an end to this duality and reopened the old frictions that Yemen had experienced throughout the twentieth century.

Chapter Five, is an outline of a series of challenges that faced Yemen in the first decade of the twenty-first century. A faltering economy, a complicated constellation of relations between the state and the tribes, the ascendance of radical Islamic movements such as al-Qa'ida in the Arabian Peninsula, a Shi'i rebellion in the north and a secessionist movement in the south all threatened the stability of the united state of Yemen and posed fundamental questions regarding the state's ability to survive.

Chapter Six, closes the book with an insight into the so-called "Arab Spring" uprisings which reached Yemen in January 2011 and the events that led to 'Ali 'Abdallah Salih's resignation in February 2012. Taking into account the history of Yemen as described in the foregoing chapters of the book, Chapter Six explains why the "Arab Spring" was in fact an escalation of the already existing tensions in Yemen. At the same time, the chapter clarifies why the uprising served as the decisive, game-changing phenomenon in Yemeni politics that turned former allies of Salih into overt rivals and led to his ouster. Subsequently, ensuing chaos led to a situation in which large swathes of Yemen fell under the de facto control of various non-government entities. Moreover, it caused a situation in which al-Qaʿida was increasingly able to operate from Yemeni territory. This final chapter contents that Yemen is more of a failed state, as opposed to a "failing" or "fragile" state, than foreign officials recognize. It remains to be seen whether the post-Salih government of Yemen will be able to reverse the erosion of state authority.

CHAPTER 1

ECOLOGICAL, CULTURAL AND HISTORICAL STRUCTURES

Topography, Geography and Socio-Demographic Features

The borders of most Middle Eastern states were drawn by the colonial powers, Britain and France, after the First World War, in the framework of the Mandate system. From this perspective, Yemen is unique. Since the dawn of Islam, Yemen has been a distinct geographical entity.[1] Yemen's geographical and topographical diversity influenced the development of the country's settlement patterns, social structures and forms of government. Therefore, it is imperative to understand Yemen's natural, ecological and topographical features.

Pre-Islamic Arabic literature uses the term "*Yaman*" to refer to the territory that extends across the coast of the Indian Ocean and the Red Sea and through the heartland of the Arabian Peninsula.[2] This pre-Islamic definition of Yemen's territory is not identical to the territory of the modern state of Yemen.[3] Today's Yemen is located south-west of the Kingdom of Saudi Arabia, and the coastline forms its western and southern borders. In the west, Yemen stretches along the Strait of Bab al-Mandab and the Red Sea shores to the Saudi Arabian border in the north. In the south, Yemen stretches along the Gulf of Aden and the Arabian Sea to the border with the Sultanate of Oman in the east. Desert lies to the north and east of Yemen.

There are three ecological regions in Yemen: the coastal plains, the mountains and the desert. The coastal plains contain the fertile lands and are located near the mountains of Ta'izz, Ibb and Jibla. The Tihama plain – a hot and humid region – is situated alongside an expansive mountainous area and along the coast of the Red Sea. A less fertile, mountainous region is in the north of the country, between Sanaa and the more northern city of Sa'da. The region of Hadramawt, located in the east of the country, contains both coastal plains and arid desert with deep wadis.[4]

There are some clear differences between Upper and Lower Yemen. Upper Yemen refers to the northern highlands that stretch from the Saudi border in the north to Damar in the south, and from Hajja in the west to Shabwa in the east. Lower Yemen refers mainly to the cities of Ta'izz, Ibb and Hudayda.[5] The mountainous area has long served as a natural defensive barrier for the tribes that dwell therein. Two main tribal confederations in the mountains are the Hashid and the Bakil. Owing to the natural defensive barrier, these two tribal confederations were never completely subjugated to the direct control of external invaders, even though their territory has been under Ottoman occupation. There was no supra-tribal authority or accepted central rule in the mountainous region, and it was inconceivable for any ruler to control Sanaa in particular and Yemen in general without the support of the heads of these two tribal confederations.[6]

In contrast to the people in the mountainous regions, the people in the plains were more easily exposed to external influence and invasions. The people of the plains were unable to develop a strong army, and in most cases they were dependent on protection from tribes in the mountains. The people who dwelled on the Tihama coastal plain were particularly exposed to foreign influences. They engaged primarily in trade and had a cosmopolitan outlook.[7]

City-states were established in south Arabia before the rise of Islam. The temperate climate and precipitation allowed cities to flourish in the mountainous areas. The largest and most ancient city in Yemen is Sanaa, located in a fertile valley about a mile and a half above sea level. It is in fact one of the oldest continuously inhabited cities in the world. Sanaa was a hub for the production of local handicrafts and was especially known for its metalwork such as swords, daggers and knives. During different historical periods of governance, Yemen's rulers have alternately transferred their seat of rule from Sanaa to Jibla and Ta'izz. In 1948, Imam Ahmad reinstated Sanaa as Yemen's capital, and it has been the political and economic centre of Yemen ever since.

Yemen's eastern mountain range was less populated than the northern mountain range: this meant that the tribes in the eastern

Map of Yemen
Source: CIA, 2010

range were unable to forge a large tribal confederation. In the eastern mountain range, Sanaa's political authority was nominal and unable to completely subdue the tribes. Also, given that Yemen is surrounded by desert in the north and east, Yemen did not have strong political relations with its neighbours (see on page 3).

Religious Characteristics

In the first centuries since the appearance of Islam, two leading religious communities developed in Yemen: Zaydiyya and Shafi'iyya. The Zaydi/Shafi'i division is of crucial importance in Yemen's history. The Zaydi community is based in the mountainous regions whereas the Shafi'i community is based in the southern part of the country and the Tihama plain. In practice, the dividing line between the "Zaydi north" and the "Shafi'i south" was the Samara Pass, just south of the city of Yarim.[8] Thus, the cities of Dhammar, Saana and Sa'da are predominantly Zaydi, while Ibb, Ta'izz and Hudayda are predominantly Shafi'i.[9]

In 628, Yemen became part of the Islamic Empire, and the vast majority of its people accepted Islam. Two centuries later, in 897, a local Zaydi dynasty wrested control of Yemen from the Islamic Empire. This would usher in a unique politico-religious tradition in Yemen. From the beginning of the tenth century, tribes from the northern mountains adopted the Zaydiyya – an offshoot of Shi'i Islam, which holds that the Shi'i imam did not disappear.[10] Zaydi Islam is named after its founder, 'Ali ibn al-Husayn, known as Zayn al-'Abidin, the grandson of Imam Husayn (and the great-grandson of the fourth caliph, 'Ali).[11]

The Zaydiyya upholds the principle that only a direct descendant of the Prophet (*ahl al-Bayt*) can be an imam and lead the Islamic community. However, in contrast to the mainstream Shi'a (the Twelvers), the Zaydi community developed more moderate views, recognized the legitimacy of the first three caliphs that proceeded 'Ali and rejected the messianic view of the "Hidden Imam". Because of its moderation, Sunnis refer to the Zaydis as the "fifth school of Islam".[12] The Zaydiyya took root in the north of the country, where it did not encounter a competing religious or political alternative. The imams, the heads of the Zaydiyya, enjoyed the status of legitimate mediators and arbitrators amongst tribes from the north. This legitimacy enabled the Zaydi leaders to solidify their political hegemony and disseminate their faith.[13]

Unlike other Shi'i offshoots, the Zaydis maintained a politico-religious structure, the Zaydi Imamate. Rule over the Imamate was inherited by members of the *sadah* (singular: *sayyid*) or *ashraf* (singular: *sharif*) families. These are families who are believed to be descendants of Zayd (the Zaydiyya's founder) and the Prophet Muhammad.[14] These families believed that the imam was the political and religious leader of the community of believers (*Amir al-Mu'minin*) which allowed the Zaydiyya to become the dominant sect in Yemen. The founder of the first Zaydi Imamate was Yahya Ibn Husayn, whose Imamate lasted over a millennium, from the year 897 until 1962. According to the Zaydi doctrine, Imam Yahya functioned simultaneously as both the political and religious leader of the community of believers and Zaydi believers referred to him as the "guide towards the truth" (*al-hadi ila al-haqq*).[15]

Imam Yahya forged a Zaydi political system in line with Zaydi doctrine. For centuries to come, the person of Yahya served as the primary example of the qualities that an imam should possess. Yahya also established the obligation for Zaydis to obey the imam:

> ... because they were born from the seed of the Prophet, because they have knowledge of God, because of their piety, because of their knowledge of what God permitted and forbade and of the needs to fulfill religious rites, because they know what their rights and obligations are, they do not covet material objects, they back down from temptations in life, because they are ready to fight the enemies of God ... and perform the commandment of the holy scriptures and tradition and establish law and order ... and finally due to the courage of their hearts in battle, and due to their uncompromising perseverance in the times of distress and their abundant generosity.[16]

The Sunni-Shafi'i population dwelled in the urban centres and along the coastline. Whereas the mountain-dwelling Zaydi population was relatively isolated from foreign influence, the Shafi'i population was more exposed. Common wisdom holds that this division between the Sunni Shafi'is and Shi'i Zaydis is what caused discord between the two communities; however, there are several major factors aside from simple geographical differences. Religiously, the Zaydiyya was perhaps the most moderate of all Shi'i offshoots; it was doctrinally close to the Sunni Islamic schools, and did not accept the mystical and messianic dimensions of Shi'i Islam. However, the cultural differences between the Zaydis and Shafi'is could be seen in the styles of dress, architecture and community life.[17] The Zaydis and the Shafi'is therefore constituted two distinct subcultures in Yemen. However, the discord between the two communities did not stem from these religious and cultural differences but was political in nature.

Throughout most of Yemen's history, the Zaydis have ruled over the Shafi'is. The superiority of the Zaydis was recognizable in every realm, and they naturally saw themselves as patrons of the country.[18] This self-perception was fundamentally in line with Zaydi political philosophy, which perceived the rule of a Zaydi imam over Zaydis and non-Zaydis alike as an inevitable reality. The Zaydi Imamate designated notables from the Zaydi community to high positions such as advisors, judges and administrators; furthermore, the Zaydi tribes in the north granted their support to the imam and joined his army. Therefore, the core of the imam's control was in regions inhabited by Zaydi tribes.

The Shafi'is recognized the imam's rule but did not accept his religious authority. They looked to Shafi'i scholars for guidance in religious matters and their children were educated in Sunni *madrasas*. Shafi'is were not appointed to key positions in the central administration or the army. Having been marginalized, many of them – students, workers and merchants (especially in Ta'izz and Hudayda) – chose to move to Aden or even to leave the country.[19] As a result, they were exposed to modern ideas, such as Arab nationalism and socialism, to a greater degree than the Zaydis who lived in relative isolation.

Tribal Structures

The centrality of the tribe as a socio-political unit and basis for individual and collective identity in Yemen is unmistakable. The exact number of tribes in Yemen is unknown; Heyworth-Dunne estimates it at around 74.[20] ʻAbdallah al-Wasiʻi and ʻAdil Nur al-Din put that number even higher, close to 100.[21] Tribal leaders (*shaykhs*) enjoyed religious legitimacy and as the *shaykh* himself was loyal to the imam, his tribesmen, in being obligated to be loyal to the *shaykh*, were loyal to the imam as well. In contrast to most tribes in the Arabian Peninsula, which were nomadic, Yemeni tribes are mostly sedentary. Tribesmen in Yemen lived in stone houses and engaged in agriculture, selling goods in order to supply their needs.[22] The number of nomads and shepherds among them was relatively small.

Anthropological studies show that while the tribes of Yemen share a similar political culture, especially those of the northern highlands ("Upper Yemen"), they also vary in size and organization.[23] Using broad generalizations such as "the tribes of Yemen" would ignore the diversity of tribes in Yemen and fail to address the environmental and historical factors of the tribal setting. There are, however, different approaches. Dresch, for example, downplays the significance of ecology in understanding Yemeni tribes, the structures of which he portrays as sets of cognitive categories on a linguistic model.[24]

Because of the centrality of tribes, tribal politics have always been central to the political and social institutions in Yemen. Usually, villages in Yemen were the exclusive territory of one tribe (a tribal *dar*).[25] Sometimes tribes became rulers of larger administrative units. Larger tribes generally subjugated smaller tribes and sometimes even a whole city district.

Yemeni tribes have historically united in large confederations. Throughout history the balance of power across Yemen between tribal confederations has shifted. Several tribal confederations broke up in the beginning of the twentieth century but the large Zaydi confederations, the Bakil and the Hashid, maintained their prominence. The original tribes in the Hashid confederation are called *hashid* while those who joined later are called *mutahashid*. Likewise, the *bakil* are the original tribes in the Bakil confederation and the *mutabakkil* are the newcomers. The imams drew governors, administrators and militiamen from the Hashid and Bakil confederations. But not all tribes of Yemen were part of a confederacy. The tribes of Khawlan, for example, formed a concentration of independent power and zealously protected their autonomy. In contrast to those in the north, tribes in the south are smaller and less cohesive and were never dominated by one tribal confederation after the manner of the Hashid and Bakil (see figure below).[26]

The Zaydi tribal confederations established tribal states that sprawled across a broad territory. However, these "states" were not characterized by the existence of a central rule that held the monopoly

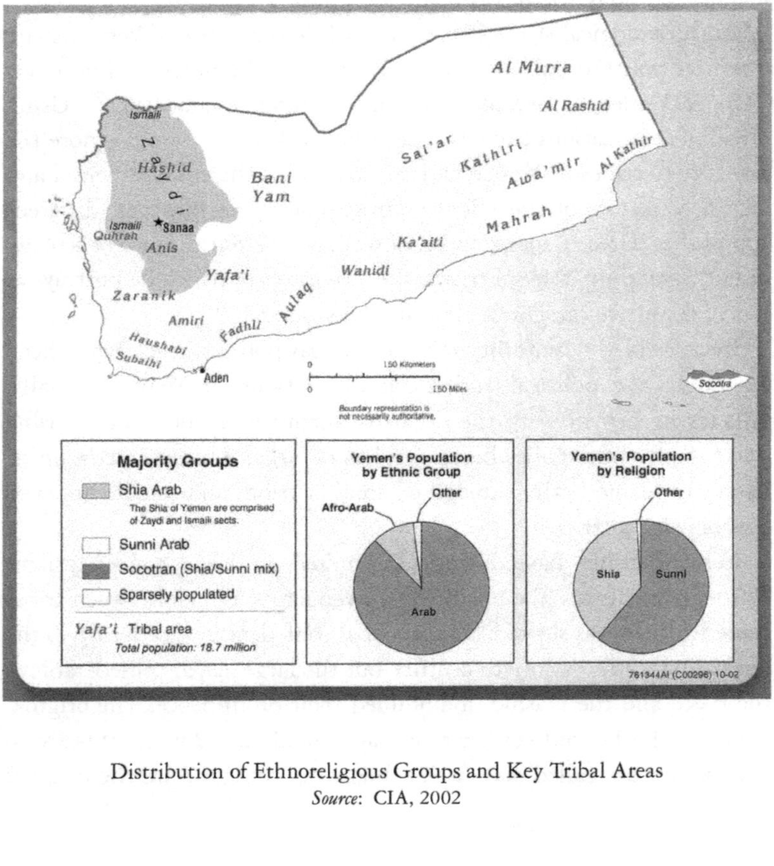

Distribution of Ethnoreligious Groups and Key Tribal Areas
Source: CIA, 2002

on the use of force. In most cases, these states had limited resources and a simple system of administration based on personal relations. These states were mainly concerned with the application of religious law and tax collecting; and thus, their control was nominal. Tribes enjoyed a discernible degree of autonomy in their own internal affairs and maintained armed tribal militias. Therefore the tribal map was in a constant state of flux.[27]

External Powers

Owing to its strategic location, Yemen was exposed to the designs of foreign forces and world powers. In Yemen's modern history, the intervention of two imperial powers – the Ottoman Empire and the British Empire – particularly left their mark on Yemen. Yemen was divided into two spheres of control beginning with the British occupation of Aden in 1839 and the Ottoman re-conquest of parts of the country in 1849.

The Ottoman Presence

Yemen's history witnessed two waves of Ottoman conquest. The Ottoman conquest of Yemen in the middle of the sixteenth century – particularly the conquest of Sanaa and the establishment of the *vilayet* of Yemen in 1547 – did not constitute Yemen's full integration into the Ottoman state. The Ottomans tried to subdue the Zaydi tribes in the northern mountains, but met tough resistance and in 1567 they gave up and withdrew from the mountain area. In 1635, they were forced to evacuate completely after suffering a defeat by the forces of Imam Qasim Bin Muhammad (known as *al-Mansur Billah*) and his son, Imam Muhammad Bin al-Mansur.[28] These imams reinstated their rule over "Greater Yemen", from Hadramawt in the south to 'Asir in the north.

By the middle of the eighteenth century, central authority had begun to wane as local tribes exploited the weakness of the Imamate and gained autonomy.[29] In the middle of the nineteenth century, the Ottomans renewed their efforts to control Yemen's coastline and major cities such as Ta'izz and Hudayda. This effort was partially successful as the Ottomans did not encounter too much opposition from the local populations, mostly because they were Sunnis like the Ottomans.

In the nineteenth century, the Wahhabi movement began to pose a challenge to Ottoman administration of the state and the Ottomans decided to embark on a second wave of conquest in the Peninsula. In their attempts to suppress the Wahhabi uprising, the Ottomans were aided by the governor of Egypt, Muhammad 'Ali. In 1837, he controlled the eastern bank of the Red Sea, from the Suez to Bab al-Mandab. The deterioration of relations between Muhammad 'Ali and the Sultan in Istanbul contributed to the Ottomans' decision to try to expel Muhammad 'Ali from his foothold in the region in the beginning of 1839. In the same year, the Ottomans occupied parts of the Tihama. In 1905, the Ottomans occupied Sanaa, but were unable to extend their hegemony over all of Yemen.[30] Their attempt to advance northwards was met with tough resistance from Zaydi tribes, and Yemen became, in the words of Paul Dresch, "the cemetery of the Ottomans".[31]

In the scholarly literature, the period of Ottoman rule in Yemen is portrayed as a tumultuous period, replete with local rebellions that were brutally put down.[32] Many of the Ottoman officials and officers lamented the view that Istanbul took of Yemen as peripheral to the empire. The Egyptian scholar Hasan Ibrahim Hasan argues that their frustration manifested itself in repression of the indigenous population.[33] This phenomenon explains the tortuous relations between the authorities and the inhabitants of the Zaydi north, but Shafi'i areas were relatively tolerant and open toward the Ottoman presence.

In some of the sources, however, the period of Ottoman rule is portrayed as bringing relative welfare and comfort to Shafi'i regions.[34] Thomas Kuhn analyses Ottoman policies from a socio-demographic perspective. He posits that from the very beginning, the Ottomans did not extend the Tanzimat (empire-wide reforms aimed at improving central rule) to Yemen and employed other means, primarily appeasing gestures to tribal leaders and "divide and rule" techniques, in order not to rouse opposition to their rule.[35]

The British Occupation

Nearly contemporaneous to the Ottomans' second occupation of Yemen, the British established a presence in the south of the country. In 1839, British forces led by Captain Haines occupied the Aden Peninsula.[36] The Sultan of Lahaj, the previous ruler of Aden, quickly recognized the reality of the new power in the region and, in 1843 and 1857, signed "friendship accords" with the British, recognizing their rule. Control of Aden allowed the British to control Bab al-Mandab, the narrow strait that divides Asia from the Horn of Africa. This strait had long been a strategic site sought after by foreign invaders. Napoleon Bonaparte's invasion of Egypt in 1798 caused the British to realize that their strategic imperial waterways to their colonies in the East could be threatened. The British were also alarmed by Egyptian rebel Muhammad 'Ali's incursions into the Hijaz, as well as his conquest of Mukha and other settlements along the Yemeni coast throughout the 1830s. Fearing that Aden would be Muhammad 'Ali's next destination, the government of British India authorized Captain Haines to occupy Aden.[37] Rapidly transformed from a destitute fishing village with a few thousand residents to a bustling cosmopolitan city with a population numbering in the hundreds of thousands, Aden became a major strategic and commercial link in the British Empire. It came to be known as its most important port east of Suez as well as a leading city in the region.

The British never aspired to full control in Arabia, but control of Aden was seen as a tool to build up British dominance in the region, and therefore they established a military base there under the direct control of the government of British India. In essence, the colony of Aden was just 75 square miles, surrounded by a hinterland in which dozens of petty emirs, sultans and *shaykhs* ruled small polities.[38] Captain Haines, as the political agent from 1839–1854, realized that securing the British presence in Aden meant that Britain would need to spread its influence in the surrounding regions. He understood that tribal heads would operate according to their individual interests, and that British policy would not succeed unless it were possible "to motivate each one of them in the territory towards a collective goal".[39]

In order to spread their influence, the British sought to form agreements with the petty rulers in the hinterland. As a result, the British were increasingly drawn into internal issues, for example while trying to end the tribal wars between the Qu'ayti and the Kathiri Sultanates. As a result, this zone of control came to be known as the "Protectorate of Aden".

Under the British, the Colony of Aden was a separate entity from the Protectorate of Aden, which included around 12 polities to the west, north and east of Aden, whose leaders had reached understandings

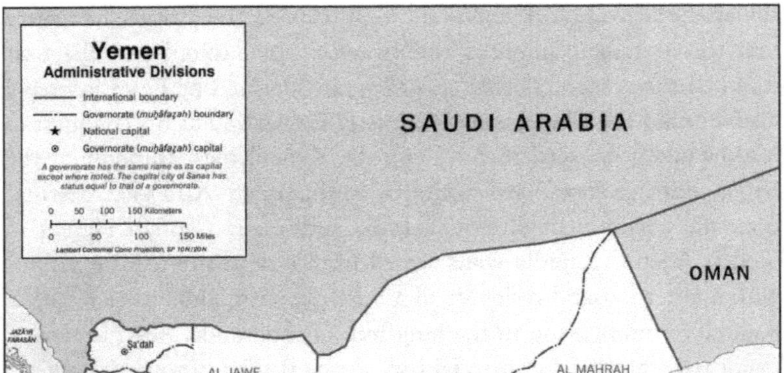

Yemen's Administrative Divisions
Source: CIA, 2002

with the British.[40] These polities served as a buffer zone that granted the British strategic depth and defense for the Colony of Aden. The boundaries of the polities within the protectorate were redefined on an ad hoc basis throughout the British presence there (1839–1967).

Early in the twentieth century, the British initiated negotiations with the Ottomans in order to establish a border between their respective territories of influence.[41] At the same time, the Zaydi resistance to the Ottoman presence in the north intensified. Finally, the Ottomans' defeat in the First World War paved the way for the establishment of an independent state in northern Yemen, ruled by an imam who claimed that he had the right to rule over the entire country.

The Imamate of Yemen in the Twentieth Century

For hundreds of years, Yemen was administered by an autocratic ruling establishment called the Imamate (*Imama*). According to the Zaydi doctrine, the imam was both the political and the religious leader. In contrast to other Shi'i sects, the Zaydi doctrine did not imbue the Imamate with a quietist, eschatological dimension. Rather it was a binding and active establishment, and therefore less sacred. The chosen imam was a descendant of one of the families of the *sadah* or the leading Zaydi families.[42] Although theoretically restricted by *sharia* and traditional practices in Yemen, in practice he enjoyed broad governing authority.

The Hamid al-Din family, dominant in Yemeni politics for over a thousand years, rose to power in 1889 and established a dynasty of imams. The first imam from this dynasty was Imam Muhammad (al-Mansur Muhammad Ibn Yahya Hamid al-Din). His primary objective was to expel the Ottomans from their strongholds in Yemen, as his antecedents had attempted to do when the Ottomans occupied the Arab provinces including parts of Yemen.

Imam Muhammad resumed the revolt against the Ottomans during his rule (1889–1904). He accused the Ottomans of deviating from true Islam by repressing the weak and drinking alcohol. At the height of the revolt, the imam's forces attacked and killed the delegations of tax collectors who had been sent by the Ottoman governor.[43]

The revolts spread quickly and the Yemeni highlands, excluding Sanaa and 'Amran, fell into the hands of the imam's forces and enabled the imam to expand his control to the plain of the Shafi'i south.

The Ottomans struck back and their armies regained the territories that had been conquered by the imam's forces. In conjunction with this successful military action, the Ottomans began a series of reforms, including the establishment of secular schools, hospitals and telegraph networks and the introduction of a Western-style system of civil laws alongside Islamic law. Despite ongoing tribal revolts, in the early years of the twentieth century the Ottomans managed to stabilize their rule in Yemen.

In the year 1904, Imam Muhammad died and was replaced by his son, Yahya bin Husayn bin Muhammad (Imam Yahya). Yahya viewed the Ottomans as foreign occupiers, and his first proclamations called for revolt against them.[44] To that end, he strove to obtain the crucial support of the two large tribal confederations – the Hashid and the Bakil. Like his father, Yahya claimed that the Ottomans had abandoned the commandments of Islamic law and that he, as a descendant of the Prophet Muhammad, was obligated to revive the Zaydi claim to rule over Yemen.

With his ascension, Yahya led the Zaydi tribes in a renewed campaign against the Ottoman occupier. In April 1905, Yahya conquered the cities of Sanaa, Ibb, Qa'taba and Yarim.[45] Fearing that the revolt in Yemen would spread throughout the empire, Istanbul dispatched forces to subdue the Yemeni uprising. In August of the same year, Sanaa was back in Ottoman hands.[46] The Ottomans tried to reach a compromise with the imam following a series of tough battles that resulted in many casualties and the destruction of many parts of central Yemen. While negotiating with the Ottomans, Yahya made claims that were indicative of his vision of the Zaydi Imamate. He demanded that the Ottomans recognize Islamic law as the sole judicial system in Yemen, and abrogate Ottoman civil law in Yemen. Towards this end, Yahya negotiated a shared sovereignty with the Ottomans. Yahya agreed to recognize the Ottoman Empire as a defending force against external occupation and the Ottoman Sultan, Abd al-Hamid II (1876–1908), as a defender of Muslim Yemen against the infidels.

However, he refused to accept the sultan as leader of the Islamic community (*amir al-mu'minin*). This was in line with Zaydi doctrine, which required that the imam, a descendant of the Prophet Muhammad, be the leader.[47] Yahya refused to recognize the borders that were determined by the British and the Ottomans in their attempt to chart out their spheres of influence in Yemen: he believed that his vision of "greater Yemen" could be realized.[48]

Yahya's acceptance of the Ottoman presence contributed to calmer relations between Yahya and the Ottomans, but not for long. When Hasan Tahsin Pasha (1908–1910) sought to impose a new order in Yemen by introducing new taxes and a stronger military presence, this led to a renewed deterioration in relations between the Ottomans and the Imam. However, this time the Ottomans were preoccupied with internal crises that followed the Young Turk Revolution (1908). Yahya capitalized on the weakness of the Ottomans. In signing the Da'an Agreement with them in 1911, he forced them to acquiesce to his demands: recognizing him as the political and spiritual leader of the Zaydi (though not the Shafi'i) community and granting him the authority to levy taxes. The Ottomans also recognized his rule from the plains of Yemen to the southern coast of Ta'izz.[49] In other words, Yahya became the sole community leader of the Zaydis and was accountable only to the ruling authorities in Istanbul.[50] The Da'an Agreement symbolized the beginnings of Yemen's autonomy under the Imamate of Yahya. Thomas Kuhn, however, views the agreement as an inextricable part of imperial policy, which was meant to bring the *vilayet* of Yemen under Ottoman imperial territory and to bring the Zaydi Imamate under Ottoman administration.[51]

With the outbreak of the First World War, the status of the Zaydi tribes was strengthened even more because the Ottomans, who intended to attack British Aden, sought a compromise with the tribes. They bribed the Zaydi tribes and sometimes even induced tribesmen to attack the British. This enabled Yahya to broaden his power and influence; he supported the Ottomans throughout the war, and did not respond favourably to the British attempts to curry his favour and obtain his support.[52]

Following their defeat in the First World War, the Ottomans evacuated Yemen. Their departure paved the way for Yemen's independence. Therefore, Yemen was one of the first independent Arab states that rose out of the ruins of the Ottoman Empire. However, in contrast to other states in the Middle East, the concept of "Yemen" was not a fictitious creation like the state of Jordan but a notion that was ingrained in the collective identity of the inhabitants.[53]

Imam Yahya shifted his centre of rule to Sanaa. From his ruling palace, Yahya staked a claim to "Greater Yemen", which included the territories of 'Asir, Aden, British protectorates, Hadramawt and parts of the present-day Sultanate of Oman. There was nothing new to this claim (see figure on page 12).[54] In the beginning of his reign as imam in 1904, Yahya had named most of the aforementioned regions "the southern part of Yemen" (*al-jiha al-janubiyya lil-yaman*). Therefore, after having signed the Da'an Agreement, Yahya sent messages to *shaykhs* in Aden and in areas under British control asking that they renew their loyalty.[55] Yahya relied on the historical claim that Zaydi imams had ruled Yemen for a millennium. Unlike his predecessors, Yahya had the power, authority and determination to make this vision a reality. With the fall of the Ottoman Empire, Imam Yahya claimed sovereignty over territories that included both the Ottoman and British spheres of influence, and in August 1919, he sent a representative to Aden to convey to the British the conditions under which he would be willing to reach a compromise.[56] Yahya's vision and his territorial claim laid out the modern, nationalist foundations for the future state of Yemen.

Yahya's rivals did not accept his territorial claims. The 'Asir and Hudayda regions were ruled by Yahya's rivals from the Idrisi House, which maintained a tribal polity that enjoyed British patronage. The British controlled the Colony of Aden and the protectorates. Even Yahya's claim to central Yemen raised questions, since only in 1835 did the important cities and the southern mountainous regions fall to Zaydi rule. The legitimacy of the Imamate was questionable especially in light of the tribal and religious schism. The Imamate's legitimacy was based on its ability to stay above the tribal and sectarian divisions; the imam would forge alliances with certain tribes, without himself becoming a player in the tribal arena.

Yahya dedicated his first years as imam to curbing Ottoman influence in Yemen. His preoccupation with them stemmed from the fact that they overshadowed his status as a religious leader, as had been established in the Da'an Agreement. The Ottomans never officially renounced their right to rule over any Islamic land and they certainly did not renounce their right to rule over Arabia and Yemen. Only when the Ottomans departed Yemen was Yahya able to establish a religious state according to his vision.

Imam Yahya invested great efforts in the cultivation of his image as a religious leader and placed Islamic motives at the centre of his doctrine. He sought to instill a feeling of affinity towards the central rule amongst the tribes of Yemen. Upon taking office, Yahya presented his philosophy of governance to his subjects:

> People of the country! I bring before you the instructions of Allah: [to follow the path] of Allah's book [the Quran], the traditions of the prophet [*hadith*], and the obligation of commanding the good and forbidding the evil (*al-amrbil-ma'ruf wal-nahi 'an al-munkar*) ... I have taken upon myself a number of obligations (conditions): to rule according to the commands of Allah and the Prophet, to prefer your good over mine on matters between us, to ensure your welfare over mine, to stand in the fore against your and my enemies. There are two obligations upon you: to consult with me and to advise me in discretion or in the open just as Allah's commands are binding upon me, and to obey me as long as I obey Allah. If I have transgressed the rules of obedience to Allah, then I do not have the right to demand obedience from you. And if I have changed or distorted Allah's and the Prophet's message, then I am no longer deserving [to rule] over you.[57]

Yahya adorned himself with the title *al-Mutawakkilbillah* (one who puts his trust in Allah) and enjoyed broad legitimacy.

The establishment of Imam Yahya's rule was based on his relations with the tribes, as is the case with the Saudi royal family. In both cases, the strength of the state was dependent on the military power of the tribes, but this is where the similarity ends.[58] While tribes from the heart of the Arabian Peninsula were primarily nomadic, the Zaydi tribes of Yemen were primarily sedentary. The Zaydi tribes had long been distinct political entities, and unlike tribes from the Arabian Peninsula, the Zaydi tribes retained much of their autonomy during the state-building process. Large groups of tribes in Yemen retained their power and operated like a state within a state during Yahya's rule. Unlike Ibn Saud whose power was derived from his alliance with the Wahhabis, Imam Yahya's power was not derived from a religious revivalist movement; the Zaydiyya did not emerge as a response to a puritan message that strove to "repair" Islam in its entirety.

Although during the 1920s, Yahya managed to conquer the portions of Yemen that had previously been part of the Ottoman sphere of influence, the tribal heads did not fully embrace the authority of the Imamate. In the 1920s and 1930s, Yahya was forced to confront many revolts in which the tribes sought to consolidate their status while gnawing away at the power of the Imamate. For example, in 1924, tribes from the Jawf region encircled Sanaa and beseiged it. The Zaranik tribes from the Tihama region appealed to the League of Nations requesting recognition as a separate, independent state.[59] Yahya sent his son, Ahmad, to suppress the Zaranik Revolt in 1928–1929.

Another pattern in tribal politics, which sometimes makes it difficult for the observer to understand local balances of power, is the phenomenon of shifting loyalties. For example, Imam Yahya had always been able to depend upon the support of the Hashid tribes. But during the First World War they split on the issue of loyalty to the imam; Yahya had reached an understanding with the Ottomans and avoided direct conflict with them, but some of the Hashid tribes did not agree with this policy.[60] They requested permission from Imam Yahya to join Muhammad al-Idrisi in his campaign against the Ottomans. The most important leaders of the Hashid and Bakil confederations (Yahya bin Yahya al-Sharif from the Bakil and Nasir bin Mabkhut al-Ahmar from the Hashid) functioned as mediators between Yahya and al-Idrisi. Imam Yahya refused to grant any of the Hashid tribes permission to attack the Ottomans. In response, the petitioning tribes left the Hashid confederation to join al-Idrisi's forces.[61]

During the 1920s, Yahya not only regained the allegiance of these rebellious Hashid tribes, but he also conquered the al-Idrisi territory. Al-Idrisi had reached an agreement with the British and they recognized his independence and extended their support to him. As the Ottomans evacuated their forces from Yemen, British forces arrived to the coast of Hudayda in order to support al-Idrisi.[62] With the death of Muhammad al-Idrisi in 1923 and the succession of his son, 'Ali, a window of opportunity presented itself to Yahya. In 1925, Yahya conquered the port of Hudayda (which had been under the control of the Idrisi household since 1919) and subdued the Hashid tribes which had supported al-Idrisi. Yahya also sent his son, Ahmad, to subdue more Hashid tribes in the north. These military expeditions laid the groundwork for the demarcation of the future Yemeni-Saudi border.

In what would become a pattern in Yemen's power game, local powers sought patron-client relationships with foreign powers and vice versa. Towards the end of the 1920s, the imperial powers used their local clients to better their position in the region. This turned Yemen into a strategic focus for colonial aspirations in the Middle East, where foreign powers including Italy sought to advance their status. From its colonies in Africa, Italy contested the British position in Yemen and in 'Asir in order to create a strategic advantage in the sea trade routes that stretched from Italy's colony in Eritrea to the Red Sea and the Arabian Peninsula. In 1923, the Italians signed a trade agreement with Imam Yahya ensuring access to the port of Mukha, which thereafter became a centre of their trade activities. Subsequently, they established telegraph lines and communication infrastructure connecting Mukha and Sanaa. They also transferred weapons and ammunition to the Imam for use against his rival, al-Idrisi.[63] Yahya captured the city of Hudayda in 1925, and the Italians shifted their activities to Hudayda a year later. Following that, the Italians signed a broader friendship and trade treaty with the imam. This treaty was not viewed favorably by the merchants in Hudayda and Sanaa, and it increased British fears of an Italian trade monopoly in Yemen. In response, the British tried to disrupt the movement of weapons within Yemen and 'Asir, and they were partially successful. Al-Idrisi turned to the British in Aden and requested aid against Imam Yahya. The British sought to reach a compromise with the Italians, the imam's new patron. In 1926, they arrived at a series of understandings, but these were shaky from their very inception.[64]

Before the end of the 1930s, Italy lost its hold in the region. They wanted to avert a confrontation with the British, but were concerned that their status would erode in the event that the British would attack Yahya's positions. Recognizing the dwindling influence of the Italians, Yahya made an agreement with the Soviets in 1928 and reached an understanding with the British in the 1934 Treaty of Sanaa.[65]

'Ali bin 'Abdallah al-Wazir, one of Yahya's important allies, conquered the Idrisi-controlled territories of Hudayda (1925) and subdued the northern part of Tihama including 'Asir and Jizan as well as Ibb, Ta'izz, Zabid and Ma'rib.[66] With these areas thus brought under Imam Yahya's control, al-Idrisi turned to the Saudis to request support and patronage. The Saudi Kingdom, at the time engrossed in its own process of state-building, was interested in aligning itself with a local player like al-Idrisi in order to improve its control on its emerging borders with Yemen. In an attempt to recover 'Asir for al-Idrisi, Ibn Saud invaded and held the territory until April 1934, when skirmishes between the Saudi and Imamate forces developed into war between Saudi Arabia and Yemen. The war ended in a compromise: in exchange for a Saudi withdrawal from the port of Hudayda, Yahya withdrew his forces from Najran, Jizan and 'Asir. This meant that Yahya lost territories that he considered to be an integral part of his "Greater Yemen".

At home, Imam Yahya stabilized his power by exploiting inter-tribal rivalries. Hostage-taking (*raha'in*) was a common practice in Zaydi political culture and Yahya adopted it as a way to make his rule more secure. After Yahya's forces suppressed a particular tribe, they took the *shaykh*'s sons and other male family members to Sanaa, far from the tribe's dwelling, and brought them to one of the imam's fortresses.[67] The treatment of the hostages was dependent upon the behaviour of their tribe. If the tribe's behaviour was good, then it was permitted to send clothing and food and fund the education of the hostages. Sometimes the hostages were given the option to see their father or patron. When a hostage reached the age of 15, and after having undergone an educational process aimed at inculcating loyalty to the imam, he was returned to his tribe and replaced with another hostage.[68] If his tribe behaved, the hostage himself was able to choose his replacement. In 1955, the number of hostages was estimated in the thousands.[69] In this manner, Yahya secured the obedience of the tribes and expanded his base of power in Yemen.

The art of bargaining with the tribes did not end with hostage-taking: coercion, bribery and the cultivation of religious affinity were also useful bargaining chips in Yahya's hand. While these tactics did facilitate cooperation between the imam and the tribesmen, intra- and inter-tribal feuds added an additional layer of complexity and hampered relations between the Imamate and the tribes, amounting to a complicated web of loyalties. Yahya's methods could be both cruel and flexible and he imposed his direct authority on the sedentary tribes of Sanaa and its environs. In more distant regions, the imam had only nominal control and, in most cases, he arrived at an understanding with the tribesmen which would not infringe upon the local practices and the measure of autonomy they had enjoyed in the past. The imam's nominal rule was based on the loyalty of *shaykhs* and the *sadah*.[70]

However, the *sadah* presented Yahya with a no less formidable challenge: they held that any one of their cohorts could declare himself an imam and undermine Yahya's rule over the Imamate. Yahya quickly and prudently appointed his son, Ahmad, as his successor, but aroused the anger of the *sadah* in doing so, because such an act was contrary to the Zaydi tradition according to which the *sadah* chose the imam's successor. In order to appease the *sadah*, Yahya granted them financial rewards and influential positions, until potential candidates for the Imamate and leading members of the *sadah* were compelled to swear their allegiance to his son, Ahmad.[71]

At times Yahya deposed commanders of his army and confidants from their positions for fear that their authority would undermine his. A good example is the Wazir family – a large *sadah* family descended from a nineteenth-century imam, which considered itself the rightful claimant to the Yemeni Imamate. Members of the family, such as 'Abdallah al-Wazir and 'Ali bin Ahmad al-Wazir, had served Imam Yahya in high military and administrative posts, but had been transferred from their positions because they posed a challenge to the Hamid al-Din family. Yahya ousted the Wazir family from their posts in his government and army, which enabled him to reorganize the administrative divisions from six to four provinces (*liwa*) whose governors (*'umara*) were appointed by the imam and subject to his direct control.

Yahya also increased his influence in areas that had traditionally been Shafi'i strongholds and acknowledged Shafi'i scholars who were willing to accept him as the supreme authority. He even codified their legal interpretations as a guide for courts and cautiously selected the judges and granted positions to those whom he considered to be loyal.

Yahya established a defense force (*jaysh al-difa'*) with the advice of Turkish officers, with the aim of stabilizing Yemen. This was not a regular army in the modern sense. Yemen's topography and tribal divisions made the task of establishing a modern army difficult. Subordinating the army to central rule would have required creating a new set of loyalties outside the existing tribal identity frameworks, as recruits for the army could only be drawn from the tribes. Therefore, the imam created military units that were homogenous in terms of tribal affinity. Thus, he did not tear down tribal affinities but rather utilized them towards strengthening the army as a whole.

The tribesmen were trained in workshops that were held for nearly six months. In 1940, the army was estimated at 50,000 soldiers, which allowed the imam to mobilize his forces when necessary. Tribesmen who completed their service in the army were transferred to the "external army" (*al-jaysh al-barrani*), a reserve force that included all of the tribal forces and was based on the framework of tribal units.[72] The Shafi'is did not serve in the highest echelons of the army. Moreover, many of them paid an alternative tax in order to purchase exemption from army service. Thus, this army institutionalized the supremacy of the Zaydi tribesmen over the Shafi'is, and also served as a new means for collecting taxes from the Shafi'i community.

In 1943, Yahya abolished the old army structure in favour of an institution that could better serve him in establishing control over the state. He retained a small reserve force and under it, he created a

3,000-man unit of career soldiers, directly subordinate to the imam. It was called the Victorious Regular Royal Army (*al-jaysh al-muthaf-far al-nithami al-malaki*).[73] Those enlisted in this army were primarily Hashid and Bakil tribesmen. Since they spent their entire lives in the army, their identification with their tribes significantly eroded. If a tribesman desired a discharge from the army, he was required to provide a replacement for himself. Often sons replaced their fathers, cultivating an army tradition amongst some families. If a certain province did not yield enough volunteers, then soldiers were drafted, as occurred more than once in Shafi'i regions and in the tribal regions in the north.[74] In addition, a special unit of about 600 men was drawn from the new army to serve as the imam's personal guard. The rest of the armed forces engaged in law enforcement, tax collection and security functions, which were aimed at extending the imam's authority over the tribes. The army did not just defend the borders of the country; it also provided protection to foreigners staying in the country. The army was not connected to other administrative systems that were run by the *sadah*; rather, it was an outlet for the imam's independent action. The advent of the telegraph even bolstered the army's usefulness as a tool by which the imam could consolidate his control internally and externally.

Throughout the 1930s, Yahya dedicated efforts to defining and securing Yemen's territory; in particular, he concerned himself with defining the borders with the Saudis in the north and the British in the south. In February 1934, Yahya and the British signed the Treaty of Sanaa according to which the 1904 Anglo-Ottoman border would become the Anglo-Yemeni border.[75] But the two sides interpreted the agreement differently. While the British assumed that their control in Aden and in the protectorates was secure, Yahya treated the British presence as temporary and never considered giving up on his idea of "Greater Yemen". In May of that year, Yahya and the Saudis signed the Treaty of Ta'if, which demarcated the northern border of Yemen and returned the Tihama region to the Imamate, although the Saudis gained the territories of 'Asir, Najran and Jizan.[76] Even though these agreements were temporary, in practice, they determined the borders of the Imamate and allowed Yahya to concentrate his efforts on state-building.

Throughout the first half of the twentieth century, Yahya strove to ensure the preservation of the tribal-Islamic character of the Zaydi Imamate. Yahya viewed isolation as the best way to secure the status quo and therefore he conducted an isolationist foreign policy and kept a particularly low profile with states in the region. Yahya prevented the onset of the modernizing spirit of the twentieth century from penetrating the realms of his Imamate. The Imamate provided a minimal civil infrastructure that did not include highways, paved roads, motor transportation, hospitals or a power-supply network. As a result, most areas of the country were characterized by relative isolation and backwardness.

Tax collecting in the Imamate reveals the convoluted nature of the relationship between the imam and the tribes. The tribes' subordination to the central rule was evident from their payment of taxes, and sometimes the government provided subsidies to reward the tribes for their ongoing loyalty. Tribal heads collected taxes for the central rule and saw the imam as a spiritual and political leader as long as he ruled in accordance with Islamic morals and values. In addition, the imam served as an accepted arbitrator and unofficial mediator between rival tribal groups.[77]

Yahya stood at the helm of the Imamate during the years 1904–1948, a period in which traditional societies throughout the Arab world coped with the forces of change and modernization. The outcome of Yahya's policies was a strong but traditional state of fewer than 3 million people in the 1930s and 1940s.[78]

At the end of the 1930s, Yemen began to witness the influence of ideologies from the outside world; Islamism was noteworthy among them. Yemeni students were going to Egypt in order to acquire a higher education at al-Azhar or Dar al-'Ulum. Ideologues such as Hasan al-Banna, the founder of the Society of the Muslim Brothers in Egypt, left a deep impression upon these students. Some of them joined the ranks of the Muslim Brothers and carried their message back to Yemen through their involvement in the "religious police" (the Association of Commanding the Good and Forbidding the Evil).[79] As a result, the Muslim Brothers had a significant influence in Yemen. Sometimes leading members of the Muslim Brothers in Egypt would come to Yemen. For example, Fudayl al-Wartalani began to disseminate the doctrine of the Muslim Brothers in Yemen throughout 1947.[80] Egyptian teachers in Yemen, some of whom were members of the Muslim Brothers, also disseminated their message in the 1940s.[81]

Young urban intellectuals who belonged to upper class families, like Muhammad Ahmad Nu'man, Muhammad Mahmud al-Zubayri and 'Abd al-Rahman al-Iryani (the future President of North Yemen) were also active during this period.[82] Their activity in the mid-1930s focused on the establishment of youth clubs that disseminated modern ideas and called for secular reforms. For example, Ahmad Nu'man founded the *al-Madrasa al-Ahliyya* which, along with other groups, criticized the imam and his governance. The imam perceived them as a threat and had them placed under house arrest, forcing some of them out of the country; they settled in Cairo, where they continued to operate. Eventually, they returned to Yemen with ideas of reform and revolution, which served as the basis for the establishment of the Free Yemenites movement, founded in Aden in 1944.

The Free Yemenites' primary influence was conceptual, and their political organization was less significant. The movement created awareness of Yemen's backwardness through its publications, *Majallat al-Hikma al-Yamaniyya*, *al-Rabita al-Arabiyya* and *al-Sadaqa*. This loose coalition suffered from numerous disagreements among its members, yet it served as a platform for opposition to the Imam in the 1940s. The Free Yemenites movement also collaborated with the Muslim Brotherhood as they both aimed to topple the Imamate. Together they formed a group and presented Imam Yahya with a petition calling for sweeping reforms in Yemen. In response, Yahya imprisoned the signatories, effectively neutralizing their challenge to his rule. Nevertheless their activism should be seen as the closest attempt at a "national" movement in Yemen.[83]

'Abdallah al-Wazir, a member of one of the strongest *sadah* families and a challenger to Yahya's crown, was well positioned to exploit the lack of cohesion amongst the Free Yemenites and to harness their momentum for his own purposes. A group of educated individuals and army officers coalesced around him. Amongst the officers were the graduates of the Military Academy in Iraq, who had been sent there by the imam in the mid-1930s following the Saudi-Yemeni war in 1934 and who benefited from the decision to establish a standing army.[84] ʻAbdallah al-Sallal (the future President of North Yemen) was prominent in this group.

In the years following the Second World War, Imam Yahya began to lose his grasp. Some of the members of the Free Yemenites blamed the army for the failure to prevent the loss of the Najran and ʻAsir provinces to the Saudis and from their centres in Taʻizz, al-Hugariyya, Sanaa, Ibb, Hajja and Aden, they fanned the flames of that resentment. Individual tribes near Sanaa also joined forces with al-Wazir.

On 17 February 1948, Imam Yahya was assassinated[85] and ʻAbdallah al-Wazir declared himself the new imam. Ahmad, Yahya's first-born and appointed successor, was nearly assassinated also, but he managed to escape, leaving his base in Taʻizz where he had served as a governor and making his way to Hajja equipped with a sizeable portion of the state coffers.[86] In a short period of time, he was able to mobilize the support of the Hashid, Bakil and other northern tribes. After a three-week siege, Sanaa fell to Ahmad, who brutally executed 35 activists from the Free Yemenites and beheaded ʻAbdallah al-Wazir. Al-Wazir's severed head was sent to Sanaa as a warning. Then Ahmad Bin Yahya began his period of rule as imam.[87]

The Transitory Period: The Road to Revolution, 1948–1962

Ahmad's Imamate faced very different challenges than those that had confronted his late father. With the political experience that Imam Ahmad obtained during his father's reign, he too was keen to maintain balance among the tribes. As most of the tribes near Sanaa were loyal to the al-Wazir family in February 1948 when Yahya was assasinated, Ahmad declared Taʻizz (his previous governorship) his base of rule. Furthermore, he continued to expand his army so that it would serve as a counterweight to the power of the hostile tribes. The tribes did not sympathize with him; for them, he symbolized central rule that sought to place restrictions on their power. In 1960, Imam Ahmad created the National Army (*al-Jaysh al-Watani*).[88] The structure, framework and equipment of the National Army were modern, and in the early 1960s, it was a 20,000-man army. As the tension between the central rule and the tribes increased, Imam Ahmad's reliance on the new army likewise increased.[89]

Having seen Egypt's dominant position and Saudi Arabia's prosperity, Ahmad wanted to propel his Imamate forward. In terms of foreign policy, he tried to bring his country into the heart of the Arab fold and, to some extent, the international scene. In 1950, he invited the first American delegation to Yemen, hoping to obtain diplomatic and material support. But his main focus was the Arab world: in the early 1950s, Yemen became a member of the Arab League and in 1954, it signed a defense pact with Egypt and sent young Yemeni officers to be trained in Cairo and Damascus. In March 1958, the Imamate even joined the United Arab Republic (the unification of Egypt and Syria), albeit not as a full member; Yemen merely cooperated on security and foreign policy issues. This did not represent an acceptance of revolutionary Arab nationalist ideology on the part of the imam, but rather his strategic calculation: such a tactic, he hoped, would dull the sting of propagandistic attacks that cast the Imamate as an anachronism and as a hindrance to the Arab revolution. He also believed that joining the Arab League would grant him Arab support in his battle against the British.[90]

The policy of trying to integrate with the Arab world had consequences of its own. The young Yemeni officers returned from their training in Cairo, Damascus and Baghdad imbued with Arab socialist ideas. They became more aware of their country's backwardness and became the chief opposition to the imam's regime. They despised the imam and his policies that benefited the Zaydi nobility, opposed traditional practices and were committed to broad social reform.[91] The imam, not trusting these officers, did not put them in positions of responsibility when they returned to Yemen. With an abundance of free time, they were able to meet and conspire against the imam.[92] At the same time, liberal exiles such as Muhammad al-Zubayri, who had fled Yemen in the aftermath of the 1948 assassination of Imam Yahya, settled in Egypt and used its media to undermine the imam's rule and call for change in Yemen. In their eyes, the Imamate was a symbol of evil and brutality and they did everything in their power to vilify it.[93]

In 1955, members of the new opposition joined forces with discontented tribal elements in order to attempt a coup. Amir 'Abdallah (*sayf al-Islam*), Yahya's seventh son, conspired with army officers led by Lieutenant Colonel Ahmad Yahya al-Thalaya, convinced that it was time to topple the imam. They forced Imam Ahmad to abdicate in favour of his brother, Amir 'Abdallah. Again, as in 1948, the northern Zaydi tribes responded quickly to save the imam. Ahmad's first-born, Muhammad al-Badr, set off northwards to Hajja and mobilized the Hashid and Bakil tribes. The 8,000-man strong tribal force defeated the opposition and Imam Ahmad returned to his palace after five days.[94] Ahmad ordered the execution of Amir 'Abdallah and Amir 'Abbas, his brothers who had conspired against him. He also ordered the execution of the tribal commanders of the conspiracy, Khawlan tribal *shaykhs* Husayn bin Nasir al-Ahmar and 'Abd al-Latif bin Qa'id.[95]

Despite their support for the imam during the 1955 coup attempt, the northern Zaydi tribes did not completely support his policies. On the one hand, they preferred Ahmad to the agenda of the reformists and therefore supported him. But they resented Ahmad's efforts to reduce their autonomy. The tribes expressed their dismay with a series of revolts throughout Yemen when Imam Ahmad became extremely ill in the beginning of 1959.

In April of the same year, Ahmad went to Italy for medical treatment and left his first-born son, Muhammad al-Badr, to rule in his place. Al-Badr proved to be a weak leader, and tribal opposition seized upon this opportunity.[96] The Hashid and Bakil tribes were the first to pose a concrete challenge to al-Badr. To appease them, al-Badr quickly allocated large financial royalties to the tribal heads of the two confederations. This did not completely end the revolt. Meanwhile, the military officers demanded "their share", and al-Badr considered provoking the Hashid and Bakil against the officers. The tribal opposition was surprised when Ahmad suddenly returned from Italy in 1959 and suppressed their revolts, calming the situation for a while.

Relations between the imam and the Hashid tribesmen deteriorated. The Hashid, who had come to Imam Ahmad's rescue in 1955 and had frustrated the coup directed against him (as they had done in 1948), were now his rivals. Ahmad's decision to execute the *shaykh* of the Khawlan, Husayn bin Nasir al-Ahmar, had unequivocally destroyed the base of tribal support built by the Hamid al-Din family. Revolts were renewed throughout Yemen. In the spring of 1960, the powerful Khawlan tribes joined the revolt, attempting to enlist support from the British in their battle against the imam's regular army. Imam Ahmad's attempts to incite other tribes against the Khawlan were unsuccessful.[97] The Bani Hashish and Bani Murad tribes refused his request to attack the Khawlan. The Jawf tribes also revolted, invading and plundering Hazm, the main city within proximity of their tribal *dar*. Yemen dissolved into an arena of tribal war.

A tribal bloc coalesced in opposition to the *al-sadah* notables and proposed an imam from its own ranks.[98] The educated middle-class and urban officers who also wished to depose Imam Ahmad supported the new tribal bloc.[99] Ahmad tried to unite his supporters, the *sadah*, and was even ready to go so far as to acquiesce to the growing influence of the al-Wazir family (which had conspired to depose his father in 1948).[100]

British Policy in the South: Federalism, Over-Involvement and War in Yemen

An examination of British policy throughout the 1950s is most important for shedding light on the final chapter of the Imamate. At the time, four distinct entities existed in Yemen: the Imamate, the British Colony of Aden, the Western Aden Protectorate and the Eastern Aden Protectorate. The Imamate of Yemen in the north was totally independent and free of any British involvement. However, the level of tension between the Imamate and the British rose steadily throughout the 1950s. As Yemen joined the Arab league, the imam started lobbying for international support in his attempt to counter the increasing British presence in the south-east and south of the country. The Western Aden Protectorate, which embraced the nape of Aden, included a number of sultanates, mainly Lahaj, Zinjibar and nine large tribes. The Eastern Aden Protectorate included the highly influential Qu'ayti Sultanate, whose central dwelling was in Mukalla on the coast of the Arabian Sea, and the Kathiri Sultanate, which was located in Hadramawt. The Eastern and Western Protectorates of Aden were thinly populated, lacked oil and were relatively undeveloped compared to other Arab states. The British neglected them in economic and geopolitical terms and exercised only nominal influence there. They served as a buffer zone between the Imamate and the Colony of Aden.

In the 1950s, the Aden colony rose in prominence economically and geopolitically after the British evacuated India in 1947 and the Suez Canal in 1956. In the 1950s, the British also sought to deepen their involvement in the south-west of the Peninsula. Two chief threats faced the British throughout this decade which jeopardized their hold in Aden. The first was Imam Ahmad's claim to full spiritual and political authority in Yemen, including Aden. The second emerged as the British were forced to cope with the winds of Arab nationalism that swept the region and undermined their presence in the Arabian Peninsula.

The British feared that the Aden protectorates – a buffer between the Imamate of Yemen and the British Colony of Aden – could be turned into fertile ground for anti-British activity from both the Imam's supporters and Arab nationalists. The British felt threatened mainly because of the Arab nationalists' attempts to create a base of operation for themselves in the protectorates. For example, the South Arabian League (*Rabitat al-Janub al-Arabi*)[101] was established in the early 1950s. The League was a political organization that opposed the expansion of Britain's authority in the protectorates and called for independence for the protectorates and Aden.[102] The head of the League, Muhammad 'Ali al-Jifri from Lahaj, tried to capitalize on grievances against the British, and appealed to both the tribes in the protectorates and young educated proponents of revolutionary ideas in Aden. The League strove to unify Yemen, including the territory of the Imamate and the British Colony of Aden. However, in the absence of an agreement with Imam Ahmad, and in light of the fact that Aden did not harbour any opposition to the British, the League had no choice but to confine its activity to the protectorates.[103] The League won crucial support from the ruler of Lahaj, Sultan 'Ali bin 'Abd al-Karim al-'Abdali, who in 1952 presented himself as an enthusiastic supporter of Arab nationalism. Because of this growing resistance, in the early 1950s the British became much more involved in the protectorates, deposing local leaders who adopted anti-British ideas drawn from radical Arab nationalism. In conjunction, British policy-makers weighed the possibility of creating states in the protectorate regions and assembling them into a federation that could preserve British interests in the region.

The very existence of the South Arabian League aroused suspicion among the British in Aden. They perceived the League as a potential ally of British enemies and also feared that the League would team up with the imam who supported the anti-British tribal players in the protectorates. They also feared that the League would collude with the Egyptians who protested the British presence in the Arabian Peninsula, or even the Soviets who, after the 1928 agreement with the imam, began to transfer arms and logistical equipment to the Imamate. Despite the fact that the Moscow-Cairo-Lahaj-Sanaa axis was not concrete, and to a large degree was a figment of the British imagination, British officials in the region began to fear that their interests were in danger.[104]

The independence of Sudan in 1956 and the creation of British Somaliland in 1960 were bad omens for British plans in Aden. British decision-makers came to believe that in order to avoid a similar scenario in Aden they should annex the colony to a broader federation led by pro-British local leaders. Throughout the 1950s, they increased their intervention in the regions of the protectorates adjacent to Aden such as Lahaj and Fadli (regions that traditionally enjoyed almost full autonomy) as well as in the Mahra region in the east and in upper 'Awlaqi near the border with the Imamate. However, this intervention, which was heavily dependent on the cooperation of local rulers in the protectorates, actually reduced the local rulers' autonomy and caused resentment. Donald Foster, a senior British official, wrote in his memoir that "in the al-Dali' settlement the authority of the *shaykh* barely stretched beyond the city of al-Dali' itself, and many of those whom the British considered to be loyal to the al-Dali' leaders ... denied their loyalty".[105]

The British were faced with a dilemma that created a rift between decision-makers in London and Aden. The British officials in Aden advocated the expansion of British involvement in the protectorates. Tom Hickinbotham (1951–1956) and William Luce (1956–1960), the two governors in Aden at the time, saw the expansion of British involvement as an effective tool with which to defend British assets in Aden, but also to stabilize the situation and make it possible for the British to withdraw in the future should they choose that course of action.[106] The two of them firmly held that tribal revolts and nationalist uprisings should be put down. Hickinbotham even believed that the creation of a federation would foster a stronger bond between the local rulers and the British.[107]

In London, policy-makers were divided on the proposed federation plan. Owing to their special ties with the governors in Aden, the Colonial Office advocated Hickinbotham's federation plan. The Foreign Office opposed it because they feared that it would entangle Britain in an additional regional war that would require a lot of attention and resources. Foreign Minister Selwyn Lloyd (1955–1960) opposed the federation plan because he believed that an intensification of this conflict between the imam and the British could fan anti-British sentiment in the Arab world and in the United Nations.[108] However, the policy was implemented because the upper echelons of the government (Prime Ministers Winston Churchill, 1951–1955, Anthony Eden, 1955–1957 and Harold Macmillan, 1957–1963) believed, drawing from experiences in Nigeria and Malaysia,[109] that the creation of such a federation was the best way to strengthen the British position vis-à-vis the immediate threat of Imam Ahmad's vision of a "Greater Yemen" and the broader threat of Arab nationalism.

Hickinbotham presented his plan for a federation on 7 January 1944.[110] According to the plan, the governor of Aden would be appointed high commissioner of the federation with broad authority at the expense of the autonomy of tribes. According to the plan, the tribes would be compensated with weapons, goods and, most importantly, protection. The federation plan was bolstered by the prospect of oil deposits in the region. Hickinbotham tried to persuade the local rulers that the federation would be a transitory phase on the path to their independence but that did not allay their suspicions. For example, the governor of Lahaj expressed his suspicion when he said, "independent rule is exactly what we have at the moment and a federation will cause us to lose it".[111] While proposing the federation plan to policy makers in London, Hickinbotham suggested that "like a chef in his kitchen, we must teach our people {rulers in the protectorates} how to prepare the pudding".[112] At this stage, London did move forward with the federation plan.

London sent a replacement for Hickinbothom. The new governor of Aden, William Luce, carried out a "wait and see" policy, fearing that delving into a discussion of the plan would increase the demand for full independence in the protectorates and would stir up nationalist agitation in the Colony of Aden. The idea of a federation was shelved for the following four years.

The Suez Crisis did not influence Luce's considerations regarding the ongoing conflict with Imam Ahmad. The fact that the imam asked the Soviets for aid made the British very anxious. In December 1956, William Luce vividly put it this way: "All the indications show that Yemen is becoming involved in the Nasirist-Soviet bloc, and I doubt whether Yemen can still extricate itself from anti-British activity in the protectorates".[113]

In the second half of 1956, Muhammad al-Badr, the imam's first-born son, visited East Germany and the Soviet Union, indicating a strengthening in relations between the Imamate and the Soviet Union. The Soviets began to equip the imam's army with tanks and missiles, although it was unclear if the army was even capable of using them.[114] The imam viewed British intervention in the protectorates, particularly their proposal to create a federation, as a violation of the Sanaa Agreement of 1934 and an attempt to banish him from the southern part of the country. In response, the imam revived his claim to the territory in the south and began to cultivate his working relations with the tribal leaders in both the Eastern and Western Protectorates. He granted moral and material support to tribes that were willing to carry out raids against the British. Local uprisings in some of the states of the protectorates, such as 'Awdali, demonstrated that the imam's policy was achieving its goal. At this stage, some British policy-makers called for an air raid against the imam's forces. In contrast, officials in the Foreign Office suggested dialogue with Imam Ahmad and supported compromise. As a matter of fact, that had been tried but to no avail.[115]

When the tension between the imam and the British increased in 1955, the British command in Aden recommended several measures: the first was to arm the local leaders in the protectorates, such as the Sultan of 'Awdali and Sharif Husayn of Bayhan, and encourage them to infiltrate the border and attack the imam's targets. Imam Ahmad was so angered by British policy that he instructed his officials to invite Western journalists to cover the conflicts that developed near the settlement of Qa'taba.[116] In December 1957, the British reported that the imam had begun to equip the tribes in Dathina and Fadli with thousands of rifles in preparation for one of the most "dangerous and massive sabotage efforts" that the British had experienced up to that point.[117] In early 1958, Luce received a green light from the British government to move forward with the federation plan and stir up tension in the Imamate.

Eventually, important regional developments gave the decision-makers in London the impetus to move forward with the federation plan. Gamal 'Abd al-Nasser's regional popularity was at its peak following the nationalization of the Suez Canal. In the beginning of 1958, he prepared for the unification of Egypt and Syria, which culminated in the Arab United Republic (UAR) in February 1958. A month later, the Imamate joined with the UAR in a loose federation known as the United Arab States (UAS). As the imam embraced Arab nationalism, the British feared that the heads of tribal states in the protectorates would also be tempted to do so. They feared that the imam could exploit the spirit of Arab nationalism to drive the tribes in the protectorates to attack the British.

However, Luce knew that most of the local sultans and *shaykhs* in the protectorates did not view the message of radical Arab nationalism favourably. The tribal polities of Bayhan, 'Awdali and Fadli agreed to unite in February 1958, bringing the idea of establishing a federation closer to realization. In Luce's view, this was the right moment to pay back the ardent opponents of the federation plan – among them the governor of Lahaj, Sultan 'Ali bin 'Abd al-Karim al-'Abdali. For the British, he epitomized an autonomous and rebellious *shaykh*, who employed Arab nationalism to reinforce his anti-British policies. Sultan 'Ali was a *shaykh* who praised Arab nationalism, but it is difficult to believe that he actually internalized the idea or considered joining Nasser's camp.[118] Nonetheless, in April 1958, the British designated him as a threat, invaded Lahaj and ousted Sultan 'Ali. He fled to Cairo where he claimed on *Sawt al-'Arab* (Voice of the Arabs) that the British plotted to oust him in order to take over the prospering cotton economy of Lahaj. What's more, the decision to oust Sultan 'Ali would later prove to hamper the effort to establish a federation.

The conservative British government was willing to adopt the federation plan, yet only as a tool with which to preserve British interests by securing the maritime route to the Persian Gulf. The British did not aim to create independent states in the protectorates. Luce emphasized that Britain would maintain its status as advisor to each one of the tribal states and to the federation as a whole. He also recommended recognition of the nominal independence of the federation.

On 11 February 1959, al-Dali', Lower Yafi' and Upper 'Awlaqi joined the three states that had supported the federation (Bayhan, 'Awdali and Fadli) in order to create the Federation of the Emirates of the South. In the beginning of the 1960s, the British combined all of the tribal states with Aden into the Federation of South Arabia, which the British hoped would succeed them if they should choose to evacuate.[119]

The British aimed to depose the imam and to appoint his brother, Amir Hasan (a former governor of Ibb and the prime minister of the Imamate from 1948–1955) in his place. Imam Ahmad's friendship agreement with Moscow, what the British perceived as his embrace of Arab nationalism and his son's pro-Soviet tilt aroused serious alarm amongst the British officials in Aden. In February 1958, a British senior officer declared that "the ousting of the present regime must be carried out by local Yemenis, although it is clear that Hasan and his supporters enjoy substantial support from the Americans, alongside our support [the British], the Italians and King Saud".[120] In July 1958, Luce submitted a proposal to distribute 25,000 shotguns to tribes that supported Hassan throughout the Imamate. Thus, the British drastically changed their policy in south-west Arabia, carrying interventionism to a greater degree than ever before.

In April 1959, when Imam Ahmad left the Imamate for medical treatment in Italy and left his son al-Badr at the helm, the British exploited the situation in order to increase unrest and to destabilize the foundation of the imam's rule. The Hashid tribes also took advantage of the imam's absence, staging a rebellion that shook the central rule of the Imamate. The Hashid tribes sought to settle some scores with the imam, who two months earlier had ordered the assassination of one of their leaders.[121] Ahmad returned and entered into a dialogue with the British and the rebelling tribes, which quelled the situation. But this was nothing more than the calm before the storm.

From the British perspective, the dialogue was a pyrrhic victory. They continued to advance the federation plan and to consolidate their power despite Imam Ahmad's resistance. Yet the British did not inquire into the imam's motives. Had they done so, they might have realized that they shared a common interest with the imam – namely, curbing Arab nationalists' ideas for reform. But they did not come together to cooperate. In choosing to oppose each other, they rendered themselves more vulnerable to Arab nationalism.

British policy in the 1950s – their over-involvement in the affairs of local rulers and their creation of a federation – reflected an attempt to impose British authority upon a region in which local rulers had been accustomed to a great deal of autonomy in their affairs. The British did not aspire to reconstitute their imperial power in the region; rather, they were forced to cope with the challenges of the day – the imam's claim to the south of Yemen, Arab nationalism and Soviet penetration into the Middle East. This policy sometimes provided a response to local problems for the short term, but in the long run it raised the level of tensions between the tribes and the British and strengthened the opposition that would eventually depose the imam.[122]

Toward the end of the 1950s and the early 1960s, Arab nationalist propaganda intensified. Nasser's revolutionary message calling for the overthrow of "reactionary Arab monarchies" did not spare Yemen and was propagated by Egyptian soldiers, teachers and doctors who arrived in Yemen. In 1961, around 500 Yemenis were registered in Egyptian educational establishments where they were exposed to Arab revolutionary propaganda. Imam Ahmad characterized Egypt's socialist ideology as anti-Islamic and publicly criticized Nasser.[123] In December 1961, Nasser announced that the unification between Egypt and Yemen was void, which only intensified the Egyptian propaganda attacks against the Imamate.[124] Nasser publicly encouraged subversion in order to turn Yemen into a revolutionary Arab republic like Egypt.

Imam Ahmad had partially responded to some of the prevailing problems, but it was too little, too late. Meanwhile, Ahmad's deteriorating health also contributed to a battle of succession within the Hamid al-Din family. The sick imam determined that his son, al-Badr, would be his successor and demanded that his brother, Amir Hasan, swear allegiance to him. However, al-Badr lacked the support of most of the tribes; they preferred Hasan. During his reign as governor of the northern districts in the beginning of the 1950s, Hasan had prudently built a strong network of loyalties amongst the tribes and exploited this network during his struggle with the imam. Ahmad had tried to alienate Hasan from Yemen's politics by appointing him ambassador to the United Nations. However, this was not sufficient to arrest the fundamental shift in the balance of power. The alliance between the Imamate and the Zaydi tribes crumbled, helping to bring about the 26 September 1962 Revolution which marked the end of the Imamate in Yemen.

The fate of the tribal-Zaydi Imamate was sealed. On the domestic front, the Imamate lost tribal support and faced increasing demands to enact liberal reforms. The Imamate was also forced to cope with a serious challenge from the British, who increased their presence in the south and south-west of Yemen, regions that Ahmad saw as integral parts of Yemen. In the Arab world, the status of the Imamate was eroded by the lure of Nasserist doctrine. Cairo was a seat and channel of inspiration for Yemeni opposition groups long before the 1952 Revolution in Egypt, and even more so after Nasser rose to power in 1954. The protest against the Imamate led to the birth of organizations such as the Free Yemenites (*al-Yaman al-Ahrar*) in the second half of the 1940s, and the Yemenite Union (*al-Ittihad al-Yamani*) in the beginning of the 1950s. These organizations criticized the regime for its backwardness, pushed for the implementation of a system of socio-economic reforms and advocated the establishment of a republic. Following the 1952 Revolution in Egypt, these groups operated branches in Aden and Cairo.

Most prominent among the activists was Ahmad Muhammad Nu'man, an influential Shafi'i who fled to Aden in the middle of the 1940s in order to join the opposition to the imam. In 1950, the imam pardoned Nu'man and he returned to the Imamate to lead the education system, but he continued to maintain his relations with the Free Yemenites. Later on he was exiled to Egypt where he served as the president of the Yemenite Union and published a newspaper called *Sawt al-Yaman* (Voice of Yemen).[125]

In Cairo Nu'man met other Yemeni exiles like Muhammad Mahmud al-Zubayri, who had settled in Cairo since his participation in the conspiracy against the imam in 1948, and Muhsin al-'Ayni, a graduate of the Sorbonne who served as the general secretary of the Union of Professional Organizations in Aden until he was expelled by the British. These individuals came together and formed the Movement for the Liberation of Yemen (*harakat tahrir al-yaman*) led by al-Zubayri. They disseminated Nasser's propaganda, which undermined the imam's rule and cast the imam as an obstacle to Arab revolution. The Yemeni exiles' movements in Egypt quickly became the hub for the coordination of logistical, moral and ideological aid between the regime in Cairo and the revolutionary activists in Yemen. The support that Nasserist Egypt granted to the instigators of the coup in Yemen in the two months before the coup was undoubtedly one of the central factors of their success.

Imam Ahmad died of natural causes on 19 September 1962. His son, Muhammad al-Badr, managed to hold the post of imam for one week. On 26 September, a group of army officers carried out a coup and established the Yemen Arab Republic. Al-Badr was the last of the imams of the house of Hamid al-Din. He narrowly escaped death at the hands of the revolutionaries. Having sought refuge in Sanaa he implored the tribes of the north and the Imamate's traditional allies to fight the revolutionaries.

For centuries, the imams, sultans and *shaykhs* in Yemen had used traditional "give and take" tactics with the semi-autonomous tribes through a governing network of a few administrators and dignitaries from leading families. The Zaydi imams had exercised authority in the northern mountains throughout the years, but they did not completely control the southern parts of Yemen, where Sunni Shafi'is constituted the majority.

In the first half of the twentieth century, the Imamate of Yemen was a renewed monarchy akin to the Saudi case. Nonetheless, Imams Yahya and, to a lesser extent, his son Ahmad did not invest in institution-building and modern means of administration. Rather they viewed their role as that of ruler, as arbitrator and mediator in accordance with Zaydi tradition. Yahya and Ahmad's conception of rule was based on the realization that tribes were foci of power that would not fully accept the imposition of central authority. Therefore they directed their efforts toward ensuring the loyalty of the tribes.[126] In times of crisis, they believed that the autonomous Hashid and Bakil confederations would support them, which they did in 1948 and 1955; nevertheless, the tribes' autonomous status contributed to the eventual downfall of the Imamate. It is important to remember that in Yemen – a poor state with meagre resources – the rulers did not have the economic capacity to channel the loyalty of most of the tribes to the central rule. This significantly affected the efficiency of Yemen's ruling system. Unlike other oil states of the Arabian Peninsula, building a welfare state and distributing rents was not an option.

Despite the difficulties of running a state in Yemen, during the first six decades of the twentieth century, Imam Yahya and Imam Ahmad administered the Imamate rather successfully. They were very pragmatic in defining boundaries even while they dreamt of "Greater Yemen". They created relative calm within those boundaries, in itself a phenomenon rarely observed in 1,000 years of Yemeni history. The imams saw the reinvigorated Imamate as a return to the glorious past of Yemen. In a period in which other traditional societies went through a process of modernization, Imam Yahya invested his efforts in the preservation and isolation of the Imamate and in maintaining a traditional agrarian economy. Imam Ahmad's attempts to ease the isolationist policy, to move closer to the Arab fold and to implement carefully-considered reforms were too little too late. In terms of the evolving circumstances in the Middle East, the result was a state in which time stood still. For this reason, the contributions of Yahya and Ahmad to the development of modern Yemen are not praised in the Arabic literature and are mentioned only peripherally in Western literature. However, Yemen witnessed the beginning of development during Yahya and Ahmad's reign, and this development was furthered by their revolutionary successors.[127]

CHAPTER 2

THE AGE OF REVOLUTIONS: 1962–1978

The Arabian Peninsula is the home of monarchical regimes which, according to many observers, are uniquely resilient due to the special features of the Arabian Peninsula – tribalism and conservative Islam.[1] Yemen – no less tribal or conservatively Islamic than its neighbours – was the exception to this rule. Throughout the 1960s, the conservative, tribal Imamate vanished, opening the way for a revolutionary regime and the creation of a new state – the Yemen Arab Republic (henceforth North Yemen).

Revolution in the North: From Imamate to Republic

On 26 September 1962, revolutionary change occurred in Yemen. A group of young officers led by Colonel 'Abdallah al-Sallal,[2] the commander of North Yemen's military forces, took over and proclaimed on Radio Sanaa:

> Instead of a rule of evil, a Yemeni republic has been established. This is a revolution of the entire nation: of soldiers and citizens, of workers and students, of the South and the North. This is a revolution of a republic that believes in Allah, in unity, and in Arab nationalism. This is a revolution that will put an end to

> factionalism. There will no longer be Zaydis, Shafi'is, Hashemites or materialism, rather there will be one nation.[3]

The Yemen Arab Republic was established and Sallal was appointed as its President.

In the months before the coup, the revolutionaries received aid from Egypt, which targeted the imam's regime in Yemen and vilified it as an obstacle to Arab revolution. Yemen became the arena in which Gamal 'Abd al-Nasser tried to recover from the blows he endured at the end of 1961: the dissolution of the United Arab Republic and, to a lesser extent, the Kuwait crisis.[4] From Nasser's perspective, developments in Yemen presented a golden opportunity to restore Egypt's waning status in the Arab world.[5] In the days following the 1962 Revolution, Nasser sent Egyptian military units to Yemen. Before the end of 1963, the Egyptian forces under the command of 'Abd al-Hakim 'Amir reached 30,000 soldiers. The Egyptians placed their advisors in every important post of the administration and military command and entrusted them with the authority to execute policy.[6] North Yemen became part and parcel of the Egyptian state. British journalist Edgar O'Ballance writes: "There was no doubt ... that the 'Voice of the Arabs' radio programme, beamed from Cairo, attracted Arabs everywhere in the Yemen; partly because Nasser's propaganda machine was both skilful and experienced and partly because there was no competitive alternative. Egyptians working in the country as military instructors, school teachers and doctors, all subtly and insidiously aided the spread of Nasser's views ... All this had a profound effect on young, restless, impressionable minds in the Yemen".[7]

From the outset of the September 1962 Revolution, signs of civil war were already palpable. Amir Hasan, the claimant to the former Imamate, returned from his position at the United Nations and coordinated the opposition against the newly-created republic in Sanaa. Soon, tribal delegations that had sworn their allegiance to Hasan began to stream into Sanaa. The assumption of power by the urban officers and educated class (amongst them prominent Shafi'is like 'Abd al-Rahman al-Baydani, Ahmad Nu'man and 'Ali 'Uthman) and the execution of clerics and tribesmen by the

Republicans aroused serious indignation and protest amongst the Zaydi tribes. Proclamations regarding the cancellation of road tolls that were commonly levied by the tribes, slogans about the need for "the abolishment of the Zaydiyya and the Shafi'iyya" and the stated aspiration to implement "far-reaching social and administrative reforms"[8] made it clear to the tribes that the Republican regime sought to create a new order that would relegate them to the sidelines of Yemen's political arena. These tribes, which aimed to topple the Republic and restore the Imamate, were the nucleus of the Royalists (*malkiyyun*). Indeed, there were also tribesmen and tribal groups that joined the Republicans (*jumhuriyyun*) including the leading *shaykh* of the Hashid confederation, Shaykh 'Abdallah al-Ahmar and parts of the Nu'aym, Bani Qays and Murad tribes. Yet these tribal groups were not significant enough to tilt the balance of power in favor of the Republicans; overall, the tribes primarily supported the Royalists.[9]

In the beginning of October 1962, Muhammad al-Badr, Imam Ahmad's first-born son, appeared in the mountains of the north. Until then, he was thought to be dead and the tribes viewed his return as a miracle.[10] Amir Hasan, who had proclaimed himself imam, renounced his claim and recognized al-Badr in order to unify their forces. In exchange, Badr appointed Hasan Prime Minister and made him a high military commander. These events cemented the Royalist support of most of the tribes. Naji al-Qadir, one of the important Bakil *shaykhs* who dwelled east of Sanaa, and other Hashid *shaykhs* came to al-Badr's residence to swear their allegiance. Others, like the Jama'ah, Bani Sahr, Khawlan al-Sham, Razik and even some of the non-Zaydi Tihama tribes, joined them.[11] The Royalists also enjoyed support from the petty rulers, such as the Sharif of Bayhan, and their influence was extended throughout the mountains and desert regions in the north-west and north-east of the country. The protracted estrangement between the tribes and the Imamate – one of the features of the pre-revolutionary reality and one of the reasons for the revolution's success – lessened during the civil war. In the civil war that ensued following the revolution, the majority of the tribes of Yemen sided with the Royalists.[12]

It soon became clear that the civil war transcended the local context, and it swiftly acquired regional and global dimensions. In Yemen, a battle between the Royalists and the Republicans developed. These camps were seen as proxies that represented the Saudis and the Egyptians respectively and they served as reflections of the tremors that rocked the Arab world at the time. Egypt – the pioneer of radical Arab nationalism led by Nasser – unequivocally sided with the Republicans and demonstrated direct involvement. In his speech in December 1962 in Port Said, Nasser highlighted the importance of the revolution in Yemen and elaborated on the need for an Egyptian presence there in order to defend the revolution and preserve its accomplishments: "The struggle for a free Yemen is our struggle, and the revolution in Yemen is our revolution".[13]

In contrast, Saudi Arabia directly supported the Royalists, albeit not with military involvement. For the Saudis, the revolution in Yemen and the subsequent Egyptian involvement in Yemen brought the threat of Arab revolution home to its southern border.[14] Neither Britain nor Saudi Arabia could impose the evacuation of Egyptian forces from Yemen. At the time the only player that could have done that was the US; however, the Kennedy administration was preoccupied with trying to prevent Nasser from tilting toward the Soviet Union and this is why the US refused Saudi Arabia's request to act against Nasser in Yemen. Moreover, in December 1962, the US officially recognized the new regime that had established itself in Sanaa after the revolution. The inaction of the US, which came at a critical phase of the civil war, largely decided the fate of the Imamate.[15]

The British supported the Royalists because they feared that Arab nationalism would sweep Aden as it did Saana. Prior to the revolution, the British and the Royalists did not view themselves as having common interests, but by the beginning of the 1960s it became clear that they indeed held a common view of the republic as a threat. However, British decision-makers could not reach a consensus on the issue of support for the Royalists and opposition to the Republicans. Initially, the Foreign Office was inclined to recognize the new republic in Sanaa in order to prevent alienation from the new regime. This would have ensured the stability of the Federation of South Arabia, which had already been established by the British in 1959 and aimed to secure the highly important, strategic post of Aden.[16] However, Alex Douglas-Home's Conservative government (1963–1964) went in a different direction beginning in October 1963. They thought that recognition of the new regime supported by Nasser in North Yemen would quickly erode the degree of legitimacy that was enjoyed by the *shaykhs*, *amirs* and *sharifs*, and would eventually jeopardize the political stability of the Federation.[17] The Colonial Office and the Ministry of Defense adopted this strategy. Since before the revolution there had been skirmishes along the border between the Federation and the Imamate, both the Colonial Office and the Ministry of Defense argued that this would occur all the more so with the new republic.[18]

The British were concerned with the policies of 'Abdallah al-Sallal, the newly-appointed President of North Yemen. He espoused a rigid and militant Arab nationalist ideology that promoted uncompromising warfare against foreign presence. Sallal was no more than a client of Cairo. In February 1963, Sanaa severed diplomatic ties with Britain in protest of their refusal to recognize the republic. A month later, Sanaa began to channel Egyptian weapons and ammunition to the tribes that dwelled on the border with the Federation. The challenge of confronting an Egyptian-backed tribal revolt against the Federation became a central component in the British regional agenda.

In spite of the lessons learnt from the Suez Crisis, the British decided to support the Royalists against the Republicans and their Egyptian patrons. One of the strongest pressure groups that lobbied for this policy was the Aden Group, which saw itself as the guardian of British interests in the south of the peninsula. Prominent among them were Julian Amery, the Minister of Aviation, and Duncan Sandys, the Secretary of State for the Colonies, both of whom were in direct contact with Kennedy Trevaskis, the governor of Aden. Amery and Sandys were of the opinion that support for the Royalists could be used to strike back at Nasser's Egypt and reciprocate the humiliation that they had suffered in the Suez. The Royalists' declining morale and imminent defeat made their argument stronger and their influence crucial.[19]

From a survey of British archival documents, it appears as though the main issue that British decision-makers grappled with was broader than the question of support for the Royalists; it was clear that the reality in the region demanded a British response that would address issues relating to the entire Arabian Peninsula. Since the 1962 Revolution, British officials had debated how they should respond to the Republicans' use of some border villages for military basing. These villages were used to launch attacks deep into the territory of the Federation and to transfer equipment and ammunition to revolting tribes within the Federation and in Aden itself. The British were particularly concerned with the scope of support and aid that was being sent to Bayhan, one of the member states of the Federation.[20] In October 1963, the British realized that guerilla organizations operating in the south were receiving broad support from the new regime in North Yemen. The British were aware that these groups were attempting to undermine their stronghold in the region, particularly by interrupting supply lines between Aden and the city of Dali'.[21] Another manifestation of their activities was the attempt to assassinate Trevaskis, the governor of Aden, on 10 December 1963.

The epicentre of developments was Radfan (about 68 miles north of Aden), a mountainous region in the territory of the Federation, which had winding and treacherous access roads. The Qu'ayti, the dominant tribal group in the region, derived most of its revenue from traditional agricultural economy and passage tolls that the Qu'aytis imposed on travellers in their territory. They resented the decision taken in 1962 to unify the Federation's taxation mechanism because it eliminated their ability to collect passage tolls. The Egyptians exploited their resentment in order to imbue the region with a spirit of revolt. They provided the Qu'aytis' *shaykh*, Sayf Maqbul, who had been exiled to North Yemen by the British, with men and ammunition. With Egyptian patronage, he led the tribes in an attack on British strongholds, namely border posts that were manned by the Federation's regular army.[22]

In London, discord between the "Aden Group" (including Amery and Sandys) and the Foreign Office regarding the appropriate British policy in Yemen reignited. The Foreign Office argued that reports on the situation in Yemen had been exaggerated in order to support the Aden Group's interpretation of events and proposed course of action. Simultaneously, the British strengthened their ruling mechanisms in Aden. In October 1963, Trevaskis, the governor of Aden, recommended that the Federation forces be expanded immediately "in order to prevent a Republican victory". The Aden Protectorate Levies were expanded to nearly 3,000 soldiers, transferred to service in the Federation and were from then on referred to as the Federal Regular Army.[23]

When North Yemen initiated an air strike on Bayhan, a member state of the Federation, the British Cabinet was forced to retaliate. The British launched a number of retaliatory operations in the summer of 1964 to some success. Prime Minister Douglas-Home declared on 14 May 1964: "Our policy in Yemen is one of non-intervention in the affairs of the state" and therefore "it is not our policy to supply arms to the Royalists in Yemen".[24] Despite this declaration, the British did intervene in the affairs of the state.

Meanwhile, the revolutionaries consolidated their power. In February 1963, the Aden branch of the Arab Nationalist movement (*al-Qawmiyyun al-Arab)* held its first conference in Sanaa, and in a second meeting in June of the same year declared the establishment of the National Liberation Front (henceforth the NLF). Youth groups and reform movements like the "Reform Movement of Yafi'" or the "Youth Movement of Mahra" were also under its auspices. The NLF was therefore an umbrella organization, which also served as a framework for inspiration and operation for the tribes that fought against the British in the South. It was led by Qahtan al-Sha'bi, an officer who was exiled from Yemen to Cairo in 1958 during the last years of the Imamate. Qahtan al-Sha'bi was loyal to the Egyptians and thus in November 1962, when Egypt declared the establishment of a national army for the liberation of the South, he was placed at its helm.[25]

The proponents of liberal reforms also proclaimed the principles of their doctrine. People such as 'Abd al-Salam Sabra and 'Abd al-Rahman al-Iryani demanded the revision of the state constitution and the insertion of liberal-spirited clauses. In order to promote their request, leading *shaykhs* like 'Abdallah al-Ahmar from the Hashid tribes joined their ranks and sent a delegation to Cairo. This initiative met with a harsh Egyptian response: some of the members of the delegation were arrested and a number of the *shaykhs* were even executed. The conclusion was clear to everybody: Saana was directly controlled by Egypt, which had turned North Yemen into a police state. The Egyptians treated the Yemenites as if they were incapable of running their own state and certainly unable to lead a struggle against the Royalists.[26] The battle between the Royalists and the Republicans – in effect the civil war that developed in North Yemen after the revolution of 1962 – turned Yemen into an arena of the "Arab Cold War". Yemen was a microcosm of the steadfast struggle between revolutionaries and traditionalists that typified Arab political culture at the time. The dimensions of the conflict widened even further when the Soviet Union sided with the Egyptians and the US and Britain sided with the Saudis. Hence, the struggle also represented the rivalry between the two superpowers dominating the world stage.

In the aftermath of the 1962 Revolution, a bloody struggle ensued in North Yemen between the Republicans and the Royalists which ran its course throughout the entire decade. Throughout the civil war, Yemen suffered heavy material and human losses. As such, it is not surprising that this period turned into one of the most formative experiences of the nation, etched in the Yemeni collective memory for at least two generations. At the battle's peak, the Republicans, who called for the creation of a modern state that would eliminate any remains of Yemen's backwardness,[27] controlled over a third of the country's territory, primarily the cities of Sanaa, Ta'izz and Hudayda, though within this triangle there were enclaves that were not under their effective control. The Royalists and their tribal allies controlled another third of the country's territory. The remaining third was in the control of tribes who maintained their traditional autonomous rule and even strengthened their autonomy during the years of battle owing to the glaring absence of central rule.[28]

This new chapter in Yemeni history highlighted the pivotal status of the tribes in local politics. Throughout the 1960s, in the labyrinth of the civil war, tribal divisions and tribal politics continued to play a key role. As a result, simply dividing the warring forces between Republicans and Royalists can be misleading. Alliances were formed in conjunction with tribal divisions or rivalries, and did not necessarily articulate an internalization – or even an outward espousal – of Republican or Royalist principles.

The Yemeni tribes, primarily the mountainous Zaydis, had always been the nucleus of the governing system and their loyalty was integral to the stability of every government. Since 1962, tribal forces branched out and assumed alternative associations with the Royalists or Republicans. For example, 'Abdallah al-Ahmar, the head of the Hashid confederation, became a distinct enemy of the imam in light of the fact that two of his family members – Husayn and Hamid al-Ahmar – had been executed at the behest of Imam Ahmad in 1960. The case of the Khawlan tribes is also instructive when it comes to understanding the influence of tribal motivations on the orientation of the Republicans or Royalists. Khawlan tribesmen were never fully subordinate to the imam, and the image of the execution of one of their leaders, 'Abd al-Latif bin Qayd al-Khawlan, on the orders of the imam was burned into their memory. Despite that, the Khawlan tribesmen sided with the imam and the Royalists when Nu'man bin Qa'id al-Rajih, one of their long-standing rivals from lower Yemen, became an ardent supporter of the Republicans. An additional example concerns the case of Shaykh Ahmad al-Siyaghi, a tribal leader who fled Yemen during the rule of the imam. Upon hearing that his brother had been executed by the Republicans, he immediately returned, joined forces with the Royalists and even became one of their commanders.[29]

Many tribes aligned themselves with the Royalists – including the Khawlan, the Arhab, the 'Ayyal, the Sufyan and others who did not accept the Egyptian presence and opposed Sallal as president. However, as explained above, the manner in which tribes formulated their positions during the civil war was complex, and this issue demands further investigation. It is clear that the Royalist ideal was not the guiding principle for the majority of tribes who aligned themselves on that side; rather what motivated them to act, at least in the beginning, was the unreliability of and their disappointment in the Republican regime. Calculations based on inter-tribal rivalries also played an instrumental role.[30] The Republicans quickly understood that lofty ideologies and revolutionary slogans could perhaps make headway, but were unable to ensure steadfastness and survival in the labyrinth of Yemeni political reality. Tribal divisions and dialogue within the tribal arena were the only keys to secure control of the country.

Sallal's Republic, 1962–1967

In its first five years (1962–1967), the Republic of North Yemen experienced a bloody civil war.[31] During these years, Sallal's Egyptian patrons were deeply involved administratively and militarily in almost all aspects of Yemen's governance. From the very beginning, Egypt institutionalized its influence through the signing of an agreement of cooperation with Yemen on 10 November 1962. However, the Yemeni officers' weight in the joint leadership was nominal at best. Yemenis did staff agencies, but their role in decision-making was peripheral. Egypt's representatives in the joint leadership dictated the pace of development in Yemen and decided issues of internal and foreign affairs. Throughout the civil war, though governments rose and fell, all of them would make decisions only after Egypt granted its approval.[32]

The revolutionary dynamics in North Yemen reflected an interesting complexity, resulting in catastrophic results for the young republic. As in other revolutions in the Middle East, revolutionaries channelled their efforts toward denouncing the *ancien régime* and systematically eradicating supporters of the toppled Imamate.[33] Notables from the ruling family, ministers and tribal heads who had supported the imam were executed. The title "*sayyid*" was abolished, the assets of the imam and his family were confiscated and their citizenship was revoked. The flag of the Imamate of Yemen, a red flag with a spear and five stars, was converted into a Republican flag modelled after the Egyptian one. It had three horizontal stripes (red, black and white) and in the centre of the flag, there was one star, instead of two like the Egyptian flag at the time.

The young officers – 'Abdallah al-Sallal, 'Abdallah Juzaylan, Hasan al-'Amri and about 50 others who took part in the coup – sought to quickly advance the affairs of Yemen and make it a "free Arab state". A number of Shafi'i leaders, who sought to break up the tribal framework and establish an urban-oriented political life, supported the officers in their plan to form a central army based on a modern officer corps. 'Abd al-Rahman al-Baydani, one of the Shafi'i leaders who was cultivated by the Egyptians prior to the coup, led this group. Al-Baydani sought to exploit the coup and to alter the Yemeni balance of forces in favor of the Shafi'is. However the Egyptians, who feared the Shafi'i-Zaydi crossfire and the pressure from the Hashid tribes, utterly disregarded him.[34]

From its early days in power, the leadership of North Yemen weighed the possibility of reliance on tribal heads, while leaning on the political-military echelons, which included the army officer corps, the coup instigators, and their Egyptian patrons. The gulf between these two opposing entities was a formidable obstacle, given that the revolution was closely identified with Egyptian involvement and with slogans that alienated the tribes and their leaders from the revolutionaries. Sallal was not inclined to involve the tribal leaders in his government. After all, the revolution declared war against the feudal regime and its philosophy of governance. This perpetuated the Zaydi tribes' hostility towards Sallal's regime. Their suspicion increased when it became clear to them that around half of the ministers of the first government were Shafi'is. Even those who dreamt of a socialist republic and supported the coup were quickly forced to admit that, in practice, there was no tangible change in the essence and philosophy of rule. The visionaries believed that the city of Ta'izz – where, in the summer of 1963, the Arab Nationalist movement established the first workers' union and where the First Popular Nationalist Congress had convened – would be the future "capital of the two revolutions", meaning they sought to join the north and the south in a comprehensive revolution.[35] Alas, the vision was not fulfilled due to the prohibitive legislation on political unions and the strict Egyptian control.

Yemen's isolation and decentralized character forced Sallal's government to confront the challenge of extending sovereignty over the entire country and its people. From the very beginning, it was preoccupied with the need to create a state that would provide security and services, a goal that was further complicated by the civil war. In light of these constraints, Sallal's government was forced to seek the support of the tribes and to promise them that their privileges would not be violated. For example, one of the first proclamations of the new regime in November 1962 ordered the establishment of the High Defense Council, comprised of tribal *shaykhs* who were charged with securing stability in their regions. This proclamation therefore awarded the tribal *shaykhs* additional power. Another example is the presidential order of 22 February 1963, which led to the establishment of the Council, composed mainly of tribal notables.[36]

These measures were also meant to subordinate the tribal structure to the political system, but they did not succeed. Throughout the civil war, the tribal units clearly demonstrated their superior power. In practice, the state's territory was divided between Republicans, Royalists and autonomous tribal *shaykhs*. The latter benefited from continued autonomy and economic profits that resulted from their successful manipulation of the two competing forces – the Republicans and the Royalists. Consequently, in spite of his aspirations for a modern state, the range of Sallal's government was limited to the Sanaa-Ta'izz-Hudayda triangle. Even within this triangular region, there were discernible pockets that evaded the scope of the government's control and influence.[37]

The civil war highlighted the vitality of tribes in Yemen's political arena, but at the same time made the shortcomings of reliance on tribal forces painfully clear. Because Yemen did not have a professional army, the only units that could be mobilized under these circumstances were tribal units. Many of the enlistees deserted before even reaching Sanaa. Their equipment was poor, people did not receive their salaries in a timely manner and sometimes some of them sold their weapons for food. Furthermore, owing to their shifting loyalties, the tribesmen capitalized on the war and benefited from the situation that was created. Shelagh Weir, whose research dealt with Jabal Razih (west of the northern plateau town of Sa'da), writes: "Most Razihis were 'royalist' by default as well as by conviction and contractual allegiance. But a small minority openly and actively supported the Republicans, and others undoubtedly did so secretly, variously motivated by resentment of *sayyid* power and privileges, exasperation at al-Badr's inadequacies, and a yearning for the development promised by the Republicans. Yet others were simply 'bought'".[38] A saying that was used to characterize the tribes' behaviour was "Republican by day, and Royalist by night".[39]

The civil war paralysed North Yemen in its incipient stage; it took precedence over any of Sallal's aspirations for political reform. What's more, Egypt's intervention left little room for national politics and for the involvement of Yemenis in the political system. In fact, the Egyptians penetrated every facet of Yemen's civil life. The Egyptian-based *Middle East News Agency* also opened a large office in Sanaa and radio commentators of *Sawt al-'Arab* broadcasted from there as well.[40] They dismissed Yemenis from their positions and replaced them with Egyptians. They downsized the state apparatus and packed it with Egyptian advisors. Even the presidential guard was comprised of Egyptian soldiers. The Egyptians also prevented other Arab states from becoming involved in Yemen's affairs.

Egypt became entangled in Yemen's complexities but believed that within a short period of time, it would be able to directly impose its government on Yemen, due to its technological advantages and its control of the sea and air routes.[41] This assumption proved to be misguided. As their stay persisted, the Egyptians realized that the war effort was squarely laid on their shoulders, and that they could not merely serve as influential advisors to Sallal's government as they initially hoped.

The Egyptian command was not sufficiently familiar with the country and its peculiarities: moreover, it is doubtful whether the Egyptians had made an effort to understand the conditions on the ground before sending in troops. The Egyptian expeditionary force was not properly equipped for Yemen's tropical climate. The long supply lines in Yemen and the treacherous paths took their toll. The life of the Egyptian soldier in Yemen became difficult and burdensome with food, equipment and medication shortages. Yemen's cliffs and mountains favored the tribal guerilla warriors, who mercilessly attacked Egyptian units. Consecutive battles in the north and east of Sanaa did not accomplish anything for the Egyptians, whose losses of life and materials rose steadily.[42]

In the second half of 1965, there were around 60,000 Egyptian soldiers in Yemen.[43] Despite their aspiration to guard the borders of the Republic, their control was confined to Sanaa and its surroundings, similar to the situation the Ottomans had faced 60 years earlier. The Egyptians pinned their hopes on North Yemen as a base from which to rejuvenate the Arab revolution's momentum and believed that in a short while they would fulfill their goals. Five years of war in Yemen did not bring the Egyptians any closer to the fulfillment of their goals. Their problems in Yemen were typical of any regular army in low-intensity conflict with guerilla forces.[44]

The legendary British explorer and researcher of the desert, Wilfred Thesiger, vividly depicts the problematic situation that faced the Egyptian army in Yemen at the time: "Nasser can never win the war in Yemen. To do so he would have to launch an all-out offensive, occupy the country and disarm the tribes – which, however many troops he brings in, he could never hope to do. He must realize by now that he has no hope of inflicting even a serious reverse on the Royalist forces, let alone of winning a victory that would influence the outcome of the war".[45] The Egyptians were submerged in the "Yemeni swamp" and they suffered hard material and human losses to the extent that Yemen became "Egypt's Vietnam".[46] Similar to what the Soviets and the Americans would experience in the battlefields of Afghanistan and Vietnam respectively, the Egyptian doctrine of warfare was unable to address the challenges that the complex Yemeni arena presented. The Egyptian soldiers' disillusionment with what ensued in Yemen also increased because the purpose of their battle was not clear. In their naiveté, the Egyptian soldiers thought that their mission was to fight against the British occupiers and expel them from the country, but reality confronted them with an entirely different enemy: their fellow Arab brothers. This was contradictory to what their leaders had repeatedly preached before they set out on their mission. Their despondency was amplified when the Yemeni attitude towards the Egyptians changed and they came to be perceived as occupiers – not saviours – of the Republic of North Yemen.

'Abdallah al-Sallal, a tool in the service of Nasser, lost credibility. Toward the end of 1964 many of his supporters – al-Iryani,

Zubayri and Nu'man – protested a "corrupt, incompetent and bankrupt government".[47] In their great dismay with Sanaa politics, some of them began to search independently for a different solution to North Yemen's problems. Zubayri tried to achieve a general ceasefire agreement amongst the northern tribes, but he was murdered on 1 April 1965.[48] As the fighting intensified, the strength of important tribal leaders increased. The balance of power between the tribal periphery and the central rule tipped in favour of the tribes. Under the pressure exerted by 'Abdallah al-Ahmar, who was both the Interior Minister and the head of the Hashid tribal confederacy, Sallal was forced to appoint Ahmad Nu'man to the office of prime minister.[49]

Immediately following his appointment, Nu'man sent a message to the Saudi King Faisal regarding the need to establish dialogue and reach a compromise that would put an end to the warfare.[50] The time was ripe for that kind of overture because 'Abd al-Nasser and King Faisal were negotiating a ceasefire, which was achieved in August of 1965. The Saudis attacked the Egyptians in the north as the Egyptians had attacked the British in the south but without fiery revolutionary ideology. The Royalists in Yemen – tribes aligned with the Saudis and anyone supported by them – did not devise a revolutionary programme but only sought to renew and rehabilitate their power. They cloaked their struggle in emotive slogans such as *al-nar qabla al-'ar* (rather fire than shame)[51] and they suspected correctly that, similarly to the British, the Egyptians viewed tribalism as a malaise that needed to be uprooted.

Egyptian forces in North Yemen faced difficult challenges and worsening conditions. The battles that were waged in the north and east of Sanaa increased their casualties, material losses and the price tag of their stay in Yemen. Their pretensions to be "defenders of the Republic of North Yemen" lacked any validity in reality. During the war, Nasser and Faisal met with the goal of reaching a ceasefire.[52] This meeting provoked Sallal and the NLF's consternation as, from their perspective, going to Riyadh was tantamount to treason and the ideological abandonment of the revolution. Due to Saudi and Egyptian pressure, Yemeni delegations of Royalists and Republicans met in November 1965 in al-Harad near the Saudi border.[53] Despite Egyptian pressure, the Republicans refused to accept the Saudi recommendation to compromise on the definition of Yemen as an "Islamic state", and negotations collapsed.[54]

These developments prompted changes amongst the revolutionary camp, primarily in the ranks of the NLF. In the conference convened in Ta'izz in June 1965, the NLF promulgated a new nationalist charter. Yemen's backwardness was now explained in Marxist-Leninist terms. For the revolutionaries, colonialism and feudalism were two systems that conspired to dominate the lands of the state. Therefore, the revolution was charged with the belief that a Marxist strategy of guerrilla warfare, as developed in North Vietnam and Cuba, offered a more successful model of organization and a proven set of tactics for gaining popular support.[55] There was an ideological shift away from Arab nationalism and towards more sophisticated messages of revolutionary socialism. This demonstrated the erosion of Egypt's status among the Republicans, particularly after Egypt had reached an agreement with Saudi Arabia. The revolutionaries recognized that Egypt was exploiting Yemen and delaying its development and independence, just like other foreign powers had done in the past.

Egypt worried about what was unfolding in the echelons of the NLF. A "bourgeoisie" pro-Egyptian faction and a "revolutionary" pro-Marxist faction emerged within the NLF. The pro-Marxists would not compromise their doctrine and rejected any accord with the Royalists and Saudis.[56] They also rejected continuing any cooperation with Egypt because they believed that Egypt had abandoned its revolutionary principles.[57] After the Egyptian leadership abandoned its ties with the pro-Marxists in the NLF, it began to strengthen its ties with the "bourgeoisie" who still pledged allegiance to Egypt. In January 1966, Egypt established an organization called the "Front for the Liberation of Occupied Southern Yemen" (henceforth FLOSY).[58]

Yemen experienced factionalism that was accompanied by a rapid and disruptive movement of immigrant workers. On the one hand, Aden absorbed a significant immigration of Yemenis from the North, and on the other, many Yemenis (around 100,000 throughout the 1960s) immigrated to Saudi Arabia. Although the Sanaa government presented itself as the sworn enemy of the Saudis (even if subject to fluctuations in Egyptian policy) until 1967, the Saudis did not block the remittances of the Yemeni workers in Saudi Arabia. Together with critical support from the Egyptians, this allowed North Yemen to survive the crisis. Having said that, the economic situation of North Yemen deteriorated throughout 1966, owing to the Federation's decision to seal the border with North Yemen and close the port of Aden, which facilitated the transfer of imports to North Yemen.

The border between the Federation and North Yemen turned into a no man's land. The NLF and FLOSY worked industriously to enlist the tribal heads' support.[59] In August 1966, Sallal returned to Yemen after a nine-month stay in Egypt. It quickly became clear that he had been detained in Egypt because of a difference of opinion regarding the most appropriate policy for North Yemen. Also, when he returned, the Prime Minister, al-'Amri, tried to prevent him from landing in Yemen. Sallal's return aroused waves of protest from the Presidential Council (*majlis al-ri'asa*), whose members left for Cairo with their staff of eight ministers.[60]

Egypt arrested these members of the Presidential Council. A new government was established in Yemen and staffed with pro-Egyptian military personnel like 'Abdallah al-Juzaylan[61] and Mahmud al-Ahnumi.[62] In October 1966, the National Guard was formed; its first order of business was to assassinate opponents of Egypt. The Arab Nationalists and professional unions, the components of which the NLF was comprised, were initially loyal to Egypt. However, as soon as they wavered in their support, the Egyptians started persecuting them. Egypt lost its networks of power and support in Yemen and the worse the situation got, the harsher the Egyptian reaction was. In September 1966, the Egyptians suppressed youth movement demonstrations using live fire.[63] The Egyptian forces renewed their bombardments in regions where there were thought to be "rebellious" tribes, and occasionally resorted to poison gas.[64]

Eric Rouleau, a journalist who visited Yemen in the beginning of 1967, illustratively described many of the facets of the struggle in Yemen and Egypt's waning status. He noted that Royalists expressed their position simply: "The 1962 revolution was ours and the Egyptians stole it from us".[65] Many Royalists held that there was a need to establish a new political order immediately following the Egyptian withdrawal, and Sallal grasped the full extent of his inevitable ruin. In a desperate effort, in January 1967, he tried to establish the "Popular Revolutionary Union" (*al-Ittihad al-Sha'bi al-Thawri*)[66] and for this purpose, he summoned 'Abd al-Qawi Makawi (a former senior official of the Aden government) and representatives of the Ba'th party (*Hizb al-Ba'th al-'Arabi al-Ishtiraki*) in Yemen and the Arab nationalists.[67]

Another meeting took place at the behest of Sinan Abu Lahum. Sinan was a tribal leader who was highly influential amongst the Bakil tribes. He had been seen as an ardent Republican after his uncompromising battle with the imam from 1959 to 1962. But this time, he joined the Royalists, as did 'Abdallah al-Ahmar, the leader of the Hashid tribes, who demanded that Sallal release Yemeni members of government who had been arrested in Cairo and political prisoners who had been apprehended and jailed since August 1966. Muhammad Ahmad Nu'man published in 1965 a book titled *Landmarks in Yemeni History: The Interested Parties in Yemen* (*Adwa 'ala tariq al-yamaniyyin: al-Atraf al-Ma'niyya fil-Yaman*), which views the conflict between tribes and villages as the cause for friction between Zaydis and Shafi'is. *The Interested Parties* is preoccupied with the Zaydi superiority in national politics, and Nu'man's views are grim and harsh. He concludes that from time immemorial, Yemen was a gathering point of "interest groups" or "parties", each of which had its own vision. Nu'man's description is applicable to millennia of politics in Yemen. The reality of the 1960s embodies Nu'man's tragic story of Yemen, and the absence of real dialogue and inability of certain groups to be attentive to the hardships of others.

During the "the Egyptian Era", Yemen opened further to the outside world. The Egyptian presence contributed to the creation of urban bureaucracy and changes in economic patterns. Merchants moved to Ibb and transitioned from exporting agricultural products to importing foreign products, and micro-trade blossomed due to the sale of food products and clothing to Egyptian soldiers. Nevertheless, the adversity and bloodshed that Yemen experienced during this period of civil war hampered the state-building process. Similar to cases of other developing countries, the task of state-building in North Yemen exceeded the need to preserve order and security and was meant to install a revolutionary order. The cultural mayhem experienced by Yemen in the wake of the sharp transition from the Imami period of isolation to dynamic activity in the Arab fold, and the absence of an organized and effective system of governance, rendered state-building nearly impossible. Sallal's government reached a dead end. A loss of legitimacy and credibility brought about his deposition at the same time that his patron, Egypt, abandoned the country. Beaten and humiliated following the defeat of the June 1967 war, Egypt evacuated its troops (at the time nearly 70,000 soldiers) from Yemen before the end of 1967.

The Path to Revolution in the South: The End of the British Era

Throughout Sallal's years of rule, and in conjunction with his attempt to stabilize his regime in North Yemen, dramatic developments in the south of the country paved the way for a revolution of a different kind. The British hold in the south came under the attack of Gamal 'Abd al-Nasser and his supporters. The battle against the British was defined in terms of decolonization and later as class struggle, but in this case too tribal considerations stood at the centre of the picture. The Radfan revolt of 14 October 1963 is key to understanding the developments in the south. In this mountainous region, on the twisting access roads deep in the lands of the Federation, sparks ignited and a flare-up that would lead to the end of the British presence in Yemen took place. Like the revolution of September 1962 in the north, the Radfan revolt constituted a critical juncture in Yemen's history.

The "Rebels of Radfan" were Qutaybi tribesman from the Radfan Hills, an area which was part of the British protectorate of Dali'. These rebels complained about the deteriorating conditions and oppressive policies of the governor of Dali', a member state of the Federation, whose leader was considered a British client. In May 1963, many of the Qutaybi tribesmen made their way north in order to arm themselves, and in October of the same year, they submitted a petition saying:

> We submit to you this complaint from all Ahl Quteib [Qutayb] Aqils [headmen] and Shaikhs against Naib [the local governor]

> Mahmud Hasson [Mahmud bin Hasan] ... We have got nothing from him except oppression ... He has changed the system of the Urfi [customary law] Court and Appeal Court ... He has also made decisions and revoked the judgement of the Urfi Court ... he has relinquished [sic] the Aqils and notables of Ahl Quteib from their responsibilities and deprived them of their stipends ...
>
> The said Naib has separated the clans of the Ahl Quteib and placed one above the other.
>
> He deals with the affairs of the treasury in a way unknown to all ...[68]

The "Rebels of Radfan" increased their attacks on the Federation's patrols, and in the spring of 1964, the conflict escalated when the British army and its tribal supporters attacked the rebels. Many on the border fled out of fear of their lives. The "Rebels of Radfan" were suppressed by the British. The British tried to appease the rebels and prevent them from joining the anti-British forces in North Yemen by developing an agricultural infrastructure in their territory; however, this was unsuccessful. The British attempt to disconnect the supply lines from the rebels aroused the indignation of the locals and incited further revolt. The NLF exploited local grievances and established posts in the region (in lower Yafi' and Dathina) for operational logistics.[69] This made the British more vulnerable.

Egypt exploited the Radfan revolt. When riots broke out in Radfan, Radio Cairo asserted that the revolt was a source of inspiration for a coming revolution:

> Tomorrow the revolution will expand its extensions in order to gather within itself all the states which comprise the Federation of South Arabia. Tomorrow the revolutionary lava will pour out of Aden's proximity, people of freedom will topple the stronghold of colonialism, and revolutionaries will set ablaze the refineries of the oil industry.[70]

Cairo condemned the petty rulers, calling them "agent sultans", accusing them of collaborating with the British to consolidate the British presence in the port of Aden and deep within the lands of the Federation. At this point in time, the British raised the status of Aden in their strategic considerations from a colonial lake to a strategic necessity.[71] The British evacuation of Kuwait in September 1961 and Iraq's attempt to claim it for itself also strengthened the importance of Aden as a vital location from which Britain could defend its interests and the maritime routes on the way to the Indian Ocean and the Persian Gulf.[72]

However, throughout the 1960s, the British presence in the south of Arabia blatantly went against the *zeitgeist*. The Yemeni and Egyptian nationalists had high expectations and grand visions. The British, in contrast, felt the signs of decline and their imperial pretensions waned. Nevertheless, as was the case in the 1950s, they were willing to act against the "rebels" and sometimes resorted to harsh punitive measures, but these did not amount to a comprehensive attack on the NLF. The British were also hesitant in their efforts to counter the actions of 'Abdallah al-Asnaj, the head of the Aden Trade Union Congress (henceforth ATUC), which was established in March 1956.[73] They displayed signs of weakness and their eroding grasp in the region was obvious. Mounting expenditures and geopolitical changes turned the overseas colonies, including Aden, into an unnecessary burden. At the time, there was discussion of a planned British withdrawal, and at a certain stage, the British even involved the leaders of the Federation in their deliberations.[74]

Analysts tend to link the struggle against the British to other decolonization processes in Asia and Africa. However, while the conflict in Yemen was laden with slogans of decolonization and the notion of class struggle, tribal motivations dictated a different rhythm in Yemen. Killings of members of other tribes on grounds of defending family honour were portrayed as assaults on feudalism and imperialism if the tribesman also happened to be loyal to the British.[75] The role of ideology in the creation of some organizations and parties in Yemen has been exaggerated. For example, the "Reform Front of Yafi'", which was established in April 1963 (and which would eventually become one of the components of the NLF) has been portrayed in the revolutionary literature as an organization that was part and parcel of class struggle in Yemen but in fact, the organizations' members did not truly internalize the Marxist-Leninist ideology.[76]

While the fighting in North Yemen and in the South can be explained in terms of tribal divisions and tribal politics, the same cannot be said for the fighting in Aden. The assassination attempt on Trevaskis, the governor of Aden, in December 1963 was an omen of the bloody war's onset that thrust the "colony" into a wave of violence, killing and assassinations. ATUC, a union of many workers from the north, stood at the centre of opposition to the British in Aden. Its leader, al-Asnaj, expected the British to consider the ATUC a partner, but instead they relegated it to the sidelines; the British were suspicious of the organization and adamantly refused to negotiate with it.[77] Instead, the British opted to negotiate with the Federation of Southern Arabia, which Aden became a part of in 1963. In response, the leaders of ATUC invested their efforts in demonstrations and strikes. Their frustration with British policies brought them closer to Egypt. Nasser's strident support for the Radfan rebels and his assertion that the British had failed to learn their lesson from the Suez Crisis found an attentive ear among ATUC and its supporters.[78]

In October 1964, there were changes in the British administration. The new leader of the Labour party, Harold Wilson, orchestrated a different policy viewing British activity beyond the sea, including Aden, as an unnecessary burden. Trevaskis's replacement in 1965 and the British readiness to negotiate with the ATUC were signs of the new policy.[79] Local elements (especially the NLF) that opposed the British, as well as some of their allies, viewed the new policy as an indication of the eminent decline of British presence in the region. The discussions that the British held with their allies regarding the question of their constitution and political future did not continue. Key players in the Federation, like the Sharif of Bayhan, stood their ground and avoided the meetings that the British arranged.[80]

The opposition to the British increased and their demands were steeper than ever before. Al-Asnaj and his supporters, a non-violent but boisterous opposition, continued to express their protest and demanded more funding for their education system, however their voice was drowned out by the militant opposition of the NLF. Hand grenades that were hurled against the British officials and their families underscored a new trend.[81] While the British dispatched emergency forces in June 1965 in order to quell the situation, people like 'Abd al-Qawi Makawi, a former senior minister in the Aden government, and al-Asnaj (who had lost his leadership role in ATUC) made their way to Cairo in order to ask for advice about how to conduct the revolt.[82] The NLF took charge of the struggle for the liberation of Yemen. In view of the mounting direct pressures, and without previous warning, in February 1966 London announced its intention to evacuate British holdings in Aden by 1968. Nevertheless, the British declaration of their future withdrawal did not improve the situation, and in fact, acts of violence and expressions of instability rose.[83]

In June 1966, a series of incidents aimed at the British occurred, including grenade attacks and the planting of mines. That same month, in what the British called "the first terrorist incident", a British officer who also served as an officer of a local legion was murdered in Mukalla.[84] In the Federation, the British still tried to suppress the uprisings by mobilizing the security forces. However, both the Federation's regular army – which had more or less undergone a process of de-tribalization – and the Federation's Guard, which was more established on the foundation of blood relations, were unreliable.[85]

In Aden itself, the British were fully involved in the struggle, and this only increased hostility towards them. Not only did dissatisfaction within the ranks of the Federation's regular army increase, but the army became a conduit through which around 400 indigenous officers with command experience developed a sense of national solidarity.[86] Other bodies like the police force of Aden or the forces of the Qu'ayti and the Kathiri, member states of the Federation, did not feel much obligation towards the British, and some of them wiped their hands clean of them. These forces, which in the 1950s had spoken and preached in terms of conservative Islamic practice, were now saturated with the NLF's revolutionary ideas. Therefore, despite the internal divisions within it, the NLF became the connecting link between the city and the countryside. Amongst people from North Yemen, there were those who did not see the point in fighting the British, who in any case intended to leave. Al-Asnaj, for example, vehemently opposed turning Aden into a "second Congo" (a colonial territory fraught with a series of coups in the first half of the 1960s). Yet 'Abd al-Nasser espoused the lines of his old policy, criticizing British imperialism.[87] Even those who abandoned Nasser's camp continued to espouse these ideas. The NLF, for example, remained committed to an armed struggle, and continued to characterize any attempt to placate or strike a compromise with the British as an act of treason or cowardice.

In February 1966, 'Ali Husayn al-Qadi, the president of the ATUC, was murdered, ostensibly under the instruction of 'Abd al-Fattah Isma'il, the leader of the NLF.[88] Even though the revolutionary factions blamed the British for the murder and announced general strikes, his murder signaled an escalation in the internal fighting between them. Aden became the battleground for the struggle between the NLF and FLOSY, and between the two organizations and the British who had already announced their intentions to leave Yemen.

The south of Yemen was thrust into a bloody battle that levied a high price. Industrial production, which was limited in its scope, ground almost to a complete stop. Heavy taxation in the Qu'ayti and Kathiri states and the crash of the educational system signalled a total deterioration. Throughout the years 1965–1966, residents of the Hadramawt region suffered from hunger and epidemics.[89] During this time, friction within the ranks of the leadership in the south persisted. Al-Sha'bi, the leader of the NLF, and al-Asnaj, the leader of ATUC, loathed each other. Some of al-Asnaj's supporters even negotiated with the "feudal" sultans, but at the same time, it became clear that the authority of the sultans, *shaykhs* and *amirs* was being overtaken by the increasing waves of revolutionary nationalism. The Sharif of Bayhan was exiled to Saudi Arabia, and his state disappeared with his departure. The sultans of Hadramawt returned from Geneva in September 1967 only to discover that NLF activists had occupied their capitals.[90] In the eyes of the revolutionaries, the hypocritical British policies were a central reason for the malaise, but both the NLF and FLOSY prepared to fill the void that the British left. The Federation's regular army made a desperate attempt to restore order but failed in this task. In October 1967, fighting broke out in Lahaj between FLOSY and the

NLF. Both were struggling for slices of control throughout the crumbling Federation.

In November 1966, in a meeting in Khamir (on the border between the north and the south), the NLF sharpened its division with the FLOSY, which in the beginning had benefited from relatively broad support from the provinces of Radfan, Jabal Jahhaf and districts of the former Western Protectorate, Bayhan, Upper 'Awlaqi and Wahidi. Strongholds of the NLF had not pinned their hopes on the population of North Yemen or on the population in Aden; rather, they counted on the middle and lower class of the provinces that connected Aden to the rural south, which gave them much broader support. The NLF quickly took over the majority of the Federation's territory and filled much of the void that the British had left.

Aden became the principal arena in the NLF-FLOSY conflict, which cost hundreds of lives. It seemed as though the revolution in Yemen had just begun. The British hastily launched an operation to evacuate their troops from Aden, and the last British soldier left the colony on 29 November 1967. What began in Radfan on 14 October 1963[91] as a tribal revolt meant to increase tribal autonomy spiralled into a general and comprehensive battle against the British. The fighting ended with a shameful British withdrawal from Aden, marking the end of 124 years of British presence in the colony and the colonial enterprise in the region as a whole.[92] The Federation the British had established in southern Arabia crashed before the might of the NLF. The sultans, *shaykhs* and *sharifs* of the Federation demonstrated leadership even weaker than usual in the provinces of North Yemen. The British attempts to impose "good government" in Aden's hinterland in the last two decades of their presence further weakened local leaders and neutralized the little power that they held at the time.

In practice, both the British initiative to establish a federation through the formation of institutional bureaucracy and the abrogation of the tribal taxation system further weakened the economic power of the tribes. Tribal leaders gradually transferred their loyalty to the NLF, which used the absence of a solid tribal leadership in order to foment rebellion in southern Arabia. In practice, Britain deprived the tribal leaders of the means of government that allowed them to control their strongholds. This did not provide them with a real alternative source of power that would allow them to retain their status and influence after the British evacuation.

The defeat of the British and their allies in Aden and in the Federation paved the way for the establishment of an entirely different regime in the south of Yemen – the only declared Marxist regime in the Arab world. On 27 November 1967, the NLF declared the establishment of the People's Republic of South Yemen, which in 1970 would be called the People's Democratic Republic of Yemen (henceforth South Yemen).

The Two Yemens: The Republican North and the Socialist South

The evacuation of Egyptian and British forces from Yemen left behind two states with different orientations. One was republican North Yemen (officially called the Yemen Arab Republic) which had exhibited signs of internal strife since the very beginning of the September 1962 Revolution. The other was the newly-created, socialist South Yemen which joined the former British protectorates, including Hadramawt, and declared Aden to be its capital. Since the two forces that objected to revolution – the tyrannical Imamate in the North and British imperialism in the South – had disappeared, unifying Yemen seemed like an achievable mission. However, unity would not happen on its own, as many Yemenis thought. Sharp ideological differences divided the governments of the North and the South, and each state worked to consolidate its independence and realize its vision for the future.

When the opportunity arose to unify the political systems of both Yemens, neither state was ideologically or politically ready. While South Yemen came into the orbit of the Eastern bloc, North Yemen did not identify with either of the superpowers and maintained a position of non-alignment. For about 20 years, during the 1970s and 1980s, the two states interacted with each other in terms that resembled the Cold War – North Yemen and South Yemen became rivals.[93] The two states wavered on the brink of conflict.

North Yemen Under the Rule of al-Iryani, al-Hamdi and al-Ghashmi, 1970–1978: A Transition Period

Egypt's defeat in June of 1967 signalled the end of the Egyptian presence in the Arabian Peninsula. In mid-October, the Egyptians completed their withdrawal from Yemen. On 5 November 1967, President 'Abdallah al-Sallal was deposed in a military coup and left the country for Moscow and later Iraq.[94] The Presidential Council headed by 'Abd al-Rahman al-Iryani filled his vacancy as the President of the Republic.[95]

The appointment of this council marked the renewal of the struggle between the Republicans and the Royalists. The Royalists, seeking to shake the foundations of the Republic, surrounded Sanaa in the beginning of December 1967. With the aid of loyal tribal units, they imposed a siege, known as the "Seventy Day Siege", which became another cornerstone in the history of modern Yemen. As in the 1962 Revolution, the activities of the rebels in Sanaa captured the imagination of Yemeni countrymen. People from the South came to the North "in order to defend the revolution", and a large number of volunteers flowed in from the Shafi'i regions.[96] In order to help the besieged, the leadership of South Yemen sprang to action and deployed around 600 volunteers to Sanaa. Aden saw the confrontation as a suitable opportunity to pave the way for its future influence there, and so they aided the besieged Republicans.[97] Sanaa was full of under-equipped volunteers. For most of them, joining the new forces in Sanaa was like a refuge. North Yemen's army expanded significantly, from hundreds to thousands in a span of only two months.

The Royalist and Republican camps existed, but loyalties were not clear-cut and adherents to each camp did not always fit the respective ideological moulds. For example, 'Abdallah al-Ahmar and Mujahid Abu Shawarib from the Hashid confederation entered into an alliance with the Prime Minister, al-'Amri, against the Royalists. Conversely, activists from the Arab Nationalist Movement, who did not view al-'Amri's measures favorably, launched an all-out conflict with his forces.[98] While treating the exchange of loyalties and the Yemeni political dynamics, Deffarge and Troeller provide tribesman's testimonies.[99]

Deffarge and Troeller show that at certain times, many Zaydi tribes identified themselves as Republicans. By the same token, there were also a considerable amount of Shafi'i tribes that identified themselves as Royalists (Murad and 'Ubayda, for example).

Discussions between the Republicans and Royalists took place, yet the fighting continued and even intensified when the Republicans received support from like-minded revolutionaries in Algeria and the USSR. The Royalists, despite their Saudi support, could not subdue the Republicans and suffered hard losses. Although the Royalists remained active in the northern parts of the country until 1970, the war reached a lull and Sanaa had the upper hand.[100] Prime Minister al-'Amri was instrumental in securing the victory of the Republic.

The Saudis reversed their position toward North Yemen, and from then on, Saudi Arabia would be very influential and crucial for the politics of North Yemen. The Saudis viewed the emergence of a Marxist-Leninist state in South Yemen as a great danger. Thus, the Republican North became the lesser of two evils. The Saudis considered North Yemen a buffer against a more dangerous challenge that emanated from South Yemen. Hence, they decided to recognize the Republic of North Yemen in 1970.

North Yemen was ready to set aside the remnants of the past and leave behind old baggage with the Saudis. A number of considerations influenced North Yemen's position and motivated it to forge relations with the Saudis. North Yemen was on the brink of a harsh economic crisis, especially incapable of levying taxes in the autonomous tribal areas. The government was forced to pay substantial subsidies to support the tribal *shaykhs*. Alongside the rising expenditures for security and military needs, support for the tribes constituted around 43 per cent of the entire budget for each of the years between 1968–1970.[101] In light of these hardships, North Yemen was forced to locate additional sources of funding. Since Egyptian aid had entirely ended, North Yemen turned to Saudi Arabia for aid. In mid-May 1970, Saudi Arabia and North Yemen signed an agreement that put an end to the civil war, brought about the reintegration of the Royalists into the political system, and ensured regular Saudi funding. Many Royalists, except for people from the Hamid al-Din family (the family of the former imams), were appointed to important posts in the Republican government. In August 1975, the Yemeni-Saudi Coordination Council was created. Within that framework, a series of annual meetings were held to enhance mutual relations, expand cooperation between the two countries and help Yemen overcome its challenges.[102]

North Yemen perceived the Saudis as a potential ally in the struggle against the leftist ideology growing in popularity among the ranks of the army, an ideology which called for uprooting the tribal foundations and creating a state of a different nature.[103] Thus, while South Yemen gradually strengthened its Marxist orientation, the government of North Yemen sought a way out of their civil war and sought a compromise with the Royalists and their patrons, the Saudis. The Saudi Kingdom's growing involvement in Yemen's internal affairs was one of the hallmarks of North Yemen's politics and foreign relations in the 1970s and 1980s.[104]

Riyadh had two contradictory aspirations for North Yemen's policy. One was the hope that it would be a state strong enough to block the exportation of Marxist ideas coming from South Yemen and the other was that it would be too weak to pose a threat to its neighbouring countries. Therefore, the Saudis aimed to make North Yemen's economic dependence a pillar of Saudi-Yemeni relations. Firstly, they supplied annual aid to Sanaa to fund its military and administrative forces. Secondly and more importantly, they financially supported influential tribes and in doing so, afforded them the ability to preserve their autonomy vis-à-vis the state. Sanaa also turned a blind eye to Saudi dealings with South Yemeni expatriate groups, northern army officers and tribal *shaykhs* who aimed to bring down the ruling NLF in Aden.[105]

Al-Iryani's Presidency: September 1971–June 1974

In September 1971, Prime Minister Hassan al-'Amri resigned and his powers were given to the Presidential Council. The council was headed by Qadi 'Abd al-Rahman al-Iryani, the son of a well-known family of judges and clerics, who had received a religious education and exposure to modern ideas. Al-Iryani, as the acting president, immediately implemented a number of significant measures. He re-adopted the 1970 constitution and imbued the government ministries and institutions that were built after the revolution with authority, thereby creating a more effective central government. With the exception of the still-excluded Hamid al-Din family, royalist elements were systematically integrated into al-Iryani's "new republic". In 1971, a consultative council (*majlis al-shura*) was established with Shaykh 'Abdallah al-Ahmar from the Hashid confederation at its head. The economic needs and complexity of politics in North Yemen engendered a preference for reform in economic institutions and bodies, and less so in public service and in the armed forces – politically sensitive sectors.[106]

Al-Iryani's term was characterized by particularly arid years without grain shipments from abroad and resultant food crises. This urgent problem and commensurate lack of response highlighted the ineffectiveness of the state apparatus. The number of officials in the administration grew from 4,000 in the first year of the 1962 Revolution to around 13,000 by 1969, and further increased to 30,000 people in the second half of the 1970s.[107] Many people managed to sustain themselves through local patronage networks, and in the provincial cities there were also occurrences of highway robbery and extortion.

A vision of a reunified Yemen emerged at the forefront of politics. Leaders from North Yemen thought that the demographic reality (6 million people in North Yemen, and a little less than 2 million in South Yemen) would ensure the North's dominance. Therefore they called for an immediate move towards unification with no preconditions.[108] In November 1971, al-Iryani mocked Aden for its refusal to immediately establish a union by suggesting that the NLF should forge a coalition with his opponents who had been exiled to the south.[109] In conjunction, the North placed a series of ministries in the hands of 'Abdallah al-Asnaj, whose cohorts from FLOSY had been defeated by the NLF. Other exile groups received support from Sanaa and border incidents became more frequent. In September 1972, the two Yemeni countries stood on the brink of renewed war.

Although North Yemen was led by cautious "liberals" or "conservative republicans" like 'Abd al-Rahman al-Iryani, Muhammad 'Ali

'Uthman and Ahmad Nu'man, there were groups that desired to see the regime's collapse. These groups defined themselves as "revolutionaries" and saw al-Iryani's government as a falsification and distortion of the revolution and its objectives. Thus, for example, in 1970 an organization called the "Revolutionary Resisters" (*al-muqawimun al-thawriyyun*), composed of former members of the Arab Nationalist Movement, declared war against "the reactionary feudal forces". The members of the organization were primarily members of the former Arab Nationalists. The odds were against them but that did not preclude them from enthusiastically renewing the battle against the influence of the Saudis and their clients in North Yemen.[110] Their activity in the Rayma province in 1972 was aptly described by an observer:

> [The Resisters] captured the lands of feudalist Shaykh Ahmad bin Ahmad al-Muntasir and distributed the lands to the masses of the poor peasants [despite heavy opposition from] the mercenaries of Shaykh (feudalist) Sinan Abu Lahum who is well known [for] his hiredom to Saudi reaction and link with the American central intelligence ...[111]

Another example of their activity was their placement of explosives in the palace of Shaykh Naji Bin Mansur Nimran, who was considered a Saudi agent. In order to understand the phenomenon of shifting loyalties, one should recall that a quarter of a century before, Imam Yahya was said to have been murdered by a member of the Murad tribe, to which the Nimran *shaykhs* belong.[112] In May 1973, one of North Yemen's senior politicians, Muhammad 'Ali 'Uthman, was murdered in Ta'izz. The Resisters called him an agent of "Saudi reactionary feudalism".[113] This prompted a wider wave of arrests and executions by the government, but that didn't dissuade the opposition.

The frequent reshuffling in the administration also contributed to political instability. More often than not, it was the Saudis who appointed and fired these state officials in North Yemen, often using financial incentives. Extensive Saudi influence was also observable in North Yemen's foreign policy. The Saudi Kingdom sought to prevent dialogue between North Yemen and the socialist south at any cost, even fanning the flames of the 1972 armed struggle between them. The Saudis orchestrated the ousting of Muhsin al-'Ayni, Prime Minister of the Yemen Arab Republic, who had drafted the proposal for unification with the south in 1972. In his place, the Saudis appointed 'Abdallah al-Hajri, a conservative judge who was well connected to them. Al-Hajri served Riyadh well; in March 1973, he ratified the Ta'if Agreement of 1934, which finalized the border between North Yemen and Saudi Arabia. His government received a generous Saudi loan for his efforts. The aid money was exploited by al-Hajri, *inter alia,* to increase security forces in lower Yemen, where executions and arrests increased and were carried out contrary to al-Iryani's request. Leaders of North Yemen were not in agreement regarding Saudi intervention, and complaints were repeatedly raised amongst government circles in North Yemen over "the influence of a foreign country", obviously Saudi Arabia.[114]

When President al-Iryani opted to convey his displeasure with Saudi intervention and left the country for Syria for a short while, the situation escalated. A coup was carried out against al-Iryani by his deputy, Col. Ibrahim al-Hamdi, who became the president on 13 June 1974. It is reasonable to assume that al-Hamdi and his cohorts acted with Saudi approval, as important measures in North Yemen generally required Saudi approval.

Al-Iryani's presidency was a formative period in modern Yemen, and it seemed as though he was the right man to transform the Imamate into a modern state, even if he did so while preserving the traces and techniques of the old regime. In Yemen, some called him the "republican imam", but as head of state, he was assigned the title President of Yemen.[115] The ratification of the border with Saudi Arabia enabled the next president to demonstrate more effective control and assert the authority of the central government on Yemen's side of the border.[116]

Ibrahim al-Hamdi's Presidency: 1974–1977

The new president, Ibrahim al-Hamdi, recognized the need to build modern state institutions and adopted a policy of more dynamic reform than his predecessor had. Immediately after he assumed power, al-Hamdi abolished the 1970 constitution, which enjoyed renewed attention during al-Iryani's premiership. In one of the most significant policy measures in North Yemen since the 1970 compromise agreement between the Republicans and Royalists, on 13 June 1974 al-Hamdi announced reforms under the name "the Corrective Movement" (*al-Haraka al-Tashihiyya*). For the first time, he initiated concrete reforms in the armed forces, believing that the infrastructure development undertaken by the state would award him great loyalty amongst the tribal leaders. Al-Hamdi recognized the unique tribal character of Yemeni society and the dominance of tribes in the political system.[117] Having recognized their skills and diligence, al-Hamdi sought to develop a comprehensive strategy that would integrate them into the state. For this purpose, he planned a series of financial and administrative reforms and established a number of committees to oversee the effective implementation of the reforms. The objective of the reforms was to strengthen the connection between the centre and periphery by building access roads, hospitals, schools and water-supply lines. The reforms introduced cooperation between local bodies and the central government in order to foster civil solidarity and a sense of participation in government decision-making with the hope of eroding the traditional tribal identity frameworks and establishing a modern state.[118]

One of al-Hamdi's bold measures was his disbanding of the Consultative Council. The Council, formed in 1971, had represented a tribal base of power, which the tribes had used to obstruct the implementation of policies that threatened their interests. In addition, al-Hamdi restricted the freedom of movement of 'Abdallah al-Ahmar, the leader of the Hashid confederation and the head of the Consultative Council. He was asked not to leave the borders of his province in the region of Khamir. The Consultative Council was replaced by a military council comprised of seven members, all of whom were army officers. As the head of the military council, al-Hamdi also became the chief commander of the army. Army commanders constituted the backbone of his support, with two of them particularly prominent. The first was Ibrahim al-Hamdi's brother, 'Abdallah, who supervised the *'amalika* (the giants) – a force that was comprised of 13,000 soldiers with its command in the Dhamar region, between Sanaa and Ta'izz. The second was 'Abdallah 'Abd al-'Alim, who aided al-Hamdi in suppressing tribal revolts. It was determined that the allocations for weaponry to tribesmen would decrease substantially. In conjunction, the regime in Sanaa asked the tribesmen to turn their weapons (artillery and mortars) over to the authorities – a measure which they ardently opposed, viewing it as tantamount to losing an essential tool for the preservation of their interests and autonomy.[119]

Al-Hamdi planned to reduce the tribes' power and strengthen the authority of the state.[120] In 1975, he deposed a few of the senior tribal heads from their positions in the government and army. In an attempt to consolidate his position, al-Hamdi fired Prime Minister Muhsin al-'Ayni (with Saudi support), blaming him for collaborating with Ba'thist and leftist elements. 'Abd al-'Aziz al-Ghani, a technocrat who had served as Minister of the Treasury in 1968, was appointed in his place. Between April and June 1975, al-Hamdi initiated a wave of firings in the echelons of the military council. He also distanced members whom he suspected of over-sympathizing with the tribes, including 'Abdallah al-Ahmar's brother-in-law, Mujahid Abu Shawarib, one of the officers who had aided al-Hamdi in assuming power. He reduced the military council to just four members – himself, Prime Minister 'Abd al-'Aziz al-'Ayni, and the deputy commanders of the armed forces, Ahmad al-Ghashmi and 'Abdallah 'Abd al-'Alim. For the tribes, these changes and the firings of members of the military council violated the rules of the game, posing a direct challenge to their status. The tribes met al-Hamdi's policies with harsh opposition leading to bloody confrontations between tribal militias and army units. In the summer of 1977, tribesmen from Sahar and Sufyan blocked the Sanaa-Sa'da road in protest.[121] The aim of the tribal heads shifted from forcing a bargain to actively attempting the removal of al-Hamdi.[122]

An additional challenge that al-Hamdi took upon himself was to reduce his dependence on Saudi Arabia. From the beginning of his rule, he tried to prevent conflict with Saudi Arabia. His first year in office saw warm relations with the Saudi Kingdom and his first state visit outside of North Yemen was to Riyadh. The Saudis also tried to mediate between al-Hamdi and the tribes as the situation deteriorated. However, in the tribes' growing bitterness with al-Hamdi's policies, the Saudis rushed to support them. They became a bargaining chip, a vehicle by which the Saudis sought to entrench their involvement in North Yemen's internal affairs.[123] The Saudis calculated that the tribes could obstruct the emergence of both leftist trends in North Yemen and the influence of individuals who had an affinity with the Marxist government in Aden, which they viewed as a threat to traditional, tribal values and to the Saudi monarchical regime.[124]

Relations between North Yemen and Saudi Arabia took a turn for the worse. The tension between the two states escalated in the second half of 1975, when North Yemen negotiated the acquisition of an arms package with the United States.[125] The Saudis, as the actual financiers of the business deal, insisted that the arms package would first be sent to Riyadh, and then they would supervise its transfer to North Yemen. By doing so, the Saudis strove to underscore their patronage and emphasize that North Yemen's foreign policy was subject to their acquiescence and approval. The capitulation of the US to these Saudi dictates damaged al-Hamdi's prestige. He turned to the Soviet Union, Iran and other Arab states in order to secure financial and military aid to reduce North Yemen's dependence on Saudi Arabia. Relations between Saudi Arabia and North Yemen further deteriorated, especially when al-Hamdi began to put out feelers for a possible unification of North and South Yemen, a development that contradicted Saudi interests.[126]

Al-Hamdi attempted to compensate for the blow to his power that was the growing estrangement between his government and Saudi Arabia by integrating his one-time friends from the left into the political system, but ultimately withdrew these initiatives. His administration was forced to confront not only the Zaydi tribes' revolt in the North, but also the rising tension between the Zaydis and the Shafi'is. The Shafi'is were relatively content during the period of al-Hamdi's rule. They enjoyed freedom of speech and activity in the political realm, and Shafi'i officers and public leaders obtained lucrative positions in the army and the state apparatus throughout this period. Simultaneously, there was a discernible reduction in the Zaydi hold over the state systems. In addition to the renewed tensions between the Zaydis and the Shafi'is, an ideological dimension was added to the battle for the future course of North Yemen. In the eyes of the Zaydis, the Shafi'is were radical leftists owing to their ties with the regime in Aden, while they, the Zaydis, supported by the Saudis, opposed every attempt at rapprochement with the Marxist regime in South Yemen.[127] In contrast, the Shafi'is feared the loss of their recent achievements in the political realm and society and the revival of Zaydi power. The Zaydi tribes' ties with the Saudis only deepened the Shafi'i fears, and according to oft-repeated arguments, the 1962 Revolution was nothing but a replacement of the Zaydi Imamate with a Zaydi republic.[128] The same period witnessed the proliferation of leftist organizations amongst the Shafi'is, such as the Revolutionary Democratic Party of Yemen (*al-Hizb al-Dimuqrati al-Thawri al-Yamani*), the Democratic Popular Union (*al-Ittihad al-Sha'bi al-Dimuqrati*), and the Yemeni Workers Party (*Hizb al-'Amal al-Yamani*). These and other movements sought to buy themselves key positions in Yemeni politics and to block tribalism. In order to add currency to their claims, these movements united in February 1976 into the National Democratic Front (*al-Jabha al-Wataniyya al-Dimuqratiyya*, henceforth NDF), which – years later – would become the core of opposition against the central government.[129]

The challenges that the regime was confronting at the time forced al-Hamdi to invest all his efforts in outmaneouvring his rivals. His efforts were unsuccessful, and his policy led to violent confrontations throughout the country. In this phase, al-Hamdi abandoned the principles of his policy and developed spontaneous tactics in an attempt to placate his opposition. Sometimes he did this through new appointments in his government. The Minister of Social, Labour and Youth Affairs, Ahmad Qasim Dahmash, who considered the tribes a threat, was replaced by Husayn 'Abd al-Salam Muhammad al-Muqbil, known for his sympathy for the tribes. This was a powerful post that granted its holder the ability to freely reward tribal groups. By the end of 1976, al-Hamdi announced the convening of the Supreme Council to discuss the possibility of holding general elections. The Council was led by the prestigious and conservative qadi, 'Abdallah al-Hajri, who had served as prime minister from the end of 1972 until the fall of 1973. As a supplementary measure, al-Hamdi declared the formation of the Assembly of Representatives, which represented the tribal sector, traders and members of the younger generation.[130] However, the gap between al-Hamdi and the tribes proved unbridgeable. When the Supreme Council for the Elimination of Corruption was created, tribal leaders interpreted this as an attempt to counter their influence and bypass tribal heads by allocating funds through government ministries. Indeed, the authorities in Sanaa tried to undermine tribal leaders' autonomy.

This policy was not in line with the interests of tribal heads. In January 1977, tribal leaders secretly assembled near Sanaa and declared jihad against al-Hamdi's "communist and atheist" regime. In light of this challenge, al-Hamdi arranged meetings with NDF leaders, which resulted in a decision to establish an effective army, end the foreign presence in North Yemen, abolish the power of the tribes and establish central control over North Yemen. The NDF also called for reducing cooperation with the Saudis, however, al-Hamdi rejected this outright. Two months later in 1977, there were reports of tribal uprisings throughout North Yemen, but al-Hamdi and his prime minister adamantly repudiated these reports. Both emphasized though that the tribes opposed the implementation of internal and administrative reforms and declared that "the moment requires a battle against the traces of reactionism".[131]

In the heat of the battle, Qadi 'Abdallah al-Hajri, the former prime minister appointed to head the aforementioned election council, was murdered in Britain while there to meet Saudi King Khalid at the height of his illness. Al-Hajri was considered one of the loyal supporters of pro-Saudi policy. Throughout his tenure as prime minister, he had dynamically operated against leftist movements and rejected any attempt at unity between the two Yemens. Conflicting versions of the details surrounding his murder emerged. The Yemeni ambassador to London, Muhammad 'Abdallah al-Iryani, implied that the murder was politically driven, but did not volunteer any information regarding the identity of the assassin. Others mentioned al-Hajri's connections to the exiled imam Muhammad al-Badr, who had lived in London since 1970, and argued that the murder had been carried out by radical leftist elements.[132]

In mid-1977, the conflict between al-Hamdi and the Zaydi tribes turned violent. Tribesmen attacked caravans of military vehicles, planted mines and imposed checkpoints on the highways from Sanaa to the north of the country. In July 1977, while the Saudis were still trying to mediate between their ally 'Abdallah al-Ahmar and al-Hamdi, the latter declared his willingness to promote unification with South Yemen. In response, 'Abdallah al-Ahmar assembled 40,000 soldiers from the tribes, sometimes called "al-Ahmar's private army", in order to attack the cities Hamir and Sa'da (known to be tribal and Zaydi strongholds in the north-east of the country). Al-Ahmar's army conquered the two cities and the surrounding mountainous provinces, but the tribes from the heart of the country and the Tihama did not respond to al-Ahmar's call to join the battle. The rebels managed to hold occupied territory for a little while but an air strike forced a retreat. The air strike restored al-Hamdi's self-confidence and exposed al-Ahmar's weakness. Also, the Saudis agreed to recognize al-Hamdi as a worthy ally under the circumstances and even reduced the scope of aid that they had delivered to the tribes. To a large extent, the Saudis were disappointed with the tribes' performance. The tribes obstructed al-Hamdi's reform policies and even jeopardized the joint Yemeni-Saudi initiatives. Thus, gradually, the Saudis transferred their support back to al-Hamdi's government. Despite the protests that broke out, the northern tribes continued to challenge the central government. However, none of the sides could claim a decisive victory in this campaign.

In September 1977, al-Hamdi and al-Ahmar reached a compromise and decided to end the bloodshed.[133] According to this agreement, al-Hamdi would hold general elections for the Representative Council (although an explicit date was not scheduled) and establish a popular army of 3,000 soldiers from amongst the tribesmen. He even permitted some of the tribal leaders to resume their positions in the government and granted them and their armed guards freedom of movement throughout the country. The changes in government and the replacement of Prime Minister 'Abd al-'Aziz al-'Ayni with a candidate more acceptable to the tribes were only added measures in the course of appeasement and reconciliation. In exchange, the tribes agreed to end the fighting, to give up their heavy weaponry and to evacuate their forces from the battlegrounds.[134] However, the fragility of this agreement was exposed when al-Hamdi refused to allow al-Ahmar to enter Sanaa with his armed guards to celebrate the anniversary of the September 1962 Revolution. The fear that this event would be interpreted as a demonstration of power and independence on al-Ahmar's part motivated al-Hamdi to pre-empt the plan.[135] In his speech on the anniversary of the revolution, al-Hamdi did not mention the agreement and chose to emphasize the importance of the Corrective Movement of 13 June 1974, which "aimed at restoring the security and stability of the state ... in accordance with the tenants of the revolution".[136]

Meanwhile, an opposition group coalesced within al-Hamdi's government; it was comprised of those who opposed the compromise agreement that had been reached with al-Ahmar. One of the ministers, Ahmad Qasim Dahmash, declared that he and the NDF opposed the return of tribal heads to their former ranks and positions, as it would undermine four years of reform that reduced the tribes' influence.[137] The subsequent firing of Dahmash further inflamed the situation.

On 11 October 1977, Ibrahim al-Hamdi and his brother 'Abdallah were murdered by unknown assassins. Some claimed that the murder was carried out as revenge for the murder of al-Hajri in London. Many connected the murder to the tribal revolt of July 1977. Al-Hamdi's attempts to compromise with South Yemen by cooperating with the NDF's activists had raised the level of tension between him and the tribal heads to an unprecedented peak. Al-Hamdi was to have visited Aden on 13 October, two days after his murder, in order to discuss the steps towards unification between the two Yemens, a move that the tribal heads sought to prevent.[138]

President al-Hamdi did not succeed in implementing the reform measures that he initiated in North Yemen. By the end of his rule, the government's reach was more limited, not less. Paradoxically, and not for the first time in twentieth-century Yemen, a policy which strove to strengthen central authority at the expense of the tribes actually resulted in a reduction of central authority and in an increase in tribal autonomy. During the reign of Ibrahim al-Hamdi, a strong attempt was made to consolidate and rebuild state and societal institutions, but the results were marginal in their impact, even if North Yemen did undergo structural changes which allowed it to absorb broad technical and economic aid from abroad and take in remittances from Yemenis working in other countries. This increased the consumption rates and brought about relative growth. However, in terms of state-building, the policy of accommodating the tribes came at a high price. The outcome was the marginalization of modernizing forces and the preservation of tribal leaders' influence in government circles.

Al-Ghashmi's Presidency: October 1977–April 1978

With al-Hamdi's murder, the military council convened and appointed the army commander, Ahmad Husayn al-Ghashmi, as the commander of the armed forces and, in effect, the next president of the state. Like his predecessor, he was also forced to try to maneouvre between rival forces with different orientations. On the one hand were the Zaydi tribes, led by 'Abdallah al-Ahmar, and on the other was the NDF, a coalition of leftist factions, primarily urban and Shafi'i and supported by South Yemen. They all sought a larger voice in the government's decision-making process. Under the patronage of the Saudi Kingdom, the Zaydi tribes sought to implement the agreement that had been reached with al-Hamdi in September 1977. They pursued greater representation in the military council and the Consultative Council, which aspired to renew its activity. Al-Ghashmi was not willing to grant rights of this magnitude to tribes and anticipated that the re-establishment of the Consultative Council, led by al-Ahmar and manned by his supporters, would nullify the spirit of the Corrective Movement.[139]

Al-Ghashmi was forced to contend with intra-tribal rivalries. Due to his membership in the Hashid tribal confederation, he had to be careful to preserve a balance between al-Ahmar and Sinan Abu Lahum, one of the stronger leaders of the Bakil tribal confederation. Even if the tension between the two did not reach all-out conflict, throughout al-Ghashmi's tenure there was concomitant tension between their respective supporters, especially over the appointment of senior officers in the army.

Though the tumultuous events had reduced its strength, al-Ghashmi still had to reckon with the NDF. Its leaders – civil and military – feared that a renewed revival of Zaydi superiority in Yemeni politics would undo the gains of leftist organizations made during the civil war and its aftermath. Thus, from the start of al-Ghashmi's rule, the NDF called for a democratic government that would allow for the operation of political parties, the release of political prisoners and the establishment of the Representative Council that would reflect the demographic composition of the country. The NDF advocated unifying the two Yemens and halting Saudi intervention in North Yemen's internal affairs.[140] Finally, the NDF called for the disarming of the tribes, which revolted when they felt their interests were being threatened.

Al-Ghashmi reached a critical juncture. His predecessor, al-Hamdi, had failed to achieve his goal of reducing the power and influence of the tribes and paid a heavy price in terms of state stability. Consequently, al-Ghashmi renewed the allocations to the tribes, and distanced himself from the NDF. He went as far as to arrest a number of NDF activists on the grounds that they promoted the idea of unification. These measures did not contribute to a stable North Yemen. Anti-government demonstrations in Ta'izz and Hudayda and the tribal revolts near the shared border with South Yemen demonstrated chronic instability. The rivalry between the Zaydi tribes and the Shafi'i left destabilized the balance of power in society and in the army.[141]

The friction in the ranks of the senior military command also undermined al-Ghashmi's rule. The fact that al-Ghashmi continued to maintain a position of command over the armed forces caused disappointment amongst Hashid tribes that preferred Mujahid Abu Shawarib, al-Ahmar's relative.[142] Al-Ghashmi's decision to disband the military council and establish The Presidential Council in its stead in April 1978, while retaining the position of commander of the armed forces, increased the tension between him and some of the senior military officers.[143] North Yemen found itself in a vortex of bloodshed and political murders, and on 24 April 1978, al-Ghashmi fell victim to the same fate as his predecessor. This was the second presidential assassination in under a year.[144]

Al-Ghashmi's assassination heightened tensions between the two Yemens and contributed to a conflagration in acts of hostility along their shared border. This was observable in North Yemen's accusations that South Yemen had a role in al-Ghashmi's assassination. Radio Sanaa blamed South Yemen for carrying out "a malicious and brutal act". The Foreign Minister, 'Abdallah al-Asnaj, announced the severance of diplomatic ties with South Yemen and requested an emergency assembly of the Arab League.[145] On 17 July 1978 'Ali 'Abdallah Salih, a commander of the province of Ta'izz, was appointed the new President of North Yemen.

Socialism in South Yemen: 1970–1978

In November 1967, when the last British soldiers left the Colony of Aden, South Yemen became an independent state under the leadership of the NLF. Until then, members of the NLF focused their struggle against British foreign rule and against their rival, FLOSY. Upon the British withdrawal, the battle that broke out between NLF and FLOSY ended in a victory for the former and in the exile of most of the leaders of the latter.[146] The NLF took the lead and its leader, Qahtan al-Sha'bi, became president of the new independent state. From the very beginning, the new leadership tried to instill the revolutionary characteristics in the state machinery. The revolutionary dogma that was expressed throughout the 1960s, but which had never been put to the test, now became an actionable plan to create a new civil society.

Having been equipped with the values of the revolution, the NLF leadership sought to undermine the traditional tribal arrangement, which had coalesced during the long period of British rule. That meant that the tribe was no longer expected to serve as an independent political power but instead to assimilate into a larger administrative unit. In December 1967, a decision was made to divide South Yemen into six administrative provinces. The rationale behind this was the creation of a new administrative framework that would blur the lines of demarcation according to which sultanates, *shaykhdoms*, emirates and tribal states had been defined for many years. The new administrative division split tribes and identified them with different administrative regions.

However, it quickly became evident that there was a lack of consensus amongst the leadership of the NLF regarding the joint path of the revolution and the state. Even before he solidified South Yemen's policy, Qahtan al-Sha'bi was faced with pressure from the far left of the NLF, which sought to strengthen the Marxist orientation of the state. The far left did support the unification of the two Yemens – an aspiration that was a centrepiece of the 1962 Revolution in the North – but demanded the immediate establishment of a socio-political order that would reflect their worldview; in other words, the break-up of the institutions that the state had inherited from the British, primarily the armed forces and police. In order to foster broad agrarian reforms that would lead to a more just distribution of land, the far left called for asserting state control over the economic system. They held a conviction that the success of their planned reforms depended on bringing the traditional tribal arrangement into line with the revolutionary dogma. They aimed to spread their revolutionary ideas to the rural, tribal regions where revolutionary ideology had not trickled down before the end of 1967. Members of the far left even dispatched political commissars to the tribal areas in order to facilitate the adoption of a new school curriculum, which aroused resistance due to its Marxist content.[147]

Salim Rubay' 'Ali, known as "Salmayn", was one of the far left's prominent leaders. The far left's pre-eminent ideologue was 'Abd al-Fattah Isma'il, who originally hailed from the North and who advocated scientific socialism. In contrast, al-Sha'bi and his supporters advocated a more practical policy asserting that the NLF had "recovered its solidarity and vitality".[148]

Deliberations surrounding the practical and ideological future of South Yemen and disagreements among NLF members plagued the leadership at a time when the young country was coping with a deep economic crisis. South Yemen's finances at the time of independence were in utter disarray. Activity in the port of Aden – the primary stimulus of the South's economy – had been badly damaged due to the closure of the Suez Canal during the 1967 War.[149] In this state of about a million and half residents, there were only 127 paved roads. The illiteracy rate outside of Aden stood at around 95 per cent. The annual income per person until the beginning of the 1970s was about 107 US dollars. Moreover, the tens of thousands of unemployed and the nearly 100,000 people who had been displaced from Aden during the British withdrawal demonstrated the magnitude of the acute economic crisis.[150]

Salim Rubay' 'Ali's Presidency: June 1969–June 1978

The conflict regarding the course of the revolution and the needs of the state deepened. In the echelons of the NLF, two camps emerged: the "puritan camp", or the far left that aspired to create state and society in strict accordance with the values of the revolution; and the "pragmatic camp", headed by Qahtan al-Sha'bi, who maintained the need to adapt revolutionary dogma according to the needs of the state. During the fourth congress of the NLF in Zinjibar in March 1968, activists from the far left dictated the tone. A special emphasis was placed on the "masses" of workers and farmers who were supposed to be led by revolutionary intellectuals, even though the "masses" were nowhere to be found, since the majority of Aden's proletariat went north and no more than a few thousand remained in the South.[151] While most of the workers and the farmers in Hadramawt and in the cotton-growing areas like Lahaj and Abyan were not tribesmen, in other regions most of the farmers were tribesmen and supporters of Qahtan al-Sha'bi, who himself was from a family of small landowners and found the far left's slogans antagonizing and threatening.

In order to placate the far left, Qahtan al-Sha'bi occasionally changed his pronouncements and declared that the property of the ousted elites who had been identified with the pre-1967 order would be distributed to the guerilla fighters of the NLF. This was not enough to satisfy his opposition, and riots quickly broke out in Aden, Ja'ar and Zinjibar which led to arrests of far left leaders at the hands of the armed forces. The storm that befell South Yemen illustrated how narrow and unstable Qahtan al-Sha'bi's base of power was. This quickly escalated into open conflict in the spring of 1968. On 22 June 1969, Qahtan al-Sha'bi was deposed from his presidency.[152] The far left took over the government and set up a Presidential Council comprised of five members, headed by Salim Rubay' 'Ali.[153]

The new leadership expanded its efforts in two realms: the practical and the ideological. In the practical realm, the government focused on shattering the framework of the tribal unit by shifting traditional loyalty from the tribal head to the central government. The notion of "tribe" became synonymous with something that blocks the progress of the revolution, and the leadership ordered the disbanding of "all organizations with a tribal character".[154] The pretension of the new leadership and the belief that it was within the government's ability to radically change the dynamics of South Yemen came to fruition in the ousting of Qahtan al-Sha'bi and his supporters within the NLF in June 1969. The far left termed his ousting the "22 June Corrective Move".[155]

The government purged the army of traditional tribal elements (some of which were trained by the British) in order to prevent local units from operating according to the directives of a local leader rather than the central government. Similarly, new units were established in the regular army. They were manned by tribesmen that were considered more loyal to the central government and relatively open to new ideas. Political rivals were accused by the regime of practicing tribalism or promoting reactionism.[156]

For example, the South Yemeni army lost some of its senior officers because they belonged to the tribes of 'Awaliq, which had supported the NLF; they were replaced with tribesmen from al-Dathina who were considered to be more loyal. Also, in mid-1970, the Popular Militia and the Revolutionary Military Headquarters were established – two bodies whose functions went beyond military activity and included civil projects such as harvesting crops, paving roads and erecting bridges. In conjunction, in December 1970 the leadership passed a law instituting agrarian reform, which led to the confiscation of the agrarian assets of notable sultans and *shaykhs* and their redistribution to villagers and tribesmen. In December 1970, the new government in the south changed the name of the state from "The Popular Republic of South Yemen" to "The Popular Democratic Republic of Yemen", or "The People's Democratic Republic of Yemen" (*Jumhuriyyat al-Yaman al-Sha'biyya al-Dimuqratiyya*).[157] This name change, as well as the legal and structural reforms, all emphasized the ascendance of the Marxist line within the leadership, which had begun with the 22 June ousting of Qahtan al-Sha'bi.

The revolutionary process gained momentum in 1972 when the Fifth Congress of the NLF convened in Aden and passed legislation that would facilitate the foundation of a pure socialist state order. The attempt to radically alter the fabric of society was evident everywhere, as described by the journalist, Eric Rouleau, who visited South Yemen throughout 1972:

> Lorries packed with workers in overalls, badu with long curly black hair wearing indigo tunics, peasants with multi-colored *futahs* wrapped around their waists ... students in shirt-sleeves, soldier[s in] khaki surge around the avenues and public squares, which are heavily decorated with posters and huge banners denouncing ... "reaction" and imperialism.[158]

Feudalism was the declared enemy everywhere and the political process was dictated from above. These changes were imposed through the rigid security apparatus that was meant to enforce a new order and abolish older practices. Fishing was barred, because it was seen as harming state property. According to the law, speaking with foreigners was forbidden.[159] Citizens of South Yemen lived under police surveillance and under the supervision of state security organs and internal military security units. The level of threats that regular citizens were exposed to was probably exaggerated in the Western media, especially at the beginning of the 1970s; nevertheless, this phenomenon was real enough.[160]

South Yemen underwent a process of dramatic change. Insurgency established its reputation as a revolutionary state where reality was often described in terms of "class struggle" against "feudal" leaders who had exploited Yemen in collaboration with the British. Some talked about a "Maoist victory" of the periphery over the large cities while trying to explain the simple fact that Aden and other large cities were flooded with people from the hinterland.[161] Indeed, prior to independence, the NLF's activity in Aden had focused on forging continuity between the centre and periphery: at this point, their goals were realized when Aden saw the migration of many people from the hinterland. These migrants sought to benefit from promises of the revolution and believed that their migration to Aden would improve their status.

However, Aden had been plagued with acute economic problems since the era of independence. The economy was further damaged by the emigration of much of the backbone of Aden's economy just as the domestic migrants arrived. Paul Dresch estimates that around one quarter of the entire population left shortly after Britain's withdrawal.[162] Therefore, at the time of victory, Aden could not deliver on the promises that it had made during the revolution.

The Two Yemens: A Futile Dialogue and Civil War, 1970–1978

Since South Yemen became independent at the end of 1967, relations between North and South Yemen oscillated between friendship and hostility, between periodic declarations about the need for unification and sporadic outbreaks of bloody violence on their common border. These ambivalent relations were the result of a number of complicated factors ranging from internal disagreements in Sanaa and in Aden to each state's relations with the Saudis.

Following the Egyptian evacuation, when Royalists had imposed a siege on the ruling Republicans in North Yemen, the NLF had been quick to come to their aid in order "to defend the revolution". The Republican leaders of North Yemen rewarded the NLF for their support by recognizing them as the legitimate leadership of South Yemen. However, the cooperation between the leadership of North Yemen and South Yemen was short-lived. It quickly became clear to the conservative groups of North Yemen's leadership that their opponents in Sanaa shared a common worldview with the NLF. The prime minister, Hasan al-'Amri, whose political power derived from his connections with the tribal system, sought to "settle the scores" with leftist activists. He saw the reforms that were proposed by the left as a dangerous threat. In a battle in Hudayda and in Sanaa, al-'Amri and his supporters had the opportunity to break the power of the left and defeat them. Hence, the leftist camp in North Yemen, which had been a potential asset for the NLF, lost its hold.[163]

The support that Aden granted to leftists in the North throughout the battle led leaders of North Yemen such as 'Abdallah al-Ahmar to treat the NLF in Aden as the declared enemy. As a result, beginning in 1968, the government of North Yemen supported each of the NLF's rivals in the South in order to undermine the regime's authority. Each side opened its borders to the exiled opponents of the other. The defeated leftists in North Yemen were displaced from Sanaa to Aden and the officers in the South who unsuccessfully relied on tribal support made their way north. In February 1969, the al-'Amri government blamed the South for initiating attacks on North Yemen's territory and for attempting to institutionalize the division between the two Yemens, thereby preventing any progress toward unification.[164]

North Yemen's leadership praised the revolution at every opportunity but was cautious not to give it a Marxist-Leninist interpretation. Unlike the South, which employed the rhetoric of class struggle and means of production and relegated tribal notions such as blood ties to the sidelines, the central motif of the leaders of North Yemen in the 1970s was reduced to condemnation of the old regime and personal rule (*hukm fardi*). In the eyes of its leaders, the North's major accomplishment was ending the rule of the Hamid al-Din household, the family of the imam, and to a certain degree the rule of Sallal, who epitomized the cult of personal rule. In North Yemen agrarian reforms were not carried out, and although committees for agrarian reform were established in Ta'izz in 1968, they merely paid lip service to reform.

Despite this, the fabric of society in the North did change. At a time when socialist policies were being implemented in South Yemen, many of Aden's merchants moved to Hudayda, the only port city in North Yemen. A Shafi'i trading class emerged in Ta'izz, whose members aligned themselves with the heads of tribal groups who had also settled in the North following the emergence of the socialist regime in the South.[165] A few migrants transferred from the north to the south after 1967. Prominent among them were ideologues, like 'Abd al-Fattah Isma'il and "Muhsin" (Muhammad Sa'id 'Abdallah), originally inhabitants of the North, who would later become key players in the political system of South Yemen. These two espoused the creation of a strong party apparatus and demanded the unification of Yemen in a much more ardent manner than their colleagues in Fadli, Abyan and Hadramawt. The South accused the North of betraying the principles of the September 1962 Revolution – a charge backed by the claim that they had cooperated willingly with the Saudis and world imperialism. The arguments of the North were less dramatic, but in June 1969, prior to the events of the "Corrective Movement", a senior official complained: "We have gotten farther away from unity than we were a year ago". Indicative of this development is that in 1969, 52 per cent of the North's exports were sent to the South and around 30 per cent of the North's imports arrived from the South.[166] Four years later, the figures decreased to 7 per cent and 6 per cent, respectively.

The Unification Initiative of June 1972 and the Causes of its Failure

In North Yemen, many hoped that border disputes and warfare would eventually cause the collapse of the Aden regime, but both states were stuck at an impasse. The North's prime minister, Muhsin al-'Ayni, bowed to political pressure and proffered a unification initiative. Al-'Ayni, a Yemeni nationalist, thought that this would improve his political standing. Under the auspices of the Arab League, he met the prime minister of the South, 'Ali Nasir Muhammad, in Cairo on 28 October 1972, and the two of them signed a ceasefire agreement. It was determined in the Cairo Agreement that a year from the signing, a united Yemeni state would be established with a democratic and republican nationalist government.[167] About a month later, the presidents of the two states – 'Abd al-Rahman al-Iryani and Salim Rubay' 'Ali – met in Tripoli,

Libya, in order to finalize the details of the agreement. In this meeting, the leaders of the South acquiesced to the North's demand to declare Islam the state religion of united Yemen and *sharia* as the principle source of its legislation. In exchange, al-Iryani adhered to the socialist character and single political organization that would stand at the helm of the united state.[168]

The government of South Yemen supported unification only as a tactical move meant to diminish the military pressure on the border and to allow itself to solidify its political position domestically. The Marxist government of Aden did not wish to hold free elections because that would lead to a loss of their power or to the strengthening of the status of the leaders of North Yemen. Therefore, after the November 1972 Tripoli Agreement was signed, the government of Aden increased the tension between the two states by endorsing the attacks of leftist organizations against North Yemeni targets. In January 1973, there were many reports of local uprisings led by armed activists from South Yemen against *shaykhs* who supported the North.[169] The government of Aden set forth its demand for unification on an entirely different basis. They hoped to nurture sympathetic political groups in North Yemen who would eventually bring about a change in the leadership, a strategy developed by 'Abd al-Fattah Isma'il, a northerner who migrated to South Yemen, where he became a key player in the NLF.[170]

In contrast to South Yemen, North Yemen took the 1972 Agreement seriously, but even there, amongst more conservative circles in the government, there was opposition to joining with the "atheist Communist South". The Consultative Council, most of whose members represented the religious and tribal sector, refused to approve the unity agreement. They argued that its rhetoric regarding the commitment to the Islamic character of the state was too diluted and insufficient and on top of that, the Saudis were not satisfied and did not give their approval. The Saudis provided financial aid to tribal leaders and army officers who acted against the unification and against Prime Minister al-'Ayni, who had initiated the unification agreement.[171]

The Saudi policy, which was designed to thwart the unity agreement, encouraged the leaders of the large tribal confederations,

Shaykh 'Abdallah al-Ahmar of the Hashid confederation, and Shaykh Sinan Abu Lahum, governor of Hudayda and *shaykh* of the Bakil confederation, to increasingly voice their opposition to the unification initiative.[172] The tribal opposition to al-'Ayni coalesced in the Consultative Council. He responded by refusing to appear before the council and address their questions. Al-'Ayni resigned on 28 December 1972.[173] His replacement, 'Abdallah al-Hajri, was known for his conservative leanings, his extensive connections in the tribal arena and his amicable relationship with the Saudis. The Saudis made their allocation of financial aid to North Yemen conditional upon the ousting of al-'Ayni, as the state reached the brink of economic crisis in December 1972, threatening the salaries of state employees. Al-'Ayni's successor, al-Hajri, immediately announced that with his assumption of power, the salaries would be paid on time as planned – and they were.[174] Two months after al-Hajri's appointment, the Saudis transferred sums of money that covered North Yemen's debts. At the same time, Al-Hajri reneged on his commitment to the unification of Yemen, marking the end of the unification initiative for the time being.[175]

In the mid-1970s, additional attempts were made to stabilize relations between the two Yemens, and the two presidents, Ibrahim al-Hamdi from the North and Salim Rubay' 'Ali from the South, continued to praise unification and cooperation. The two leaders, relatively young and full of aspirations to advance their states, saw unification as a formula by which to extricate themselves from the thicket of internal politics that posed a threat to their governments and frustrated the development of a foreign policy that would reduce their reliance on external patrons. In February 1977, the two leaders met in Qa'taba, a town adjacent to their common border. The meeting produced an agreement on the establishment of a joint council headed by al-Hamdi and Salim Rubay' 'Ali that was supposed to convene twice a year in Aden and Sanaa alternately in order to ensure the progress of their joint effort. Two months after this meeting, the two leaders declared their intentions to advance the matter of unification.[176] Their calls for unity overshadowed remaining controversial issues like the ownership of Perim Island (at the head of the Bab al-Mandab Strait), which had been controlled by the South since 1967, or their divergent policies regarding the conflict between Ethiopia and Somalia.[177]

This time, the Saudis supported the unification initiative. The Saudi state, which had previously striven to undermine the leadership of South Yemen, started to focus on dissuading South Yemen from its pro-Soviet orientation through petro-dollars. Despite the socialist character of the South and its ties with the Soviet Union, there was a relatively complex system of relations between South Yemen and Saudi Arabia. Many people from the South used their North Yemeni passports to work in the Saudi Kingdom. In the second half of the 1970s the Saudis began to reduce their support for exile groups in North Yemen and became more accommodating toward Salim Rubay‘ ‘Ali in Aden. In March 1976, the Saudis even established full diplomatic relations with South Yemen, which contributed to the improvement of relations between the two Yemens.[178]

Education and Popular Culture in the 1970s

One of the important developments in both Yemens in the 1970s was the expansion of the education system, a task that both states undertook throughout the decade. On the eve of the revolution of September 1962, there were only four state high schools, which focused primarily on religious studies (alongside a number of private schools that had been established in the 1940s and 1950s). The students were mainly from upper-class families. Many Yemenis moved to British Aden, and those who settled in the more established neighbourhoods sent their boys to public schools in Aden.

After the revolution there were dramatic changes in the scope of the education system in North Yemen. The school system was structured according to the Egyptian model – six years of primary education, three years of middle school and three years of high school. The curriculum was also formulated according to the Egyptian model and Egyptians made up a large portion of the teaching staff. Between the years 1962–1963 and 1981–1982, the number of students multiplied almost tenfold, from 61,000 to almost 590,000 students. In 1971–1972, only 12 per cent of the children in Yemen were enrolled in school. By 1981–1982, 48 per cent were enrolled. The number of girls enrolled increased as well, reaching 12 per cent of the overall student population by 1981. The most dominant province in the field of education was Ta'izz, which contained half of the middle and high schools in the state.[179]

In South Yemen, the numbers were even more impressive. While the North claimed that as of the 1976–1977 school year, around 30 per cent of children aged 10 were enrolled in school, the government of the South reported 60 per cent. In South Yemen the official pronouncements and rhetoric focused on the "creation of a new human being" and on "building a new culture that would serve as the basis for the creation of a new awareness and a new mentality".[180] The prevailing perception in the South which manifested itself in the curriculum was that the North and its residents were in a period of stagnation.[181]

The 1970s was an era during which Arab nationalist and Marxist-Leninist ideologies swept the region. In both parts of Yemen, it seemed as though Islam was marginalized and less relevant in shaping the political culture. North Yemen did emphasize its commitment to "official" Islam and called for righteous government and leaders, but this was motivated by political considerations. Though sidelined in the political realm, popular Islam was experiencing a revival. In the early 1970s, during al-Iryani's presidency, Wahhabi groups appeared in the North. The government of North Yemen even approved their activities, and perceived them as a counterweight to the negative influence of the NDF. With Saudi aid, Quranic schools and religious institutions (*ma'ahid 'ilmiyya*) sprouted up throughout North Yemen and began to disseminate Wahhabi Islam in an attempt to thwart the influence of the NDF.[182] Since the 1940s, 30 years prior to the emergence of this Wahhabi presence, the Egyptian Muslim Brothers also found Yemen attractive – an Islamic state whose attributes had not been destroyed by the influence of foreign culture. The Wahhabis and Muslim Brothers found a common enemy in Yemen – secular Arab Marxism – around which to coalesce in opposition.

Youth who had been sent to Cairo to acquire a religious education in the 1950s and 1960s returned, more often than not, as leftists inspired by Marxist-Leninist ideology. Yet some internalized the religious message of the Muslim Brothers. Under Nasser's instruction, many of the Brothers were exiled from both Egypt and Yemen in the second half of the 1960s. Even those who stayed in Yemen did not find support for their ideas until the beginning of the 1970s, hampered by the dominant ideologies of Pan-Arabism and revolutionary socialism. With the changing circumstances and the North Yemeni leadership turning a blind eye to the Saudis' cultivation of Wahhabi groups as a counterbalance to the NDF, they found it easier to disseminate their messages to the public.[183] During al-Hamdi's presidency, Shaykh 'Abd al-Majid al-Zindani gained prominence. He emerged from the ranks of the Brotherhood as a "guide" (*murshid*). This man and his doctrine of religious activism would become instrumental in Yemen at the turn of the twenty-first century.

Meanwhile, South Yemen prepared for a greater attack on religious learning and its activists. In the early 1970s, the holy shrines in Hadramawt were vandalized and preachers and religious scholars were murdered. Even though state officials did hold prayers on various occasions, and despite celebrations of religious ceremonies during the holidays and commemorations, the Southern leadership perceived religion as a fading phenomenon. A lenient interpretation treated religion as an earlier or more primitive expression of socialism. In the beginning of 1974, 'Abd al-Fattah Isma'il, one of the main spokespersons for the NLF, tried to attribute a revolutionary spirit and new thinking to well-known Yemeni scholars such as Abu Muhammad al-Hasan bin Ahmad al-Hamdani. Such scholars had been referred to by the Zaydiyya as *Qaramita*, a Zaydi term for infidels who exploited Islamic ideas in order to develop an unethical message.[184] In contrast, the new, Southern paradigm presented these scholars as pioneers of socialism who espoused the idea of land cooperatives. Although they never took root among the broader public, these claims were a prime example of the manner in which leaders of the South tried to discredit the Zaydiyya and uproot religion from the public sphere and private life in South Yemen.

The education system in both the North and the South, each in its own way, raised the banner of Yemen's rich past and tried to imbue it with a new interpretation. The Ministry of Culture in Sanaa rehabilitated and published classical works of literature and poetry. In the early 1970s, several studies on Yemen's civil war and its implications were published. Zayd bin 'Ali al-Wazir's book *An Attempt to Understand the Yemeni Problem* (1971), which presents an interesting analysis of political and ideological structures in the state, is a good example of this. *Yemen: Nation and Culture*, a book that was published in 1972 by Abubakr al-Shamahi, chronologically presents Yemen's history and characterizes the shift from the Imamate to the Republic through an explanation of intergenerational conflict. In both official and popular discourse, the revolution was presented as a transition from backwardness to progress. The usage of the phrases "before the revolution" and "after the revolution" referred to North Yemen's development. The vision of a united Yemen was a central motif in the textbooks. Students of the North and South learned from the same history books, whose introductions carried the signatures of the presidents of the North and the South, Ibrahim al-Hamdi and Salim Rubay' 'Ali, and were described as "The first practical step on the road toward unity".[185]

In South Yemen, where people annually celebrated the revolution's anniversary on 14 October 1963, the main streets of every city were named "Liberty Street" and "Democracy Street". Slogans were seen everywhere, exhorting the people: "Let us struggle" – struggle for the defense of the revolution, activate a five-year plan and build the party of the pioneers.[186] Nevertheless, beyond the slogans and banners of the revolution, there was literature and poetry that was written according to familiar and accepted values in Yemen before the age of revolution. In 1977 near the Hadramawt coast, a museum was opened which commemorated the memory of the seven warriors, people of Yemen who bravely stood against the Portuguese conquerors in the beginning of the sixteenth century. *Epochs in Hadrami History*, a book by Muhammad bin Ahmad al-Shatiri re-printed in 1970, was one of many books that participated in and exemplified the literary renaissance in Hadramawt. In other areas of the South, such as Yafi', local traditions, like cultural dances and songs, were introduced as official folklore to glorify Yemeni achievements and defend the homeland.[187]

However, there was no breakthrough in the issue of unification. It became evident how complicated the domestic political arena in each of the states was. This was especially true for the North, where tribal heads adamantly tried to torpedo the idea of unity. The President of the North, al-Hamdi, was assassinated in October 1977, two days before his first planned visit to Aden. The President of the South, Salim Rubay' 'Ali, was ousted in a bloody coup in Aden a year later. Parallel to that, the North witnessed the murder of Ahmad al-Ghashmi, al-Hamdi's successor, eight months after his ascension. The idea of unity faded, swept away by the spate of political assassinations that befell the North and the South alike.

CHAPTER 3

THE DECLINE OF THE SOCIALIST AND ARAB NATIONALIST REVOLUTIONS: 1978–1990

1978 was a critical year in the dynamics of the struggle between both Yemens. Not only did two new leaders assume power ('Ali 'Abdallah Salih in North Yemen and 'Abd al-Fattah Isma'il in South Yemen), but their ideological differences and foreign policy discrepancies led to an intensification of their strained relations and the outbreak of a new civil war. If for North Yemen, 1978 was marked by the rise of 'Ali 'Abdallah Salih and the building of a patrimonial governmental system akin to his "family rule", then for South Yemen, 1978 signified the founding of the Yemeni Socialist Party (henceforth YSP) and a new constitution that granted legitimacy to the state's rule over the people and the country. The NDF, which had originated in North Yemen and was instrumental in the South's struggle against the North, was defeated, marginalized and pushed into South Yemen, where it became an important force in Aden politics. The new leader of South Yemen, 'Abd al-Fattah Isma'il, originally a northerner and devoted spokesperson for the revolution, charted a stronger doctrinal course than ever before and consequently, deepened the rift between the North and South.

Civil War: February 1979

In June 1978, North Yemen was thrust into crisis. President Ahmad al-Ghashmi was assassinated, leaving a vacuum in the political system. About a month later, on 17 July 1978, Major 'Ali 'Abdallah Salih was appointed the new President of North Yemen. Like his predecessors, al-Ghashmi and al-Hamdi, 'Ali 'Abdallah Salih ascended to power from the army. He hailed from the Sanhan tribe, whose lands lay on the southern flank of Sanaa and which was part of the Hashid confederation. Although his tribe traditionally provided the imam's army with soldiers, it did not wield prestige and influence in the tribal arena. Thus, their rise through the ranks of the Republican Army during the 1962–1970 civil war gained the Sanhan tribesmen better positions than they had ever held.

Salih was a protégé of the assassinated president, Ahmad al-Ghashmi. Before then, during al-Hamdi's presidency (1974–1977), he was appointed the military governor of Ta'izz and held this position until he became president. 'Ali 'Abdallah Salih was not particularly admired during his tenure as governor of Ta'izz and his name was even mentioned in connection with al-Hamdi's assassination. He was known to be an instrumental player in the tribal power network as well as a servant of Saudi interests.[1] The political system that he inherited from al-Ghashmi was fraught with difficulties. The army was divided into various power centres and was under the sway of external forces. The first coup against 'Ali 'Abdallah Salih was planned in October 1978 by supporters of the former president, Ibrahim al-Hamdi.[2] Although this coup attempt was discovered in its planning phase and thwarted, it illustrated the fragility of 'Ali 'Abdallah Salih's regime.

At the same time, South Yemen underwent changes in its leadership ranks. The appointment of 'Abd al-Fattah Isma'il as president and the establishment of the Yemeni Socialist Party (YSP) in October 1978 were accompanied by a strengthened doctrinal emphasis.[3] Armed with the pure principles of Marxist-Leninist socialism, the YSP emphasized its exclusiveness and centrality in the realms of state and society and insisted that "the state shall direct the society's activity with the aim of achieving the tasks of the national democratic revolution".[4] It was also argued that Yemen's history was dialectically in tandem with the Arab world's struggle and that the revolutionary struggle in both parts of Yemen was toward the goal of unity. As was emphasized in the preamble to the constitution, the goal was the unity of Yemen under the leadership of the YSP.[5] Some of the arguments for the new doctrinal emphasis were practical: a united Yemen would be economically viable in a way that the South on its own was not, and would, with a population close to 9 million, be the most populous state in the Arabian Peninsula. All other policies relating to the Gulf, the Horn of Africa and the major world powers were comprehensible only within the perspective of the incomplete, ongoing Yemeni revolution.[6]

The regime in Aden tried to exploit the weakness of North Yemen's government in order to impose political changes in Sanaa, hoping that this could later lead to unification under Southern leadership. 'Abd al-Fattah Isma'il and high officials in South Yemen saw the NDF as a useful means of realizing their vision. Its operatives sincerely sympathized with the Aden government. As mentioned, leftist elements in the North – mainly composed of Shafi'i and secular socialist activists – were outlawed during al-Iryani's tenure (1971–1974) and returned to the field during al-Hamdi's premiership. Al-Hamdi's assassination disrupted their march back into the political system in North Yemen. In 1976, the leftist elements united under one umbrella, the NDF. They even had a hand in the attempted overthrow of 'Ali 'Abdallah Salih in October 1978. The leader of the NDF, Sultan Ahmad 'Umar, was a former senior leader of the NLF and he was very familiar with South Yemen's politics.[7] Therefore, South Yemen's army cooperated with the NDF and allowed its activists to use territory in the South as a base from which to launch attacks on North Yemen's forces. Border incidents quickly escalated into general war. This conflagration resembled that of 1972, but this time the strong connection between the domestic affairs in North Yemen and the extent of its external threat was evident. The renewal of border incidents sharply illuminated the internal schism in North Yemen and the fact that power centres were supported by external forces: the tribal confederacies were supported by the Saudis against the leftist coalition of the NDF which in turn was supported by the government of South Yemen.[8]

The confrontation that developed in Yemen prompted a response from the international community. American air support was sent urgently to North Yemen in an "attempt to block the Soviet threat". The US believed accurately that North Yemen would side with it against the USSR, even though the Sanaa government – in what it described as an attempt to preserve the balance – engaged in ongoing negotiations with the Soviet Union and was on the brink of signing a large arms deal with countries from the Eastern bloc. Nevertheless, this did not develop into a conflict between the superpowers, primarily because the Soviet Union, which duly procured an arrangement of cooperation with North Yemen, did not want to lose what looked like an advantage.[9]

Under Arab mediation, the fighting between the two Yemens finally ended in March 1979. Arab states such as Iraq and Syria sought to take advantage of Egypt's ousting from the Arab League (after having signed a peace treaty with Israel) and to demonstrate Arab leadership by bringing both Yemens into an agreement.[10] The representatives of the two Yemens met in Kuwait, which culminated in the "Kuwait Agreement". The signing of a definitive agreement was a surprise to many onlookers. The agreement included not only the declaration of a ceasefire, but also a joint statement of willingness to clarify intentions and expectations for unification. As had happened in 1972, in 1979 the fighting ended with the promise to discuss unification. On 29 March 1979, the two leaders, 'Ali 'Abdallah Salih and 'Abd al-Fattah Isma'il, announced their willingness to abide by the Cairo Agreement of October 1972 and their commitment to the formulation of a constitution for the new state within a number of months.[11]

The motivation that drove 'Ali 'Abdallah Salih to settle differences with Aden was all too clear. In less than a year in office, the young president had already experienced circumstances that had undermined his regime's stability, including the coup attempt of October 1978 and a domestic scene fraught with local uprisings and skirmishes on the border with South Yemen. The fate of his predecessors could have told Salih that his willingness to promote unification was laden with dangers, but it seemed like the only way to reduce his opponents' room to maneouvre in Sanaa and the best way to consolidate his position against them.

South Yemen, in contrast, sought to exploit its military gains and aimed to unify under the assumption that their allies from the NDF would be included in the new government in Sanaa. The need to create a "single Yemeni pioneering party" as the first measure toward achieving unification had already been emphasized in the 1975 and 1978 NLF summits.[12] Initially, it seemed as though the NDF in North Yemen, crafted by Aden, would make its way into the Sanaa government. North Yemeni government officials who were declared enemies of the NDF, especially the foreign minister, 'Abdallah al-Asnaj, were ousted from the government. Joint summits between the North and the South were held regularly. In February 1980, NDF leader Sultan Ahmad 'Umar even announced an agreement with President 'Ali 'Abdallah Salih to establish a joint coalition. In response to the Saudi attempt to block shipments of American arms to North Yemen during the fighting of 1979, North Yemen signed an arms acquisition agreement with Aden's patron, the Soviet Union, in August of the same year.[13] Simultaneously, in October 1979, Aden underscored its relations with Moscow by signing a Friendship and Cooperation Pact.

As their predecessors had done in 1972, the presidents of the "two parts" (*shatrayn*) of Yemen promised to act for the unification of Yemen, but the difficulty of implementing the Kuwait Agreement quickly became evident. Saudi Arabia and opponents of unification in North Yemen realized that unification would bring about a tilt to the left in Yemeni politics, and therefore tried to block the initiative. Tribal heads stridently opposed the incorporation of the NDF into North Yemen's government. Having played an important role in the fighting during February and March 1979 when the weakness of North Yemen's regular army was exposed, the tribal heads had created a powerful position for themselves and vehemently expressed their opposition to unification.[14] Their long-standing relations with the Saudis and their emphasis on Islamic values provided them moral and financial support from Saudi Arabia.[15] With Saudi backing, the tribal heads established the Islamic Front (*al-Jabha al-Islamiyya*) in mid-1979. Their two main goals were to shatter the understanding of the Kuwait Agreement and to exert pressure on 'Ali 'Abdallah Salih to change his domestic policies. The Saudis also exerted similar pressure on 'Ali 'Abdallah Salih. In late 1979, the Saudis went so far as to suspend their financial support for North Yemen and the Sanaa government fell behind in its payments to state employees for two months in December 1979 and January 1980. Additionally, the Saudis indicated that American arms intended for North Yemen would not be delivered. In March 1980, Salih was forced to acquiesce to the Saudi demand to significantly decelerate both unification measures and the progress of relations with the Soviet Union.[16]

Meanwhile, Salih's regime neither expanded its military ties with the Soviet Union, nor severed them. Discussions on unification were held, but at a sluggish pace. In April 1980, associates of the Islamic Front together with units from North Yemen's regular army attacked the NDF's military strongholds. In the summer of 1982, they pushed the NDF operatives back into South Yemen.[17] However, the attack against the NDF did not escalate into a new border war, owing to changes in the Aden government.

In April 1980, 'Abd al-Fattah Isma'il was replaced as President of South Yemen by 'Ali Nasir Muhammad, the leader of the YSP. Despite the lesson that should have been learned from the bitter experience of former President Salim Rubay' 'Ali, who was deposed and executed as a result of his attempt to centralize political power at the expense of his colleagues, 'Ali Nasir Muhammad also held the three key positions in South Yemen at the end of 1980: president, prime minister and general secretary of the ruling party, the YSP. As 'Abd al-Fattah Isma'il resigned and left for Moscow, hundreds of activists and members of the ruling party were forced to leave their positions for 'Ali Nasir Muhammad's cohorts.[18]

The ongoing economic crisis and the floods that plagued South Yemen were placed at the top of the agenda by 'Ali Nasir Muhammad. 'Ali Nasir Muhammad shifted his focus, striving to improve relations between South Yemen and the rich oil states of the Gulf, and toward this end, he emphasized his willingness to cooperate with North Yemen and reduce his support for the NDF.[19] This policy was in line with the Soviet Union's interests: the Soviet Union hoped that rapprochement with the oil states would prevent them from strengthening their relations with the United States in light of the Soviet invasion of Afghanistan.

Even if many of Aden's residents viewed these measures favourably, it was not possible to ignore the economic gaps between various groups in society. With the discovery of oil, residents of the shanty towns on the outskirts of Aden complained about the creation of a culture of consumerism and "a state within a state" ruled by 'Ali Nasir Muhammad and his supporters. For example, his detractors criticized one of 'Ali Nasir Muhammad's associates, the governor of Abyan, who built a palace with magnificent gardens, pools, and fancy rooms for chewing *gat*.[20] Although the regime invested in development, there was a serious imbalance in this area because the funding was channeled to places that were identified with the regime. For example, in late 1985, South Yemen's government signed an agreement worth 50 million dollars with foreign companies from the Soviet Union, China and Britain for the development of regions such as Abyan and Shabwa, strongholds of support for 'Ali Nasir Muhammad. In contrast, regions like Lahaj and Hadramawt did not experience a significant development drive.[21]

Despite this, 'Ali Nasir Muhammad's presidency attenuated the tensions and brought the two Yemens to the point of cooperation. The issue of unification reemerged again as the order of the day, but not in the same manner as it did in 1979. Committees charged with evaluating various aspects of the issue were established, and one of them even published a draft proposal for a constitution for a united Yemen. In their meetings, the presidents emphasized the importance of economic cooperation, shared cultural bonds and the dialogue concerning the path to future unification.[22] This time, in contrast, the initiative came closer to receiving the blessing of the Saudis, who reacted positively to 'Ali Nasir Muhammad's desire to thaw relations between Riyadh and Aden.[23]

The Inter-Elitist Rivalries within Aden: 1986

The crisis in the balance of payments and the severe predicament that the economy of South Yemen found itself in, especially during

1985, sharpened factional rivalries. 'Ali 'Antar, the former defense minister who had supported the dismissal of 'Abd al-Fattah Isma'il, demanded in 1984 that Isma'il be permitted to return since 'Ali Nasir Muhammad's extravagant fiscal policies had pushed South Yemen to the brink of collapse. The competing factions of the YSP posed a challenge to 'Ali Nasir Muhammad's rule. In an attempt to pre-empt a coup, 'Ali Nasir Muhammad called on his supporters to purge opposing factions from the YSP. On 13 January 1986, several leaders of the YSP were murdered. A wave of violence flooded Aden and escalated into a civil war that forced 'Ali Nasir Muhammad to leave the country with tens of thousands of his supporters.[24]

Control of the party and the state passed to 'Ali Salim al-Bayd (the general secretary of the YSP) and Haydar Abu Bakr al-'Attas, who became the new President of South Yemen. It seemed as though the new government would reinstate the Marxist character and policies that had been outlined during the tenure of 'Abd al-Fattah Isma'il, but instead, the new leaders continued with the policy of the ousted President 'Ali Nasir Muhammad. This was an admission that the Aden public had never fully supported the YSP. The cumbersome bureaucracy hampered the effort to expand development and industry. Rising unemployment and poverty were indicative of the perilous state of South Yemen's economy. The years 1986–1989 were also marked by the absence of a clear state orientation and the decay of the education and health care systems. South Yemen was thrust into a chaotic reality from which the socialist regime would not recover.

South Yemen lay tucked away in the south-western corner of the Arabian Peninsula, the first and only regime of its kind in the modern Middle East. Three distinctive features were prominent in South Yemen throughout its existence: a Marxist orientation, a strong organizational apparatus and chronic rivalry amongst the ruling elite. The YSP presented itself as "the driving force in the echelons of society and state" in accordance with the theory of scientific socialism. This found distinct expression in 'Abd al-Fattah Isma'il's pronouncements and in the YSP's rhetoric that claimed, "The party should rule the state until it can become the highest authority in the state, and the state apparatus will become part of the party's apparatus".[25] From the time that the NLF assumed leadership until transforming into the YSP at the end of 1978, the party imposed itself on the state in order to fully control both the political and cultural arenas.

South Yemen utilized a network of organizational institutions to mobilize the masses. The party secured the full loyalty of the army to the Marxist ideal by purging "rightist" elements and "traitors from among the petty bourgeoisie".[26] The YSP's ideologues identified tribalism as an anachronism of the old feudal order. Peasants, students, women, workers, writers and other social groups assembled into their own organizations. As in other instances in the modern history of the Middle East, the pretentious goal of erasing primordial identities and creating a new human being was not attained. Ironically, the bloody purges of 1986, which led to a civil war that claimed 13,000 lives, divided the YSP's rival factions according to regional affiliation and not according to class or ideological differences.

The YSP failed to achieve its goals of social change. Its secularization policy was only partially successful. The religious establishment lost its power and the *waqf* (religious endowment) system was nationalized by the state, but the grandiose attempt to build a society devoid of religion proved detrimental to the YSP. When the NLF (later the YSP) encountered sharp opposition to its policy, it attempted to present Islam as a "liberating theology" and as a social and political system that is not contradictory to Marxist ideology.[27] Yet it was difficult for the NLF and subsequently the YSP to undo its image as a party and indeed a government that opposed religion.

In spite of the failure of their ideological aims, the YSP did have an effective ruling apparatus that retained relative stability in South Yemen from 1967 to 1990. The ruling mechanism's effectiveness was derived from the British colonial legacy in the region. British hegemony in Aden had rested on a strong central rule that overshadowed tribal feudal society and repressed any threat to the central authority of the state. Therefore, when the NLF assumed the leadership in South Yemen, it inherited a relatively strong ruling infrastructure. By employing various means of coercion, the party managed to effectively penetrate society and create a system of laws and procedures that consolidated their power. In South Yemen, the YSP became synonymous with the state; the state maintained strong and effective control as long as the party remained powerful.[28]

In contrast to its organizational efficacy, and in a paradox that plagued South Yemen throughout its existence, its leadership was hampered by friction and disputes. Power struggles among the YSP reflected a struggle between different visions for the state. The party was essentially divided into two camps: one advocated the preservation of revolutionary dogma and a strict interpretation of Marxism; the other sought to improve the governing system and society, even at the expense of modifying the dogma to meet the needs of the state. Between the years 1967–1986, five presidents served in South Yemen, three of whom were ousted by violent means. These rivalries and cleavages characterized South Yemen and led up to the 1986 civil war and the loss of the state's vitality. This ongoing conflict between revolutionary dogma and the immediate needs of the state plagued South Yemen and was detrimental to its development. The revolutionary ideals and the reality of the state were out of step; the revolutionary dogma sometimes dictated a rhythm and logic that were not congruent with state interests.[29]

South Yemen's foreign policy provides an appropriate example of the discrepancy between dogma and state interests. As a client of the Soviet Union, South Yemen tilted toward the Eastern bloc. From the very beginning, the state was obligated to disseminate Marxist-Leninist doctrine throughout the Arabian Peninsula, especially to its neighbouring countries, North Yemen and the Sultanate of Oman, and was expected to support underground and opposition movements there.[30] South Yemen adopted a pro-Soviet orientation which its neighbours perceived as an ongoing threat. From the outset, this precluded the possibility of stable foreign relations with other states in the Arabian Peninsula, and South Yemen was doomed to remain outside of the Arabian Peninsula's economic system.

During the 1970s the Soviet Union fiercely guarded its position in South Yemen to maintain its strategic interests in the port of Aden. In the late 1980s, as the Soviet Union edged closer to disintegration, Gorbachev's emphasis on domestic openness (*glasnost*) and reform (*perestroika*) were accompanied by a reduction of commitment to costly and labour-intensive overseas commitments. Britain had gone through a similar experience two decades earlier during their withdrawal from Aden. In South Yemen socialist enthusiasm entirely faded out, and with the exception of scattered pro forma institutional expressions, nothing remained of the country's former zeal.

'Ali 'Abdallah Salih: The Victorious Leader

The prevailing political reality in North Yemen, like that of South Yemen, was problematic and complex during the 1970s and 1980s. While in South Yemen there was a good deal of reshuffling in the political leadership, in North Yemen the leadership of 'Ali 'Abdallah Salih was a constant factor. With his ascension to power, 'Ali 'Abdallah Salih was faced with a political system fraught with difficulties, and few thought that he would be able to survive as president very long. Given the upheavals and instability in the political system in North Yemen, as well as the fates of his predecessors, this assessment was entirely reasonable. However, 'Ali 'Abdallah Salih would alter the configuration of power and successfully establish his place as the President of North Yemen and later as the president of a united Yemen in May 1990.

From the beginning, 'Ali 'Abdallah Salih's attempt to build an effective system of governance was met with concrete resistance. The threat from South Yemen grew – namely its adoption of the rigid Marxist line and its aim of subsuming the North and establishing one state under Southern hegemony. In April 1979, border clashes between the two Yemens escalated into a real war.[31] Were it not for the intervention of Saudi Arabia, the United States, the Arab League and the imposition of a ceasefire between the warring sides, Salih's rule would likely have ended in disaster only months after he took office.

Salih successfully exploited the interval of time that foreign involvement afforded him in order to consolidate his rule in North Yemen. First, he reorganized the ranks of the army in view of their poor performance in the border clashes with South Yemen. In a new round of appointments in the senior officer ranks, he removed his rivals and inserted many of his fellow Sanhan tribesmen in their place. He placed his confidants and relatives in the most important positions. For example, he appointed his half-brother, 'Ali Salih, Governor of Haziz ("the Gate of Sanhan"), a settlement located at the outskirts of the tribal territory of Sanhan. His brother, Muhammad 'Abdallah Salih, became head of Central Security. Control by the "ruling family" (*al-usra al-hakima*) was sustained by retaining the leadership and control over military and administrative institutions. His half-brother 'Ali Muhsin al-Ahmar and members of the houses of Isma'ili and al-Qadi (with whom the president had connections through marriage) were integrated into the government. Tribal notables, particularly from the Hashid confederation, were also integrated into advisory positions and their presence in government institutions was prevalent. A broad patronage network of Salih's clients ran North Yemen's security forces and public administration.[32]

An additional important dimension of 'Ali 'Abdallah Salih's strategy was to broaden his base of legitimacy. Salih's efforts to expand political participation stemmed from the shadow of threat that he lived under, and the longer he stayed in power, the more he improved his politics of survival. In 1979, Salih had scant political support outside of the army, so he fostered an environment of national reconciliation. For example, in 1981, he requested that the two former presidents, 'Abdallah al-Sallal and 'Abd al-Rahman al-Iryani, be allowed to return from exile. This gesture won him public approval, particularly when the two indeed returned. But this was not sufficient to mobilize concrete support for his rule. To this aim, Salih initiated impressive reforms in the first half of the 1980s, at the centre of which stood the national charter (*al-mithaq al-watani*), which included the fundamental principles of the state and a call to expand the circles of political participation.[33] In conjunction, he established the Committee for National Dialogue (*lajnat al-hiwar al-watani*), whose members – all senior politicians – were supposed to finalize the articles of the national charter and disseminate it among the public in order to receive feedback.[34] The entire measure ended successfully in 1982 with the holding of general elections for the General People's Congress (*al-Mu'tamar al-Sha'bi al-'Amm,* henceforth GPC). The GPC was declared as a permanent political body, whose members stood for election every four years and whose council was composed of 75 members and headed by President Salih. Although the GPC was not initially founded and presented as a political party, all of its activities and characteristics were typical of a political party and intended to reach a wide constituency. In effect, the GPC became an umbrella party, but was not always effective in light of the national challenges that marked the reality of North Yemen.[35]

Salih continuously improved the rule of the central government in different areas of the state, and for the first time its practical authority was more than nominally recognized. The regime tightened its grip in the territories that were controlled by the tribes, especially in the regions north and east of Sanaa. Proof of the regime's effective control was the defeat of the NDF. This rebellion occurred because the NDF had been marginalized but at the same time, the battle became a struggle for the future direction of North Yemen at the beginning of the 1980s. The riots were put down in 1982 and the state succeeded in establishing its effective presence on the shared border with South Yemen. In the first years of his rule, Salih displayed flexibility and political skill. The suppression of the NDF in 1982 facilitated the co-option and integration of some elements from the left into governmental systems.[36] A dialogue developed between the regime, the defeated NDF leaders and broad circles of Yemeni society, fostering an environment conducive to amending the national charter.[37]

The decline in oil prices, the world recession and the decline in remittances from Yemeni workers abroad all reduced the financial aid that North Yemen was accustomed to receiving. In light of the economic crisis, the regime resorted to restrictive policies in order to adjust to the new economic reality. When oil was discovered in 1984, the economic forecast improved. The oil also set demanding requirements for accelerated development that the state was not prepared for. Also, in the transition period between the discovery of oil (1984) and the production of oil for export (1987), the regime made sure that it would not exceed its economic ability and not increase the importation of consumer products or increase government expenditures despite the expectations that rose in specific parts of society.[38] The state's improving capability and the modernization effort throughout the 1980s provided the state with more tangible access to regions that were traditionally considered strongholds of the NDF or enclaves of autonomous tribes. New access roads and the beginnings of development throughout the country improved the regime's ability to rule. President Salih attributed great importance to the development effort in terms of national integration and state building. Army forces went through a process of expansion in 1979 and again from 1986 to 1988.

Developments in regional and international politics in the 1980s played out positively for North Yemen. For example, during the Iran-Iraq War (1980–1988), North Yemen supported Iraq while South Yemen demonstrated neutrality and sometimes tilted toward Iran. The pro-Iraq policy that led North Yemen to deploy a volunteer unit for logistical aid helped it achieve an important status for itself in mainstream Arab politics. Saudi Arabia and other Gulf states viewed North Yemen's policy favourably and increased the scope of their economic aid to North Yemen. Some of the aid money was channeled to the tens of thousands of loyalists of the ousted President of South Yemen, 'Ali Nasir Muhammad, who moved to the north following the January 1986 civil war in South Yemen. 'Ali Nasir Muhammad left for exile and tried to consolidate opposition power from abroad. Around 12,000 of his loyalists crossed into North Yemen and were billeted north of the border, adding another source of friction between the two Yemens.[39]

The economic crisis in North Yemen in 1986 was attenuated mainly by the Saudis, who had an interest in stable and quiet relations between Sanaa and Aden, but not in unification.[40] Saudi support became part of a complex network of aid. Around 200 million dollars in the form of a loan arrived from Europe and a similar amount was promised by the Arab Bank in 1987 in order to finance oil exports when the North Yemeni oil industry was in its developmental stage. As North Yemen became more integrated into the regional economy, it became a distinctive part of the inter-state system. When the Iran-Iraq War ended in August 1988, Iraq sought to expand upon its new array of allegiances in the Arab world in the name of Arab unity, and Egypt sought to restore its status as the leading Arab state. The alliance that was constructed carried the title the Arab Cooperation Council (*Majlis al-Ta'awun al-'Arabi*), and North Yemen was a member together with Egypt, Iraq and Jordan. 'Ali 'Abdallah Salih aligned his country with the regional policy-makers. The summit meeting of the Arab Cooperation Council was held in Sanaa in September 1989 under North Yemen's flag, which still praised "God, the nation and the revolution".

The Ascendance of the Islamists in North Yemen

Throughout the 1980s, the influence of Islamist groups in North Yemen grew. "The religious groups", wrote the late YSP leader Jaralla 'Umar in 1989, "have, within a decade and a half, been transformed into a major power centre exercising extensive political and ideological influence and undertaking active propaganda work".[41] The presence of Islamist groups in North Yemen grew also because the government, with Saudi financing, saw them as a tool to undermine the grip of the leftists on the state. The Islamic Front, which was established in 1979 by tribal heads, was especially supported by 'Abdallah al-Ahmar, and enjoyed Saudi support as well. It sided with the government in the struggle against the NDF and was used as a tool by Salih to goad the regime in South Yemen.[42]

Activists from the Muslim Brothers, who until then had been organized in small cells and operated sporadically, also joined the ranks of the Islamic Front. Throughout the 1970s, the Brothers became more active in Yemeni politics and even took part in formulating the constitution during 'Abd al-Rahman al-Iryani's tenure.[43] During Ibrahim al-Hamdi's rule, religious institutions were established in which the Muslim Brotherhood took quite an active part, and they served as a basis for the creation of a political party. These years witnessed the rise of Shaykh 'Abd al-Majid al-Zindani as a prominent activist. Al-Zindani joined the ranks of the Islamic Front as the leader of the military wing. He was appointed Minister of Education in 1983, and despite his short-lived term, he managed to found a series of Islamic institutions. During the years 1986–1987, there were already 1,126 religious schools, whose students numbered 118,000.[44] In the same years, Yemen became a destination for Saudi, Sudanese and Egyptian preachers.[45]

The approaching compromise between the NDF and Salih's regime aroused the suspicion of the Islamist Front, whose activists had already acquired a significant presence in the security apparatus to the extent of threatening Salih's regime. In response, the regime sought to limit their influence and offered some of them titles and political positions in order to strengthen their allegiance and lessen their resistance. When the GPC was established as the government party in 1982, representatives of the Islamic Front participated in the formulation of the national charter.[46] However, these measures were not sufficient to contain the Islamic Front activists. In the 1980s, they deepened their penetration into the education system. Throughout the years 1986–1987, the religious establishment housed 4,000 teachers who taught more than 100,000 students. Most of the teachers were members of Islamic movements in their homelands, primarily Egypt, Sudan and Syria.[47]

Nevertheless, North Yemen encouraged Islamic movements and viewed them as part of "the national charter". In the Islamic schools for girls in North Yemen, there were around 25,000 students as of 1984, a fifth of whom were from Sanaa. Gender division was a controversial issue that was raised primarily by the Islamists. In the University of Sanaa, an Islamic dress code was introduced and Islamist activists took over the student union. Radical preachers were encouraged by 'Ali 'Abdallah Salih's associates and did not encounter any resistance from the president himself. Operatives identified with the Islamic Front were even permitted to establish a newspaper in 1985, *al-Sahwa* (The Awakening).[48] The Islamic Front gained momentum in light of the informal overlap between its activists and the state and not because of formal alliances. For example, the Soviet invasion of Afghanistan loomed large in the public discourse throughout the Middle East and the Muslim world, and in Yemen debates on this issue proliferated. In the villages of North Yemen, there were dozens of journals (most of which were published in Pakistan) that debated at length the question of Afghanistan and the permissibility of taking a life in the name of the Islamic cause. Yemenis working in Saudi Arabia and in the Arab Gulf states were also exposed to this and shared their views with their close friends and family members in Yemen.[49] In the elections for the

Consultative Council of 1988, the Islamic candidates won in Sanaa and took six out of seven election districts, a result that the GPC had not been prepared for. In other parts of North Yemen, only a few members of the previous councils were re-elected.[50]

It seemed as though the public longed for a change, and the Islamists were perceived as the precursors of just such a change. By the late 1980s, Sanaa had undergone dramatic population growth. Estimates differ, but most of them showed that in the late 1970s, there were 200,000 residents in Sanaa, compared to 780,000 in the late 1980s. Within a decade, Sanaa went from a Zaydi-dominated central government hub to a cosmopolitan centre. Africans, Europeans and Arabs wandered its streets and modern stores gave it a new look. The state that replaced the Imamate was a state with presidential palaces and lavish vehicles for government ministers. The Yemeni historian, Muhammad al-Akwaʿ, aptly described the evolving circumstances of the time:

> If we compare the condition of the Imam [Imam Yahya] with that of the revolution's great ones and the heads of the Yemen Republic we find a huge difference. On the one hand, parsimony, stinginess, a [certain] greediness and yet sticking to one sort of food; on the other hand, luxury and expenditure, a profusion of variety, any number of kitchens and cooks, so there is no end to it. It's as if you were in a dream or at a feast of the ʿAbbasids or Barmecides. So it was with the Kings of Himyar and the sons of Himyaritic nobles, God spare them and help them! [51]

Despite the fact that some groups were given the opportunity to consolidate their economic position, most of the population experienced economic hardships and a vast group of unemployed workers emerged. The decline in the Yemeni Riyal's value against the American dollar (at the end of 1986 it reached a ratio of 1:18) made the situation very difficult, primarily because basic commodities like sugar and tea were imported. The decline in Yemeni workers' remittances to their families contributed to the hardships. The socio-economic hardships were all the more significant owing to a simultaneous socio-demographic change. The number of students in North Yemen grew dramatically. In the beginning of the 1980s, there were 567,000 students, and this number rose above a million in the 1985–1986 school year and to about 1,300,000 in the following school year. Half of the population of North Yemen was 15 years old and younger (as of 1981), and in 1989 around 62 per cent of the entire population was 20 years old or younger, meaning that they had not been exposed to the scenes of the revolutionary era of the 1960s. The ousting of the Imam in the North and the British departure from the South were for them no more than chapters in Yemen's history books.[52]

CHAPTER 4

UNITED YEMEN

The Path to Unification

The two Yemeni leaders continued to speak of the need for unification and exalted the idea of "united Yemen", but in practice, each of them took merely symbolic measures that lacked practical meaning in the direction of attaining this goal. The period 1967–1990 witnessed very few intervals of cooperation and relative stability between the two Yemens. Each state tried to capitalize on the other's domestic weaknesses and sought to impose its own version of unification. For both, the primary strategy was to manipulate the other state's domestic opposition forces and employ them as proxies. Leaders who tried to stabilize relations between the two and advance normalization were denounced for serving reactionary forces or "atheists" on the other side of the border. For example, Sanaa allowed exiles from the South, who were supported by the Saudis, to use its territory as a base for attacks on the NLF (and later the YSP), the leading party of South Yemen. Alternatively, in 1977, Aden tried to capitalize on the tremors in Sanaa in the aftermath of Ibrahim al-Hamdi's assassination by promoting the NDF, which was located in North Yemen, as a military opposition.[1]

In 1979, South Yemen even sent its forces to the front to fight against the North and tried to dictate its version of unification as a condition for a ceasefire. However, in practice, neither of the two had the military or political capability that was needed to impose unification on the other. The period of relative stability in the second half of the 1970s ended with the assassination of Ibrahim al-Hamdi, the President of North Yemen, in 1977 and the violent ousting of Salim Rubay' 'Ali, the leader of South Yemen in 1978. Salim Rubay' 'Ali's domestic rivals came out against what they called his "appeasement approach" toward unification.[2] Positions for and against unification were therefore tools for obtaining local support or goading rival forces.

Attempts at unification in the 1970s and 1980s were met with constant resistance from the Saudis and some powerful tribal heads from the North. The Saudis' desire to preserve the two separate states was clear. United Yemen could have adopted the ideology of the NLF in Aden, or developed an irredentist claim to return to territories such as 'Asir, Najran and Jizan, or undermined the validity of the 1934 Ta'if treaty which stipulated Saudi sovereignty over the three areas. These scenarios had negative implications for the status of Saudi Arabia in the entire region. Therefore, Riyadh cultivated the tribal leaders in the North, who viewed the ideas of the NLF as a recipe for disaster for the values of the tribal culture, not to mention the tribal autonomy that tribes had long enjoyed throughout the years.

'Ali Nasir Muhammad's tenure as President of South Yemen from 1982 constituted the longest interval of stability and cooperation between the two Yemens. Unification was frequently talked about, but negotiations were postponed until a later time. 'Ali Nasir Muhammad's opponents, mainly 'Abd al-Fattah Isma'il, scathingly criticized him, and NDF activists that had been forced to withdraw from the North to the South in 1982 also joined the critics.[3] This led to the ousting of 'Ali Nasir Muhammad who, together with thousands of his supporters, was forced to leave the South, finding refuge in North Yemen. 'Ali Nasir Muhammad's ousting darkened the relations between the two states. The influx of refugees from the South, who gathered in the North, only complicated the situation. But the new government in Aden continued, to a large extent, with the predecessor's policy in order to prevent a new crisis and stabilize its ranks. That policy was also in line with the Soviet Union's preference for strengthening its ties with the oil-rich states in the Gulf. For two years afterwards, the new regime in Aden disguised its policies in slogans glorifying unification, but there was no response from Sanaa.[4]

The discovery of oil in North Yemen changed the balance of power and lessened the central government's dependence on both the prominent tribal leaders and on the Saudis.[5] This had an implication for the relations between the two Yemens. The tension between the two Yemens sharpened in 1987 against the backdrop of discoveries of oil fields on both sides of the border, in the North in Ma'rib and in the South in the region of Shabwa. In March 1988, the two states concentrated their forces on the shared border. The crisis was resolved with an agreement that was signed between 'Ali 'Abdallah Salih and 'Ali Salim al-Bayd, the leader of South Yemen. The agreement established a 930-mile neutral zone between Ma'rib and Shabwa, as well as a joint company for the development and exploitation of the minerals in these regions.[6]

This pattern of dialogue between the two Yemens was translated dramatically and unexpectedly into the act of unification at the end of 1989. In October 1989, the joint committee that was charged with implementing the unity agreement of 1972 convened. A November meeting between the leaders of the North and the South furnished a memorandum of the constitution of the united state – the same constitution that had been completed in 1981 and since then had been shelved in light of the series of conflicts between the two Yemens.[7] The constitution was supposed to be ratified by both states and at the end of the year to approve the establishment of the unified state – the Republic of Yemen. The political and economic change that North Yemen experienced under the leadership of 'Ali 'Abdallah Salih and in conjunction, the weakness of South Yemen and the erosion of the YSP, created the possibility of uniting the two Yemens.

In the two months following the November meeting, the contacts between Sanaa and Aden grew. Within the framework of the joint committee's mandate, discussions were held for the establishment of a multi-party system. The leaders of the two Yemens even authorized the committee to hold talks with the various political currents in order to reach an acceptable formula. They also agreed – or at least declared – that democracy and political pluralism were conditions for the success of unification. In South Yemen, a process of liberalization that included the expansion of civil freedoms and the holding of local municipality elections was underway. The YSP permitted the establishment of a multi-party system and removed the limitations on citizens going abroad. It also introduced new land laws and investments such as making the port of Aden a free-trade zone. In foreign relations, as well, South Yemen underwent dramatic change. The border conflict with the Sultanate of Oman was resolved and diplomatic ties were established with the United States in April 1990.

The changes that took place in the regional and international arena, particularly the events that led to the fall of the Berlin Wall in November 1989, prompted the leaders of both North and South Yemen to convene in Aden.[8] This meeting resulted in a renewed memorandum of unification. Only two years before, an official from North Yemen had declared what was until then commonly assumed, that "unification would be achieved only after a long time, unless there is an historic accident".[9] In effect, a number of dramatic developments contributed to the unification of Yemen. The pattern of inter-Arab relations changed, and the Soviet Union entered the process of dissolution. The measure of unification also reflected South Yemen's understanding that if it did not do so, it was liable to lose its power altogether.

The Act of Unification

On 22 April 1990, the two Yemeni states signed the "Sanaa Agreement", which authorized the transition to a democratic multi-party system and the implementation of free speech and a free press. On 13 May 1990, the two states decided to unify their armies and on 21 May, the two parliaments ratified the agreement.[10] On 22 May, the banner of United Yemen was raised. From then on, the only colours of united Yemen were red, white and black. The star that until then had ornamented North Yemen's flag and the triangle that decorated South Yemen no longer appeared. The leader of former North Yemen, 'Ali 'Abdallah Salih, was appointed president of united Yemen and the general secretary of former South Yemen, 'Ali Salim al-Bayd, was appointed his vice-president.

For most Yemenis, the act of unification came as a complete surprise, even though the idea of a united Yemen was certainly not new for them. In the two months prior to the official unification in 1990, various groups in the North and South had discussed ways of cooperation. Oil companies in the North and the South, for example, cooperated in various oil exploration initiatives along the shared border (in Ma'rib-Shabwa).[11] Unification allowed the leaderships of the North and the South to present themselves as marching along the path toward the fulfillment of a historical dream. It was clear that evolving geopolitical and geo-economic circumstances led to the process of unification, and that unification was conceived of as being in the shared interest of both states.

Geopolitics played a crucial role in both Yemens' march toward unification. The decay of the Soviet Union in the early 1980s removed the ground from underneath South Yemen's feet. Soviet economic aid suddenly ceased, jarring the economy into an intense recession and slowing South Yemen's market. Furthermore, workers' remittances decreased by almost half and the state's balance of payment was in arrears.[12] This served as a final stamp of failure for the centralized economy that had been administered by the government. The departure of Soviet and East German advisors from Aden left South Yemen vulnerable and in disarray. This sharpened the dimensions of the ideological and political crisis that faced South Yemen since the civil war of January 1986. The Marxist ideological lines that had been blurred and the loss of faith in the socialist government spawned a need for a new reality. From the perspective of 'Ali Salim al-Bayd, the general secretary of South Yemen, entering unification was a response to the need of the hour and was, to a large degree, a relief from the exhausting confrontation with the opposition to his regime led by former president 'Ali Nasir Muhammad.[13]

As for North Yemen, unification was perceived as a fitting opportunity to strengthen the legitimacy of the regime. North Yemen's leadership (which ruled over a population that until 1990 was four times that of the South) under the stewardship of 'Ali 'Abdallah Salih saw unification as a measure that could broaden North Yemen's resources quota and procure access to the Far East via the port of Aden. From a demographic perspective, unification could create an impression of a stronger and more stable state. 'Ali 'Abdallah Salih's sense of security, which grew higher throughout the 1980s, found expression in the aspiration "to swallow" the South and rule a larger and stronger country. Comfortable regional and international circumstances motivated Salih to fulfill this vision of unification. Saudi opposition to the process of unification was largely weakened; Arab states, such as Iraq, now viewed unification favourably. The United States also favoured unification. These circumstances encouraged Salih in further promoting unification.[14] In his various speeches, 'Ali 'Abdallah Salih presented unity as a measure that embodies a zenith in the Yemeni experience. As such, each time that he addressed the citizens of Yemen he referred to them as "the descendants of Sheba and Himyar, who had rehabilitated the golden age of their history".[15]

United Yemen was to have been built according to the model of a multi-party democratic system. Ostensibly, this was the natural by-product of the declarations and discussions that had been held before the unification by Sanaa and Aden. However, political elites in both North and South Yemen, who from the beginning had been inspired by Arab revolutionary regimes and Marxist-Leninist ideology, had not experienced political liberalization and treated democratic rule as a foreign idea. In effect, the common ground between the two regimes was their hostility to pluralist, multi-party systems. In the beginning of the civil war in North Yemen in 1962, President 'Abdallah Sallal had outlawed all political parties, including the Arab Nationalists. In South Yemen, the pro-Marxist NLF (and later the YSP) displaced all other political parties – including the Nasserists and Ba'thists – and functioned as the sole party. Although elections were held for the parliament and local municipalities in both North and South Yemen, in both cases the process was carefully administered and monitored by the central government, which controlled the pace of the elections and determined their results. The fall of the Imamate in the north and the British departure from the south of the country paved the way for the creation of authoritarian "peoples" republics.

The newly united Yemen was quickly swept into the labyrinthine system of regional relations. Yemen abstained from condemning Iraq for its aggression in the August 1990 invasion of Kuwait, a position at odds with the other members of the Arab League. It seemed as though

'Ali 'Abdallah Salih was captivated by components of the discourse on unity – Yemen's exalted past, the fight against imperialism and slogans of Arab unity. Support for Saddam Hussein strengthened and embodied the values expressed in the unification of Yemen. Huge demonstrations in front of the American and Saudi embassies in Sanaa (actively encouraged by the Iraqi embassy) made it all too clear that united Yemen did not belong to the moderate, pro-Western camp. The slogan that was featured at all of the demonstrations, "From now on, no more America" (*ba'd al-yawm ma 'ad amrika*), reflected the *zeitgeist* in Yemen. In the Yemeni parliament, there were passionate arguments on the question of whether or not to support Iraq, and 'Ali 'Abdallah Salih, who was at the time on a state visit to Egypt and Jordan, seemed hesitant to decide upon an appropriate course of action. But as two Iraqi oil tankers anchored in the port of Aden in the end of August 1990,[16] it became clear that Salih was tilting toward Iraq, thereby deviating from the line adopted by the Arab League. Yemen subsequently expressed this position in the Security Council of the United Nations.[17]

The spirit of disapproval with Yemen's position was expressed by the Arab Gulf States, in particular the Saudi Kingdom, in September 1990 through a mass expulsion of Yemeni foreign workers.[18] Foreign aid from the Gulf States and from the West that was supposed to be delivered to Yemen was cancelled. Such measures severely hindered Yemen's economy (one of the four poorest countries in the Arab world at the time of the unification) and its standing in the Arab world. Signs of economic crisis were discernible in the rate of the Yemeni Riyal, which was devalued; between 1990 and 1991, it was at 30 Riyal to the dollar, whereas it had hovered around 5 Riyal to the dollar a decade before. Thus, at the very beginning of its statehood, united Yemen was faced with economic and political hardships.[19] Nevertheless, unification contained hope for future prosperity. Unlike previous unifications that the Arab world had witnessed (for example the unification of Egypt and Syria in February 1958 which culminated in the United Arab Republic), Yemenis shared a lot of common ground. Salih travelled extensively throughout the united country and declared that North Yemen and South Yemen were entities of the past that had been superseded by "Greater Yemen" (*al-Yaman al-Kubra*).[20] However, in the first years of unification, there was a discrepancy between word and practice.

The fact that the currencies of former North and South Yemen (the Riyal and the Dinar, respectively) were preserved was a reflection of the ongoing duality in united Yemen. In practice, the united government operated according to equal representation, which made it difficult to function and this resulted in ambiguous policies. The most dominant issue was the amalgamation of the armed forces. Salih adopted delaying tactics and prevented officers from former South Yemen from acquiring positions of power. In the first years of unification, Salih did not grant southerners a foothold in the internal security apparatus or elite army units. He placed many of his fellow tribesmen (members of the tribe of Sanhan and his allies from the Hamdan tribes) and family members in key positions in the security forces. His half-brother Muhammad was the head of the central security apparatus, and his half-brother, 'Ali, was one of the senior commanders of the Republican Guard.[21] For Salih, the unification served as a tool for consolidating his dominance in the political arena. His declarations on democracy and multi-party pluralism did not receive concrete expression on the ground and it seemed as though he was only paying lip service to advance unification as a means to swallow up the South and strengthen his regime.

'Ali 'Abdallah Salih hailed from the army and took over the government after his political rivals from the South assassinated his predecessor. In the 12 years prior to unification, his government had survived a number of coup attempts. Granting political freedom to potential rivals and allowing their ascendance in the state system was not in line with his politics of survival; it only undermined his rule and intensified instability in Yemen. Likewise, his vice-president, 'Ali Salim al-Bayd, who espoused Marxist-Leninist ideology (at least until the collapse of the Soviet Union) did not emerge on the heels of the liberal democratic ideal.

The number of newspapers and their circulation grew, as did the number of parties that took part in the political process. But there were two large dominant parties who previously led the North and the South – the GPC and the YSP respectively – while the rest were small and lacked backing during this phase. The third largest was the al-Islah party (*al-tajammu' al-yamani lil-Islah*), which relied on the tribal aegis of the Hashid and Bakil confederations in the North and enjoyed aid from the Saudis. This party, which was sometimes identified as an Islamic-tribal power, served as 'Ali 'Abdallah Salih's tool which he used to goad the YSP, the erstwhile enemy of the al-Islah party. The al-Islah party (formerly the Islamic Front) drew its power from two main sources. The first of these was the conservative tribal opposition, supported by the Saudis against the YSP that had ruled South Yemen. The leader of the Hashid confederation, Shaykh 'Abdallah al-Ahmar, was appointed secretary-general of the al-Islah party and enjoyed monumental support in the north of Sanaa and significant influence in the territories that stretched between Sanaa and Ta'izz. The second element of support was the Muslim Brotherhood, and in parallel, the members of the military wing of the former Islamic Front, under the leadership of Shaykh 'Abd al-Majid al-Zindani, 'Abd al-Wahhab al-Anisi and 'Abd al-'Aziz Yasin, who was the "Supreme Guide" (*al-murshid al-'amm*) of the Muslim Brothers in Yemen. During the elections for the Consultative Council in North Yemen (1988), the Muslim Brothers operated independently, but their failure was devastating; they won only 25 of the 301 seats. In order to strengthen their power, they cut a deal with the tribal leaders, and thus, not long after the unification of Yemen, the al-Islah party was formed.[22]

Nevertheless, the al-Islah party was created largely from members of the GPC in an effort to marginalize the YSP and provide some of the GPC's more religiously inclined members with a political voice.[23] The al-Islah's centrality increased because of its adherence to the principles of political Islam, and also owing to the political position of its leader, Shaykh 'Abdallah al-Ahmar, who also served as speaker of the parliament. The movement published three journals, *al-Islah*, *al-Sahwa* and *al-Manar*. In December 1992, the Unification and Peace Committee organized by Islah propagated slogans such as "the Quran and the Sunna are above the constitution and the law", and "support unity and preserve Islam".[24] The committee's resolutions emphasized

Islah's objectives to undermine "those who dared to place the will of the people above the will of God".[25]

The distribution of the 301 seats in the April 1993 elections reflected a change in the political map of Yemen. The GPC officially won 123 seats (actually 140 if its "independent" supporters are counted) and the YSP won 69 seats (82 if the independents are counted). The al-Islah party won 68 seats. The Ba'th won seven seats, the Nasserists won three and the al-Haqq Party won two.[26] When the election results were announced, 'Ali Salim al-Bayd, the leader of the YSP, made the conciliatory suggestion of establishing a broad coalition that would include the three large blocs.[27] The coalition agreed that 'Ali 'Abdallah Salih would continue to serve as president. Haydar al-'Attas from the YSP would continue to serve as prime minister, and 'Abdallah al-Ahmar, the leader of the al-Islah party, would serve as speaker of the parliament. Government ministries were also distributed proportionately – 15 for the GPC, 9 for the YSP and four for the al-Islah party.[28]

Save for the loss of a few ballot boxes, the elections were uneventful and organized, and it seemed as though the democratic process had taken root in united Yemen. Around 2.7 million eligible voters (including 77 per cent of eligible males and 15 per cent of eligible females) exercised their right to vote. Around 4,800 candidates, most of whom were independents, presented their candidacy. Around 3,600 of the candidates (though only 50 of them were women) persisted until the end of the race.[29] Despite these elections, liberal democracy in the Western sense did not develop in Yemen. During the first three years of unification (May 1990–May 1993), the GPC and the YSP colluded, forming a two-pronged government. Their tacit agreement received expression in the March 1993 document, the "Joint Political Action Order" (*mithaq al-'amal al-siyasi*). This agreement stated that the parties welcomed anyone who accepted the principles and goals of the two Yemeni revolutions, democracy and national integration. However, in the Yemeni leaders' view, as Kostiner writes, "democratization meant unlimited and unstructured debate. The result was a proliferation of proposals and amendments and counterproposals over an unrestricted time span."[30]

Unification of the parliaments and the governments did not lead to a representative government that expressed the full range of interests of the populations in the North and the South. The unification was not an integration of political systems with the aim of creating a broad-based democracy, but rather the expression of an alliance between Northern and Southern elites who found unification to be in their interest. The cautious optimism regarding the future of Yemen quickly gave way to gloomy predictions as the fragility of the agreement was exposed. The problematic nature of the arrangement was apparent from the very beginning: the unification process and the democratic process held contradictory premises. While unification rhetoric focused on democratic ideals, the reality of unification meant that the dominant North and South parties were able to further arrogate and concentrate their power, with little thought of expanding their constituencies. Even the election results were indicative of the structural contradiction that existed between the two processes; the GPC and the al-Islah party won significant support in the northern and western districts of Yemen and the YSP had a victory in the southern and eastern provinces of the country. But neither the GPC nor the YSP succeeded in creating support for itself in territories that were previously identified with the other party.[31]

After the elections, Salih tried to reduce the power of the YSP to a degree that would be proportionate to the South's demographic weight (around 20 per cent of the population in Yemen), but the former leadership of the South desired equal partnership. In the meeting of the party's Central Committee in May 1993, the YSP issued pronouncements lauding their dedication to united Yemen. They argued that they had contributed a full state, its resources, its people and two-thirds of the territory of united Yemen, and therefore they demanded equal distribution of positions and authority.[32] In protest, YSP leader 'Ali Salim al-Bayd resorted to repeated acts of *i'tikaf* (retirement), sequestering himself in his home district in South Yemen, but not officially resigning. His most significant *i'tikaf* was in August 1993, when al-Bayd and his cohorts in the YSP blamed 'Ali 'Abdallah Salih for authoritarianism, alleging that his agents were responsible for the recurring murders of activists from the YSP. Many Southern activists who had previously called for unification (*wahda*) began to clamour instead for secession (*infisal*).[33]

The numerically inferior South had been tempted to unify with the North through promises of equality in government, particularly in the assignment of bureaucratic posts. But when the transition period ended with the 1993 elections, there was no guarantee of equality between the South and the dominant North. The inclusion of the YSP's bitter rival, the tribal-Islamic Islah Party, into the ruling coalition with a comparable number of seats reinforced the YSP's feelings of disillusionment.[34] The bitter arguments that Prime Minister al-ʻAttas had with the parliament regarding the range of his authority served as a vivid indication of his eroding power in the political system of united Yemen.[35]

In an attempt to rehabilitate its status, the YSP put forth a number of proposals for a more equitable power-sharing agreement. Some of the proposals, such as the creation of a local and more flexible government system, were well received, but other proposals – like the one for new elections for the president and vice-president – were immediately shelved.[36]

Civil society in Yemen was well ahead of the state institutions in the promotion of ideas of unification and pluralism. Public debate was tangible at all levels. The 30-member Dialogue Committee, which was comprised of esteemed notables from the government and from non-political circles, was appointed to facilitate dialogue that would promote unification. In the beginning of 1994, the committee issued the Document of Consent and Reconciliation (*wathiqat al-ʻahd wal-wifaq*), which detailed the required reforms and was well received among intellectuals and in most public sectors.[37] However, despite the fact that the document carried the signatures of the two leaders of Yemen, neither side was willing to implement far-reaching reforms and it had little impact on society at large.[38]

The historical experience and the sense of shared identity amongst Yemenis was not enough to foster full cohesion and solidarity. State institutions reflected the reality of an artificial union; to use Michael Hudson's words, this created a "homeland by force of law" (*watan shariʻ*) and not a "real homeland" (*watan hakiki*).[39] The inter-elitist rivalry was another by-product of the artificial unification. Also, the economic promise that was bound up in the vision for united Yemen was not realized. High unemployment, price increases and the widening gap between the elite and the lower classes were signs of the times. In the years 1991–1992, reports of murder and armed robbery in Yemen's main cities increased. Arms smuggling and widespread housing difficulties (especially in the cities of former South Yemen that did not recover from the 1986 civil war) contributed to an atmosphere of crisis.[40]

A new wave of demonstrations flooded the cities of Yemen in September 1992, and in conjunction with the scope of violence and targeted killings, the economic situation deteriorated and the Yemeni Riyal lost half of its value. Instability paved the way for the next civil war. In March 1994, Sinan Abu Lahum and Mujahid Abu Shawarib, senior tribal leaders of the two largest confederations, published the following:

> We hoped that logic and common sense will triumph at the end of the day ... and that the rights of 14 million civilians would get preference over particularlist interest of various rulers ... We did not spare any effort to reach an agreement with those who wished to lead the state to destruction and calamity, but unfortunately, all we found was a bunch of lies ...[41]

Most of the understandings fell apart, and regional and international efforts to reconcile the opposing parties were unsuccessful. Since the military organs of the North and South were never united, the path was paved for renewed violent conflict. In the spring of 1994, Northern and Southern units positioned themselves across from each other on key junctures along the old borderline. The war that broke out embodied the fragility of the 1990 unification and demonstrated that in practice, two distinct ruling apparatuses continued to exist. The new constitution dedicated little space to the fusion of the abysmal differences between the two. The states of the North and South had simply agreed on full partnership for a period of two and a half years under the assumption that later issues would work themselves out on their own, despite the North's arrogation of power at the expense of the South from the very beginning of the process. The unification agreements themselves had determined that Salih would be the president of the united state, while in the Presidential Council, three seats were granted to representatives from the North and only two to the South.

Civil War Returns: May 1994

Four years after the declaration of unification, in May 1994, civil war broke out again. Salih's regime was confronted with secessionist demands from Southerners, whom he described as "the opposing forces to legitimacy and unification".[42] In the early stages of the civil war, the YSP leader, 'Ali Salim al-Bayd, declared secession from the union. He also declared the establishment of an independent southern state called the Democratic Yemeni Republic (*jumhuriyyat al-yaman al-dimuqratiyya*), and demanded that the international community recognize it. Haydar al-'Attas was appointed prime minister and declared the establishment of the Committee for National Salvation (*lajnat al-inqaz al-watani*), a committee that was entrusted with granting representation to all sectors of the population, including the religious sector. This announcement played into the hands of 'Ali 'Abdallah Salih, who framed these events not as a North-South conflict but rather the Yemeni nation's struggle against a secessionist group, "traitors" in his words, who strove to divide Yemen. Salih's forces penetrated the Southern lines and established uncontested control in several provinces.[43] The northern forces' takeover of Aden and Hadramawt on 7 July 1994 ended the war. The bloody war had lasted two months and inflicted over 10,000 casualties. As the YSP leaders fled to Egypt and various states in Europe, Salih imposed unification on the state of Yemen by force.[44]

Salih's victory stemmed, primarily, from the scope of his army, which was far larger than that of the South. In contrast to the Southern forces, which stood at about 50,000 soldiers, Salih had an army of about 120,000 soldiers, half of which were from the Hashid confederation. Some of them saw the war against the Marxist South as a sacred commandment and an opportunity to finally destroy a regime which, throughout the second half of the twentieth century, had sought to uproot the fundamentals of tribal culture. Not all tribes joined Salih's forces – the Bakil, Yafi' and Radfan did not fight for the North, but withheld support from the South in fear of Salih's retribution.

The leadership crisis in the South also influenced the results of the fighting. The South's main command was unqualified and lacked operational experience because most of its prominent figures had left after the January 1986 civil war. The people who gathered around 'Ali al-Bayd had only recently become acquainted with him. This included Foreign Minister 'Abdallah al-Asnaj, (who in his early career was the foreign minister of North Yemen) and Interior Minister Muhammad 'Ali Ahmad, who had been considered al-Bayd's rival during the events of January 1986. In contrast, supporting Salih were skilled politicians like 'Abd al-Karim al-Iryani and 'Abd al-'Aziz al-Ghani and tribal leaders like 'Abdallah al-Ahmar who, throughout the 1980s, became important clients in Salih's patronage networks. During the first unity period (1990–1994), Salih systematically acted to constrain and marginalize the YSP, while praising the unification on public occasions.[45] In addition, he continuously strove to create an independent base of support in the South, both amongst the tribes and among the factions that opposed the YSP. In contrast, the YSP remained committed to its ideals and continued to espouse ideas that had no concrete grounding among the Yemeni public. This mismatch of ambitions led to a power imbalance, which was reified in the North-led government structures. In practice, in the four years of the unification, effective cohesion was not created in Yemen. Furthermore, the democratic model that the two states agreed to in 1990 was, to a large degree, a solution based on convenience and not principle. Hundreds of years of colonial control had turned the South and the North into different entities due to their historical experience, and it was difficult in such a short time to bridge the differences in worldviews and political aspirations. The 1994 civil war made it clear that the institutions of the respective states had not merged; rather they operated in parallel to expand their power at the other's expense. The war ended this duality and unification was forcefully imposed.[46]

Unification through Coercion

Following the 1994 civil war, Salih sought to fulfill the unification in practical terms through the GPC's takeover of the political system. On 23 May 1994, in a message of conciliation, Salih declared a general pardon for all soldiers and citizens who had supported the leaders of the south. Through sophisticated use of amendments to the constitution, Salih harnessed the political system to his needs and acted to weaken rival parties, including those that had supported him during the war. Salih's dominance was absolute.

After the war and the defeat of the south, Salih adopted a number of measures to abolish the institutional duality that had persisted during the first four years of unification. First, he dismissed the Presidential Council, whose activities had fostered bitter friction in the period prior to the civil war and in which he had been no more than the "first among equals". He amended the constitution so that from then on the president would appoint the vice-president. In conjunction, he strove to further divide the state districts (24 instead of 18), primarily in the south, in order to encourage division and prevent a new concentration of power there. A single currency was established and the two airlines were combined into a single national airline. Salih also unified the army: in March 1995, he managed to combine the remains of the southern army with the northern one. Until then, this army had been comprised mainly of officers from the south who had identified with the YSP. Now it was built on a more tribal base, and key positions were filled by Salih's family and associates. The YSP lost its vitality and was no longer a factor in the political system. Its senior officials were arrested and its assets were confiscated. Its leaders – al-Bayd, al-'Attas and 'Abd al-Rahman al-Jifri – were forced to leave Yemen and established the National Resistance Front (*al-jabha al-wataniyya lil-mu'arada*) from their exile in London, led by al-Jifri. In order to present the government with a national vision and advance the message of unity, the GPC absorbed a number of former supporters of 'Ali Nasir Muhammad, the former President of South Yemen, who had been ousted in the 1986 coup. Salih viewed them as fit for his purposes because they shared a rivalry with the exiled southern leaders, so he appointed some of them ministers in his new government. 'Abd Rabbu Mansur Hadi, also one of 'Ali Nasir Muhammad's confidants, was even appointed vice-president. Having done so, Salih acquired an effective grasp on the various provinces of the state.

The GPC's political ally was the al-Islah party, which had sided with the winners at the end of the civil war. Salih rewarded them by a series of gestures, the most prominent of which were the permanent changes to the constitution, namely that *sharia* would be the fundamental basis for legislation in the new nation. These gestures led the al-Islah to believe that the government would accept its status as a growing political force. At the same time, Islah activists, mainly Shaykh al-Zindani's people, began to harass the secular population in the south and stoke unrest. They also opposed the establishment of the Aden Free Trade Zone on the grounds that it would attract a large number of foreigners to the country and undermine Yemen's Islamic character.[47] Their special relations with the Saudis became another source of concern for Salih. Slowly, it became clear to Salih that the al-Islah party was posing a concrete challenge to his rule in Yemen. Salih felt confident that the Marxist-Leninist threat had disappeared, but what he did not anticipate was that his alliance with Islah would come back to haunt Yemen in the future.

Salih certainly did not envision an Islamic republic in Yemen's future. In order to thwart the rising power of Islah and strengthen his own, he made a new round of personal appointments, and adopted measures to strengthen the connection with the Bakil tribes who also feared the power of al-Islah, most of whose activists and supporters were identified with the Hashid tribes. In conjunction, confidence building measures aimed at the populations of the south and improving relations with the former members of the YSP became Salih's priorities. Alongside his personal appointments of southern representatives, Salih carried out measures in the south that were not acceptable to Islah members such as promising compensation to Adenis whose houses had been destroyed during the civil war. He also thwarted their attempt to subject the economic and banking system to a process of Islamization.[48]

In 1996, Salih's relations with the al-Islah party deteriorated. The al-Islah's attempt to take over the curriculum in the south and to

Islamize spheres of life, and its granting of patronage to the Yemenis who had returned from the battlefields of Afghanistan, turned Yemen into a target for worldwide criticism.[49] Yemen was now perceived as a safe house for Islamic extremism and terror. This was underscored by the Egyptian charge that Salih provided refuge to Islamic terrorist groups following the June 1995 attempted assassination of Husni Mubarak in Addis Ababa.[50]

The 1997 elections provided Salih with an opportunity to consolidate his power. Through his use of effective tactics – political appointments, corruption, and the prevention of his rivals from running – his party won a sweeping victory and received 187 seats (62.1 per cent), including considerable support from the southern districts. The al-Islah party won 53 seats (17.6 per cent) and the rest were divided between smaller, fragmented parties and independent candidates.[51] The YSP did not participate in the elections. One of the most interesting features of the 1997 elections was the division in the ranks of Islah between the moderates (headed by 'Abdallah al-Ahmar) and the radicals (headed by Shaykh al-Zindani). The disagreement between the two camps was whether or not to act as part of the government or to quit it and act as opposition from outside the establishment.[52]

Salih strove to establish a single-party political system, not a multiparty or democratic one, as was discussed following the unification of 1990. In May 1997, Salih established a new government without partners from the al-Islah. The government was headed by Faraj bin Ghanim, an independent politician from Hadramawt, who had a doctorate in economics and who had broad public support. Ahmad al-Shami, the leader of the al-Haqq Party, a small Zaydi party that did not win any seats but was a declared enemy of the al-Islah party, was appointed Minister of Awqaf (religious endowments).[53] Salih appointed 'Abdallah al-Ahmar, the leader of the al-Islah party, to a position devoid of any real power – the parliament speakership.[54] He tried to placate al-Ahmar, who towed a relatively moderate line in contrast to the radical faction headed by Shaykh al-Zindani. The al-Islah party lost its nine ministerial posts and officially joined the ranks of the opposition. Sarah Phillips writes: "After being cast out by the GPC, Islah began to seek alliances with other opposition groups, even those to which it was ideologically opposed, most notably the YSP".[55] Nevertheless, despite its fierce criticism of the GPC, from 1997 Islah remained more concerned with opening and reforming the political system rather than radically altering it. Most of its leaders remained connected to the regime's patronage networks and maintained strong ties with the GPC as they had during the 1999 presidential elections when Islah had nominated President Salih as its own candidate. Islah's ambiguity was a by-product of its make-up – the tribal elements, the more religiously inclined former GPC members who had joined Islah and the conservative hardliners. Phillips correctly ascertains: "... the real balance of power within the party is determined more by political pragmatism and patronage ties to the regime than by religious ideology".[56]

In conjunction with the establishment of a government, Salih also established the Assembly of Representatives (*majlis al-nuwwab*), a consultative body to the president and parliament. The Assembly of Representatives was an appointed body, not an elected body, and was staffed by people approved by Salih (for example, 'Abd al-'Aziz al-Ghani, the former prime minister who became one of Salih's loyalists in the 1980s, and tribal leaders who had maintained extensive relations with Salih for over two decades). Ostensibly, the establishment of the Assembly of Representatives was intended to expand the base of political relations and the scope of political participation, but in practice, it was meant to chip away at the authority that the parliament continued to exert and thereby consolidate Salih's power. In August 2000, for example, Salih dictated that the number of members in the Assembly would grow from 59 to 111 and that members would vote on matters pertaining to foreign relations and security. Also, when Prime Minister Faraj bin Ghanim resigned, Salih established a new government headed by 'Abd al-Karim al-Iryani, one of his long time associates.[57] Thus, Salih consolidated his status in Yemen.

In the presidential elections that were held in September 1999 – the first ever direct elections in Yemen – Salih was re-elected. The elections embodied the tensions between the power of the state and the civic experience in unified Yemen. The elections were preceded by a declaration that they would be the first ever direct and free elections for the president. But there was no doubt about 'Ali 'Abdallah

Salih's ability to obtain a clear majority. Despite this, Salih cunningly manipulated the laws in order to prevent the opposition candidates from running in the election. To guarantee a competitive election, the constitution insisted that there must be at least two candidates. But the constitution also required nominees to be approved by at least 10 per cent of the members of parliament. Since Islah supported Salih's candidacy, the YSP was the only party that demanded to present a rival candidate but since they did not take part in the 1997 elections, they did not occupy any parliamentary seats – the constitutional condition for running.[58] A further 23 presidential nominees did not get the required approval to run. Salih's "opponent", Najib Qahtan al-Sha'bi, was the eldest son of the former president of South Yemen who had joined the GPC after unification and become a member of parliament without significant influence. Unsurprisingly, Salih won with 96.3 per cent of the vote in what he hailed as "a great democratic victory".[59]

The election campaigns of 1997 and 1999 revealed that Yemen was a state fraught with contrasts: it was a state in which a lively public debate existed but the multi-party system was very weak; it had a relatively free press in comparison to other Arab states; and there were many civil bodies that operated in the absence of free and fair elections.[60]

Salih's ultimate victory in the 1999 elections crowned him as the unquestioned leader of Yemen. He continued to goad and entice other parties into obeying his wishes. Thus, for example, when it seemed like the YSP was ready to settle differences and even convened a committee in Sanaa, Salih was upset with its members because they had appointed al-Bayd, the exiled leader, a member of the Central Committee. Salih further declared that if the YSP continued to pursue this policy, it would be outlawed.

Throughout that period, Salih continued to consolidate his family's position through nepotism. His nephew, Tariq Muhammad 'Abdallah, was appointed Commander of the Special Guards, and other close associates were given command posts in both the army and the civil system. 'Abdallah al-Ahmar's associates also won important posts and became managers of state-owned companies such as the national airlines and pharmaceutical companies. The most dominant issue was the preparation of Ahmad, 'Ali 'Abdallah Salih's son, as the designated successor. A personality cult rose up around the person of Salih, and under him Yemen abandoned the principles and rhetoric that had given birth to the revolution and became a state where tribal politics were used as an effective tool for consolidating power. At the beginning of the twenty-first century, Yemen appeared to be a hereditary republic (*jumhuriyya wirathiyya*) similar to Syria, which was ruled by the al-Assad family. It was as if the September 1962 Revolution, with its animus against personal power and its hopes of a Yemen united in freedom, had never happened.

CHAPTER 5

HEADING TOWARD A "FAILED STATE"

'Ali 'Abdallah Salih honed his survival skills over 33 years of rule (1978–1990 as President of North Yemen, 1990–2011 as the head of united Yemen). Through the careful juggling of different and often contradictory interests among tribal confederations, military and urban constituencies, he developed a pragmatic and balanced stance toward the various power centres inside and outside of Yemen – Islamists, socialists, Saudi Arabia and the West. The unification also contributed to the strengthening of his power. However, Salih's victory, impressive as it was, did not resolve the long-term challenges facing the country. The opposite was true. The first decade of the twenty-first century ushered a set of new and exacerbated obstacles into Yemen's path – a dwindling economy, a complex relationship between state and society, the strengthening of radical Islamic movements, a secessionist movement in the south – all of which posed a threat to the very stability of the unified state.

Tribe and State: Between Confrontation and Accommodation

The relationship between the state and the tribal system has always been complex and multifaceted. Salih's regime used tribes for its ongoing needs and viewed tribalism as an alternative to a party system.

This was seen especially during the years 1990–1994. The regime did not confiscate the tribes' weapons and used the tribal heads as mediators between the regime and rival groups. But when the civil war was over, it became clear that armed tribes and their leaders posed a real threat to the state in certain areas.

Tribes all over the Arabian Peninsula have acquired their positions in accordance with the type and volume of weapons that they possessed. In Yemen, this phenomenon became widespread as a result of the state's history. During the Ottoman era, weapons were widely distributed to facilitate civilian resistance against foreign powers. Carrying weapons became an important ingredient in Yemeni identity and a status symbol in the eyes of Yemenis – much more than a tool for defense: "Just as you [a Westerner] have your tie, the Yemeni will carry his gun",[1] a Yemeni professor claimed. This trend was strengthened during the 1962 Revolution and in its aftermath when there was a drastic increase in the number of weapons. A culture of violence, including organized crime, became widespread in Yemen. The authorities tried to enforce laws to limit the possession of weapons but not with great success.[2]

The attempt to disarm tribal power centres did not succeed. Tribesmen recognized that carrying a gun was necessary for self-defense as well as being an expression of power and autonomy. A tribal activist from the Ma'rib area illustrated the clash between the tribe and the state on the issue of the legitimate use of violence: "The tribes ... blame the government for trying to enforce laws to disarm the tribes while simultaneously allowing the military to do whatever they want".[3]

The tribes did not offer an alternative to Salih's rule but created an additional power centre that had to be bargained with; the very existence of armed tribal enclaves was a persistent source of instability. Attacks on oil installations in the provinces of Ma'rib and al-Jawf highlighted just how limited was the regime's reach and served as an indicator that in united Yemen, there were many tribal enclaves that the regime could not penetrate. The proliferation of weapons in the hands of ordinary citizens contributed to instability, and local disputes often became bloody. According to various estimates, the citizens possessed about nine million weapons – approximately two weapons per person over the age of 16.[4]

In view of the instability caused by the proliferation of weapons, the number of people calling for the reduction of arms and the enforcement of public security increased. In their demonstrations, civil society organizations carried slogans such as "Let's make Yemen a land free of arms", and "our Yemen is beautiful without arms".[5] The government initiated several policies in order to gain control over medium to heavy weapons, but confrontations between the authorities and armed tribal groups in many cases ended in clashes and bloodshed.[6]

One of the most remarkable phenomena in Yemen regarding tribe and state relations is the kidnapping of foreigners, tourists, diplomats or workers in multinational companies. This phenomenon was evident in Yemen's history but its scope was significantly broadened after the 1994 civil war. In most cases, the "rules of the game" are known. The kidnappers treated their hostages fairly while negotiating with the government for their release. Kidnapping was intended to turn the regime's attention toward the tribe's dissatisfaction with the prevailing situation.[7] In January 2000, a French tourist couple was kidnapped by a tribal group near the town of 'Amran, north of Sanaa. In March 2000, the Polish ambassador to Sanaa was kidnapped by the Qiyari tribal group. He was released several days later, but only after the release of the Qiyari's *shaykh*, Khalid al-Qiyari, who had been detained earlier by the authorities.[8] Usually when the government met the kidnappers' demands, the hostages were released and a lull followed. However, in some cases, hostages got hurt and a bloody struggle ensued between the army and members of a given tribe. The regime saw injuries to hostages as tarnishing Yemen's international image, and the regime retaliated in order to preserve what remained of its prestige. Ultimately, hostage-taking and power politics among the tribes form a dynamic in which, as Sanaa University sociologist Hammud al-'Awdi theorizes, the strength of tribes compared with that of the state fluctuates with the economic circumstances and the extent of the centre's penetration into the periphery through administrative, infrastructure and welfare systems.[9]

In spite of the Arab nationalist and Marxist-Leninist rhetoric that prevailed in the North and the South during the 1970s and 1980s,

Yemen remained, in essence, a tribal state. The ecological structures of the country facilitated regional divisions, where local loyalties overshadowed national loyalties. The central government never managed to achieve a breakthrough among the tribes and failed to impose central authority over the whole country. Salih, however, did succeed in creating a coalition between his family and other prominent families, in co-opting traditional groups through a socio-economic partnership and in enlarging the patron-client network by appointing his relatives to positions in the government. The return to the tactic of the patron-client network strengthened sub-state actors, such as tribes, and even anti-state actors, like radical Islamic movements which strove to undermine the regime.[10]

The Socio-Economic Crisis

At the threshold of the twenty-first century, Yemen faced one of the most difficult economic crises in its history. While the North and the South had weathered economic issues during the 1970s and 1980s, this downturn was substantially different. Yemen has become a state where over half of the population lives in conditions of deep poverty: one-third of the potential workforce is unemployed. Half of the population is illiterate and the GNP per capita for 2009 was around $460.[11]

Yemen faced a steep monetary crisis: the damages from the civil war amounted to $11 billion, Yemen's foreign debt was expanding, and the Riyal saw continual inflation, falling from 140 Riyal to the dollar in 1995 to approximately 160 to the dollar at the turn of the century. On top of that, Yemen's support for Saddam Hussein during the 1990 Iraqi invasion of Kuwait meant that Yemen's financial support from the Gulf oil states and the US had been dramatically cut. Millions of Yemenis who had been employed in the Gulf oil states were asked to return to Yemen, raising the unemployment rate even higher.[12]

The regime was duly aware of the economic crisis and its implications for the stability of the state and the legitimacy of the regime. When Salih managed to bolster his political position he also tried to bring about a shift in the economy to save Yemen from disaster. The government joined the Extractive Industries Transparency Initiative

(EITI), established the Supreme National Anti-Corruption Committee (SNACC), laid of public service personnel and implemented effective measures in the public spending budget.[13] Also, it implemented a development program for the years 2006–2010 with the aim of reducing the poverty rate and creating job opportunities in sectors such as fisheries, agriculture, natural gas and municipal services.[14] The efforts to make the state apparatus more efficient culminated in violent demonstrations in Aden, Hadramawt and Sanaa, with demonstrators blocking main roads and shouting slogans directed against Prime Minister 'Abd al-Qadir Ba-Jamal.[15] The failure of political and economic reforms, the removal of subsidies from gasoline and the consequent rise in fuel prices in July of 2005 led to huge riots all over the country. Increased poverty and pockets of corruption at the heart of the ruling system in Yemen also contributed to the instability.[16]

Following the 1994 civil war, Salih promised to fight corruption. Indeed, he attempted to uproot corruption in the bureaucracy. He reportedly carried out surprise evaluations of government workers in their workplaces. He also reportedly went through checkpoints in disguise in order to try to catch officials in the act of bribery. It was too little too late. Salih's attempts to uproot the institutional corruption which had become one of the main perils of the ruling system in Yemen were unsuccessful. In trying to appease the public, Salih declared his intention to hold new elections for the office of president and seats in parliament in 2006. But for most Yemenis, this declaration did not herald change, especially owing to the public's memory of the promises he had made on the eve of the 1999 presidential elections, in which he had won 96.3 per cent of the vote.[17]

Yemen's budget depends on oil revenues and foreign aid, but the best estimates predict that Yemen's oil revenues will run out in 2017.[18] Because oil revenues have been used as a means of appeasing separatist and oppositionist groups, reaching the bottom of the barrel would only make it more difficult for the regime to keep those groups at bay.

The rising fertility rate, a rising unemployment rate and the harsh demands for improving the state's efficiency made by the World Bank, rendered Yemen's prospects for the twenty-first century gloomy. On top of the economic woes, the existence of intransigent tribal enclaves prevented Sanaa from asserting its authority throughout the country. On the threshold of the twenty-first century, three new threats to the Sanaa regime emerged: the first was a secessionist movement in the south made up of people who were disappointed with the unification and who advocated the creation of an independent state in the south. The second threat was the eruption of a Shi'i rebellion in the northern province of Sa'da, which has come to be known as the "Huthi Rebellion", named after the family whose charismatic members have been at the forefront of the movement. The third threat derived from al-Qa'ida's increased presence in Yemen. Seen as a failed state in the making, radical movements such as al-Qa'ida viewed Yemen as an area ripe for their activities. For many of the Afghani veterans,[19] Yemen became a hub for rejuvenating their influence after having suffered blows in Iraq and other parts of the region.

The Free South (al-Janub al-Hurr)

In the southern provinces, the economic crisis set the stage for a secessionist movement. This movement strove to secede from the unified state, which it believed had been forced on the south by the regime of Sanaa. Calling itself the Free South movement (*al-janub al-hurr*, sometimes referred to as *al-hirak*), the movement demanded a more just government with real equality. As matters stood, the unified state was clearly prejudiced toward the south: there was no balance in channeling the resources for development. On these grounds, the Free South argued that there was no other choice but to return to the formula of two states.

The Free South, later on also known as al-Hirak al-Janubi, was established in 2005 but became active only in early 2007 when influential figures from the seven southern provinces (Aden, Lahaj, Abyan, al-Dali', Shabwa, Hadramawt and al-Mahra) met. The meeting was titled *liqa al-tasaluh wal-tasamuh* (a meeting of appeasement and forgiveness). It aimed to clear the atmosphere of past frictions and build up an understanding that would pave the way for joint activity.[20] The birth of the Free South was accompanied by the publication of a magazine having the same name.

The economic predicament that Yemen faced and the decline of industry in the south added to the resentment of the people. Factories were shut down and a great portion of the lands were purchased by elites of the north. Unemployment and poverty culminated in widespread protests. Many southerners argued that the unified state had treated them unfairly with regards to property disputes, jobs and pensions.[21]

A harsh economic situation and political frustration were not the only reasons for protest among the demonstrators. Their slogan, "we will get back our land using non-violent means", aptly sums up the modus operandi of the Free South.[22] In this way, al-Hirak al-Janubi posed a unique challenge for the regime in Sanaa. As a grassroots movement, it was not simply a matter of co-opting or intimidating southern elites.[23] The activists of the Free South emphasized the differences between the north and south in terms of worldview and perceptions. Many of them acted under the conviction that the forced unification did not succeed because both parts of Yemen were representing different cultures. While northerners widely held that the southerners were "unbelievers", southerners viewed northerners as "ignorant" or "land robbers".[24] The southerners perceived the north as a tribal society run by a tribal code, and perceived themselves as true nation-builders. Moreover, they believed that the government in the north was plagued with inefficiency and corruption.[25] They further called attention to the deterioration in the status of women and argued that women paid the price for unification.[26] In contrast to other states in the Arabian Peninsula, socialist South Yemen had implemented many reforms that bettered women's status: polygamy was prohibited, schools were integrated in terms of gender and women were encouraged to involve themselves in the workforce. Now, argued the activists of the "Free South", the government of Sanaa was imposing an Islamic character on Aden. Many mosques were built. In many public spaces including cafés and restaurants owners implemented "family areas" where bachelors were not allowed, similar to a Saudi practice. According to southerners, the north had long been the fiefdom of an archaic society:

> Don't forget Imams had been cutting us out of the civilization for ages ...

> Don't forget that when Europeans invaded the country, the Imams argued that they were demons with blue eyes and warned against interacting with them ...
>
> How would you like that a government that rules over a population where 90 per cent of it is illiterate will run the state? Shame on you that your leader did not manage to complete his high school education. This was not a matter of struggle between south and north, but one of tenets and worldviews.[27]

Symbolically, the Free South movement chose al-Dali' as their base. This was the place where the 1963 revolution began which eventually led to the British evacuation and the creation of South Yemen. The Free South was a diverse movement in terms of the social classes and political profiles of its members. The military backbone of the Free South Movement was made up of former officers of the southern army who had been dismissed following the unification of the state and the creation of its army. They were accompanied by educated but unemployed young people, and civil servants who had lost their jobs. The movement's leaders were Hasan Ahmad Ba'um and Nasir 'Ali al-Nuba, whose activity focused most of the time on preaching the tenants of the secessionist struggle first to the people of Hadramawt and later to the inhabitants of the south. In November of 2008, al-Nuba asserted that the solution to the issue of the south could be found only by returning sovereignty and independence to the south and obtaining the right of self-determination.[28]

The magazine, *al-Janub al-Hurr*, became the centre of activity for the secessionists and also an arena for accusations and complaints against the regime. For example, in early 2009, an analysis by a researcher from the south, exposed the way the regime in Sanaa had deepened its control in the south. His report included a list of the names of the army commanders of the north that had enjoyed cooperation with army officials from the south and who had become informers and had paved the way for the penetration of the conquering army of the north.[29] The report also presented the methods of trickery and deception that had been used by the Sanaa regime, including the restoration of political figures from the south after having ensured that they would serve the regime's interests. The report accused Dr. Sa'id Yasin Nu'man, the secretary-general of the YSP, of doing nothing to bring back the "stolen properties" of the YSP. Others like Salim Salih Muhammad, the president's advisor and the chair of the committee which dealt with the implications of the civil war, and 'Abd al-Rahman al-Jifri, the chair of the "Sons of the Arab South", were both introduced as people who flaunted their titles but were merely puppets of the Sanaa regime.[30]

The Free South activists referred to their homeland as if it were a region which had been conquered and occupied since the 1994 civil war. A diverse group of activists who believed that unification had been a grave mistake came together under Ahmad Ba'um in order to restore the rights and self-determination of the south. The very fact that the people of Hadramawt kept using their own currency, the southern Dinar, rather than the Yemeni Riyal, served as another indication of their desire to stick to their original identity and not to be assimilated into the "conquest project" of Sanaa.[31]

The activists of the Free South emphasized the gloomy results of the conquest that had been going on since 1994. They believed that the soldiers of the south had paid a heavy price; their pensions had been reduced and the regime in Sanaa was afraid that they would join the rebels of either the north or the south. These soldiers were the skeleton of the army of former South Yemen and after unification, some had been retired against their will. They saw themselves as the "victims of unification" and unsurprisingly became one of the main forces in the demonstrations and parades that strove for an independent south. One of the most conspicuous expressions of their discontent was a demonstration in al-Hurriyya Square in Khormaksar in July 2007.[32]

In the spring of 2007, there were many demonstrations throughout the south calling for secession (*infisal*). The Free South's activity focused on Hadramawt, where most of Yemen's oil was located. What stood out was its attempt to prevent property sales to the people of the north, the blocking of roads and the harassment of vehicles having a license plate from the north. In July 2008, the security forces fired live ammunition and used tear gas against the demonstrators whose demands included pensions for the retired, improvement of the public services and the release of more than 80 activists who had been apprehended in former protests. Dozens of demonstrators were arrested in the demonstration in Radfan and Lahaj, including Hasan Ba'um, the leader. The authorities in Yemen announced that the arrested activists would be tried for violent acts and they were expected to be sentenced to ten years in prison. Three other activists that called for the secession of the south, Ahmad 'Umar bin Farid, Muhammad Hasan Zayd and 'Abd Rabbu Hasan al-Khamis were tried on charges of sabotaging Yemen's unification and inciting a civil war.[33] A similar demonstration was held in Aden in December 2008 during which dozens of demonstrators were arrested, but still the Free South emphasized the non-violent character of their demonstrations and accused the regime of carrying out cruel attacks against them, especially one that took place in Sanaa, where the regime used live ammunition.[34] In mid-April 2009, the regime quashed a massive demonstration, killing a female student from Radfan. The activists of the Free South called this a "declaration of war" against the south. Salih al-Shu'aybi, a columnist, wrote:

> History repeats itself in the same tone, same means, same bloody narcissistic mentality, destruction and bloodshed. This time 'Ali 'Abdallah Salih declared a war without his historical allies whom he ignored the same way that he had ignored the values, principles and agreements of the "slaughtered" unification and thereby declared a second war against the south.[35]

It was symbolic that the event took place in the region of Radfan, the same place where in 1963 the revolt which eventually led to the British withdrawal, had erupted. A former army officer and one of the leaders of the army's pensioners (who had been retired against his will) expressed the way that the scenes of the past and the crises of the present were converging:

> I feel proud that in view of the capabilities of the heroes of Radfan who died as martyrs, expressing nobility, courage and

> honor, as is known from our history, they had the same unique courage and performance which they inherited from their ancestors throughout history.[36]

The magazine, *al-Janub al-Hurr*, also became a platform for discussion about the unification and its failure. A thorough investigation of the magazine and its articles vividly reveals the way that the past has been interpreted by the people of the south. They highlighted the unique identity and history of the south in order to prevent the north from blurring the lines. One of the columnists, Abu Muhammad al-Dirjaji, claimed that the "conquering regime of Sanaa was trying to unnaturally 'graft the [southern] branch onto the [northern] root'".[37] Sanaa was introduced as the "historical capital" in order to emphasize that the south was an integral part of Yemen. Al-Dirjaji also argued that the "conquest aimed to twist the modern history by re-writing the events of the September 1962 Revolution and the 14th of October 1963 Glorious Revolution".[38] He put forward as an example the fact that the propagandists of the north mentioned that the leaders of the south chose Ta'izz, a city in the north, as the headquarters for their activity – a choice which the propagandists proclaimed stood for the unity of the struggle and unity of Yemen. Darjaji went on to say that this was not an indication of either a joint struggle or a revolution any more than Fidel Castro's use of Mexico for the Cuban Revolution was an indicator of a joint struggle between Mexico and Cuba.[39]

The Free South activists focused on strengthening the dimensions of the southern identity, in order to pre-empt what they viewed as a conspiracy that strove to erode the south's identity. At the same time they highlighted the non-violent and liberal character of their struggle. Personalities like Muhammad Ahmad al-Qama', a well-known writer who had been apprehended in the city of Zinjibar, asserted that the struggle was a direct continuation of the south's struggle for independence and that reality forces one to sacrifice personal interests for the greater cause.[40] The Free South activists also brought the story of their struggle and its character into the international limelight. They emphasized that there were two states (North Yemen and South Yemen) and that this issue had been discussed in the UN Security

Council. They cited UN Resolutions 924 and 931, which had determined that the north's war against the south was unjust, and they called for sanctions against Salih's regime if he would not comply with these resolutions.[41] At times they repeated statements made by leaders such as President of the UAE, Khalifa bin Zayid al-Nuhayyan, who asserted that "the south is a state that should not be forced to accept unification through aggressive methods and power of weaponry".[42]

The incompetence of the Yemeni regime in dealing with regional and international problems was viewed by the Free South activists as an indicator that the Sanaa regime was not able to lead. Thus, for example, the UN resolution which called for the internationalization of the Gulf of Aden in order to more effectively cope with piracy was a result of Salih's attempt to foster cooperation between Yemen, Somalia, Sudan, Djibouti and Ethiopia. His failure to do so was harshly criticized by columnists of *al-Janub al-Hurr.* His initiative, which was raised under the banner of the Sanaa Declaration,[43] was depicted by one of the statesman of the south as an "alliance of the poor" in view of these states' dire economic circumstances and an unsuccessful attempt to gain regional influence.[44] Others, like Lutfi Shatara, understood this initiative as another attempt to cover up harsh internal problems and a failed foreign policy:

> One of the conspicuous signs of the failure of Yemen's foreign policy, and what turns Yemen into a paper tiger, is Salih's ongoing initiatives to resolve regional and international conflicts, such as Iran's nuclear file, while in effect, he cannot even release one hostage kidnapped by local tribes without carrying out humiliating acts including paying the ransom to the kidnappers.[45]

The clear conclusion of the activists was that the only solution was secession (*infisal*) and the re-establishment of two states in Yemen. They launched an international campaign that exposed the plots of the Salih-led unified state in order to gain international support for the restoration of their one-time homeland in the south. The activists framed their protests as an international concern. As such, they tried to taint Sanaa by consistently referencing the attack on the USS *Cole* in

October 2000 and the terrorist attacks on hotels in Aden and tourist groups.[46] The activists also reiterated Salih's policy during the 1990 Iraqi invasion of Kuwait as another indication of what they viewed as flawed policy. Yusuf Khalid, a columnist for *al-Janub al-Hurr* magazine, warned the Gulf's inhabitants:

> Drink from the same glass, but this time it would come from the regime of 'Ali 'Abdallah Salih. Oh the people of the Gulf, do something before the axe hits your head. Have you forgotten Salih's policy toward the Iraqi invasion of Kuwait? Salih's regime does not believe in the rights of the neighboring states, does not believe in Islam and Arabness ... this regime believes only in its particular interests and the day he gets the position as a crucial decision-maker, what you are going to get is abuse and robbery, as was the fate of the state of the south and its people who believed the slogans of unification until each citizen of the south realized that he became a stranger in his country and a third-class citizen, stripped of rights and peace of mind.[47]

People of the south restructured their history by highlighting past correspondences that could attest to the deep-seated differences between the south and the north. For example, a letter endorsed by the people of the Yafi'i tribe was sent to Imam Yahya. It read:

> [This letter is from] all the *shaykhs*, people and tribes of Yafi' small and large, rich and poor, to his Excellency, Yahya Hamid al-Din. His Excellency should realize, and so his disciples, brothers, the lands of Yemen and its surroundings, should know that Allah is making his army out of his anger, and take into account your deeds in this world. We are determined and you should know that we have conquered the valley of Hadramawt and we have purified the country of corruption. We have eliminated most of the heretics and the enemies and now it is your turn. Any way you are going to be rescued by any state that will give you shelter and in any state that will protect you, you won't be able to run away from our swords or get rest from our arrows. Our swords

> hit like lightening and our arrows go deep. The soldiers that would confront us would be of no use and your prayers will not be heard here. That is because you violated agreements and used unjust and corrupt methods. You should know that you attacked our country and killed our people. Beware of Allah before the war begins and your flesh will be scattered everywhere. Thank Allah that we had warned you and informed you by this letter. [Signed] the *shaykhs*, the illuminated ones, notables and all tribes of Yafi'.[48]

It is difficult to ascertain the extent to which the call of the Free South appealed to Yemenites at large. *Al-Janub al-Hurr* consistently reported that the movement was growing. It reported that southern officials who had previously cooperated with the north now joined the Free South because they came to believe unification had been a mirage. The magazine cited declarations made by *shaykhs*, emirs and sultans that they had joined the Free South, expressing their goal to restore the independence of the south. One of the sultans, Tariq bin Nasir al-Fadli, stated:

> We thought of building our homeland from scratch. We thought of paving the way for our people to get closer to stability and an honorable life, that our homeland will get what it deserves, that we'll show the world that we are the land of wisdom. This is how we understood unity and so we acted in favor of it. But unfortunately, what we are witnessing is [*sic*] rights that are being stripped or evaporated, a land which is robbed and people who have been taken captive by false national principles.[49]

Other disappointed tribal heads expressed their support for the Free South. An example is the declaration that was made on behalf of Shaykh 'Idrus Sa'id al-Sabihi, from the Hamdan tribe, which argued that the people of the south had tasted the horrors of the 1994 civil war and that theirs was a just issue of political, judicial and historical rights. Unity failed after the southern identity was confiscated and the people of the south had been discriminated against. The conquerors carved the land up into feudal portions, which turned the people of the south into virtual strangers in their own country.[50] A leading *shaykh* from the province of al-Shu'ayb put it bluntly after the Friday sermon:

> Today, I announce my joining the ranks of the Free South and I am expressing my pride of being today amongst my brothers and people in this movement. Starting from today, I am joining [the Free South] in order to restore through it the justice and the rights to the south that was robbed and taken by the regime of the 7th of July that conquered the south.[51]

There were, however, southerners who did not side with the secessionists and did not see the formula of two states as a fitting solution. They criticized the poor performance of the regime and called for a change in its policy in an effort to save unity. They did not perceive the April 2009 parliamentary elections (which had gone relatively smoothly) as anything more than another attempt "to make use of the public cache in order to buy them off and to drive the security forces to missions far away from what they were primed to in order to enforce election results that did not represent the people's will and which would eventually end in bloodshed and resistance in the streets".[52]

Al-Sahwa.net, a news website that was established in October 2002, recommended that the regime "quit the sporadic reforms because they [merely] conceal [the mismanagement of the government] and start acting for the interest of unified Yemen and go on with the unification program even if the office of the president would be sacrificed for that".[53] Others suggested the creation of a federal government, where each of the 21 provinces would enjoy autonomy in many areas and would have the authority to shape the public order in its own province.[54]

Another critic, Da'ud al-Sharyan, emphasized in his article "Yemen: Between Negligence and Abuse" that to portray events in Yemen in terms of a north-south dichotomy is misleading. Events in unified Yemen have often been described as the marginalization of southerners and the preference for northerners who are taking over the decision-making apparatus and high-ranking posts, but this is not the only interpretation of events. Al-Sharyan points out that most of the prime ministers during the post-unification era were southerners, and that the situation of the southern provinces was not that different from the situation of the northern provinces. The problems which Yemen suffered from remained intact: unemployment, poverty, corruption, the absence of vision for economic growth and a vague implementation of democracy.[55] He concludes that the regime did not cope with those problems but rather provided ammunition to the enemies of unification. Al-Sharyan also mentions that the feeling of discrimination against the south was not fabricated; that there was regional discrimination in Yemen, but that those feelings of sectarianism did not justify the use of violence or the delegitimization of the state. He calls for accountability and a re-examination of the ruling system especially with regard to the appointment of officials on a meritocratic basis rather than a sectarian or geographic one. Al-Sharyan concludes that "the essence of the regime that created unification should change in order to fulfill the needs of [the unified state's] existence".[56]

Most of the criticisms and the protests in the south were perceived by the spokesmen of the regime in Sanaa as "direct and indirect incitement of elements ... that had lost their position and were now fanning the flame of the conflict for their individual interests using their dire economic conditions, inflation and unemployment".[57] They mainly accused the former President of South Yemen, 'Ali Nasir Muhammad (1980–1986), who sat in exile in Damascus, of standing behind the southerners' agitation and of lending logistical support to the Free South. The fact that his picture was repeatedly displayed as part of demonstrations in the south (much more than the photos of 'Ali Salim al-Bayd, another former president of South Yemen) proved to the Sanaa regime how deeply involved 'Ali Nasir Muhammad was. However, although 'Ali Nasir Muhammad made some statements in favour of the south, he called for a non-violent struggle.[58]

Beyond that the regime in Sanaa tried to foster a "business as usual" atmosphere in the provinces of the south. The president, 'Ali 'Abdallah Salih, accused the media of over-dramatization and added that the situation in the south was under control, not because of the presence of the army but rather because of the southerners' authentic support for unification in much higher numbers than in 1994. Clerics who were identified with the regime responded assertively against the demonstrations that were carried out by the Free South. Nasir al-Shaybani, for example, formerly the minister for endowments (*awqaf*) who became a preacher in a mosque in the north of the country, depicted the demonstrators as "heretics" and "communists" and also "Westernizers" that would like to inject the state with a Christian and American nature.[59] The Vice-President of Yemen, 'Abd Rabbu Mansur Hadi, said: "The sowing of chaos and destruction and the incitement to hatred in the south are carried out in accordance with an external agenda and regional and separatist interests that do not reflect the will of the inhabitants or the people of the southern and eastern provinces of Yemen".[60] In the opening session of the third gathering of the ruling party he claimed, "What happens is that there are calls for restoring the era of separatism and secession that we had experienced before the revolution of the 14th of October".[61]

In conclusion, it would be safe to assume that the Free South, through non-violent political activity, fostered a harsh picture of the results of the 1994 civil war and called for secession. Many of the inhabitants of the south did support the non-violent struggle for independence. Haydar Abu Bakr al-'Attas, who was Yemen's prime minister from 1990–1994, summed up the problematic reality: he emphasized the illegitimacy of the unification because from the early stages the people of the south were not able to express their opinion through a plebiscite. But even so, al-'Attas argues that the unification could have worked if it had not been for the systematic marginalization of the southern leaders in 1994 which culminated in the destruction of the state, army and institutions of the south. He goes on to say that Sanaa had completed its takeover of the southern provinces with the aid of collaborators from the south.[62]

The painful realization that unification had been an illusion was the basis for the creation of the non-violent movement in the south. Political activists, such as 'Abd al-'Aziz al-Dali'i, observed that more and more people in the south were becoming disillusioned even though there were others who were still captivated by the dream of unification. Society in the south became, in the eyes of the Free South activists, divided in two: the disillusioned and those who unfortunately still talked about the need for unification.[63]

In an interview with *al-Janub al-Hurr*, Salah al-Saqaldi, a prominent member of the YSP who had formerly served as a vice-minister and political advisor to 'Ali Salim al-Bayd (the former President of South Yemen) summed up why unification had failed. He argued that the unification of Yemen had indeed been one of the aims of the YSP but that its vision of unification was based on regime change in Sanaa. The south gave up the state, the land and the resources for unification but what was created was a state, under which the banner of unification was becoming corrupt and inefficient. In the aftermath of unification, the south's leaders were marginalized and more than 150 of the YSP leaders were eliminated. On top of that, some of the southerners within the leadership of the unified state were acting in accordance with their personal interests, which served to further weaken the south's position in the unified government.[64] Salah Al-Saqaldi blamed the north for the civil war of 1994 that brutally crushed the understandings of unification. Salah Al-Saqaldi emphasized the cultural and societal differences between the north and south and defined the non-violent movement of the south as "a demonstration of power that must grow and eventually bring about the downfall of despotism".[65] He went on to say, "history tells [of] many other occasions where tyrants were toppled by an un-armed public. Haile Selassie of Ethiopia was ousted, the Shah of Iran, Ceausescu, Pol Pot and many others for whom cruelty and weaponry could not prevent their downfall".[66]

The nature of the activities and statements of the Free South provided the impression that they assumed their struggle would be long and gradual but in the end they would prevail. Alongside the denunciation of the repressive regime in Sanaa, they urged more cooperation from all movements and organizations in society. They also urged the fostering of a national pact based on the principles of the south's legacy. Salih al-'Asa'i, a member of the Democratic Union of the South (*al-Tajamu'al-Dimuqrati lil-Janub*), explained the need for such a measure, saying:

> We are a people who lost our homeland and identity. Our country was ravished and our history and identity were deliberately twisted in the name of unification that was declared in

> May 1990. The south is not a party to the regime of Sanaa but a state with boundaries and recognized sovereignty, geographically, regionally and internationally. The regime of Sanaa buried the aims of unification and has been trying to bury the honor and courage of the people of the south by its armed forces and tanks since the civil war.[67]

The Free South posed a new challenge to the regime of Sanaa because it was a non-violent movement which used the new media and offered a new political platform. Its protest was against inequality, poverty and corruption, which fell on listening ears in many sectors.[68] They criticized the project of the unification – Salih's main agenda. Ultimately, the Free South contended that unification had revealed the real nature of the Sanaa regime – the regime was repressive and the President was unable to lead. Moreover, in the opening years of the twenty-first century, the Sanaa regime also faced other threats such as the Shi'i revolt in the north and radical Islamism in the south, which made Sanaa's politics of survival much more difficult.

The Shi'i Revolt in Sa'da

In June 2004, the Zaydi cleric Husayn Badr al-Din al-Huthi challenged the regime's authority in the northern province of Sa'da. By depicting 'Ali 'Abdallah Salih as "a tyrant ... who wants to please America and Israel by sacrificing the blood of his own people", al-Huthi gathered momentum which culminated in a revolt throughout Sa'da.[69] The Sanaa government attempted to stop the rebels but it soon became clear that it was not a spontaneous revolt but rather something that had been carefully planned. Middlemen failed in their attempts to convince the rebel leaders to put an end to the revolt and to get closer to the negotiating table. Salih's public announcement that he was willing to moderate his stances and listen to the rebels' grievances did not help. As matters stood, the revolt of the Huthi people was derived from their belief that the legitimacy of the regime in Yemen was null and void and that it was time for change. They did not declare that publicly but just focused on several demands of a bargaining nature. Still, the devotion and enthusiasm with which they conducted their struggle made it clear that this was much more than a local tribal revolt. The causes of this conflict could be traced throughout the 1980s and 1990s where a flow of pious Wahhabis made their way from Saudi Arabia to Yemen. The Zaydi-Shi'i community (which some view as the fifth school of Sunni Islam because of its moderation) found itself hemmed in by radical Salafi Islam on the one hand and suppressed by the Sanaa government on the other hand. Husayn al-Huthi's declaration that his struggle aimed to protect the Zaydiyya from the Salafi presence in Sa'da, and his praise of the Islamic Republic of Iran and the Hizballah movement in Lebanon was an indication of that.[70] The Sa'da province, located adjacent to the Saudi border, had long been considered the "peace province" even before the advent of Islam owing to the fertility of its lands and the vital trade that its inhabitants had conducted for years. Later on, Sa'da became one of the main strongholds of the Zaydi Imamate and was the last province to fall in the 1962 Revolution. The eruption of the revolt there in 2004 dramatically changed the posture of the one-time "peace province" and turned it into a bloody theatre of violence, damaging its economy and agriculture.

The conflict in Sa'da experienced several rounds of warfare. The first one erupted in May 2004 in the Maran Mountains under the leadership of Husayn Badr al-Din al-Huthi, one of the forefathers of a movement that came to be known as the "young believers" (*al-Shabab al-Mu'min*). Husayn al-Huthi had been a prominent member of the GPC and a member of parliament who represented the province of Maran in Sa'da throughout the years 1994–1997.[71]

In its early beginnings, the Young Believers movement benefited from Sanaa's manipulative policy of using new political players to goad competing power centres. The government nurtured the new movement to counterbalance the al-Islah party, which had "politically divorced" the GPC in 1997. By doing so, the government tried to limit the influence of al-Islah in Sa'da and other northern provinces. For years the government turned a blind eye to the movement's establishment of schools and colleges, which promoted the restoration of the Shi'i Zaydi Imamate. These schools did not come under the surveillance of the state and they acted freely owing to logistical and financial support from the government.[72]

As far as Husayn al-Huthi was concerned, the government of Sanaa remained the principal enemy. His acts and ideas and the way he preached to young students raised anxiety among the traditional Zaydi *'ulama* and threatened to create a rift among the Zaydiyya. The traditional *'ulama* viewed al-Huthi as an intolerant radical contrary to Zaydi tradition, which throughout history had been an adaptive and moderate school of Islam. They tried to prevent him from preaching, but to no avail. Zaydi youth from Sa'da and the surrounding area were attracted to al-Huthi's ideas. The religious establishment's anxiety was justified when it became clear that al-Huthi was attacking the regime and calling for his disciples to capture the mosques. When the security forces tried to prevent demonstrators from propagating such slogans, al-Huthi's disciples acted violently and their actions culminated in bloodshed.[73]

The first round of violence lasted three months and was suppressed in September 2004, but at a heavy price (800 people died, 400 of them soldiers).[74] The army's magazine, *The 26th of September*, published a set of documents that proved that al-Huthi was being aided by external elements, which made the regime much more aggressive in suppressing the revolt, going so far as to apprehend journalists. Among the dead was Husayn al-Huthi, the leader of the revolt.[75]

The revolt was renewed in March 2005, this time under the leadership of Badr al-Din al-Huthi, Husayn's father. The rebels tried to disrupt the public order by blocking roads and attacking state institutions and army installations. This time the bloodshed went beyond Sa'da, with Sanaa becoming the focus of a series of attacks against the security forces.[76]

At this stage, events in Yemen drew some responses from the regional scene. In April 2005, the main Shi'i *madrasah* in Najaf, Iraq, criticized the Sanaa government, claiming that it had attempted to extinguish the Shi'i community in Yemen. In late 2006, the fighting resumed under the leadership of another member of the al-Huthi family, 'Abd al-Malik, and this round ended with the ceasefire of February 2006. In September 2006, 'Ali 'Abdallah Salih declared an overall pardon for Huthis if they would set down their arms and reach an agreement with the regime. Parallel to that, he released hundreds of prisoners and compensated those whose property had been damaged during the battles.

While trying to eradicate the rebellion, the regime adopted a known modus operandi – collaboration with any actor that would be willing to go against the Shi'i rebels, including radical Sunni groups. The regime's weakness and inability to exert influence in different parts of the country was exposed. The government of Sanaa no longer stood above the different forces that comprised Yemen's political map, but rather became an element that collaborated through ad hoc alliances against rivals. This phenomenon was already seen during the 1994 civil war. In an attempt to erase the socialist power centre, Salih had nurtured al-Islah and the disciples of Shaykh al-Zindani. Salih had rewarded them after the war, which caused them to think that the regime accepted their activity and was aware of their strengthening position. The members of the al-Islah party, especially the disciples of al-Zindani, who was nominated by Salih to the chair of the Committee for the Reconstruction of Yemen, acted to strengthen the "modesty policy" in Yemen and became importers of a Salafi-influenced Islam. Soon it became clear to Salih that al-Islah posed a real challenge to its authority. The alliance that he built up after the civil war cast a shadow on the future course of Yemen. Even now, in view of the Shi'i revolt in Sa'da, those patterns of activity were used again. Salih's regime mobilized the support of Sunni-Salafi actors in its struggle against the rebels in Sa'da. This measure did not allay the tension but rather helped drag Yemen into the group of Middle Eastern states which were being rocked by the Sunni-Shi'i conflict.

The fourth round of violence began in 2007 under the leadership of 'Abd al-Malik al-Huthi. The battles centred on several areas in the province of Sa'da, especially Razih, Dayhan, Ghamar and Bani Mu'adh.[77] The ongoing deterioration in Yemen's security was also felt by the Jewish community. This community, entrenched in Yemen from time immemorial, became a target for the "young believers" movement. In the beginning of 2007, it was reported that 80 Yemenite Jews, inhabitants of the area of al-Salam in the province of Sa'da, left the region after having received a ten-day ultimatum demanding their departure from the "young believers". In one of the threatening letters that was distributed by the "young believers", it was claimed:

> They [the Jews] took part in acts and deeds that serve first and foremost, global Zionism. They also systematically act to further corrupt the virtues and morals of the people of the country and incite them to desert their religious values and their morality.[78]

The local authorities in Sa'da held a meeting in the presence of several *shaykhs* after a complaint was brought forward by several Jews that had been threatened and abused. They demanded that the authorities treat them justly as Yemenite citizens. At the end of this meeting, a fatwa was published that set the rules for relationships between Muslims and Jews but this fatwa did not provide the Jews with security, and eventually caused them to leave the region in order to save their lives.

The government did not ignore the Jews' predicament and even offered them support and alternative housing in other parts of the country. The prime minister, 'Abd al-Qadir Ba-Jamal, declared "we will never allow one of our Jewish citizens to be hurt or damaged" because "the Jews are like brothers to us ... the Jews are the people of this country even before the advent of Islam and they have full rights to live among us".[79] This was no more than moral support. The Yemeni government was between a rock and a hard place. On the one hand, Israel and the US were quick to depict Yemen as backward, and on the other hand, Yemen was attacked from within on grounds of appeasing the West and "global Zionism". The critics capitalized on Israel's responses and used them as an indication of the existence of a damaging link between the Zionist Jews and the Jews of Yemen.

The leaders of the Jewish community in Yemen were quick to declare their loyalty to Yemen and did not wish to be identified with the state of Israel. The chief rabbi, Yahya bin Ya'ish Yahya, declared: "We [the Jews] are Yemenites who live under the banner of the state and the government of Yemen. Israel's declarations in our regard do not concern us since we have no connection with it and it [Israel] has no connection with us".[80]

The fate of the Jewish community in Yemen remained uncertain even after the chief rabbi's declaration. Periods of stability and harmony between both Jewish and Muslim communities in Yemen were now seen as relics of a distant past.[81] The Jewish issue attested to the fragility of both the political system and the regime in Yemen. Local tribes and in this case, religious militias, dictated the rhythm in provinces like Sa'da, far away from the scope of the Sanaa regime's control.

The rebellion in Sa'da was becoming a consistent nuisance for the regime in Sanaa and even an existential threat. Yemen was dragged into the Sunni-Shi'i conflict that had been sweeping the Middle East since the downfall of Saddam Husayn in April 2003. In March 2007, Iranian students demonstrated in front of the Yemeni embassy in Tehran demanding the expulsion of the Yemeni ambassador from Iran. The Iranian government also changed the name of the street adjacent to the Yemeni Embassy in Tehran, naming it after the "martyr" Husayn al-Huthi. In February 2007, the Yemeni parliament authorized the government to use whatever means necessary in order to stabilize the situation in Sa'da. The state-run media called for the extradition of Yahya al-Huthi, a former member of parliament whose immunity had been stripped after having been a source of inspiration for the rebels. In May 2007, the army escalated its activity in the province of Sa'da to the extent of intense rocketing over rebel camps in al-Mazru', al-Dayhan, al-Mudawwara, al-Hamra and others. The simple fact that some of these areas, especially the Razih area, had fallen under the rebels' control and the fear that the Huthis' supporters would penetrate the province's capital led to an unprecedented concentration of army forces in Sa'da. These forces were strengthened even further when it became clear that al-Ahmar's call to the tribes of Khawlan bin 'Amr in Sa'da to side with the state had not worked.[82] The army forces shelled different areas in Khawlan, especially villages that were put under siege. The tough war that the regime waged against the rebels drew threats from 'Abd al-Malik al-Huthi that it would lead to a fifth round of warfare that could be disastrous for Yemen, militarily, economically and socially. It was only in June 2007 that there was a lull in the escalation of events owing to the mediation of Qatar.[83]

The ceasefire agreement was welcomed by many in Yemen, including opposition parties that had published an announcement in support of the ceasefire. At the same time, some saw Doha's nine-point pact[84] as a victory for the government of Yemen and a sign of the weakening of the rebellion, enabling the government in Sanaa to impose state authority on the no man's land.[85] Nevertheless, the relative relaxation that ensued in the aftermath of the ceasefire evaporated after several months when the violence in Sa'da was renewed with increased intensity.

In January 2008, clashes broke out between the regime's armed forces and the Huthi supporters in Matra, one of the main strongholds of the Huthi supporters.[86] In February 2008, it seemed as if the warring parties had reached a ceasefire that limited the fighting to one month and set the priorities for the reconstruction of the regions that had been damaged. The agreement called for disarming the Huthis, withdrawing the army from the villages, releasing the arrested rebels and expelling the rebellion's leaders, 'Abd al-Malik al-Huthi, his brother 'Abd al-Karim and 'Abdallah al-Rizami, to the Emirate of Qatar. The agreement also specified that the rebels would stop demanding the return of Yahya al-Huthi who had lived outside of Yemen.[87] Nevertheless, this was another agreement that did not manage to prevent the outbreak of a new confrontation.

In March 2008, the Yemeni authorities declared that the Huthi rebel movement had violated the Doha agreement.[88] This violation, according to the authorities, was reflected by the rebels' expulsion of 3,200 students and 91 teachers from 22 schools in the areas of Awlad 'Ayyash, Duwayb al-'Ulya, Duwayb al-Sufla, al-Ghabar and Awlad Nuwwar – all of them in the Sa'da region. The Director of the Education Ministry in Sa'da, Naji al-Ghaythi, claimed that the "young believers" took control of the schools after the expulsion of the students and the teachers and warned them not to come back.[89] In April 2008, in Sa'da, the rebels assassinated Salih al-Hindi, a member of parliament, his son and three of their companions. This event attested to the ongoing dispute between the rebels and the Presidential Committee who were authorized to renew the negotiation with the rebels in order to implement the agreement. Al-Hindi was considered a staunch supporter in the fight against the Huthis. His assassination was carried out a day after the Presidential Committee declared that it refused to go back to Sa'da, putting the blame for the failure of the agreement on the rebels' leadership.[90]

The situation deteriorated further in May 2008 after a lethal explosion in the Bin Salman Mosque in Sa'da which resulted in 16 dead and 45 wounded.[91] Hundreds of citizens and members of the political and military leadership accompanied the victims in the funeral while using slogans in support of the government and denouncing the Huthis. The phrase "there is no God but God" and "al-Huthi is the enemy of God" expressed both disappointment and frustration after the high expectations that had been created by the Doha Agreement. The renewed tension was the result of a two-day siege that the rebels imposed on a complex of government buildings including the ministries of education, health and defense. Dozens were killed in a confrontation in the province of Sa'da. The army bombarded the Huthi territory including the areas in Sahar where the rebels renewed efforts to cut the transportation lines between Sa'da and Sanaa.[92] Mediation efforts went on in parallel to the fighting. Pro-government tribes that had a connection with the Huthis were asked by the government to negotiate with the Huthis.[93] Both the Qataris and the presidential delegation returned to Sa'da in an attempt to save the ceasefire agreement. The Presidential Committee asked the local authorities in Sa'da to use restraint and prevent escalation.[94]

The confrontation and the intense negotiations to put an end to the fighting ran parallel to each other. When there was a setback in the rebels' position, the leadership declared its willingness to change its policy; thus for example, 'Abd al-Malik al-Huthi sent a message in August 2008 to 'Ali 'Abdallah Salih saying that he intended to stand by the agreement that called for an end to fighting in Sa'da. Al-Huthi clarified that he was fully committed to the articles set out by President Salih: stopping the military activities in the region of Sa'da, opening up the roads, gathering the mines, ending the armed demonstrations, delivering the Huthis' weapons to the state, allowing refugees to return to their homes and villages and returning the civilian and military hostages to the local authorities. Al-Huthi clarified in his letter that he and his supporters were "fully committed to the preservation of stability and security all over the province of Sa'da", and that they would "repay good for good and justice for justice", and would "preserve the homeland's interests and the peace of its citizens".[95] In spite of hopes for an agreement, the fifth round of violence continued throughout 2008. The rebels in Sa'da again issued belligerent statements and both sides prepared themselves to renew the fighting in the second half of the year. This was another indication that the attempt to put an end to the fighting had failed. The fifth round of fighting created additional refugees and the economic situation deteriorated further. The anxiety that prevailed among leaders in Yemen was uniquely deep. This time the renewed fighting came after intensive mediation efforts on the part of *shaykhs*, notables and members of parliament in Sa'da who had met with the rebels' leadership with Salih's approval after the stagnation of the Qatari mediation.[96]

Salih's regime tried to heal the wounds and repair the war damages. A governmental committee was nominated to take care of the damages that resulted from the armed confrontations between the government and the Huthis. Alongside the establishment of a fund for reconstructing areas that had been damaged throughout the war, the committee approved regulations that would make it easier for refugees to return to their villages, and also reopened service centres that were closed during the war. A parliamentary investigation committee was established to discuss the fate of the absentees that had disappeared during the years of war. Speaker of Parliament and head of the investigative committee Shaykh Hamid al-Ahmar sped up the activities of the committee in response to ongoing demonstrations by NGOs and human rights activists in the public squares in Sanaa. Family members of absentees also joined the demonstrations, carrying photos of the absentees. The committee did investigate some of the allegations regarding people who went missing during the fighting in Sa'da.[97] Ultimately, the committee could do little to help the families of the missing persons.

Salih's regime identified the Huthi rebellion as the source of an existential threat that was overshadowing Yemen. The security organs tried to arrange a meeting between the "young believers" who had been arrested, and the notables who represented the Zaydi school, in order to encourage moderation (*wasatiyya*) and abstention from violence, but to no avail. The "young believers" answered the authorities' proposals by saying that they would honor the requests only if they had approval from Sayyid Husayn (Husayn Badr al-Din al-Huthi), the late leader of the rebels. They believed he was still alive and that the government's announcement of his death in September 2004 was no more than false propaganda.[98]

The name of the "young believers" points to an identification with Islamic causes outside of Yemen. In several mosques in Sanaa, as in al-Hadi Mosque in Sa'da, the main stronghold of the movement, activists concluded their prayers with slogans that had become the mottos of Islamist movements: "Death to America, death to Israel, victory for Islam" (*al-mawt li-amrika, al-mawt li-isra'il, al-nasr lil-islam*).[99] Under interrogation, members of the "young believers" were offered pardons in exchange for abandoning their rebel activities, but their refusals reflected their zeal for their cause.[100] In keeping with its "divide and rule" tactics, Salih's regime tried to explore whether it would be possible to support the "young believers" as a counterweight to religious parties and Salafi organizations that were opposing the Huthis. This was another case where the instrument turned against its designer and the price demanded from Yemen was heavy.[101]

In April 2009, the tension between the government and the Huthis in Sa'da grew. The governmental authority in the Sa'da province accused the Huthis of killing and wounding more than 120 people since the ceasefire.[102] The governor, Faris Manna', blamed the Huthis for the the murder of a shaykh who had been appointed by the President to examine the findings of the Presidential Committee in the province of Ghamar. The government added that the assassination was carried out parallel to the Huthis' takeover of public and private buildings in the province of Ghamar including the properties of the shaykh. These activities against tribal *shaykhs* and public figures that were identified with Salih's regime were intended to create divisions among the tribal elements who supported his regime and to gather new support for the rebels.[103]

The Huthis' attack in the province of Ghamar and the subsequent takeover of various buildings and institutions as well as the central market in the main city of the province signaled the beginning of the sixth round of fighting starting from August 2009. The frustration with the renewed fighting, and the fact that "Huthi saboteurs" (as they were described by the regime) were attacking targets which had been identified with the regime as well as regular Yemenis, brought the regime and its leaders to admit that the ceasefire agreement would fail again.[104] Now they argued that the Huthis had used the *hudna* (temporary truce) months to strengthen and recuperate. The simple fact that in several incidents in late 2008 the rebels had made use of heavy weapons, shells and mines attested to that.[105] In parallel to the renewal of the propaganda war between the government and the Huthis, there were many reports of battles between the Huthis and pro-government tribes, especially the Khawlan bin 'Amr and al-Hamati tribes. The people of al-Hamati joined in as a result of their desire to take revenge on the killing of two of their *shayhks* by Huthi supporters from the al-Dibb area. Along with that, at least five people were killed and others were wounded with the renewal of fighting between the Sufyan and al-'Usaymat tribes in the region of 'Amran. In this case, mediation efforts also failed.[106] In August, it was reported that nine tribesmen, presumably Hashid, that were fighting side by side with the army were killed by the Huthi rebels. It is very difficult to ascertain the number of tribesmen who fought with the army against the Huthis, even though there are estimations that by late 2009 thousands of army soldiers and supporting tribesmen had been killed. These reports, in addition to the information they provide about what had transpired in Sa'da, attested to the complexity of Yemen's problems: the complex situation between tribe and state, the arms caches possessed by the tribes, inter-tribal disputes, vendettas of tribesmen against the government or the Huthis – all these turned the tribes into handy militias that were used cynically by both the regime and anti-government elements.

The Huthis were depicted by the official media as "the *fitna* (civil strife) group" which had ignored the regime's bid to bring peace to the province of Sa'da. The official media argued that this group which lived by its sword and enjoyed the support of Yemen's enemies continued to carry out terrorist attacks against the armed forces and innocent civilians. Road robberies and the takeover of public institutions were means of defying the state.[107] The declaration went on to argue that the "*fitna* group" would bear the responsibility for its evil deeds, which would lead to its self-destruction, since this group was no more than a gang that was aiming to shed innocent blood and undermine stability.[108] The frustration of the Yemeni leadership found expression in the words of the prime minister, 'Ali Muhammad Mujawar, who combined the various opposing forces to the regime and titled them the "Satanic Triangle Alliance" – a formulation in which the Huthis are just one of the axes in a triangle which also included the secessionists from the south and al-Qa'ida.[109]

The rebellion in Sa'da topped the agenda of the public discourse. A public survey that was carried out by the Centre for Strategic Studies in Sanaa in December 2008 showed that 45 per cent of the population in Yemen believed that the war was a result of the authorities' poor performance while 43 per cent of the population put the blame on the Huthis. 72 per cent of the respondents believed that the war in Sa'da was avoidable.[110] However, the Huthi rebellion ignited resentment and anger among several groups in Yemen. Many of the inhabitants of Sa'da and the surrounding area commemorated their loved ones who died in the battle for "the unification of Yemen" by displaying their photos in shops, cars and public areas. The mourning families gathered as "Sons of the Martyrs for Unity" and strongly criticized some government officials who called for pardoning separatists, mercenaries and rebels, for fear that they might "resume spreading the venom of sedition, separation and treason".[111] The "Sons of the Martyrs for Unity" also attacked the advocates of secession who adhered to a two-state solution, which had prevailed prior to 1990. A statement issued by the group in Lahaj said: "We pledge to God, the homeland, and President 'Ali 'Abdallah Salih that we will stand in the first line in defense of unity and its gain against thugs and plotters who only live on bloodshed. We will be the strong shield defending the dignity and pride of our people".[112]

These groups were frustrated because they didn't have a clear picture of what the Huthis were trying to achieve: was it a struggle for the restoration of a Shi'i Imamate? Did the Huthi rebels desire autonomy for themselves in the north of Yemen? Had they been turned into a tool for external forces that were striving to advance their interests at the expense of the collapsing state of Yemen? The slogans which were gleaned from Iran's vocabulary, "Death to America, Death to Israel", were easy to identify and reverberated throughout Sa'da. Opposing slogans were heard in the streets of Sanaa, such as "no more terrorism", and those who carried such slogans viewed the Huthis and Salafi Islamic extremists as equally responsible for the collapse of united Yemen. Supporters of unification and the mourning families did not conceal their criticism of the poor performance of the regime in Sanaa. They were also of the opinion that Yemen's problems were an outcome of injustice and inequality. Most of them were upset with the socio-economic situation and their low pensions which were not paid in time. However, especially as their sons found their deaths in the "battle for unity", they were not willing to go to the extreme of leading Yemen to a renewed division. The well-known Yemeni poet, Ahmad Ba-Majbur, a southerner from Shabwa, extensively toured the country and wrote poems praising the unification. One of his aphorisms which many Yemenites admire is "pride despite poverty". Ba-Majbur discussed this theme in an interview given to *al-Sharq al-Awsat*:

> I always wonder if I should take a stand against Yemen's unity so that the state might seek to please and honor me as it does with others. But then I say "no", I will not retract; I will not spoil my poetic gift. I will devote my gift to the end, advocating the unity, not division of Yemen. Even if my reward was mere remarks in official papers then I am the poet of national unity.[113]

At times various reports referred to the government of 'Ali 'Abdallah Salih as a Sunni-dominated Yemeni government;[114] that is, struggling against a Shi'i rebellion – although in effect this was not true. A great portion of the tribesmen who fought against the Huthis were Shi'i Zaydis rather than Sunnis. President Salih himself was a Shi'i Zaydi, as most government members were. At the same time, many from the Sunni Shafi'i community in the south viewed the government as a "Zaydi-dominated Yemeni government". The Sa'da region has long been the stronghold of the Shi'i Zaydiyya, but since the early 1980s it had witnessed Salafi penetrations which were reflected in the sermons of Wahhabi preachers. Shelagh Weir, an anthropologist who carried out her field research in the Razih region of the Sa'da governorate, referred in her research to the Wahhabi movement and phrased it as "a clash of fundamentalisms". Weir also added that the Zaydi revival was partially a result of financial and missionary efforts on the part of Salafi elements.[115] She also explained that Wahhabism appealed to some of the tribes in Sa'da, who felt inferior to the traditional Zaydi elite.

The increased tension in Sa'da was quickly interpreted as a proxy war between Saudi Arabia and Iran. The Yemeni government accused Iran of providing financial and logistical support to the Huthis and was especially furious about the wide media coverage that Iran granted to the Huthi rebels in Sa'da. In an interview with *al-Hayat*, Salih clarified that the Lebanese-based Hizballah had transferred support to the rebels, including guidance in planting mines and preparing explosives. He went on to say that the blatant Iranian involvement in the internal affairs of other states was a result of the lack of Arab cohesion and that Iran was trying to promote the trend of Shi'itization of the Arab world.[116] Yemen's minister of communication, Hasan al-Lawzi, attacked Iranian media channels such as *al-Kawthar*, *al-'Alam* and the *Voice of Tehran*, and said that their bold involvement in the internal affairs of Yemen was tantamount to an international crime. He added that there were leading Iranian clerics who granted financial and political support to the rebels of Sa'da.[117] Even if there had been an exaggeration on the part of the regime in Yemen regarding the volume of Iranian support, there is no doubt that this conflict bore within it the potential to develop into a proxy war between Saudi Arabia and Iran similar to what was going on in Lebanon.[118]

The rebellion in Sa'da was of local origin, though at later stages of the rebellion external influences began to intrude. It is difficult to ascertain the volume of Iranian involvement even though Iran's state-owned media outlets were backing the rebels. Husayn Shariatmadari, the editor of the newspaper *Kayhan*, used the Iranian TV channel *al-'Alam* to attack Saudi Arabia "for its anti-Iranian campaign which was in line with the interests of Israel and the West".[119]

The Iranians, for their part, argued that Saudi armed forces were active in the fighting alongside the Yemeni authorities. The Saudis, of course, denied involvement, but they admitted having consulted with the Yemeni government because of the escalation of the scale of violence.[120] It would be very difficult to ignore the Saudi involvement. There were reports that the Saudis tried to relocate Sunni Yemenites in the south of the Kingdom near the border with Yemen and that this measure raised fears among Shi'a in Saudi Arabia that this was an attempt to change the demographic composition of the Kingdom and to further reduce the weight of the Shi'a.[121] It seems doubtful that this was the Saudis' main motivation especially since the Saudis were responsible for the expulsion of many Yemenis from the Kingdom in the early 1990s. However, there were Saudi attempts to relocate Salafis and Sunnis (some of them released from Guantanamo), who were known as "rehabilitated Salafis", but still, the number was minor, so it cannot be explained by geographical considerations. This Saudi program was based upon two main goals: an extensive hunt for extremists and financial incentives for extremists willing to hand over their weapons and disassociate from radical organizations.

Toward the end of 2009, there was a stern war of words, which indicated the ongoing tension between the pro-Saudi camp and the pro-Iranian camp in the Middle East. The silence that the Saudi media imposed on itself regarding Iran since the elections that had been held there in June 2009 was replaced, beginning in August of that year, with a blatant attack against Iran's involvement in Yemen. Saudi Arabia accused Iran of financing and arming the rebels of Sa'da in order to undermine the security and the stability of both Yemen and Saudi Arabia, adding that the whole thing was primed to provide Iran with control over the maritime route to Sudan and northwards.[122] In an editorial in the daily newspaper *Watan*, it was argued that "the identification of the Huthis with the Iranian ideology, the Iranian protection given to them and the Iranian weapons that were found on both land and sea – all these attest to the fact that the Huthis are proxies of Iran".[123] Some of the analysts viewed the whole thing as an Iranian attempt to create a Hizballah-style Iranian proxy on the mutual border between Saudi Arabia and Yemen. Thus, for example, the Saudi columnist Muhammad bin 'Abd al-Latif al-Shaykh declared that "the Huthis are nothing but a Yemenite Hizballah and 'Abd al-Malik al-Huthi is nothing but a Yemenite Hasan Nasrallah".[124] A warning was sent to the authorities in Saudi Arabia by this columnist who argued that there should be no "soft hand" in dealing with the Huthis and "the gangs of the Huthi rebels in Sa'da should understand that playing with fire in the boundaries of Saudi Arabia would be very pricey for them ... "[125]

The long and ill-defended borders that Saudi Arabia shares with Yemen and Iraq caused ongoing difficulty with preventing Islamists from moving between Yemen and Saudi Arabia. In the process Saudi Arabia was bitterly reminded that in its war against Islamic extremists, the road was still fraught with fierce challenges. In late August 2009, 'Abdullah Hassan al-'Asiri, a terrorist, called Prince Muhammad bin Na'if, at that time senior assistant to the Minister of the Interior for security issues, and expressed his desire to turn himself in as part of the terrorist rehabilitation program. The Prince accepted his offer. An al-Qa'ida website claimed that the Prince flew al-'Asiri to his palace on his own private jet. After he arrived, al-'Asiri blew himself up in the presence of the prince, in an attempt to take his life.

Ibrahim al-Rubaysh, one of the religious ideologues of al-Qa'ida in the Arabian Peninsula,[126] justified the assassination attempt in a tape titled, "Why Muhammad bin Na'if?" In the tape he stated that Muhammad bin Na'if was responsible for a war against the *mujahideen* and wages that war against them on behalf of the "enemies of Islam". Al-Rubaysh went on to describe the reasons behind the failed assassination attempt against Prince Muhammad bin Na'if, the leader of Saudi Arabia's counterterrorism campaign since 2003:

> Why Muhammad bin Na'if? Allah has favored me in the fact that I have never met Muhammad bin Na'if, may Allah deal with him as he deserves, but I have been in his prisons, I have dealt with his wardens and I have lived with those charred by the fire of his tyranny. I along with others have witnessed, while we are the witnesses of Allah on His earth, how he has waged

> war against jihad and the Mujahideen, something that even the media affirms. Muhammad bin Na'if stood alongside his troops guarding and protecting the Americans, preventing the Mujahideen from reaching them. He could have assumed the role of a bystander, but instead defended them, just as a good child defends his father's possessions.[127]

The attempt on Muhammad bin Na'if's life proved that Saudi Arabia was still far from the end of the battle against Islamic terrorism and that the Kingdom, itself, was the main incubator of terrorism.[128] At the same time, Saudi Arabia was one of the most effective states in the war against terrorism.[129] The Saudis introduced figures according to which 45 wanted men were captured since 2003. Some of the individuals on the "most wanted" list that was published in February 2009 were also targeted and captured.[130] Beginning in 2005, Saudi Arabia strengthened its cooperation with US intelligence and improved its skills by training special units to gather intelligence and combat terrorism. It is no wonder that Saudi Arabia – a state where the regime is committed to fighting local terror networks without reservation – turned into a model that the US desired for Afghanistan, Pakistan and Yemen to emulate.[131] This is why the US avoided criticizing Saudi Arabia harshly even though it was known that many Islamic extremists were crossing its southern and northern borders.

The Saudi effort to combat terrorism was especially evident in Yemen, where the Saudis were hunting terrorists who had taken shelter there. During that time, the cooperation between the Saudi and Yemeni authorities improved. The ongoing conflict in Sa'da, with its sectarian dimension, fostered additional avenues of Saudi-Yemeni cooperation. So while the rebellion in Sa'da could be viewed as a local conflict, its wider dimensions should not be ignored, especially as regards the Saudi involvement and the Saudis' siding with the government of Sanaa.

Iran viewed the Huthi rebellion positively, occasionally expressed its support and sympathy to the Huthis and at times provided logistical support. It is difficult to ascertain the volume of Iranian support, but the Yemeni government suspected deep Iranian involvement and reported finding Iranian arms caches.[132] One should take into account though that for Salih it was pretty comfortable to rely on arguments about outside involvement, especially Iranian, that fanned the flames in Sa'da. The Huthis denied receiving any support from Iran, Libya or any other external player.[133] The rebellion in Sa'da was initiated by Husayn Badr al-Din al-Huthi, a former MP who instigated a violent reaction against the corruption of Salih's regime and his confidants. However, as happens from time to time in the different parts of the Middle East, these local protests, especially if they bear a religious character, also bear anti-American and anti-Zionist elements and the regime is denounced for cooperating with the West. Anti-Zionism found expression in the attack against the Jewish community in Sa'da and the surroundings.

As with the secessionist movement in the south, so it was in Sa'da. The regime tried to keep a posture of "business as usual" and to convey the impression that everything was under control. Addressing a local gathering in the south of the country, Yemeni Vice-President, 'Abd Rabbu Mansur Hadi, said:

> Yemen has made great achievements; we must be capable of accommodating change. But what is going on here and there in the south or in Sa'da in the north, will not affect the march of construction and investment. These incidents cannot harm our country. The local government will address all problems and will end centralization. The day to day administration and planning will be in the hands of local authorities.[134]

With the renewal of fighting there were many reports on behalf of the news agencies of the Yemeni government, such as this one: "Masses from many tribes of all the country's governorates are heading willingly for the Sa'da governorate to take part in the fight against the Huthi rebels ..."[135] It was also argued that businessmen and merchants began donating money to the security and armed forces fighting against the rebels and that hundreds of thousands of young people had announced their readiness to battle the insurgents in Sa'da.[136]

Nevertheless, the regime in Yemen internalized the fact that only significant improvement in all areas of life would pave a new way for Yemen. Poor incomes, the lack of a suitable health system and medical insurance, dwindling water supplies – all these were problems that Yemeni society was experiencing day by day. The regime's representatives made promises to different sectors of the Yemeni society that the hoped-for change was close, but under the circumstances it was very difficult to start the process of reconstruction. The rounds of fighting in Sa'da and its surroundings left 100,000 citizens refugees in their own state and their own governorate.[137] In spite of the optimistic declarations, the representatives of the government occasionally voiced their view that the goal of getting back to square one in Sa'da would be more than difficult. Coping with the challenges that the rebellion posed – reconstructing the damages of the war, incorporating the Huthis in legitimate political activity, dealing with the Huthi supporters' religious worldview and overcoming familial loyalties – promised to be very difficult, no less of a challenge than the war itself.[138] The old baggage from the ongoing bloodshed, especially the links between warring parties and tribal networks inside Yemen as well as their links with states and movements outside of Yemen, served to widen the conflict and created friction that made the mission of dealing with Yemen's economic and social problems difficult if not impossible. The ideology that Husayn Badr al-Din al-Huthi sowed among his disciples and its socio-economic dimensions could attest to a challenge of a different sort and required a much more creative policy from the regime. Not only did the decision to fight the rebels fail to eliminate them ideologically; it even served to strengthen their cause.[139]

The Challenge of Radical Islam: al-Qa'ida

The presence of radical Islamic movements in Yemen became evident in the aftermath of the unification and even more so during the civil war. Because at that time the YSP was its main rival, the Yemeni regime welcomed the assistance of any player which could weaken the YSP, including radical Islamic movements. As long as the activists of the Islamic movements directed their criticism against the YSP, Salih's regime turned a blind eye to their activity and this allowed them to gain momentum. Soon, the regime found itself in trouble because the Islamists unleashed a vitriolic attack on all regional players who they identified as pro-Western. Yemeni Islamists went so far as to try to assassinate Egyptian President Husni Mubarak while he was visiting Addis Ababa, the capital of Ethiopia, in June 1995. This affair placed Salih's regime in the international limelight.

The increasing influence of the Islamic movements was seen in the day-to-day activities in the south. The "Modesty Committee", headed by Shaykh 'Abd al-Majid al-Zindani, intensified its activities. For example, in the port city of Hudayda, committee officers were ordered to restrain "prostitution and obscenity". They were authorized to stop couples on the streets and require them to provide proof that they were either married or immediate family members. In Aden, the former socialist-Marxist capital, al-Zindani and his supporters bluntly demanded that Salih's government should end the "moral corruption that could be found everywhere" – social dancing, alcohol consumption, soap operas, fashion shows and store-front mannequins. In July 2008, al-Zindani established the Committee for the Propagation of Virtue and Prevention of Vice (based on the Saudi model),[140] which conducted surprise inspections of restaurants to ensure that they were not selling alcoholic beverages.[141]

One of the major questions that remained unanswered concerns the relationship between the Yemeni leadership and al-Zindani.[142] He has definitely been one of the more influential figures in Yemen, well connected with Islamists, but well accepted among non-Islamist Yemenis. It was repeatedly argued that he provided moral and spiritual support to Islamists, including a fatwa which approved the suicide attack against the USS *Cole* in October 2000. There was a surge of militant, Salafi activity in the north in July 2001, after the demise of Shaykh Muqbil bin Hadi al-Wadi'i, the founder of the Salafi movement in Yemen. After his death, divisions emerged in the Salafi camp and the friction intensified between people like Muhammad al-Imam, Abu Hasan al-Ma'ribi and the Islamist group *jam'iyyat al-hikma al-yamaniyya* which was founded by Shaykh 'Aqil al-Maqtari.[143] One of the main causes of disagreement was the extent to which the Salafis should be involved in Yemeni politics. Shaykh Muqbil, for example, had refused to be involved at all.

Journalists often use the term "Islamist" as a substitute for al-Qa'ida, though there is a plethora of Islamist movements in Yemen. However, al-Qa'ida is the most militant and has the most extreme ideology of these groups.[144] It is clear that not all Islamists in Yemen are al-Qa'ida members and it is difficult to measure al-Qa'ida's volume of activity and its number of activists, but it can definitely be said that al-Qa'ida has strengthened its position in Yemen in recent years and its presence has become conspicuous.[145]

Al-Qa'ida's attack on the USS *Cole* in October 2000 in the port of Aden constituted a watershed in al-Qa'ida's modus operandi. The regime in Yemen found itself at a crossroads, which required a different strategic decision. Salih must have recalled the lesson of the early 1990s when he supported Saddam Husayn and paid a heavy political and economic price, which resulted in a mass expulsion of Yemeni workers from the Gulf States. This time Salih realized that it would be in his regime's best interest not to go against the flow, and thus he declared himself a full partner with the US in its counterterrorism operations. The shift in Salih's policy was reflected in a flood of arrests of suspects in the USS *Cole* attack and the freezing of their bank accounts, as well as the arrival of American advisors to help create a counterterrorism unit. The establishment of a joint programme to monitor the entrances and exits at Yemen's airports and seaports further strengthened the impression that Yemen had become an active partner in what would come to be called the "war on terror".[146]

However, it became clear that Yemen's promise to fight terrorism was empty simply because the Yemeni government only had a grip on the main cities of the state. The central regime's inability to impose itself in certain territories which had become enclaves run by tribal militias turned Yemen into an attractive arena for organizations like al-Qa'ida. Many Yemeni citizens fought for al-Qa'ida throughout the world, especially in Iraq, Afghanistan and Pakistan. Yemen was now a safe haven for many of these Yemeni al-Qa'ida volunteers.[147]

Yemen, the ancestral homeland of the bin Laden family, was viewed as an attractive area because of the lack of state control in several regions, and many (particularly native Yemenis) made their way there after having fought against the Americans in Iraq or Afghanistan. Afghan veterans were just one component in the widening base of support of al-Qa'ida's network in Yemen. Tribal groups outside of Sanaa's reach became an attraction for al-Qa'ida. And each one of these groups that took a decision to cooperate with al-Qa'ida viewed the cooperation as a measure that would contribute to bettering its position in the land of Yemen. For example, tribal groups in Ma'rib, approximately 170 kilometres east of Sanaa, whose relationship with the Sanaa government was characterized by friction, viewed cooperation with al-Qa'ida as a tool that could strengthen their position. Other tribal areas in the Ma'rib, Jawf and Shabwa regions became places of shelter and protection for the leaders of the organization and its activists. Such a pattern can be found in abundance in Yemen's history. Tribes would side with a certain player in accordance to their evaluation of the local power game and their attempt to improve their positions and not because of ideological motives.

A publication issued by al-Qa'ida entitled *Sada al-Malahim* provided an explanation for the rebellion against Salih's regime and asserted that this was one of the greatest commitments taken on by the Salafiyya. In all declarations and references made by al-Qa'ida activists, Salih's regime was depicted as a tyranny that should be uprooted. It was explained that attacking this regime was not a deviation from Islam but rather a commandment according to a known tradition that calls for action against apostates; according to the *hadith*, the Prophet Muhammad said, "whoever changed his religion, kill him".[148] The teachings of well-known clerics like Ibn 'Aqil and Ibn al-Jawzi, who permitted rebellion against such rulers and even preached for killing them, were used to substantiate the argument. Al-'Ustaz 'Abdallah, for example, preached that there was an obligation to rebel against Salih, explained,

> ... Today we see that Ali 'Abdallah Salih replaced Islam with secularism, which by itself means heretics and apostates. Whoever wishes any religion other than Islam, his apostasy will be refused and he'll loose everything in the next world (*Surat*

> *al-'Imran*, 85). He denies the fact that he recognizes the UN as a judicial authority and he acts in accordance with its pacts and resolutions made by human beings that sharply contradict the ordinances of Allah. He is a heretic since he forged an alliance with the Jews and the Christians and not with the believers. He stayed away from the believers, helped the heretics and turned a cold shoulder to the jihad warriors.[149]

Salih was depicted as a tool in the service of the Zionists and one who spied on the jihad warriors and practically supported the American presence in the Red Sea. The source of al-'Ustaz 'Abdallah's discontent with Salih, and that of those he represents, was not only that Salih did not fulfill his duties as a Muslim ruler who rules according to the Islamic law but also that he paved the way for immoral behaviours such as prostitution and alcohol consumption. Therefore al-'Ustaz 'Abdallah concluded, "It is our obligation to mobilize the Muslims to topple 'Ali 'Abdallah Salih ... and to show the people what Allah's verdict is regarding apostates such as 'Ali 'Abdallah Salih".[150]

Al-'Ustaz 'Abdallah and other Islamists viewed Salih as an apostate partly owing to his policy toward the neighbouring state of Somalia, which had become a zone of conflict between the American forces and Islamists. One of the main lines of attack against Salih was his treacherous cooperation with the Americans in Somalia. Al-Qa'ida's publications and declarations referred to Salih as "al-Aswad al-'Ansi", one of the most notorious figures in Islam who was considered the first to become an apostate, and who had committed many transgressions.[151] It was also argued that Salih gathered armies and put them under the authority of an American officer to be used against the Muslims in Somalia. "Our desertion of our brothers in Somalia today is our desertion of Allah tomorrow", suggested Abu Hurayra al-San'ani, one of the most conspicuous columnists of *Sada al-Malahim.* He went on to praise the jihad warriors in Somalia for their heroic struggle against the enemies of the *umma* and called upon Muslims, wherever they were, to find a way to support the brothers in Somalia.[152]

To a large extent, al-Qa'ida's success in bolstering its presence in Yemen resulted from a joint failure of both the Yemeni government and the Americans. The first phase of the American-Yemeni battle against al-Qa'ida began in October 2000 after the attack on the USS *Cole* that resulted in the deaths of 17 American sailors. That, together with the events of 9/11, brought the Yemeni government into cooperation with the Americans in conducting a war on al-Qa'ida and their supporters in Yemen. The most conspicuous action took place in November 2002. Six al-Qa'ida activists were killed in an air attack in the Ma'rib province including 'Ali Salim Sinan al-Harithi who was considered the leader of al-Qa'ida in Yemen and the commander of the squad that attacked the USS *Cole*.[153] The arrest one year later of al-Harithi's replacement, Muhammad Hamdi al-Ahdal (known as Abu 'Asim al-Makki),[154] was another blow for al-Qa'ida. The lethal blow to the skeleton of al-Qa'ida's leadership in Yemen gave both the American and the Yemeni governments a feeling of victory and the belief that they had delivered a bitter lesson to al-Qa'ida's activists that would prevent them from quickly returning to their operations in Yemen. In the years after that, the issue of al-Qa'ida in Yemen did not top the agendas of the Yemeni government or the American administration.[155] Salih's regime realized how destructive al-Qa'ida could be, but the regime identified al-Qa'ida as a transnational movement that fights against Crusaders and Zionists and not a movement confined to a given territory. Unlike the other challenges that the regime faced and perceived as existential threats – the Huthi rebellion and the secessionist movement in the south – the problem of al-Qa'ida was of a different nature and coping with Islamic militants was, in the mind of Salih, a global or Western problem that could not be solved by Yemen alone. Despite the detrimental effects al-Qa'ida's activity had on Yemen – after all, its activists attacked not only Western targets, but also army installations and institutions identified with the regime[156] – they were still not considered by the regime as a critical threat which demanded an immediate response such as the Huthi rebellion in the north and the secessionist movement in the south. The last two were taken at the time as an existential threat that was gleaned from the unique Yemeni experience. Throughout

2004, Yemen directed its efforts against the Huthi rebellion in Sa'da and in parallel implemented an economic policy which cut subsidies and aimed to repair the economy which resulted in demonstrations and riots in the central cities.

The United States rose to the occasion and pressed for democratic reforms in an attempt to eradicate pockets of corruption in Yemen as part of its overall policy in the Middle East. During his visit to the US in November 2005, Salih was informed that the aid for Yemen in the framework of USAID was frozen. The news shocked Salih who had been under the impression that his arrival in Washington was a gesture and reward for his activity against al-Qa'ida. Instead he was informed of the loss of 20 million dollars of aid money. His anger grew when he was told that there was a decision to severely cut the degree of support to Yemen and to place it at 280 million dollars instead of 420 million. These punitive steps were intended to signal to the regime that it had not dealt with the corruption in its government. Instead of taking advantage of the situation and delivering a blow to al-Qa'ida, the Americans and the Yemeni government quarrelled between themselves; al-Qa'ida used the time period to regroup and reorganize. Both the Americans and the Yemeni government assumed, based on their past experience, that if and when al-Qa'ida recovered, they could overcome it. Both governments would be surprised at al-Qa'ida's growth during 2004–2005.

The escape of 23 al-Qa'ida prisoners in February 2006 signified the renewal of al-Qa'ida's activity in Yemen in an unprecedented capacity. Among the escapees were Jamal Ahmad Badawi and Jaber al-Banna, two senior activists whose names topped America's most-wanted list.[157] The Americans pressured the Yemeni government to arrest them. But after the killing of Badawi and al-Banna, it became clear to both the Americans and the Yemeni regime that the escapees still at large – such as Nasir al-Wahayshi, Qassim al-Raymi and Muhammad al-'Umda – filled the gap that had been created by the demise of Badawi and al-Banna. Several months after their escape from prison, the growth of al-Qa'ida was undeniable. Al-Qa'ida focused its activity on state infrastructure before moving on to acts of sabotage that were much more cruel and professional.[158]

In March 2007, the attorney general of the Ma'rib region was assassinated. In the summer of the same year, al-Qa'ida activists carried out an attack on Spanish tourists which resulted in the death and injury of 17 people.[159] This happened in accordance with the appointment of Nasir al-Wahayshi and Qassim al-Raymi as the leader and deputy leader of the Yemeni branch of al-Qa'ida.

Nasir al-Wahayshi was appointed to leadership at the relatively young age of 33. He acquired his basic education in religious institutions in Yemen before leaving for Afghanistan in the late 1990s and becoming one of Osama bin Laden's entourage. He even took part in the fighting in the Tora Bora caves and in 2002, he went to Iran where he was arrested by the Iranian authorities and extradited to Yemen in 2003.[160] The fact that people like al-Wahayshi and al-Raymi reached the top of the leadership of al-Qa'ida in Yemen attested to al-Qa'ida's large constituency in Yemen. Al-Qa'ida proved to be an organization that could cross tribal and regional lines in a manner that was unprecedented for any other movement or political actor in Yemen. The narrative that was brought into the public discourse by al-Wahayshi and others proved to be much more attractive than any other message that had been propagated by either the Americans or the Yemeni government.[161]

In January 2008, al-Qa'ida published the first copy of its bi-monthly magazine, *Sada al-Malahim*, and in the same month, it carried out a lethal attack against a group of tourists from South Korea and thereafter against the policemen appointed to investigate the event.[162]

In late 2008 Ayman al-Zawahiri, second in command of al-Qa'ida, granted an official appointment to al-Wahayshi, the leader of al-Qa'ida in Yemen. Al-Zawahiri highlighted Yemen's importance in the reorganization of al-Qa'ida and argued that the organization was acting in order to rescue the people of Yemen when it became clear that the "heretical forces strove to turn Yemen – the land of faith, wisdom and devotion to Islam – into a storage, supply and support base for the march of Crusaders and Zionists". Therefore al-Zawahiri sent his congratulations to the activists of al-Qa'ida in Yemen and urged the people of the country to help "the jihad, the jihad fighters and their *amir*, Abu Basir Nasir al-Wahayshi".[163] Al-Wahayshi adopted expressions and perceptions of Osama bin Laden's school and strengthened his position as the leader of al-Qa'ida in Yemen while delegitimizing the regime in Sanaa.[164] By recounting his personal experience from the period when he stayed near Osama bin Laden, al-Wahayshi praised the bravery of Yemeni warriors that had fought in Afghanistan throughout the 1980s, including the story of a Yemeni from Ma'rib who despite being more than 60 years of age went to Afghanistan and found his death there. He was portrayed as a devoted Muslim warrior that had understood how critical the time was and did not hesitate to sacrifice himself for the *umma*.[165]

The dynamic events in Yemen were interpreted by al-Wahayshi in a way that fitted his vision. The May 1990 unification was portrayed by him as a blessed development since it signalled the demise of socialism and paved the way for a united nation returning to its Islamic origins. But as al-Wahayshi argued, it soon it became clear that

> [...] Yemen was taken captive by a crook named 'Ali 'Abdallah Salih who had promised to the people that he would implement Islamic law and a just rule and equally distribute the resources of the state. Instead, the treasonous agent abolished the Islamic law, and committed obscenities under the guise of tourist projects – hotels, dancing balls, the mixing of men and women – and closed educational institutions that trained clerics and people of knowledge. This deceit was more so exposed when he decided to conduct a stern war against the brave jihad fighters who had fought side by side with their brothers in Iraq and Afghanistan, and he did that to appease his master, [George] Bush.[166]

Al-Wahayshi compared the way that Salih took control of Yemen to what happened in Baghdad and the Gaza Strip. Al-Wahayshi named the President "al-Ruwaybda", a derogatory nickname from Islamic tradition which was given to a particularly foolish and evil person, and he argued that Salih conducted a cruel struggle in Ma'rib, Jawf, Shabwa, Abyan, Sanaa and Hadramawt in order to damage the tribes, to disarm them, to take control over their lands or territories, rob the oil, gas and other resources of the land and in effect, to perpetuate a crime against the Yemeni people as the Jews did in Gaza.[167] The struggle over Yemen was characterized by al-Wahayshi as a sacred war, which strove to spread Islam from the very place it was given birth. Yemen, therefore, was perceived as a point of departure for the renewal of the Islamic conquest, and the first step in returning to *bayt al-maqdas* (an Islamic title for Jerusalem). Sacrificing one's life in a struggle over the territory of the Arabian Peninsula was a huge privilege that could ensure honour in this world and the next. Al-Wahayshi focused his words toward soldiers and people serving the security forces in Yemen who, according to him, were living in a twisted reality and instead of fighting the Jews, were fighting their own people.[168]

One of the more conspicuous writers in *Sada al-Malahim*, whose pen name was Hamil al-Mask, borrowed a quote from Ayman al-Zawahiri for the title of his article "From here we do begin". Al-Mask said that although in reality Muslim peoples gathered around the jihad fighters – as demonstrated in Afghanistan and Pakistan under the leadership of Amir Mullah 'Umar, and in the cases of the spread of the jihad to north Pakistan, Iraq, Somalia, north Africa and Chechnya – this was not the case in the Arabian Peninsula. Yemen, argued al-Mask, has a strong tribal culture, where tribes are devoted to their religion and principles. The land is mountainous and has long borders, a long seashore, and it is very difficult to take control of it; hence, it is a most comfortable area for the jihad fighters. On top of that, the state is ruled by a regime that adopted discrimination, robbery and abuse and the Yemeni people are being run over by the wheels of corruption and suppression with no one to protect them. It was therefore obvious how critical and important was the mission that the jihad fighters took upon themselves. Al-Mask described the ideological breach where "the heretic socialists of yesterday met with the Muslim cleric". These political leaders relied on the help of "the shoe guy" (a derogatory nickname given to Bush following the "shoe-throwing incident")[169] who reiterated that Yemen is an ally of the US.[170] Al-Mask briefly described the history of the jihad in Yemen starting from the year 2000 and emphasized that in spite of the suppression and proliferation of arrests, jihad cells grew up, such as that led by Abu 'Ali al-Harithi, who carried out heroic acts. Under the leadership of al-Wahayshi, concluded al-Mask, the jihadist struggle became more resilient, as the movement managed to increase its power and connect itself to the different sectors of the Yemeni society and under the circumstances, one should hope for the jihad fighters' full control of the Arabian Peninsula.[171]

One of al-Qa'ida's more calculated operational conclusions was al-Wahayshi's support for al-Janub al-Hurr, the secessionist movement of the south. In a video clip posted on his website, al-Wahayshi declared his support for the people of the south in view of their struggle against 'Ali 'Abdallah Salih. Salih al-Shanfara, one of the leaders of the secessionists, was quick to repudiate al-Wahayshi's words, saying "we [the secessionist movement] have no connection to al-Qa'ida and we will never accept such things or such stances".[172] This did not change al-Wahayshi's behaviour and in spite of the fact that his vision was totally opposite to that of the secessionists, he claimed that the secessionists' argument was an echo of his own argument about the suppressive and corrupt nature of the Sanaa regime. Al-Wahayshi's arguments did not express authentic support for the ideas and worldview of the secessionists but were an attempt to capitalize on the event and weave them into al-Qa'ida's narrative.[173]

Al-Qa'ida activists recalled the bitter and painful memory of the first phase of the US and Yemeni joint attack (October 2000–late 2003). At the time, both the Yemeni regime and the Americans perceived the presence of al-Qa'ida as a critical issue and effectively collaborated in a strategic attack against al-Qa'ida targets in Yemen. At the time, al-Qa'ida was not that skilled nor able to cope with this effective attack. Al-Wahayshi drew some bitter lessons from this attack and managed to build up a power base that went on the offensive and hit targets identified with both the regime and the Americans in order to emphasize that the defensive phase was over and that al-Qa'ida was able to influence events in Yemen. Al-Qa'ida leaders knew how deeply the regime was involved in coping with challenges from the south (the secessionists) and the north (the Huthi rebellion) and that the dwindling economy had turned the running of the state into an impossible mission. Al-Qa'ida leaders simply concluded that the more chaotic the situation in Yemen was, the better it would be for them.

Al-Wahayshi tried to capitalize on regional crises and tried to use weak states in the Arabian Peninsula and the Horn of Africa as bases for action. In January 2009, the Saudi and Yemeni branches of al-Qa'ida were formally merged. The release of *Sada al-Malahim* provided an extract from an interview with al-Wahayshi who said the Saudi *mujahideen* had pledged allegiance to him and agreed to form a united organization called "al-Qa'ida in the Arabian Peninsula" (AQAP, *al-Qa'ida fi Jazirat al-'Arab*).[174] The amalgamation was created because the Yemeni activists needed knowledge and financial support and the Saudi activists who were being hunted by the Saudi authorities needed a safe haven.[175] Al-Qa'ida provided from then on a reservoir of volunteers willing to carry out terrorist attacks outside of Yemen, especially in the oil fields of Kuwait, Saudi Arabia and Iraq, in order to create "economic terrorism" to disrupt the oil supply from the Middle East to the different parts of the world. The Western governments' warnings to their citizens not to travel to Yemen increased the Yemeni regime's embarrassment and exposed its weakness. The Americans' aerial attacks on senior al-Qa'ida figures in November 2006 violated Yemen's sovereignty and drew criticism from both Yemeni opposition groups and underground groups who believed that the regime had been turned into a servant of Western interests. State officials, as well as security forces, became a target for al-Qa'ida.

In July 2007 activists of Islamic Jihad, a group identified with al-Qa'ida, carried out a suicide attack which resulted in the killing of eight Spanish tourists. In June 2009, the bodies of two German tourists and three South Koreans that had been kidnapped were found in Sa'da. For the first time, foreigners were not merely being kidnapped but almost immediately executed. As mentioned, the phenomenon of kidnapping foreigners for ransom characterized Yemen during the 1994 civil war, but was intensified starting from 2006. More often than not, however, these acts were carried out with the aim of getting ransom and did not end in execution, certainly not immediate execution. The fact that these events, especially the last one, took place in the north of Yemen urged the regime to put the blame on the Huthi rebels. A short while after that, however, al-Qa'ida released video clips of the terrorist attacks against the South Korean tourists. They subsequently attacked the police who were investigating the incident. Al-Qa'ida therefore expanded its area of activity in Yemen and along with forging alliances with certain tribes, especially in the Ma'rib region, it also stirred the pot in Sa'da. This is why 'Ali 'Abdallah Salih asked the tribal leaders in Ma'rib not to provide shelter to the escaped al-Qa'ida leaders but to turn them over to the authorities.[176] In July 2009, the Yemeni foreign minister accused al-Qa'ida of fanning the flames of the Shi'i rebellion in the north and initiating violence in the south. Both al-Qa'ida's activity in Yemen and the Shi'i rebellion in Sa'da exacerbated Saudi fears and resulted in a Saudi interventionist policy that was also expressed by increased support for the regime in Sanaa.[177] Saudi Arabia published a list of 85 people, including two Yemenis, wanted for terrorist attacks, 26 of whom had found shelter in Yemen. That list served as a pretext for the Saudis to intervene in Yemen.[178]

After April 2008, there was a relative lull in al-Qa'ida's terrorist attacks. This could be partially explained by the success of the Yemeni security apparatus in pre-empting the group's activity, but it was mainly due to the internal friction in al-Qa'ida's ranks between Hamza al-Qa'iti's faction and the leader of the group, Nasir al-Wahayshi. The regime tried to open a dialogue with al-Qa'ida in order to obtain a working compromise, for example that those affiliated with the group would stop attacking the security forces and state institutions. 'Ali 'Abdallah Salih authorized one of his relatives, a member of the Khawlan tribe, to strike a deal with al-Qa'ida and to negotiate with al-Wahayshi, with the understanding that al-Qa'ida's prisoners were not to be tortured and that some of them would be released in return for stopping the attacks against Yemen's security forces.[179]

'Ali 'Abdallah Salih used manipulative tactics in keeping with his politics of survival. In the early stages of al-Qa'ida's presence in Yemen, he found al-Qa'ida to be a fitting tool in his hands. Salih's use of al-Qa'ida as a tool substantiated the impression that the regime viewed both the secessionists in the south and the Huthi rebels in the north as existential threats. In spite of the fact that al-Qa'ida strengthened its presence in Yemen, in Salih's view, al-Qa'ida did not strive to topple the regime and replace it, but rather to settle into some areas where the regime was weak and could not penetrate. On top of that, al-Qa'ida attracted many people from Yemeni society, including tribal, urban and village people. For most Yemenis, most al-Qa'ida activists were brothers, nephews or members of the same tribe that should have been talked to or negotiated with.[180] In addition to alliances that were forged with tribal militias, 'Ali 'Abdallah Salih was also aided by al-Qa'ida activists or other Sunni-Islamist groups while fighting against the Huthis in the north. The paradoxical nature of Yemen's power game meant that 'Ali 'Abdallah Salih contributed to the strengthening of al-Qa'ida in Yemen and to the emergence of the extended body of al-Qa'ida in the Arabian Peninsula.

In Yemen's power game, ad hoc alliances and shifting loyalties constituted an important component. The volatility of power configurations culminated in "impossible alliances" and shifting loyalties. Thus, for example, the possibility of an ad hoc alliance between the Huthi rebels and al-Qa'ida activists could not be overlooked; both had an interest in hitting Yemeni and Saudi targets. In his confession, Muhammad al-'Awfi, a jihadist and a former prisoner at Guantanamo Bay, convincingly pointed to a linkage between the Huthi rebels and al-Qa'ida, saying that the Huthis and their Iranian patron had offered him support and aid if he would assist them in demolishing the regime in Yemen.[181] Al-'Awfi also mentioned the new strategy that was developed by al-Qa'ida: to carry out terrorist attacks in Saudi Arabia in order to undermine the stability of the Kingdom. The Huthi's spokesperson argued that the Saudi media was "weaving a net of accusations between the Huthis and what is called the 'al-Qa'ida organization' without having one piece of hard evidence", and that in effect, these accusations were primed to "justify hostile policies that both the Saudi and Yemeni regime carried out as part of the Zionst projects in the region".[182] It is difficult to ascertain whether or not there is a link between the Huthis and al-Qa'ida. On the surface, it is not reasonable that Salafis would commit themselves to an alliance of cooperation with the Zaydi Shi'i camp; further credence is lent to this view by the fact that both sides' representatives denied such a contact. However, this possibility cannot be ignored in view of the fact that both parties had common enemies (the regimes in Yemen and Saudi Arabia).

Yemen's politics were characterized by conflicting alliances, which made it very difficult for the observer to identify the lines by which the alliances were drawn or ascertain their logic and motivation. A case in point is that of Tariq al-Fadli, the son of one of the last sultans of al-Fadli in the province of Abyan, who had been identified with jihadist groups.[183] Tariq al-Fadli later on expressed his support for the secessionist movement in the south, saying that it is "an issue of a people that was conquered and whose wealth was confiscated". As for his former activity in jihadist groups, he said, "this is an issue of more than 20 years which has terminated. Now we are living in our land and we have no connection whatsoever to Afghanistan".[184] Al-Fadli was not considered a terrorist by the regime when he was a member of jihadist or other groups, but when he joined the secessionists of the south, the regime suddenly depicted him as a terrorist. 'Ali 'Abdallah Salih, while pointing an accusing finger toward the secessionist movement in the south, argued that it was connected to al-Qa'ida. This was an indication that Salih was beginning to view al-Qa'ida as a threat that could destroy Yemen.

In its magazine, *Sada al-Malahim*, al-Qa'ida continued to doctrinally and psychologically depict Salih as a ruler supported by the Americans. The treasonous role of Saudi Arabia and its interventionist policy in Yemen's affairs also did not go unnoticed by al-Qa'ida spokesmen. They labelled the Saudi royal family as the "government of al-Salul" (the leader of the *Munafiqun*),[185] and they argued that the Saudi influence had invaded Yemen and was fighting Islamic warriors.[186]

Towards the end of the first decade of the twenty-first century, it seemed that al-Qa'ida had reached its strongest position in Yemen. Al-Qa'ida's presence in Yemen validated the argument that Yemen was becoming the next Somalia or Afghanistan. Similar to the Afghanistan-Pakistan complex, Yemen and Somalia, as a pair, became another focus in the global map in terms of the "war on terror". Al-Qa'ida's activity placed Yemen in the limelight, especially in view of Yemen's increased geo-strategic importance: Yemen is adjacent to Saudi Arabia, the greatest oil exporter in the world. Yemen faced and still faces a complicated set of obstacles, including Shi'i challenges in Sa'da and the piracy in the Red Sea near the Strait of Bab al-Mandab.

The state of Yemen had reached the point of no return. While the state's apparatus was eroded and the government's influence was confined to the urban areas, a wide arena remained for al-Qa'ida's activities. The security situation in Yemen deteriorated significantly. Adding to the economic problems and difficulties in the water supply programme, Yemen had to cope with the phenomena of porous boundaries, lack of security in the maritime routes and lack of effective control in large parts of the state. Arms trafficking and the easy procurement of weapons all over Yemen (60 million weapons in a state of 22 million people),[187] goes some way to explaining the lack of stability in Yemen and the surrounding states. The capabilities of the Yemeni government were indeed limited and it was desperately in need of support. The American awareness of Yemen's needs was reflected in its raising of support from 9.3 million dollars in 2008 to 24 million in 2009. The support was given for improving the health, education and welfare systems in Yemen. Investing in Yemen was intended to prevent the exportation of instability to the Arabian Peninsula and the Persian Gulf or alternatively to the Horn of Africa, especially Somalia. The paradox of an aid regime predicated on security meant that for Yemen to top the USAID agenda and receive more funds it must be viewed as a security threat. To that end, the regime produced a list of wanted men, including Huthi rebels and al-Qa'ida activists. However, cozying up to the Americans for aid by crushing popular figures led to a backlash and gave rise to the characterization of the Salih regime as a treasonous collaborator.

Al-Qa'ida's explanation of the 2008 attack on the American embassy in Sanaa is indicative of the response to increased Yemeni cooperation with American forces. It was explained that embassies had been turned into "centres of conspiracy which strive through apostate rulers to extinguish what remains of Islam. They [the embassies] kill our children under the cover of family planning and distribute obscenities such as alcohol, drugs, prostitutes and homosexuality among the Muslim society".[188] They went on to say that, among other things, the embassies provided services and financial aid for groups they saw as heretical, such as the Isma'iliyya, the *Ithna 'Ashariyya* and the Sufis, and that among their personnel were military attachés who were deeply involved in strengthening the military presence of their state in Muslim lands. Al-Qa'ida's spokesmen in Yemen argued that alongside the establishment of CIA and FBI offices in Yemen, the American embassies put special effort into mobilizing Yemeni agents in order to use them against the Muslims and Islam. According to al-Qa'ida, the damage to Yemen and its sovereignty was exposed in October 2003 when an unmanned aerial vehicle attacked al-Qa'ida's senior officials in Ma'rib and killed a prominent member of al-Qa'ida in Yemen, Sinan al-Harithi, suspected of having planned the USS *Cole* bombing in 2000.[189]

States such as Afghanistan, Iraq and Somalia,[190] where the ethno-religious complexities threaten to crush the state, have become an attractive arena of activity for al-Qa'ida. Yemen was seen as a new-comer to the "failed states club". Al-Qa'ida has long viewed Yemen as an important territory. 'Umar 'Abd al-Hakim, known as Abu Mus'ib al-Suri, was one of al-Qa'ida's most important ideologues. He wrote a brief essay entitled "The responsibility of Yemen's people toward the sacred sites of Muslims" where he claimed that the demographic composition of Yemen and its mountainous nature turns it into a natural fortress that could provide shelter to the jihadist warriors.[191] Being a poor, tribal, religious and conservative state, Yemen became a fitting arena for ideological and organizational usage by al-Qa'ida where they could carry out a long-term, systematic effort of the ideological mobilization of young people who constitute most of the rapidly growing Yemeni population. In early 2009, al-Qa'ida continued to bolster its presence in Yemen.[192] The Salih regime had little authority outside the cities, and in a state that is fraught with territorial enclaves, mainly mountainous, it is obvious why Yemen became a convenient shelter for al-Qa'ida activists.

In line with its programme, which strives to undermine nation states, especially where societies are divided along tribal, ethnic or territorial lines, al-Qa'ida viewed the dismembered Yemen as a tool to strengthen its presence and its logistical system in a region which is adjacent to Bab al-Mandab Strait, a highly important geo-strategic maritime route.[193] The threat that was posed to the whole region by the strengthened presence of al-Qa'ida in the Arabian Peninsula encouraged the Saudis to foster an assertive policy that supported 'Ali 'Abdallah Salih and strove to uproot al-Qa'ida's presence in the region. The chief editor of the Saudi paper, *al-Sharq al-Awsat*, Tariq al-Humayd, explained, "Today, support of Yemen's leadership became a necessity and is not just a bargaining chip or an issue that could be neglected or postponed. The danger is much more grave than what some of the people think and the worst-case scenario could happen. If and when it happens, it would influence not only Yemen and Saudi Arabia, but the whole region".[194]

The signs of a joint Saudi-Yemeni effort to expose al-Qa'ida activists' shelters were evident. This activity grew further in view of the estimation that dozens of activists had followed their leaders' orders and made their way from Saudi Arabia to Yemen.[195] The deputy leader of al-Qa'ida in the Arabian Peninsula, Sa'id al-Shahari, also known as Abu Sufyan al-Azdi, was a former prisoner at Guantanamo Bay and number 31 on the Saudis' list of 85 most wanted terrorists. He called on Muslims to fight against the Western presence and especially to hit the heretics that help them while indirectly alluding to Saudi Arabia.[196] One of the most wanted was Na'if al-Qahtani, a Saudi who was considered to be the liaison officer connecting the different arms of al-Qa'ida in the Arabian Peninsula and the financier of the terrorist infrastructure of al-Qa'ida in Yemen.[197] The hunt for the wanted and the demise of some of them did not contribute to a relaxation but just refuelled the bloodshed and gave birth to squads that carried the name of the martyrs. The squads also tried to retaliate by carrying out some other terror acts, such as the squad of the martyr Hamza al-Qa'iti, an al-Qa'ida leader who was killed together with his five companions by the security forces in Hadramawt in August 2008.[198]

Al-Qa'ida came to be perceived as an entity that strove to undermine the state and threatened its existence. The attack on the South Korean tourists in March 2009 was perceived as crossing a line and drew criticism from clerics and education officials, especially in Hadramawt. One of the columnists depicted the terror act as satanic and argued that only a huge "popular revolution, against terrorism and extremism and a full scale social campaign against the distribution and trade of weapons can rescue Yemen from oblivion".[199] He went on to argue that a resistance movement should be created in order to rescue the country, which would include all sectors of society – parties, civil society organizations, clerics, politicians, students and intellectuals – as a last resort "against the expansion of those groups which hold dangerous and radical views determined to go on in the satanic evil road".[200]

Shaykh al-Habib Abu Bakr al-Mashhur argued that the phenomenon of terrorism originated from the political intervention of outsiders and that there was a false interpretation of Islamic law aimed at undermining the very pillars of the country. Husayn al-Jaylani, the chairman of an educational club in Hadramawt, called for this phenomenon to be dealt with systematically through educational and religious training that is based on a moderate outlook. He added that the civil society organizations should have an instrumental role in that. Muhammad Saqqaf al-Hadr argued that attacking tourist groups contradicts the religious spirit and Muslim toleration and that the argument that the foreign tourist is an enemy is false, based on stupidity and ignorance. Dr. Sa'id al-Jariri, the head of the writers' association in Hadramawt, said that the struggle against terrorism should be carried out through joint efforts by the security organs and the educational system since terrorism is an ideological problem in nature and its origin can be found in a twisted consciousness that aims to turn young people into ticking time bombs.[201]

In May 2009, the deputy prime minister, Rashad al-'Alimi, declared that Yemen was facing a threefold challenge – terrorism, the rebellion against democracy and the economic crisis. The more the plethora of threats expanded, the more the regime became committed to the 22 May 1990 unification as the only path to securing the future of the state. It is no wonder that the state's enemies were defined by the regime as the enemies of unification. Al-'Alimi emphasized that any attempt to solve problems by violent means contradicted the pluralist spirit that the unification of Yemen provided the country with. Al-'Alimi's statements regarding al-Qa'ida should be further emphasized since they can attest to the regime's belief that al-Qa'ida has gone beyond the pale and threatens to become "an alternative in case of a societal political, economic collapse. Then al-Qa'ida could raise

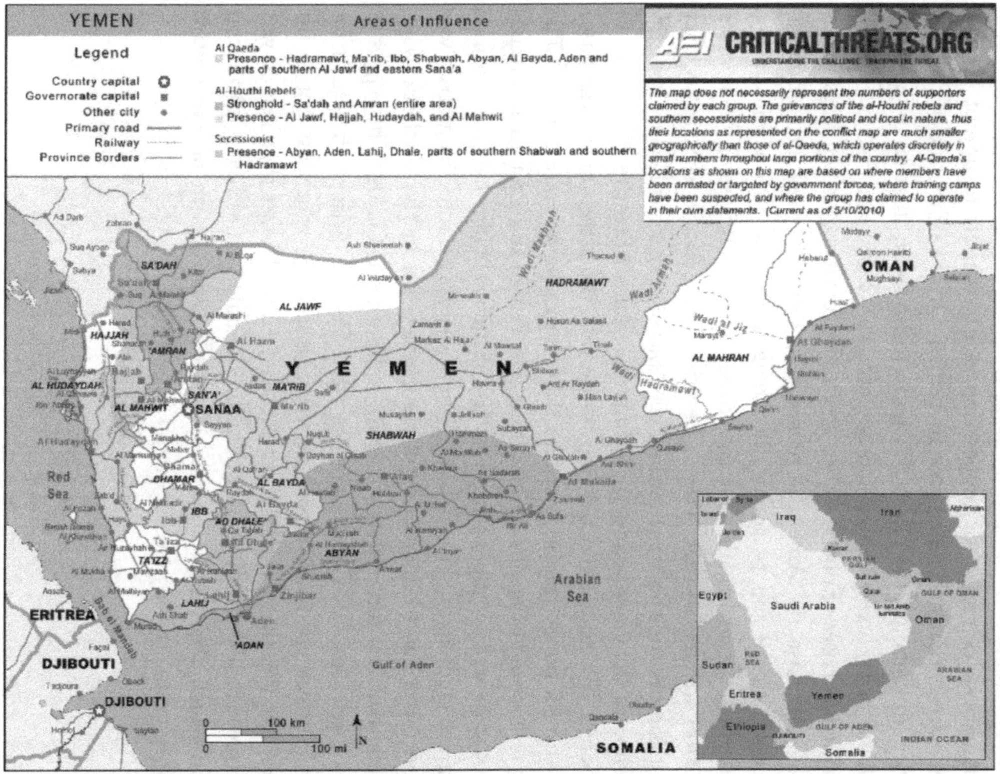

The Power Centres in Yemen
Source: www.criticalthreats.org

its voice and rule and it could use this place as a point-for-departure for its terrorist activity, both regionally and internationally as happens today in Somalia, Afghanistan and other states".[202]

Throughout these years, the regime in Yemen was facing tough American demands for cooperation in its struggle to uproot Islamic terrorism that had taken root in Yemen. On the other side of the Red Sea, in Djibouti, the US established a military installation designed to monitor events in Yemen and Somalia, two states that had been identified as bases of operation for al-Qa'ida. Similar to other cases in the Middle East, the American presence in Yemen turned into a double-edged sword and paradoxically strengthened the radical forces. The terrorist attacks against the American Embassy in Sanaa in September 2008 attested to that. The cooperation between the Yemeni security apparatus and the US regarding the "war on terror" had been strengthened in the years before, including the establishment of FBI offices in Sanaa, but still it did not help to prevent the attack on the embassy where a booby-trapped car and heavy armaments were used.[203] The presence of al-Qa'ida's senior officials in Yemen and a tough and impatient American response proved that Yemen is being shaken by various grave challenges. This is how Yemen was drawn into the global "war on terror" and became one of the battlefields in the battle between international forces that strove to undermine al-Qa'ida. The report of the release of al-Qa'ida activists from Yemeni prisons in return for a promise not to take part in terrorist activity or at least not to hit targets identified with the regime attested to the fact that Yemen was drawn into the well-known dynamics of failed states like Afghanistan in which short-term compromises are brokered with no eye toward long-term strategy (see figure on page 191).

CHAPTER 6

THE ARAB SPRING: NEW CHALLENGES EXACERBATE THE OLD

In hindsight, 'Ali 'Abdallah Salih's rule over Yemen seemed destined to have expired before he chose to step down. Even before the Arab Spring began in Yemen, the government was faced with the aforementioned challenges to its legitimacy, to wit: the Huthi rebellion in the north, the secessionist movement in the south and al-Qa'ida in the Arabian Peninsula seemingly everywhere. When a popular uprising started in the major cities in January 2011, it would grow into yet another challenge to Salih, as grave as any of those previously mentioned. The Arab Spring was an unforeseen, game-changing phenomenon in Yemeni politics that turned former allies of Salih into overt rivals. The ensuing chaos over the course of the year led to a situation in which large swathes of Yemen were indeed under the de facto control of various non-government entities.

As a result, the argument that Yemen is in fact already a failed state, as opposed to a "failing" or "fragile" state, has never been stronger. While there is no universally agreed-upon definition for what constitutes a failed state,[1] it is contended here that Yemen is more of a failed state on the ground than foreign officials recognize. To put it another way, Salih might still have been the "address" for Yemen in 2011, but he did not control every room in the house.

The Early Days

After less than a month of protests in Tunisia, President Zayn al-'Abidin bin 'Ali fled to Saudi Arabia on 14 January. He was the first Arab dictator to be the target of, and removed by, the popular protests known collectively as the "Arab Spring". If the sight of the Tunisian demonstrations inspired their fellow Arabs to emulation, the actual *success* of the Tunisian demonstrators in effecting a change in government compelled millions more Middle Easterners to take to the streets with greater intensity. Such was the case in Yemen in January 2011.

Protestors in the thousands took to the streets of Sanaa in January 2011. The protests were organized by the Joint Meeting Parties (JMP), a coalition of opposition parties in Yemen's parliament which included the Islamist al-Islah party and the Yemeni Socialist Party among others. One of the most notable figures in the early days of the protest movement was Tawakul Kirman, a journalist, women's rights activist and, for a time, member of al-Islah. She had called for protests in Sanaa in January, and was briefly detained by security forces. Her detention provoked more demonstrations in the major cities of Yemen, which likely explains her release two days later.[2] Kirman would later go on to receive the 2011 Nobel Peace Prize with two other women's rights activists.[3]

Upon her release, Kirman called for a "day of rage" to be held throughout the country on 3 February. On 2 February, President Salih made offers that fell far short of satisfying the protestors' demands. Shortly before the Arab Spring had spread to Yemen, the GPC made a poorly-timed proposal to change the constitution; the change would have removed presidential term limits, allowing Salih to remain in power after his latest term expired in 2013.[4] It was also well known that Salih had been, in recent years, grooming his son Ahmad to be his successor as president, despite the objections of other powerful figures in the government. Now, less than two months after the attempt to change the term limits, Salih pledged to his people that he would not seek another term, and that Ahmad 'Abdallah Salih would not succeed his father to the presidency. The protestors did not rescind their demand that Salih step down immediately.

On 3 February, an estimated 20,000 protestors marched in Sanaa. Change Square (*maydan al-taghyir*) near Sanaa University became the hub of the anti-regime demonstrators. A reportedly equal number of pro-Salih demonstrators also took to the streets that day. It was also reported that the government used buses to bring in more Salih-supporters from outside of Sanaa.[5] Smaller anti-government protests also took place in Aden and Ta'izz.

In the early days of the uprising, protestors would be met with riot police using tear gas and batons. But as it became clear that the movement would not quickly abate, more violent means were to follow. The first fatalities of the Arab Spring in Yemen occurred on 23 February, when two students were shot dead and another 21 were wounded by pro-government gunmen wearing civilian clothing. The police failed to prevent the gunmen from getting through a barricade separating them from the protestors.[6] The violence on 23 February foreshadowed the greater carnage that would come to Sanaa less than one month later.

By the end of February, 'Ali 'Abdallah Salih proposed the formation of a national unity government in accordance with the law and the Yemeni constitution, in order to prevent the country from descending into chaos. The opposition, however, refused this offer and demanded Salih's resignation. In the streets of Sanaa, the protests continued as demonstrators gathered for the "Friday of Defiance" (*jum'at al-thibat*), using the slogan "Here we are to plant the seeds of the freedom tree", and calling for the ouster of the dictator.[7]

In a speech in front of high-ranking *'ulama*, President Salih blamed the opposition for not being willing to cooperate in forming a national unity government. He declared that he was willing to resign, since: "... The country is not 'Ali 'Abdallah Salih's property, nor the opposition party's property, neither does it belong to the *'ulama* or to the *shaykhs*. It is the property of the *umma* ... ".[8] Nevertheless, neither his statements nor his choice of language resonated sufficiently with the opposition or the protestors to satisfy them.

The 18 March Turning Point

On 18 March, the ranks of the protestors in Sanaa had swelled to 100,000. In the late afternoon, this large procession was fired upon by uniformed security personnel and plain-clothed gunmen perched on rooftops. By the end of what many described as a "massacre", 52 people had been killed and hundreds were wounded. This was greater than the combined total of protest-related deaths that preceded 18 March. The government was widely blamed, though it denied all responsibility. President Salih spoke of the victims as "martyrs of democracy".[9] He also sacked his entire cabinet, yet asked them to remain until a replacement cabinet could be assembled.[10]

The 18 March violence would prove to be a turning point in the uprising against Salih. Government and military figures began defecting to the opposition and demanded Salih's resignation.[11] Yemen's ambassador to the UN, 'Abdallah al-Sa'id, quit on 20 March, along with four other government ministers as well as the foreign ambassadors to China, the Czech Republic, Japan, Jordan, Kuwait, Saudi Arabia and Syria.[12] There were pre-existing rivalries between Salih and other elites, and the events of 18 March gave them the opportunity to openly challenge Salih's legitimacy to an unprecedented extent.

Before the Arab Spring, it was no secret that 'Ali 'Abdallah Salih was grooming his son Ahmad to replace him as president. Nor was it a secret that this angered other men who wanted the job, like General 'Ali Muhsin al-Ahmar, who by some accounts had been promised that he would succeed Salih after he leaves office.[13] Salih's other notable opponents in recent years included Shaykh Hamid al-Ahmar and his brother, Shaykh Sadiq, of the al-'Usaymat tribe. They were prominent *shaykhs* of the Hashid tribal confederation, which included Salih's tribe, the Sanhan. Hamid was also a prominent member of the opposition al-Islah party. During the 2006 presidential election campaign, Hamid al-Ahmar was an outspoken critic of Salih and supporter of his opponent. In a 2009 interview on al-Jazeera, al-Ahmar went as far as to call for Salih's resignation.[14] Hamid's brother Sadiq was also described in some reports as the top *shaykh* of the Hashid confederation. The consensus among Yemen's elites was that the Sanhan tribe was taking more and more slices from a shrinking pie. Men like 'Ali Muhsin al-Ahmar, and Shaykhs Hamid and Sadiq, were alienated by Salih's consolidation of power within his family. When the first protests began in January, some supporters of Salih blamed the al-Ahmar family for orchestrating the unrest. It had also been reported that

Hamid al-Ahmar paid for food to be brought to protestors camped out in Sanaa's Change Square.[15]

On 21 March, General 'Ali Muhsin al-Ahmar dispatched forces under his command to protect protestors in the capital. Ten other senior military commanders also resigned. The protestors' encampment at Sanaa University was the scene of a rally in which former soldiers and policemen took turns announcing their resignations and denouncing the regime. Sadiq al-Ahmar also called on Salih to step down. His brother Husayn had resigned from the government a month earlier in protest. The prospect of a civil war loomed ever larger as tanks belonging to 'Ali Muhsin al-Ahmar's First Armoured Division, and those of the loyalist Republican Guard, took up positions in the Yemeni capital. Al-Ahmar's forces were concentrated around Sanaa University to protect the protestors, while Salih's forces were concentrated around the presidential palace and the Ministry of Defense.

Before the Arab Spring, President Salih had maintained power through a patrimonial system of corruption.[16] The most trusted officials, such as relatives or fellow members of the Sanhan tribe, were given the most sensitive positions in the military and apparatuses of state security. Other allies were both enriched – and held in check – by crony capitalism. Often this system co-opted figures of opposition parties as well as the GPC. This system ensured that no serious threats to Salih formed within the government. Not only were potential rivals brought into Salih's circle of corruption, they could easily be subjected to campaigns of intimidation or have their privileges revoked if they stepped out of line. But this patrimonial system could not mitigate widespread, grassroots opposition. Indeed, foreshadowing the Arab Spring was the government's impotence in dispersing the Free South movement. April Longley Alley described it this way: "At its heart, the movement is an indictment of Salih's mode of rule, which relies on elite patronage, corruption, divide-and-rule politics, and the manipulation of regional and tribal identities ... Given current levels of animosity, and the decentralized, grassroots nature of the *hirak's* [the Free South Movement's] leadership, it is unclear whether co-opting individual leaders is a sufficient strategy for quelling the movement".[17]

The violence against protestors on 18 March decisively eliminated any remaining legitimacy of Salih's rule in the eyes of the vast majority of the population. It also provided popular cover for Salih's rivals like 'Ali Muhsin al-Ahmar and Sadiq al-Ahmar to openly call on the President to resign. The patrimonial system of co-opting potential rivals could not endure in the face of such widespread and total condemnation of the regime.

Another casualty of the 18 March violence was the United States' tacit support of President Salih. Because Salih had been a staunch ally in the "war on terror", the Obama administration was reluctant to openly call on Salih to step down as it had with Husni Mubarak in Egypt. The rising toll in dead and wounded in Yemen convinced US policy-makers that Salih's obstinacy would only lead to increasing instability and violence. The Yemeni government's preoccupation with anti-regime protestors went against US interests, which were chiefly invested in the struggle against al-Qa'ida in the Arabian Peninsula. Though it was reported that the US supported a transfer of power since the early days of the protests, after 18 March, US officials began signalling to its regional allies and the media off the record that Salih's hold on power was untenable and that in the interests of stability, he should step down.[18]

The Gulf Initiative

In April, the Gulf Cooperation Council (GCC), consisting of Bahrain, Kuwait, Oman, Qatar, Saudi Arabia and the United Arab Emirates, began efforts to negotiate a peaceful transition of power in Yemen. Salih was invited to a conference in Riyadh along with the leaders of the JMP, a coalition of Yemen's opposition political parties. The basic principles of the deal, which came to be known as the Gulf Initiative, were widely known before they were officially made public on 7 April.[19] Salih was to transfer the powers of the presidency to Vice President 'Abd Rabbu Mansur Hadi. Simultaneously, a coalition government led by the JMP would be put in place, and new elections for both the presidency and parliament would be held two months after the deal went into effect. Last but not least, the Gulf Initiative stipulated that Salih and his relatives would be immune from future prosecution.

While Salih's government made statements that were apparently receptive to the Gulf Initiative, stating that he would "positively embrace" a compromise, in a speech to a crowd of supporters on April 8, Salih explicitly attacked the Prime Minister of Qatar for meddling in Yemen's domestic affairs. Earlier in the week, Qatar's prime minister told the media that the GCC wanted Salih gone. Salih seized on this, accusing the GCC of attempting a coup against him.[20] The opposition's reaction to the Gulf Initiative was also mixed. The leaders of the JMP accepted the deal, but the grassroots opposition rejected immunity for Salih and his relatives. The Gulf Initiative in effect exposed a political rift between the anti-establishment protestors, and the opposition parliamentarians of the JMP who, while wanting Salih out of power, did not desire the same revolutionary upheaval to which grassroots organizations aspired.[21] Some protestors were also suspicious of the Gulf Initiative because they counted the governments of the GCC among the repressive regimes of the Middle East. Some even viewed Salih as a shill for the Saudis.[22]

Salih's defiance continued throughout April. He praised the Gulf Initiative while simultaneously insisting that he would not step down until the scheduled end of his term in 2013. These mixed signals aroused the cynicism of the protestors. A statement from the grassroots Youth Revolutionary Council read: "This is the 12th time this month Ali {Salih} has told us he is ready to quit, yet he is still here. His promises are worthless to us now. This is political jockeying, nothing else".[23] It was mistakenly reported on 23 April that Salih had signed off on the Gulf Initiative. Again, on 2 May, Salih backed out of signing the agreement at the last moment.

The Violence Escalates

The first reported clash between Muhsin al-Ahmar's soldiers and the Republican Guard was on 13 April, when Republican Guard soldiers seized a checkpoint being manned by soldiers of the First Armoured Division north of Sanaa. One opposition soldier was reported to have been killed, and six wounded.[24] The two sides traded shots again on 12 May, again in Sanaa, when al-Ahmar's men came to the aid of protestors who were being fired upon by loyalist forces.[25] These fire-fights would pale in comparison, however, to the violence that would break out one week later between Salih's loyalist forces and armed tribesmen of the Hashid tribal confederation.

Being one of two large tribal groups in northern Yemen, the Hashid tribal confederation included President Salih's own tribe, the Sanhan. The al-Ahmar family was the paramount family of *shaykhs* that leads this confederation. The involvement of this elite family demonstrates that the Arab Spring in Yemen was not simply a struggle between the masses and elites, but also a struggle that pitted elites against each other. Hailing from the Amran Province north of Sanaa, the patriarch was 'Abdallah bin Husayn al-Ahmar until his death in 2007. Even though he was one of the founders of the Islamist party, al-Islah, 'Abdallah al-Ahmar and President Salih were political allies throughout much of Salih's rule. From 1993 up to his death, 'Abdallah was Speaker of Parliament. Most of his ten surviving sons continued to be active in Yemeni politics.

Tension between the Salih and al-Ahmar families grew in the years leading up to the Arab Spring. Among the al-Ahmar brothers, the most outspoken critic of President Salih was Hamid al-Ahmar. In another interview with al-Jazeera in 2010, Hamid repeated his call on President Salih to resign, accusing him of running the state like a family business, even going so far as to accuse Salih of committing high treason.[26] Indeed, well before the events of May 2011, there was an Arabic pun going around in reference to the rivalry "between the two Bayt al-Ahmars ... The reference is to Shaykh 'Abdallah's surname and the President's home village, Bayt al-Ahmar".[27]

Another brother, Husayn al-Ahmar, was a member of Salih's own GPC party, but he defected to the opposition in February, weeks before the wave of defections that followed the 18 March killings. When announcing his resignation to a crowd of supporters in the Hashid heartland of Amran Province, Husayn called for the overthrow of the regime.[28]

The inevitable clash between the regime and armed tribesmen loyal to the al-Ahmar family came in late May, after the third and final time that Salih backed out of signing the Gulf Initiative. On 22 May, in a televized signing ceremony at the presidential palace in Sanaa, members of Salih's General People's Congress signed the document, but Salih conspicuously did not. The event was meant to be a face-saving spectacle for Salih, who insisted on opposition leaders being present to sign the agreement. The opposition leaders had signed the document the previous evening on 21 May. Since they refused to attend, Salih refused to sign. In his remarks on state television, Salih made a statement that encapsulated his strategy in dealing with the mounting crises: to convince Yemenis and the world that he was the only alternative to civil war and chaos. "If they [the opposition leaders] don't bow, and want to take the country into a civil war, let them be responsible for it and for the blood that was shed and that will be shed if they insist on their stupidity", he said.[29] At this point, the GCC announced that it was halting its efforts at mediation.

Earlier that day, a crowd of Salih's supporters surrounded the United Arab Emirates' embassy in Sanaa, trapping American, European and Arab diplomats inside. They were to rendezvous at the UAE embassy before proceeding to the presidential palace for the signing ceremony. Eventually the diplomats were removed from the embassy by helicopter and brought to their respective residences.[30]

On 23 May heavy fighting erupted between soldiers loyal to Salih and approximately 500 gunmen loyal to Sadiq al-Ahmar. The fighting was concentrated around al-Ahmar's residence in Sanaa as well as several government ministry buildings. Both sides used heavy weapons, including artillery and mortars. The Interior Ministry and al-Ahmar's residential compound were shelled. Both sides accused each other of being the first to fire upon the other. Opposition leaders also accused Salih of intentionally trying to provoke a civil war in order to remain in power.[31] After several days of fighting, dozens were dead and Hashid gunmen claimed to have taken over the Interior Ministry building, the headquarters of the state-run television station and the headquarters of Yemen Airways.[32]

Fighting had also spread beyond the capital by 26 May, with Hashid tribesmen engaging Republican Guard forces. Thousands of fighters were trying to reach the capital, while Salih's soldiers attempted to stop them.[33] A truce established on 27 May had broken down by 31 May. Throughout much of this period, 'Ali Muhsin al-Ahmar's First Armoured Division remained neutral. Most of the fighting was concentrated in the Hasaba District in the north-eastern part of the city.

The Retreat of Central Authority

The elite units of Yemen's military were meant to defend the regime as much as Yemen itself. With the regime facing unprecedented threats to its existence, the military units that were still loyal to Salih were concentrated against the forces of Sadiq al-Ahmar, mainly in and around Sanaa.

On 27 May, militants belonging to an Islamist militant group called *Ansar al-Shari'a* (Support of Islamic Law) seized control of the town of Zinjibar, the capital of the province of Abyan. This was the most alarming signal up to that point that al-Qa'ida-affiliated groups were filling the vacuum left by the shrinking presence of 'Ali 'Abdallah Salih's government outside of the major cities. Perhaps due to US pressure, the Yemeni air force and some ground forces did confront *Ansar al-Shari'a*, but the town was only brought back under government control after nearly two months of continuous fighting, by which time many of the town's 54,000 inhabitants had fled.[34] By contrast, the evolving crisis in the northern province of Sa'da went unmitigated.

Before the Arab Spring, two of the forces most often employed to combat the Huthi insurgency in Sa'da Province were 'Ali Muhsin al-Ahmar's First Armoured Division and Hashid tribal militias loyal to Sadiq al-Ahmar. With both of these forces now confronting Salih in Sanaa, Sa'da Province came under the de facto control of the Huthis. This shift in energy by al-Ahmar's forces was a pivotal event that was to seal the fate of Salih's presidency. Two days after 'Ali Muhsin al-Ahmar defected, on 20 March, the Huthis took control of Sa'da and installed their own governor in Sa'da Province, the government-appointed governor having fled.[35]

3 June, 2011

On 3 June, shortly after Friday prayers, there was an explosion at the entrance to the mosque in the presidential compound where Salih was attending Friday prayers. The cause of the blast could not be determined; it may have been a mortar shell, a rocket-propelled grenade or a bomb that had been smuggled in. Whatever caused the explosion, it claimed the lives of 11 guards, and five other senior officials were seriously wounded.[36]

Initial reports described Salih's injuries as light,[37] but after he was flown to Riyadh for medical treatment on 5 June, it became clear that Salih was gravely injured. Although the al-Ahmars never claimed responsibility for the attack, the government immediately blamed them. Heavy fighting resumed in the capital.

The remainder of 2011 witnessed additional instances of AQAP taking over towns, the Huthi consolidation of their hold on Sa'da Province and a stalemate in Sanaa between loyalist forces, anti-government Hashid tribesmen and Muhsin al-Ahmar's First Armoured Division. There would not be any more dramatic political realignments such as that which followed the 18 March shootings. In early June when Salih flew to Riyadh for medical treatment, anti-government protestors rejoiced in the belief that Salih would not return. However, in September Salih surprised many when he returned to Yemen, as defiant as ever. Although Salih's return prompted a temporary surge in violence in the capital, he inevitably acquiesced to the Gulf Initiative on 23 November. On 22 January, Salih left Yemen for medical treatment in the US. He returned in February to be present when 'Abd Rabbu Mansur Hadi was officially sworn in as Yemen's new president.

Although Salih's tenure as President of Yemen finally came to an end, his family's enduring influence over the government, especially the most well-trained, well-equipped units of Yemen's military, portend that the Salih family will continue to play an influential role in the expected transfer of power from the GPC to the JMP. Meanwhile, it remains to be seen whether the post-Salih government of Yemen will be able to reverse the erosion of state authority in the face of the Huthis, the successionists (*al-hirak*) and al Qa'ida.

CONCLUSION

Throughout the twentieth century, Yemen witnessed dramatic upheavals. In the north of the country, a traditional Imamate existed until 1962, followed by a period characterized by foreign intervention and a bloody civil war that culminated in the rise of a series of conservative military leaders. The South had long been under British control and developed separately from the North. Following the war of independence against the British in 1967, the state in the South became the only Marxist-Leninist state in the Arab world and existed as such for a quarter of a century. In contrast to the conservative Republic of North Yemen, which was supported by the Saudis, South Yemen developed as a secular state that praised the Marxist order and strove to uproot the tribal organizations of society. Thus, alongside the religious and geographical divisions, Yemen witnessed the emergence of two states of different orientations, and the effort to unify the two was fraught with difficulties.

When the two Yemens united in May 1990, it was hoped that the union would emphasize a nation of a common language, a wide geographical expanse and a common written tradition. The aspiration for unity was in the hearts and souls of the Yemeni public, but the shared historical experience and common language were not enough to create cohesion and full solidarity. The southern and northern elites each dictated a political rhythm that suited their particular sets of interests. The institutions of the unified state reflected an artificial union of two different entities, with a lot of overlapping institutions. To use Michael Hudson's terms, "this is how a homeland 'by force of law' (*watan shar'i*) was created and not a 'true homeland' (*watan haqiqi*)".[1]

The story of Yemen is also the story of the decline of revolutionary ideas, the victory of the primordial identities and pre-revolutionary patterns. Pretentious revolutionary ideologues striving for the creation of a new "Arab human being" swept the Middle East throughout the century. The revolutionary regimes in Egypt, Iraq, Syria and Yemen tried to broaden their bases of legitimacy by casting tradition as an anachronism and creating a socialist system and a new sense of solidarity, but this ended in failure.

'Ali 'Abdallah Salih tried to create state cohesion by cutting himself off from the socialist ideology and placing a new emphasis on the centrality of tribes in Yemen. Paradoxically, the ongoing existence of primordial groups – sub-state actors consisting of extended families and tribes having different loyalties – constituted an instrumental element in Salih's state-building process. This is how in the post-revolutionary era, Salih created a coalition between his family and other important families through political-economic partnership and the appointment of relatives in line with patron-client networking. This mechanism, in which primordial groups were co-opted into a wide network or coalition, fostered better control for the regime in different spheres such as public administration, political elites, trade unions and businessmen.

In this sense, the story of Yemen could serve as an example of the resilience and importance of tribal identities.[2] After years of futile attempts to uproot the tribal system, united Yemen under the leadership of 'Ali 'Abdallah Salih renewed the reliance on traditional affinities and turned the familial divisions into a legitimate characteristic of the regime. Unified Yemen was, therefore, based on accommodation of rather than alteration of the state reality. However, reliance on traditional affinities was accompanied by the strengthening of sub-state actors, such as the tribes, or anti-state actors, such as radical Islamic movements that challenged the state order. In a state of around 23 million people and a huge amount of weapons in private hands, the regime found it difficult to provide welfare, security and education to all segments of society. Yemen witnessed a lack of security (*aman*) and stability (*istiqrar*). The state was unable to secure freedom of movement, unable to end autonomous judicial systems and unable to disarm militias. The absence of the state in the "no man's land" enabled the Islamists to build up a web of strong loyalties by offering what the central regime could not offer – welfare, infrastructure, schools and clinics.

Yemen, one of the least economically developed states in the Middle East, has suffered from ongoing instability. The tribal wars, the persistence of autonomous enclaves where the state's law cannot penetrate, arms smuggling and al-Qa'ida terrorist attacks – all these nipped in the bud any attempt to stabilize the Yemeni system. Terrorist attacks in the port of Aden, against the USS *Cole* in 2000 and a French tanker in October 2002 for example, heavily damaged the state economy that was based on oil export as one of the main sources of income. Western companies suffered significant loss of life and property, but the most severely damaged was the state of Yemen and its dwindling economy. The high premiums that were demanded by the insurance companies turned the import of oil or any other commodity into a very pricy and dangerous transaction. The lack of tangible resources made it more difficult for the state to co-opt and appease tribal centres in order to buy relative stability.

Following the events of 9/11, the international community diverted its attention to states such as Yemen that were viewed not only as sad humanitarian cases but also as "failed states" and a threat to regional and international stability. In Yemen, for example, the absence of law in several autonomous enclaves (for example, the province of Hadramawt, the origin of the bin Laden family) created a huge industry of arms smuggling. Yemen was a sovereign state but was unable to secure safe movement and stability within its borders. It is no wonder that its long and ill-defended border of 1,400 kilometres with the Saudi Kingdom became a source of attraction for Islamic movements.[3]

Voices from a distant past flooding the north of Yemen, the demand to restore a Zaydi Shi'i Imamate and the rounds of bloodshed that erupted since June 2004 between the regime and the Huthi rebels in Sa'da, became a real threat to Salih's regime. The situation became further complicated when it became clear that this conflict, which had a local origin, invited the involvement of foreign interests and turned

Yemen into a battlefield in the Sunni-Shi'i struggle that swept the Middle East in the beginning of the twenty-first century.

The presence of the secessionist movement in the south and its refusal to accept the idea of a unified state constituted a source of consistent criticism against the regime in Sanaa. The Free South's non-violent patterns and its detailed explanations regarding the failure of unification – a forced and arbitrary measure in their mind – contributed to the delegitimizing of the regime in Sanaa. These explanations were appropriated and often cynically used as tools in the service of some radical movements, such as al-Qa'ida, that strove to undermine the regime. The threatening scenario of returning to two Yemeni states as well as memories of the years of cold war between both Yemens created an active public discourse and provided a stage for groups that aimed to promote their status in Yemen. The discussion surrounding the division of Yemen or its reorganization on a federal basis posed some questions for Yemen's future course. Getting back to the former division of North and South does not seem viable. South Yemen, which was dismembered in the late 1980s, was swallowed up by the North and will not be able to stand on independent feet in spite of the oil which was discovered in some areas of the south. Such a scenario, if it were to occur, would be the beginning of state fragmentation, a reality that could become more dangerous for Yemen and the region.

When Salih came to power in 1978, astute political observers did not believe that he would complete even a year of his term, but Salih did prove himself a leader who could weather grave challenges. He managed to survive exactly where his predecessors failed. However, the Arab Spring proved to be the game-changing phenomenon in Yemeni politics, exacerbating already existing tensions and causing a shift of alliances once again, thereby eroding Salih's presence and status to the point of no return. Eventually, Salih's regime did not prevail.

In the post-Salih era, it seemed as if the political system in Yemen had entered a new phase where the state's future would not be determined by the ordinances of the past. Yemen is portrayed as a stateless area, in other words, a territory which is fraught with poverty and lack of resources, rapidly becoming a greenhouse for radical movements which use terrorism to promote their vision. The growing presence of al-Qa'ida, the inability to negotiate an acceptable compromise with the Huthis in the north and the activities of the secessionist movement in the south – all these make it much more difficult for Yemen to strike out a path for its future. Yemen has not yet reached the stage of states like Yugoslavia or Rwanda, where the community crashed because the delicate ethnic balance at the very heart of those states' existence was demolished under pressure. Owing to its ethno-demographic complexities, its institutional weakness and its marginal position in the global economic network, Yemen barely manages to keep its head above water. Yemen – a fragile and weak state, fraught with economic difficulties, where the central authority lacks the ability to exert its influence over different areas – could easily devolve into a failed state.

Yemen is a state at risk – at high risk. The questions surrounding the future path of Yemen are numerous. Will Yemen crumble in front of the set of pressures from within and from without and become another tragic case such as Afghanistan or Somalia, or will it find the way to a better future? Time will tell if and when this can be achieved by its leaders and people.

NOTES

Preface

1. Fred Halliday, "The Formation of Yemeni Nationalism: Initial Reflections", *Rethinking Nationalism in the Arab Middle East.* Eds. Israel Gershoni and James Jankowski. New York: Columbia University Press, 1997, pp. 30–31.
2. A thorough debate on the unification of Yemen appears in an article by 'Abd al-Karim al-Iryani, a man who served in various positions in the public political system of North Yemen, as Foreign Minister (for three terms) and as Prime Minister of North Yemen in 1980–1983. "Tatawwur al-Awda' al-Iqtisadiyya fi Shatray al-Yaman wa-Mustaqbal al-Wahda al-Wataniyya", *Dirasat fil- Tarikh wal-Siyasa wal-Iqtisad – al-Nadwa al-Diplomasiyya al-Ithna 'Ashariyya.* Ed. 'Ali Humaydan. Abu Dhabi: Foreign Ministry, 1992, pp. 80–94, 108–150.
3. Muhammad 'Abd al-Salam, *Al-Jumhuriyya Bayna al-Sultana wal-Kabila fil-Yaman al-Shimaliyya.* Cairo: Sharikat al-Amal lil-Tiba'a wal-Nashr wal-Tawzi', 1988, p. 193. 'Abd al-Salam is the pen name associated with Abu Bakr al-Saqqaf, a Yemeni sociologist.

Chapter 1. Ecological, Cultural and Historical Structures

1. Christian Julien Robin, "Yemen", *Encyclopedia of the Qur'an.* Ed. Jane Dammen McAuliffe. http://www.paulyonline.brill.nl/entries/encyclopaedia-of-the-quran/yemen-COM_00223. Last accessed 1 May 2013.
2. For a thorough discussion of the extended definition of al-Yaman or *Bilad al-Yaman*, see 'Adnan Tarsisi, *Bilad Saba wa-Hadarat al-'Arab al-'Ula.* Beirut: Dar al-Fikr al-Mu'asir, 1990, pp. 10–11, 24–29.

3. Robin, "Yemen".
4. Ibn Khaldun chose to divide Yemen into seven central kingdoms: Zabid (in Tihama), Aden, Sanaa, Sa'da, Yamama, Najran and Hadramawt. In his discussion, Ibn Khaldun also mentions the debate over whether or not the last three provinces belong to Yemen. See Muhammad Husayn al-Farah, *Al-Yaman fi ta'rikh Ibn Khaldun*. Sanaa: al-Hay'a al-'Amma lil-Kitab, 2001, pp. 644–672.
5. Upper and Lower Yemen are separated by the mountainous ridge that severs Ta'izz and Ibb from the arid northern highland region. Others identify the cut-off point differently. See, for example, D. Thomas Gochenour, "Towards Sociology of the Islamization of Yemen", *Contemporary Yemen: Politics and Historical Background*. Ed. B.R. Pridham. London: Croom Helm, 1984, pp. 1–19.
6. W. H. Ingrams, *The Yemen: Imams, Rulers, and Revolutions*. New York and London: Praeger, 1964, p. 12.
7. For example, along the strip from the north – from Jizan to Hudayda – sugar, tea, matches, weaponry, ammunition, silver and incense were imported. See Shelagh Weir, *A Tribal Order: Politics and Law in the Mountains of Yemen*. 1st ed. Modern Middle East Series no. 23. Austin: University of Texas Press, 2007, p. 20.
8. Yarim is a major town located on the main road about halfway between Sanaa and Ta'izz. See Robert D. Burrowes, *Historical Dictionary of Yemen*. 2nd ed. Historical Dictionaries of Asia, Oceania, and the Middle East no. 72. Lanham, MD: Scarecrow Press, 2010, p. 332.
9. Fu'ad al-Banna, *Al-Haraka al-Siyasiyya al-Shi'iyya fil-Yaman*. Dubai, 2009.
10. J. Leigh Douglas, "The Free Yemeni Movement, 1935–1962", *Contemporary Yemen: Politics and Historical Background*. Ed. B. R. Pridham. London: Croom Helm, 1984, p. 7.
11. For more on the beginning of the Zaydiyya and its main tenets, see Hasan Hudayri Ahmad, *Qiyam al-Dawla al-Zaydiyya fil-Yaman*. Cairo: Madbuli, 1996, pp. 25–50.
12. In the first few centuries of its existence, the Zaydiyya experienced internal struggles as a division emerged between two different schools of thought about the future of the Zaydiyya. The divisive issue was the great influence of the Mu'tazila upon the Zaydiyya, with the first camp seeking to preserve it, the second rejecting the Mu'tazila influence and seeking to restore the pure, original Zaydiyya school. See Muhammad 'Isa al-Hariri, *Dirasat wa-Buhuth fi ta'rikh al-Yaman al-Islami*. Cairo: 'Alam al-Kutub lil-Tiba'a wal-Nashr wal-Tawzi', 1998, pp. 65–71.

13. Weir, *A Tribal Order: Politics and Law in the Mountains of Yemen*, pp. 229–236.
14. An additional Shi'i offshoot consisting of tens of thousands of believers, historically identified with Yemen by most accounts, is the Sulaymani branch of the Isma'ilis. Unlike Zaydis, the Sulaymani Isma'ilis believe that the Mahdi (the hidden imam) will return from the place of his occultation to lead the community. According to the Isma'ili view, the last imam was Isma'il ibn Ja'far al-Sadiq, the seventh in the dynasty of the *Ithna 'Ashariyya* (the Twelvers).
15. Amin al-Rihani, *Muluk al-Arab: Rihla fil-Bilad al-Arabiyya*. Beirut: Dar al-Jil, 1987, pp. 177–182.
16. Cornelis van Arendonk, *Les debuts de l'imamat zaidite au Yemen*. Leyden: E. J. Brill, 1960, p. 256.
17. Weir, *A Tribal Order: Politics and Law in the Mountains of Yemen*, p. 11.
18. Robert W. Stookey, *Yemen: The Politics of the Yemen Arab Republic*. Westview Special Studies on the Middle East. Boulder: Westview Press, 1978, p. 173.
19. Ibid.
20. James Heyworth-Dunne, *Al-Yemen: A General Social, Political and Economic Survey*. Cairo: Renaissance Bookshop, 1952.
21. 'Abd al-Wasi' Ibn Yahya al-Wasi'i, *Ta'rikh al-Yaman: Al-Musamma' Furjat al-Humum wal-Huznfi Hawadith wa-Tarikh al-Yaman*. Cairo: Al-Matba'ah Salafiyah wa-Maktabatuha, 1927, pp. 319–320.
22. Manfred W. Wenner, *Modern Yemen, 1918–1966*. Johns Hopkins University Studies in Historical and Political Science v. 85, no. 1. Baltimore: Johns Hopkins University Press, 1967, p. 38.
23. Weir, *A Tribal Order: Politics and Law in the Mountains of Yemen*, pp. 2–3.
24. Paul Dresch, *Tribes, Government, and History in Yemen*. Oxford: Clarendon Press, 1989, pp. 330–338.
25. 'Adil Nur al-Din, *al-Yaman, Madiha wa-Hadiruha wa-Mustaqbaluha*. Cairo: Idarat al-Shu'un al-'Amma wal-Tawzi' al-Ma'anawi, 1964, p. 19.
26. Barak A. Salmoni, Bryce Loidolt and Madeleine Wells, *Regime and Periphery in Northern Yemen: The Huthi Phenomenon*. Santa Monica: RAND Corporation, 2010, pp. 47–48.
27. Weir, *A Tribal Order: Politics and Law in the Mountains of Yemen*, pp. 1–6.
28. A. S. Tritton, *The Rise of the Imams of Sanaa*. Hyperion reprint ed. Westport, Conn: Hyperion Press, 1981, p. 110.
29. John Baldry, "Al-Yaman and the Turkish Occupation 1849–1914", *Arabica* 23.2 (1976): 156–196 (158).

30. Ibid, pp. 160–163; Wenner, *Modern Yemen*, pp. 42–43; for a thorough and interesting discussion on the Ottoman presence in Yemen, see Caesar E. Farah, *The Sultan's Yemen: Nineteenth-Century Challenges to Ottoman Rule*. London: I.B.Tauris, 2002, p. 26.
31. Paul Dresch, *A History of Modern Yemen*. Cambridge: Cambridge University Press, 2000, p. 6.
32. For example, see Farah, *The Sultan's Yemen: Nineteenth-Century Challenges to Ottoman Rule*.
33. Hasan Ibrahim Hasan, *al-Yaman: al-Bilad al-Sa'ida*. Cairo: Dar al-Ma'arif, N.D., p. 124.
34. For example, see Muhammad ibn Ahmad Nahrawali and Clive K. Smith, *Lightning over Yemen: A History of the Ottoman Campaign (1569–71)*. The Library of Ottoman Studies Vol. 3. London, New York: I.B.Tauris, 2002.
35. Thomas Kühn, "Shaping and Reshaping Colonial Ottomanism: Contesting Boundaries of Difference and Integration in Ottoman Yemen, 1872–1919". *Comparative Studies of South Asia, Africa and the Middle East* 27.2 (2007): 315–331 (316).
36. Commander A. B. Haines headed the Bombay Marines and from the 1830s strongly promoted the establishment of a British base in Aden. Haines had a grand vision of Aden as a port, commercial centre and military base. After the occupation, he served as the British political agent in Aden until 1854. See Burrowes, *Historical Dictionary of Yemen*, p. 162.
37. For further details on the negotiation between Captain Haines and Aden's previous owner, the Sultan of Lahaj, see Dresch, *A History of Modern Yemen*, pp. 18–20.
38. The Venetian explorer Marco Polo (1254–1323), who stumbled upon Aden in his journey, described it as sitting on the most open, narrow and rigid route, which was preferred by the returning traders from India and the East. The discovery of the Cape of Good Hope and the opening of alternative trade routes to the East marked the beginning of Aden's decline, which continued until the appearance of the British, who held on determinedly to the coast of the Gulf of Aden in 1839.
39. Note by Lt. Col. Jacob, Assistant Resident Aden, *Arab Bulletin*, no. 49, 30 April 1917.
40. By 1954, when the British signed their last protectorate agreement, they had already signed around 90 separate agreements with small polities whose combined populations did not exceed 750,000.
41. The border that was established would become, with minor changes, the border between the two Yemens in 1967.
42. Al-Rihani, *Muluk al-Arab*, p. 178.

43. Robin Leonard Bidwell, *The Two Yemens*. Harlow, Essex; Boulder, CO: Longman; Westview Press, 1983, p. 55.
44. Wenner, *Modern Yemen*, p. 44.
45. Muhammad Yahya al-Haddad, *Ta'rikh al-Yaman al-Siyasi al-Mu'asir*. Beirut: Manshurat al-Madina, 1986, p. 91.
46. Bidwell, *The Two Yemens,* p. 57; al-Haddad, *Ta'rikh al-Yaman al-Siyasi al-Mu'asir*, p. 91.
47. Dresch, *A History of Modern Yemen*, p. 6.
48. Wenner, *Modern Yemen*, p. 45; an interesting discussion about the various geographical definitions of "Greater Yemen" can be found in Husayn bin 'Ali al-Wasi', *al-Yaman al-Kubra: Kitab Jughrafi Jiuluji Tahribi*. Cairo: Matba'at Al-Nahdha Al-Arabiyya, 1962.
49. Bidwell, *The Two Yemens*, p. 57; Stookey, *Yemen: The Politics of the Yemen Arab Republic*, p. 163.
50. Wenner, *Modern Yemen*, p. 47.
51. Thomas Kühn, however, views the agreement as an inextricable part of imperial policy, which was meant to bring the *vilayet* of Yemen under Ottoman imperial territory and to bring the Zaydi Imamate under Ottoman administration. See Kühn, "Shaping and Reshaping Colonial Ottomanism", pp. 315–317.
52. Bidwell, *The Two Yemens*, p. 58; Wenner, *Modern Yemen*, p. 49.
53. Benedict Anderson, *Imagined Communities: Reflections on the Origin and Spread of Nationalism*. London, New York: Verso, 1991.
54. Al-Wasi', *Al-Yaman al-Kubra*, pp. 11–21.
55. Sultan Nagi, "The Genesis of the Call for Yemeni Unity", *Contemporary Yemen: Politics and Historical Background*. Ed. B. R. Pridham. London: Croom Helm, 1984, pp. 240–260.
56. For further elaboration on Yahya's territorial claims and British reactions, see *Arab Bulletin*, "Yemen: Overtures from the Imam". 58 (5 August 1917): n.pag.
57. Richard Sanger, *The Arabian Peninsula*. Select Bibliographies Reprint Series. New York: Books for Libraries Press, 1970, p. 111.
58. For a comprehensive analysis of the formation of the Saudi state, see Joseph Kostiner, *The Making of Saudi Arabia, 1916–1936: From Chieftaincy to Monarchical State*. New York: Oxford University Press, 1993.
59. Bidwell, *The Two Yemens*, p. 106.
60. Robert W. Stookey, *South Yemen: A Marxist Republic in Arabia*. Profiles: Nations of the Contemporary Middle East. Boulder: Westview Press, 1982, pp. 40–43.
61. *Arab Bulletin*, "Idrisi and Imam", 13 (1 August 1916): n.pag.; *Arab Bulletin*, "Notes: Yemen News", 60 (20 August 1917), n.pag.; *Arab Bulletin*, "Untitled", 61 (1 September 1917).

62. Dresch, *A History of Modern Yemen*, pp. 28–29; Wenner, *Modern Yemen*, pp. 142–143, 149–150.
63. In 1912, on the eve of the war and in the framework of the struggle between the Ottomans and the Italians on the coastline, the Italians lent similar support to Muhammad al-Idrisi and even bombed Hudayda and its port in their battle against the Ottomans.
64. John Baldry, "Anglo-Italian Rivalry in Yemen and 'Asir, 1900–1934". *Die Welt des Islams* 17.1/4 (1976): 155–193 (156, 160, 164–166, 171–175, 178–179).
65. This treaty put an end to the conflict between the signatories and provided for the withdrawal of the imam's forces to north of the Anglo-Ottoman line of 1904.
66. Al-Haddad, *Ta'rikh al-Yaman al-Siyasi al-Mu'asir*, p. 92–94.
67. Hostage-taking was also seen within tribal confederations. Dana Adams Schmidt explains that Shaykh 'Abdallah al-Ahmar's hold on the Hashid confederation began to break up in the spring of 1964 when the traditional system of hostages by which he ensured the loyalty of other tribal *shaykhs* suddenly broke up. See Dana Adams Schmidt, *Yemen: The Unknown War.* London: Bodley Head, 1968, p. 175.
68. A more detailed explanation on the hostage system can be found in Weir, *A Tribal Order: Politics and Law in the Mountains of Yemen*, pp. 273–275. In her extended anthropological fieldwork on Jabal Razih, Weir argues that the hostage system shows how easily the tribal structures of Razih could be harnessed to new administrative purposes.
69. Heyworth-Dunne in *Al-Yemen: A General Social, Political and Economic Survey* shows that the imam not only took tribesman as hostages but also members of *sadah* families.
70. For a more detailed analysis of Yahya's rule with regard to the tribes, see Fadhl 'Ali Ahmad Abu Ghanim, *al-Buniyya al-Qibaliyya fil-Yaman bayn al-'Istimrar wal-Taghayyur.* Cairo: Dar al-Hikma al-Yamaniyya, 1991, pp. 161–169.
71. J. E. Peterson, *Yemen: The Search for a Modern State.* London: Croom Helm, 1982, p. 41.
72. In 1953, the reserve force totalled around 40,000 soldiers. For comprehensive research on the army and its divisions, see Sultan Nagi, *al-Ta'rikh al-'Askari lil-Yaman: 1839–1967.* Publisher unknown, 1967, pp. 113–115.
73. Ibid, pp. 108–129.
74. Edgar O'Ballance, *The War in the Yemen.* Connecticut: Archon Books, 1971, p. 40.
75. Sultan Nagi, *al-Ta'rikh al-'Askari lil-Yaman*, pp. 90–91; see also FO 94/1261, 1939. All archival documents cited are from the Public Records Office, London.

76. Samir Muhammad Ahmad al-'Abday, *al-Wahda al-Yamaniyya wal-Nitham al-Iqlimi al-'Arabi*. Cairo: Madbuli, 1997, p. 20.
77. For a discussion on Yahya's Imamate and the various challenges that he confronted, from the vantage point of a researcher of the emergence of the nationalist movement in Yemen, see 'Ali 'Abd al-Qawi al-Ghafari, *al-Wahda al-Yamaniyya: al-Waqi wal-Mustaqbal*. Sanaa: Kitab al-Thawabit, 1997, pp. 59–75.
78. The first population census was carried out in North Yemen in 1975. The total population was calculated at 4,705,336. See M. W. Wenner, *The Yemen Arab Republic: Development and Change in an Ancient Land*. Boulder CO: Westview Press, 1991, p. 20.
79. Members of the movement did not identify themselves as members of the "Brotherhood" and did not call their movement by this name. However, they were perceived and treated by the population as the Muslim Brotherhood. See J. Leigh Douglas, "The Free Yemeni Movement, 1935–1962", *Contemporary Yemen: Politics and Historical Background*. Ed. B. R. Pridham. London: Croom Helm, 1984, pp. 36–37.
80. Al-Wartalani allegedly inspired the group of conspirators who planned and carried out the 1948 revolution.
81. Shukri Hassan, "Al-Ikhwan al-Muslimun fil-Yaman". *Al-Tali'a al-Yamaniyya*, no. 8 (September-October 1984), pp. 76–77.
82. Al-'Abdali, *al-Wahda al-Yamaniyya wal-Nitham al-Iqlimi al-'Arabi*, p. 21.
83. J. Leigh Douglas, and G. Chimienti, *The Free Yemeni Movement, 1935–1962*. Beirut: The American University of Beirut, 1987, pp. 242–243.
84. Al-'Abdali, al-Wahda *al-Yamaniyya wal-Nitham al-Iqlimi al-'Arabi*, pp. 21–22; Sultan Nagi, *al-Ta'rikh al-'Askari lil-Yaman*, pp. 119–122.
85. Some of the sources pointed to Shaykh 'Ali Nasir al-Qarda'i of the Murad tribe as the perpetrator. Rivalries between Imami forces and the Murad tribe, which was known for its autonomous posture, had led to a fierce struggle between the regime and this tribe by the end of the 1920s. Most sources, however, agree that Abdallah al-Wazir had conspired against the imam and had a hand in his assassination.
86. Gene Currivan, "New Yemen Regime Seizes $40,000,000 Carried Away Just Before Assassination". *The New York Times*, 21 February 1948: 6; see also al-Ghafari, *al-Wahda al-Yamaniyya*, pp. 59–71.
87. Douglas provides the names of those that were executed and their organizational affilitation. See Douglas and Chimienti, *The Free Yemeni Movement, 1935–1962*, p. 156.
88. Yitzhak Oron, ed., *Middle East Record*. Vol. 2. Tel Aviv: The Moshe Dayan Center, 1961, p. 696.

89. Ibrahim Rashid, *Yemen under the Rule of Imam Ahmad.* Documents on the History of Arabia. Chapel Hill: Documentary Publications, 1985, pp. 67–69.
90. Haydar 'Ali Naji al-'Izzi, *Inqilab 'Amm 1955 fil-Yaman.* Aden: Wizarat al-Thaqafah wal-Siyaha, 2004, pp. 60–67.
91. For a concise discussion of the phenomenon of the centrality of the Arab officers in various Middle Eastern countries, see Manfred Halpern, *The Politics of Social Change in the Middle East and North Africa.* A Rand Corporation Research Study Series. Scranton: Princeton University Press, 1963, pp. 53–57, 257–259.
92. Stookey, *Yemen: The Politics of the Yemen Arab Republic*, pp. 190–91; Wenner, *Modern Yemen*, pp. 83–85.
93. See, for example, Dresch, *A History of Modern Yemen*, p. 78.
94. Ahmad al-Saqqaf, *Ana 'A'id min al-Yaman.* Cairo: Dar-al-Katib al-'Arabi, 1962, pp. 27–46; for additional information on the events of 1955, see al-Ghafari, *al-Wahda al-Yamaniyya*, p. 70.
95. Al-Haddad, *Ta'rikh al-Yaman al-Siyasi al-Mu'asir*, p. 287.
96. Fu'ad al-Ba'dani, 'Al-Zaydiyyun wal-Thawra al-Yamaniyya', in: *Al-Huthiyyun fil-Yaman.* Dubai: Markaz al-Misbar lil-Dirasat wal-Buhuth, 2010, pp. 212–215; 'Abdallah Ahmad al-Thawr, *Hadhihi Hiyya al-Yaman.* Beirut: Dar al-Fikr al-'Arabi lil-Tiba'a wal-Nashr, 1976, pp. 25–32.
97. For further details about the al-Khawlan Revolt, see Nagi, *al-Ta'rikh al-'Askari lil-Yaman*, pp. 187–190.
98. *Al-Difa'*, 8 October 1959.
99. *Al-Hayat*, 22 January 1961.
100. Al-'Izzi, *Inqilab 'Amm 1955*, pp. 41–49.
101. At first, the League was named "The League of the Sons of South Arabia" (*Rabitat Abna' al-Janub al-'Arabi*). Other prominent members of the League were 'Abdallah Nadhib, Shaykhan al-Habashi and Qahtan al-Sha'bi. The League developed its activity out of Aden and included elements from the nationalist and Marxist groups. For further details, see al-Ghafari, *al-Wahda al-Yamaniyya*, pp. 77–78.
102. Burrowes, *Historical Dictionary of Yemen*, p. 344.
103. To a large extent the League's agenda was similar to that of other workers' unions that strove for the creation of an independent entity in the south of Yemen. The League did not stick to its original messages and toward the end of the 1950s the Saudis managed to win the loyalty of its activists.
104. Spencer Mawby, "Britain's Last Imperial Frontier: The Aden Protectorates, 1952–1959". *The Journal of Imperial and Commonwealth History* 29.2 (2001): 75–100. http://www.tandfonline.com/doi/pdf/10.1080/03086530108583120. Last accessed 12 June 2013, pp. 79–81.

105. For Foster's impressions and experiences, see Donald Foster, *Landscape with Arabs: Travels in Aden and South Arabia*. Brighton: Clifton Books, 1969, p. 51.
106. A. N. Porter and A. J. Stockwell, *British Imperial Policy and Decolonization, 1938–1964, Vol. 1. 1938–51*. Basingstoke: Macmillan, 1987, p. 375.
107. There were high command officials in the British imperial system who also shared Hickinbotham's opinion, particularly Kennedy Trevaskis and Hugh Boustead.
108. For such voices within the British policy-making apparatus, see "Record of a Meeting between CO and FO", 19 August 1954, CO 1015/829.
109. For an interesting comparative debate on the British idea of a federation and similar endeavours that were carried out in other colonies, see Fred Halliday, *Arabia Without Sultans*. London: Saqi Books, 2002, p. 185.
110. Ibid., pp. 181–182.
111. Ibid.
112. Hickinbotham to Lennox-Boyd, 28 October 1954, CO 1015/830.
113. Luce to Morgan, 23 December 1956, CO 1015/809.
114. Ingrams, *The Yemen: Imams, Rulers, and Revolutions*, p. 99.
115. Hickinbotham had met with the imam in Ta'izz in October 1954. See Ta'izz to FO, 19 October 1954, CO 1015/830; Hickinbotham to Lennox-Boyd, 28 October 1954, CO 1015/830.
116. Luce to Secretary of State, 28 January 1957, CO 1015/1298.
117. Luce to Secretary of State, 2 December 1957, CO 1015/1304.
118. Al-Ghafari, *al-Wahda al-Yamaniyya*, p. 74.
119. In September 1962, a programme to establish the Federation of South Arabia was proclaimed and in the beginning of 1963 it was completed.
120. Note by Kemp, February 1958, CO 1015/1266.
121. Wenner, *Modern Yemen*, pp. 125–126.
122. The British deliberations and the policy that they eventually carried out included confidential operations to provide support to the Royalists in the north. See Clive Jones, "Where the State Feared to Tread: Britain, Britons, Covert Action and the Yemen Civil War, 1962–1964". *Intelligence and National Security*, 21.5 (2006): 717–737. http://www.tandfonline.com/doi/pdf/10.1080/02684520600957688. Last accessed 12 June 2013. One of the arguments that Jones raises refers to the Israeli involvement alongside the British in support of the Royalists in order to deepen the Egyptian entanglement in Yemen.
123. Ahmad broke off the alliance with Nasser with a publicized poem that criticized Nasser for not being Islamic enough. See Dresch, *A History of Modern Yemen*, p. 86.
124. Nagi, *al-Ta'rikh al-'Askari lil-Yaman*, p. 207.

125. For more on the activity of the movements in the 1940s, see al-Ghafari, *al-Wahda al-Yamaniyya*, p. 55–56.
126. Sarah Phillips, *Yemen's Democracy Experiment in Regional Perspective: Patronage and Pluralized Authoritarianism*. New York: Palgrave Macmillan, 2008, pp. 90–91.
127. Other leaders in the region also enjoyed a similar fate. Their attempts to pass conservative reforms drowned in the sea of change and were not acknowledged by their critics and other historians. Another case of this is the Omani ruler, Sa'id bin Taymur (1932–1970), who tried to traditionally navigate his state in view of the waves of change and the oil economy. See U. Rabi, *The Emergence of States in a Tribal Society: Oman under Sa'id Bin Taymur, 1932–1970*. Portland: Sussex Academic Press, 2006.

Chapter 2. The Age of Revolutions: 1962–1978

1. For more on how the monarchies coped with the challenges of the day in the Arab World, see Joseph Kostiner, "Introduction", *Middle East Monarchies: The Challenge of Modernity*. Ed. Joseph Kostiner. Boulder: Lynne Rienner Publishers, 2000, pp. 1–12.
2. 'Abdallah al-Sallal was one of 13 young men who had been sent by Imam Yahya to Iraq in the mid-1930s, the first group of that sort. From that time forward he was very active in the army and led a group of army officers that aspired towards reform and change.
3. On the goals of the revolution and the aspiration to establish a new order, see 'Ali 'Abd al-Qawi al-Ghafari, *Al-Wahda al-Yamaniyya: al-Waqi' wal-Mustaqbal*. Sanaa: Kitab al-Thawabit, 1997, pp. 86–90; Radio Sanaa, 26 September 1962 in BBC Worldwide Monitoring, 26 September 1962.
4. In 1961, the British withdrew from Kuwait and Kuwait became an independent state. Immediately, Iraq attempted to occupy Kuwait. This event was instructive for the British as they considered their policy and presence in Yemen. For details on the Kuwait crisis and British policy there, see Uzi Rabi, "Kuwait's Changing Strategic Posture: Historical Patterns". *Journal of South Asian and Middle Eastern Studies* 27.4 (2004): 52–65.
5. On the roots of Egyptian involvement in Yemen from the Saudi viewpoint, see Saeed M. Badeeb, *The Saudi Egyptian Conflict Over North Yemen, 1962–1970*. Boulder: Westview Press, 1986. For the Egyptian viewpoint, see the memoirs of an Egyptian officer who served in North Yemen during the Egyptian invasion. Ali Abdel Rahman Rahmy, *The Egyptian Policy in the Arab World: Intervention in Yemen 1962–1967: Case Study*. Washington DC: University Press of America, 1983.

6. Mahmud 'Adil Ahmad, *Dhikrayat Harb al-Yaman, 1962–1967*, p. 290. Ahmad was an Egyptian officer who served in North Yemen during the Egyptian invasion.
7. Edgar O'Ballance, *The War in the Yemen*. Connecticut: Archon Books, 1971, p. 63. See also, Claude Deffarge and Gordian Troeller, *Yemen 62–69: de la révolution "sauvage" à la trêve des guerriers*. L'Histoire que nous vivons. Paris: R. Laffont, 1969, pp. 25–26, 122–124, 209–216. Deffarge and Troeller argue that President Nasser was instrumental before and during the revolution and that the revolution was a clear reflection of his vision.
8. *Ruz al-Yusuf*, 1 October 1962; *Al-Jarida*, 2 October 1962.
9. Paul Dresch, "The Tribal Factor in Yemeni Politics", *The Yemeni War of 1994: Causes and Consequences*. Ed. Jamal S. al-Suwaidi. London: Saqi Books, 1995, p. 43.
10. Dana Adams Schmidt, *Yemen: The Unknown War*. London: Bodley Head, 1968, pp. 48–49.
11. Not all tribes joined in for ideological reasons. For example, the Tihama tribes joined in because their leading *shaykh*, Muhammad 'Abdallah al-'Ammuri, had been executed in Sanaa by the Republicans.
12. Sultan Nagi, *al-Ta'rikh al-'Askari lil-Yaman: 1839–1967*. Publisher unknown, 1967, pp. 220–241.
13. Nasser's speech in Port Said, Radio Cairo, 23 December 1962 in BBC Worldwide Monitoring, 24 December 1962.
14. For more on the Saudi security perception on this issue, see Mark N. Katz, "Yemeni Unity and Saudi Security". *Middle East Policy* 1.1 (1992): 117–135. http://digilib.gmu.edu/jspui/bitstream/1920/3118/1/yemeni%20unity%20and%20saudi%20security.pdf. Last accessed 13 June 2013.
15. On American policy in Yemen, see Edward F. Prados, *The US and Yemen: A Half-Century of Engagement*. Washington: Center for Contemporary Arab Studies, 2005, pp. 10–12.
16. See a report on the British Cabinet meeting of 5 February 1963: CAB 130/189 GEN 776, "Cabinet Meeting 5 Feb. 1963".
17. For example, see the Foreign Minister's letter to one of the Members of Parliament in which he argues that the British should not recognize the republic. FO 371/174639 BM 1051/2.
18. CO 1055/11 80075, "Research Department Memorandum: The Yemen Claim to Aden", 12 June 1964.
19. O'Ballance, *The War in the Yemen*, p. 127.
20. Karl Pieragostini, "Britain, Aden and South Arabia: Abandoning Empire", *British Policy in Aden and the Protectorates 1955–67: Last Outpost of a Middle East Empire*. Vol. 10. London: Routledge, 2004, pp. 46–47.

21. Ibid., p. 46.
22. O'Ballance, *The War in the Yemen*, p. 127.
23. See the letter from the governor of Aden, Trevaskis, to the state treasurer regarding the colonies. 14 October 1963, CO 1055/213; Paul Dresch, *A History of Modern Yemen.* Cambridge: Cambridge University Press, 2000, p. 237. For a comprehensive account of all the military and paramilitary units which existed in Aden and the Protectorates throughout the British period, see Frank Edwards, *The Gaysh: A History of the Aden Protectorate Levies 1927–61 and the Federal Regular Army of South Arabia 1961–67.* Solihull: HELION & Company, 2003.
24. For the British Prime Minister's memorandum on this issue, see: FO 371/174639 BM/1051/10.
25. Yemeni scholars who published in Yemen before the end of the twentieth century depicted the NLF as a movement whose goal was to unite Yemen. For example al-Ghafari describes the Nationalist Front as a genuine Yemeni movement rather than a product of Egyptian influence. See al-Ghafari, *al-Wahda al-Yamaniyya*, pp. 70–77.
26. For a thorough analysis of Egyptian policies in North Yemen, see Dresch, *A History of Modern Yemen*, pp. 89–96.
27. Robert W. Stookey, *Yemen: The Politics of the Yemen Arab Republic.* Westview Special Studies on the Middle East. Boulder: Westview Press, 1978, pp. 226–228.
28. On the eve of the revolution North Yemen's population was around 4.5 million people. Sanaa, the capital, had a population of around 60,000. Hudayda, a central port city, had a population of about 35,000. Ta'izz, a trade city in the south-west of the country, had a population of 20,000; another sparsely populated city, Sa'da, was a Zaydi stronghold in the north of the country close to the Saudi-Yemeni border. City dwellers, therefore, represent a small slice of the general population. The majority of the population belonged to tribes from the mountains or villages.
29. Dresch, *A History of Modern Yemen*, p. 94.
30. Dresch, "The Tribal Factor in the Yemeni Crisis". Dresch demonstrates how there can be differences of opinion between and within tribes.
31. For more details on the events that preceded the coup of the Free Yemenites, see Ahmad Yusuf Ahmad, *al-Dawr al-Masri fil-Yaman: 1962–1967.* Cairo: General Egyptian Book Organization (GEBO), 1981, pp. 110–111.
32. For a thorough discussion of Egypt's policy during these years, see Deffarge and Troeller, *Yemen 62–69: de la Revolution 'Sauvage' a la Treve des Guerriers*, pp. 109–121.

33. See for example Fred Halliday, *Arabia without Sultans*, pp. 108–115; and al-Ghafari, *al-Wahda al-Yamaniyya*, pp. 79–83.
34. At the end of 1963 al-Baydani left Yemen, and toward the end of 1966 the Egyptians appointed him the Yemeni Ambassador to Lebanon.
35. Nagi, *al-Ta'rikh al-'Askari lil-Yaman*, p. 207.
36. Radio Sanaa, 22 February in BBC Worldwide Monitoring, 24 February 1963.
37. Robert D. Burrowes, "Prelude to Unification: The Yemen Arab Republic, 1962–1990". *International Journal of Middle East Studies* 23.4 (1991): 483–506.
38. Shelagh Weir, *A Tribal Order: Politics and Law in the Mountains of Yemen*. 1st ed. Modern Middle East Series no. 23. Austin: University of Texas Press, 2007, p. 281.
39. Donna Lee Bowen and Evelyn A. Early, *Everyday Life in the Muslim Middle East*. Indiana Series in Middle East Studies. Bloomington: Indiana University Press, 2002, p. 367.
40. For more details on the Egyptian presence in Yemen, see Joseph Kostiner, *The Struggle for South Yemen*. London: Croom Helm, 1984, pp. 109–142. See also Ahmad, *al-Dawr al-Masri fil-Yaman: 1962–1967*.
41. For a brief report of Egypt's motivations and goals while invading Yemen, see Muhammah 'Ali al-Shahari and Ibrahim Wahib Fahmi, *Jamal 'Abd al-Nasir wa-Haqa'iq min Harb al-Yaman*. Beirut: Antun Jamil Saba, 1997.
42. Deffarge and Troeller, *Yemen 62–69: de la Revolution 'Sauvage' a la Treve des Guerriers*, pp. 189–196.
43. Ahmad, *Dhikrayat Harb al-Yaman, 1962–1967*, pp. 286, 290, 591–597.
44. David M. Witty, "A Regular Army in Counterinsurgency Operations: Egypt in North Yemen, 1962–1967". *Journal of Military History* 65.2 (2001): 401–440.
45. Wilfred Thesiger, "War in Yemen – 2: Tribesmen Acknowledge the Imam's Rule". *The Times*, 22 December 1966, p. 11.
46. Youssef Aboul-Enein, "The Egyptian-Yemen War (1962–67): Egyptian Perspectives on Guerrilla Warfare". *Infantry Magazine* 93.1 (2004): 19–23.
47. Dresch, *A History of Modern Yemen*, p. 103.
48. 'Abd al-Malik al-Tayyib, *Al-Thawra wal-Nafaq al-Muthlim*.Sanaa: 'Abd al-Malik bin Muhammad al-Tayyib, 1995, p. 9.
49. For more details on the composition of Nu'man's government, see al-Tayyib, *Al-Thawra wal-Nafaq al-Muthlim*, pp. 21–31.
50. Gregory F. Gause, *Saudi-Yemeni Relations: Domestic Structures and Foreign Influence*. New York: Columbia University Press, 1990, p. 66.
51. Dresch, *A History of Modern Yemen*, p. 99.

52. Peter Hinchcliffe, John T. Ducker and Maria Holt, *Without Glory in Arabia: The British Retreat from Aden*. International Library of Colonial History. London: I.B.Tauris, 2006, pp. 65–66.
53. Schmidt, *Yemen: The Unknown War*, p. 182.
54. For a detailed report on the Harad Conference see O'Ballance, *The War in the Yemen*, pp. 153–170.
55. Joseph Kostiner, *South Yemen's Revolutionary Strategy, 1970–1985: From Insurgency to Bloc Politics*. Boulder: Westview Press, 1990, pp. 13–18. See also H. Lackner, *P.D.R. Yemen: Outpost of Socialist Development in Arabia*. Political Science of the Middle East, no. 27. London: Ithaca Press, 1985, pp. 40–42.
56. For more discussion of the rifts within the NLF leadership on this issue, see Sultan Ahmad 'Umar, *Nathra fi-Tatawwur al-Mujtama' al-Yamani*. Beirut: Dar al-Tali'a lil-Tiba'a wal-Nashr, 1970, p. 182. 'Umar treats the group of traders and *shaykhs* as a "bourgeoisie faction".
57. The rivalry of the camps can be exemplified by the actions of a pro-Marxist member of the NLF, Muti' al-Dammaj. Al-Dammaj, a resident of Ibb, was exiled to Aden during the imam's rule, returned and conquered Ibb during the 1962 Revolution, and now rejected cooperation with Egypt. People like al-Dammaj became staunch ideological and financial supporters of the NLF in the south, when Egypt cold-shouldered the NLF. Dresch, *A History of Modern Yemen*, p. 107.
58. According to the majority of the academic literature, the two fronts are known by their initials. Hence, it is NLF for the Nationalist Liberation Front and FLOSY for the Front for the Liberation of South Yemen.
59. On the tribal maneouvring between the two fronts, see al-Tayyib, *Al-Thawra wal-Nafaq al-Muthlim*, pp. 215–216; and Kostiner, *The Struggle for South Yemen*, pp. 135–136.
60. *Al-Hayat*, 23 and 27 June 1969.
61. Juzaylan was a staunch supporter of Egypt and declared from the beginning that the 1962 Revolution should follow the lines of the 1952 Revolution in Egypt. He wrote a memoir. See 'Abdalla al-Juzaylan, *Al-Tarikh al-Sirri lil-Thawra al-Yamaniyya: 1956–1962*. Beirut: Dar al-'Awda, 1977, pp. 91–103.
62. Dresch, *A Modern History of Yemen*, p. 105.
63. For a narrative of the "the Egyptian Era" in Yemen, see Deffarge and Troeller, *Yemen 62–69: de la Revolution 'Sauvage' a la Treve des Guerriers*.
64. Andrew James McGregor, *A Military History of Modern Egypt: From the Ottoman Conquest to the Ramadan War*. Westport: Praeger Security International, 2006, p. 261.

65. Eric Rouleau, "Le Yemen: Voyage a Travers le Moyen Age", *Le Monde*, 11 May 1967.
66. O'Ballance, *The War in the Yemen*, p. 176.
67. Walid Mahmud 'Abd al-Nasir, "Awwal Tajriba Marksiyya 'Arabiyya", *Wujahat Nathar*, May 2010.
68. CO 1055/ 277 quoted in Dresch, *A History of Modern Yemen*, p. 97. It appears that the *na'ib* (Mahmud bin Hasan) was the brother of the Qutaybi *shaykh*, Sayf bin Hasan, who led the protest.
69. For example in the al-Dathina region, the British detained a camel convoy equipped with 45 land mines, 150 hand grenades and 200 rifles. See 'Adil Rida, *Muhawala li-Fahm al-Thawra al-Yamaniyya*. Cairo: al-Maktab al-Masri al-Hadith, 1974, p. 43. See also CO 1055/196, CO 1055/195.
70. Radio Cairo, 3 May 1964 in Summary of World Broadcasts (SWB), 3 May 1964.
71. Pieragostini, "Britain, Aden and South Arabia: Abandoning Empire", pp. 12–13, 48–51.
72. Rabi, "Kuwait's Changing Strategic Posture: Historical Patterns", pp. 52–65.
73. For more on the ATUC's sources of inspiration and its establishment, see Robert D. Burrowes, *Historical Dictionary of Yemen*. 2nd ed. Historical Dictionaries of Asia, Oceania, and the Middle East no. 72. Lanham, Md: Scarecrow Press, 2010, p. 66.
74. FO 371 174634 (BM 1041/3/G), 2 January 1964.
75. For example, Dresch, *A History of Modern Yemen*, pp. 96–97.
76. Fawwaz Traboulsi, "Les Transformations des Structures Tribales depuis l'independance du Yemen du Sud". *Cahier du Gremamo* 10 (1991): 226, p. 33.
77. For more details, see Spencer Mawby, *British Policy in Aden and the Protectorates 1955–67: Last Outpost of a Middle East Empire*. Vol. 10. London and New York: Routledge, 2004, pp. 90–126.
78. Ibid., p. 103.
79. The Labour government in London dismissed Trevaskis. This signalled a fresh approach to the issues of independence and security of South Arabia. Kennedy Trevaskis wrote his memoirs from South Arabia in *Shades of Amber: A South Arabian Episode*. London: Hutchinson, 1968.
80. Dresch, *A History of Modern Yemen*, p. 100.
81. Manifestations of this period and of the events that transpired in the south of Yemen are introduced in three books that summarize the abundance of sources and provide a reliable picture of the situation. See Shakir al-Jawhari, *Al-Sira' fi*

Aden. Cairo: Madbuli, 1992; Kostiner, *South Yemen's Revolutionary Strategy*; and Pieragostini, "Britain, Aden and South Arabia: Abandoning Empire". Among Yemeni writers there is no consensus regarding the events and their interpretation. Two contradictory versions can be found in Husayn Sulayman al-Adhal, *al-Istiqlal al-Da'i'*. Cairo: Dar al-Wazzan lil-Tiba'a wal-Nashr, 1988; and Muhammad Sa'id 'Abdallah (known as "Muhsin", who served for years as the head of the security apparatus), *Aden: Kifah Sha'bi wa-Hazima Imbaraturiyya*.

82. See al-Nasir, "Awwal Tajriba Marksiyya 'Arabiyya".
83. Robert W. Stookey, *South Yemen: A Marxist Republic in Arabia*. Profiles: Nations of the Contemporary Middle East. Boulder: Westview Press, 1982, pp. 54–57.
84. Dresch, *A History of Modern Yemen*, p. 112.
85. An interesting and thorough analysis of these policies can be found in D. Ledger, *Shifting Sands: The British in South Arabia*. London: Peninsular Pub., 1983.
86. M. Crouch, *An Element of Luck: To South Arabia and Beyond*. London: Radcliffe Press, 1993, p. 55.
87. Kostiner, *South Yemen's Revolutionary Strategy*, pp. 13–18.
88. Ledger, *Shifting Sands: The British in South Arabia*, p. 69; al-Adhal, *al-Istiqlal al-Da'i'*, p. 203.
89. CO 1055/74, FO 371/185241, 185243, 185244.
90. Al-Adhal, *Al-Istiqlal al- Da'i'*, pp. 213, 222–225, 232, 245.
91. For a more thorough explanation of the Radfan events, see J. Walker, *Aden Insurgency: The Savage War in South Arabia 1962–1967*. Kent: Spellmount, 2005, pp. 202–270.
92. For a summary of Britain's colonial chapter in Aden and a comparative view of the British presence in the Persian Gulf, see Uzi Rabi, "British Possessions in the Persian Gulf and Southwest Arabia: The Last Abandoned in the Middle East", *Britain and the Middle East: From Imperial Power to Junior Partner*. Eds. Zach Levey and Elie Podeh. Portland: Sussex Academic Press, 2008, pp. 264–279.
93. Muhammad 'Abd al-Salam, *Al-Jumhuriyya Bayna al-Sultana wal-Kabila fil-Yaman al-Shimaliyya*. Cairo: Sharikat al-Amal lil-Tiba'a wal-Nashr wal-Tawzi', 1988, p. 193.
94. Al-Sallal returned from exile in 1981 and died in March 1994.
95. Burrowes, *Historical Dictionary of Yemen*, p. 189–190.
96. Dresch, *A History of Modern Yemen*, p. 114.
97. O'Ballance, *The War in the Yemen*, p. 195.
98. Sa'id Ahmad al-Janahi, *Al-Haraka al-Wataniyya al-Yamaniyya: Min al-Thawra ila al-Wahda*. Aden: Markaz al-'Amal lil-Dirasat wal-Nashr, 1992, pp. 481–482.

99. Deffarge and Troeller, *Yemen 62–69: de la Revolution 'Sauvage' a la Treve des Guerriers*, pp. 264–265.
100. Leaders who were fully devoted to the revolutionary message, like 'Abd al-Fattah Isma'il, explained the conflict as one of the main reasons for the failure of attempts to unify Yemen.
101. Elham Manea, *Regional Politics in the Gulf: Saudi Arabia, Oman, Yemen.* London: Saqi Books, 2005, p. 37.
102. Abdul-Malik al-Thawr, "YSCC's upcoming round due on sideline of Riyadh meeting", *Yemen News Agency (SABA)*, 24 February 2010. http://www.sabanews.net/ar/print206916.htm. Last accessed 19 June 2013.
103. Robin Leonard Bidwell, *The Two Yemens.* Harlow, Essex; Boulder, CO: Longman; Westview Press, 1983, pp. 243–244.
104. Ibid.
105. Stookey, *South Yemen: A Marxist Republic in Arabia*, pp. 67–68.
106. Yasir al-'Arami, "Tanthim al-Qa'ida fil-Yaman: Min al-Hamish ila al-Matn", *Al-Huthiyyun fil-Yaman.* Dubai: Markaz al-Misbar lil-Dirasat wal-Buhuth, 2010, pp. 268–278.
107. Stookey, *Yemen: The Politics of the Yemen Arab Republic*, p. 262; Kiren Aziz Chaudhry, *The Price of Wealth: Economies and Institutions in the Middle East.* Cornell Studies in Political Economy. New York: Cornell University Press, 1997, pp. 125, 200.
108. *Al-Nahar*, 8 December 1970, p. 10.
109. Muhammad 'Ali al-Shahari, *al-Yaman: Al-Thawra fil-Janub wal-Intikasa fil-Shimal.* Beirut: Dar Ibn Khaldun, 1972, p. 226.
110. Al-Janahi, *al-Haraka al-Wataniyya al-Yamaniyya: Min al-Thawra ila al-Wahda*, p. 514.
111. Military Communiqué from the "Volunteers" Organization, February 1973, p. 211, quoted in Dresch, *A History of Modern Yemen*, p. 125.
112. Ibid., pp. 125–126.
113. Ibid., p. 126.
114. Michael Field, ed. "Saudi Arabia". *Middle East Annual Review.* Ann Arbor: University of Michigan, 1977, p. 292.
115. Robert D. Burrowes, *The Yemen Arab Republic: The Politics of Development, 1962–1986.* Boulder, CO: Westview Press, 1986, p. 29.
116. Burrowes, *Historical Dictionary of Yemen*, p. 188–194.
117. See *al-Sayyad* (Beirut), "Interview with Ibrahim al-Hamdi". 2 February 1975.
118. Sarah Phillips, *Yemen's Democracy Experiment in Regional Perspective*, p. 44.
119. *Ruz al-Yusuf*, 28 March 1977; *al-Ahram*, 13 April 1977.
120. Bidwell, *The Two Yemens*, p. 487.

121. Weir, *A Tribal Order: Politics and Law in the Mountains of Yemen*, p. 293.
122. *Al-Qabas* (Kuwait), 12, 13, 18 January 1977.
123. Gause, *Saudi-Yemeni Relations*, pp. 114–117.
124. *Al-Dustur* (London), 21–27 November 1977.
125. Ahmad Noman Qasim Al-Madhagi, *Yemen and the USA: A Super-Power and a Small-state Relationship, 1962–1992*. BAR International. London: I.B.Tauris, 1996, p. 96.
126. *Al-Dustur* (London), 21–27 November 1977.
127. *Al-Qabas*, 18 January 1977.
128. Burrowes, *The Yemen Arab Republic: The Politics of Development, 1962–1986*, p. 27.
129. For further details on the foundation of the NDF, see Burrowes, *Historical Dictionary of Yemen*, p. 243.
130. Tamar Yegnes, "The Yemeni Arab Republic". *Middle East Contemporary Survey*. Ed. Colin Legum. Vol. 1. New York: Holmes and Meier, 1976, pp. 652–655.
131. *Al-Qabas* (Kuwait), 18 January 1977. *Ruz al-Yusuf* (Cairo), 28 March 1977.
132. The suspect in the assassination of al-Hajri, Zuhayr Yusuf 'Akash, was identified by British security as a member of the PLO. His name was mentioned later in relation to the hijacking of a Lufthansa airplane in October 1977. Other reports in the Egyptian press attribute the assassination to an internal leadership struggle. The reports argued that the assassination was committed by followers of the former prime minister Muhsin al-'Ayni. *Al-Ahram*, 26 April 1977.
133. *Ruz al-Yusuf*, 5 September 1977.
134. *Al-Siyasa* (Kuwait), 13 October 1977.
135. *Al-Siyasa*, 25 September 1977.
136. *Radio Sanaa*, 25 September 1977, Daily Report: Near East and South Asia (DR), 27 September 1977.
137. *Al-Siyasa*, 6 October 1977.
138. *Al-Ahram*, 14 October 1977.
139. Burrowes, *Historical Dictionary of Yemen*, p. 157.
140. *Al-Nahar al-'Arabi wal-Duwali*, 19 November 1977.
141. *Ruz al-Yusuf*, 24 October 1977.
142. Ibid.
143. Two officers played a central role in al-Ghashmi's regime: Deputy Chief of General Staff 'Ali al-Shayba and Major 'Ali 'Abdallah Salih, the military commander of the Ta'izz province: Radio Sanaa, 26 October 1977, World News Connection, 28 October 1977.

144. *Al-Ahram*, 20 October 1977.
145. *Al-Ra'y al-'Amm*, 28 June 1978.
146. *Al-Hayat*, 21 March 1968.
147. *Al-Hayat*, 21 May 1969; *al-Ra'y al-'Amm*, 10 April 1969.
148. *Al-Hayat,* 10 April 1969.
149. For the centrality of the port in Aden's economy, see CO 725/97/4, CO 1055/157, "The Petrie Report", September 1959.
150. Michael C. Hudson, *Arab Politics: The Search for Legitimacy*. A Yale Paperbound. New Haven: Yale University Press, 1977, p. 352.
151. Dresch, *A History of Modern Yemen,* p. 121; Burrowes, *Historical Dictionary of Yemen*, p. 366.
152. For more on this see Ahmad 'Atiyya al-Masri, *Tajribat al-Yaman al-Dimuqratiyya*. Cairo: Dar al-Madani lil-Tiba'a wal-Nashr, 1974, pp. 548–550; Fathi 'Abd al-Fattah, *Tajribat al-Thawra fil-Yaman al-Dimuqratiyya*. Beirut: Dar Ibn Khaldun, 1974, pp. 99–104.
153. Further details about the 22 June events were given in an interview to an Egyptian paper by 'Abd al-Fattah Isma'il; see *al-Jumhuriyya*, "Interview with 'Abd al-Fattah Isma'il". 25 June 1969.
154. *Al-Ra'y al-'Amm*, 2 November 1970.
155. *Al-Jumhuriyya*, "Interview with 'Abd al-Fattah Isma'il".
156. See, for example, *al-Hayat*, 22 June 1969; *al-Hurriyya*, 23 June 1969.
157. Radio Aden, 2 November 1970, in BBC Worldwide Monitoring, 13 December 1970.
158. Eric Rouleau, "L'etoile Rouge sur le Yemen du Sud", *Le Monde*, 27 May 1972; Lackner, *P.D.R. Yemen: Outpost of Socialist Development*, pp. 64, 67.
159. Habib Abdulrab, *La Reine Étripée*. Paris: L'Harmattan littératures, 1998, pp. 14, 35, 136.
160. Al-Adhal, *al-Istiqlal al-Da'i'*, p. 408.
161. Fred Halliday, "Yemen's Unfinished Revolution: Socialism in the South". *Middle East Research & Information Project (MERIP)* 81 (1979): 3–20.
162. Dresch, *A History of Modern Yemen*, p. 122.
163. For a discussion on sectarianism within the new regime in the north, see 'Umar, *Nathra fi-Tatawwur al-Mujtama' al-Yamani*, pp. 194–195; Stookey, *Yemen: The Politics of the Yemen Arab Republic*, p. 253.
164. Halliday, *Arabia Without Sultans*, pp. 335–336.
165. Political leaders in the south determined that the number of migrants was one million, but this was obviously an exaggeration. The entire population of the south stood at less than two million, and according to Halliday, even 500,000 seemed exaggerated. Halliday, "Yemen's Unfinished Revolution", pp. 5–15.

166. Bidwell, *The Two Yemens*, pp. 256–257; Lackner, *P.D.R. Yemen: Outpost of Socialist Development*, p. 59.
167. The text of the "Cairo Agreement" can be found in Rida, *Muhawala li-fahm al-thawra al-Yamaniyya*, pp. 290–295.
168. *Al-Nahar*, 30 November 1972, p. 2.
169. *Al-Nahar*, 12 January 1973, p. 12; *al-Nahar*, 27 June 1973, p. 9: *al-Hawadith*, No. 485, 19 January 1973, p. 23; *al-Hawadith*, No. 865, 8 June 1973, pp. 25–26.
170. Halliday, *Arabia Without Sultans*, p. 269–270.
171. Bidwell, *The Two Yemens*, p. 263.
172. *Al-Hawadith*, No. 846, 26 January 1973, pp. 22–25.
173. *Al-Nahar*, 29 December 1972, p. 13; *al-Nahar*, 30 December 1972; *al-Nahar*, 15 January 1973, p. 10.
174. *Al-Nahar*, 10 January 1973, p. 8; *al-Nahar*, 14 January 1973, p. 10.
175. J. E. Peterson, *Yemen: The Search for a Modern State*. London: Croom Helm, 1982, pp. 144, 166, n. 16. On al-Hajri's nomination, see: *Al-Nahar*, 23 September 1973, p. 9; Bidwell, *The Two Yemens*, pp. 263–264; *al-Hawadith*, No. 847, 2 February 1973, pp. 2–30.
176. *Ruz al-Yusuf*, 28 March 1977.
177. *Al-Ahram*, 26 August 1977.
178. The Saudis reportedly provided South Yemen with $400 million in early 1976. See *al-Siyasa*, 13 March 1976.
179. Dresch, *A History of Modern Yemen*, p. 175; for more details on girls' education, see Cynthia Myntti, *Women and Development in Yemen Arab Republic*. Schriftenreihe Der Deutschen Gesellschaft Für Technische Zusammenarbeit. Eschborn: German Agency for Technical Cooperation, 1979.
180. 'Abd al-Fattah Isma'il, *Al-Turath wal-Thaqafa al-Wataniyya*. Beirut: Dar Ibn Khaldun, 1986, p. 64.
181. This new trend did not go unnoticed in traditional circles. A senior *qadi* in the city of Ibb lamented the decay of traditional morals. He complained that before the revolution, Yemeni people had knowledge of and familiarity with religion. He felt that youngsters didn't have a clue about the Qur'an, Sunna and religion in general: "They [were] going toward Communism, but they [didn't] know what that is". Quoted in Dresch, *A History of Modern Yemen*, p. 149.
182. A detailed report on the establishment and development of the religious institutions can be found in Ahmad al-Daghshi, "Al-Ma'ahid al-'Ilmiyya – Nash'atan wa-Waqi'an wa-Mustaqbalan", *Majallat Shu'un al-'Asr*, No. 13, October-December 2003, p. 34.

183. Nasser, in conjuction with his struggle against the Muslim Brothers in Egypt (and the execution of Sayyid Qutb, the ideologue of the Muslim Brothers in 1965) intensified the monitoring of Muslim Brothers operatives in Yemen. A number of Yemenis were exiled from Yemen following this, including 'Abd Mahmud al-Mahlafi and 'Abd al-Salam Khalid, both of whom were from the same regions in lower Yemen. For an illuminating discussion on this topic, see al-Janahi, *al-Haraka al-Wataniyya al-Yamaniyya: Min al-Thawra ila al-Wahda*, pp. 516–517.
184. Dresch, *A History of Modern Yemen*, pp. 142–143.
185. Ibid., p. 143.
186. Ibid., p. 144.
187. Ibid.

Chapter 3. The Decline of the Socialist and Arab Nationalist Revolutions: 1978–1990

1. Joseph Kostiner, *Yemen: The Tortuous Quest for Unity, 1990–94*. Chatham House Papers. London: Royal Institute of International Affairs, 1996, pp. 28–29.
2. Robert D. Burrowes, *Historical Dictionary of Yemen*. 2nd ed. Historical Dictionaries of Asia, Oceania, and the Middle East no. 72. Lanham, Md: Scarecrow Press, 2010, p. 95; Robin Leonard Bidwell, *The Two Yemens*. Harlow, Essex; Boulder, CO: Longman; Westview Press, 1983, p. 282.
3. In 1978, the NLF absorbed the local Ba'th Party and the Communist Party into its ranks. From then on, it was called the Yemeni Socialist Party.
4. Constitution of the People's Democratic Republic of Yemen (Aden, amended in 1978). *World Statesmen*, "Constitution of the People's Democratic Republic of Yemen". 1978. http://www.worldstatesmen.org/YemenPDR 1978.pdf. Last accessed 16 June 2013.
5. Ibid.
6. Fred Halliday, "Yemen's Unfinished Revolution: Socialism in the South". *Middle East Research & Information Project (MERIP)* 81 (1979): 3–20 (14).
7. For details of the creation and establishment of the organization of the National NDF see Fred Halliday, "The Arabian Peninsula Opposition Movements". *MERIP Reports* 130 (February 1985). *CrossRef.* http://www.jstor.org/stable/pdfplus/3011110.pdf?acceptTC=true. Last accessed 16 June 2013.
8. *Al-Nahar*, 3 March 1979, p. 1, No. 8; *Al-Hawadith*, 2 March 1979, p. 23, No. 1165.

9. For more details on the relations between North Yemen and the Soviet Union, see Stephen Page, *The Soviet Union and the Yemens: Influence on Asymmetrical Relationships*. Studies of Influence in International Relations. New York: Praeger, 1985.
10. *Al-Nahar*, 3 March 1979, pp. 1, 6, 8; 6 March 1979, pp. 1, 10.
11. *Al-Nahar*, 6 March 1979, p. 1; 19 March 1979, p. 1; 31 March 1979, pp. 1, 10.
12. 'Abd al-Fattah Isma'il, *Al-Jabha al-Qawmiyya – al-Tanthim al-Siyasi lil-Mu'tamar al-Tawhidi* – October 1975, Beirut: Dar Ibn Khaldoun, 1976, pp. 135, 181.
13. *Al-Nahar*, 6 January 1980, p. 1; 2 February 1980, p. 1; 18 February 1980 p. 1.
14. Fadhl 'Ali Ahmad Abu Ghanim, *Al-Buniyya al-Qibaliyya fil-Yaman bayn al-Istimrar wal-Taghayyur*. Cairo: Dar al-Hikma al-Yamaniyya, 1991, p. 332.
15. *Al-Nahar*, 13 May 1979, p. 16.
16. *Al-Nahar*, 8 February 1980, pp. 1, 10; 20 March 1980, pp. 1, 10.
17. *Al-Ba'th*, "Interview with Sultan Ahmad 'Umar". 22 March 1982: 1–10.
18. For more on the events that led to the consolidation of 'Ali Nasir Muhammad's rule, see *Al-Madina* (Jeddah), 6 August 1980; Radio Aden, 29 December 1980, World News Connection, 30 December 1980; *al-Mustaqbal*, 31 January 1981.
19. *Al-Nahar al-'Arabi wal-Duwali*, No. 182 (27 October–1 November 1980), p. 23.
20. Nasir Qandil, *Hakadha Tafajjara al-Burkan*, p. 46, quoted in Paul Dresch, *A History of Modern Yemen*, p. 168.
21. Joseph Kostiner, *South Yemen's Revolutionary Strategy, 1970–1985: From Insurgency to Bloc Politics*. Boulder: Westview Press, 1990, pp. 107–109.
22. See for example declarations that appeared in *Al-Nahar*, 14 June 1980, p. 1; 4 December 1981, p. 9.
23. *Al-Nahar*, 11 May 1980, p. 1. Yemeni Prime Minister 'Abd al-Karim al-Iryani argued in December 1981 that he had received the blessing of the Saudis to complete the process of unification with the South. Also see Elizabeth Collard, ed. *Middle East Economic Digest*. London: Middle East Economic Digest, Ltd., 1981. 68. Vol. 25, p. 68.
24. For further details, see Mark Katz, "Civil Conflict in South Yemen". *Middle East Review* 19.1 (1986): 7–13.
25. Gregory F. Gause, "Yemen", *The Middle East and North Africa*, General Surveys, 43rd edition, London: Emerald Group Publishing Limited, 1977, p. 79.
26. Marius Deeb, "Radical Political Ideologies and Concepts of Property in Libya and South Yemen". *The Middle East Journal*, 40.3 (1986): 445–461 (458).

27. Norman Cigar, "Islam and the State in South Yemen: The Uneasy Coexistence". *Middle Eastern Studies* 26.2 (1990): 185–203 (185–88). http://www.tandfonline.com/doi/pdf/10.1080/00263209008700814#.UjGRfNJkOvI. Last accessed 17 June 2013.
28. Kostiner, *Yemen: The Tortuous Quest for Unity*, pp. 3–4.
29. For more on the discrepancy between state needs and revolutionary dogma, see *The Times*, 11 February 1986.
30. For further details about the Dhofari rebellion and the assistance given to the opposition in Oman by outsiders such as South Yemen, see Uzi Rabi, *The Emergence of States in Tribal Society,* 2006, pp. 183–214.
31. *The New York Times*, 20 January 1980.
32. Kostiner, *Yemen: The Tortuous Quest for Unity*, pp. 27–29.
33. Dresch, *A History of Modern Yemen*, pp. 154, 160 and 174.
34. Radio Sanaa, 27 May 1980, in WNC, 28 May 1980.
35. Salih spoke of these decisions as "the completion of the democracy process in Yemen", Radio Sanaa, 30 August 1982 in Daily Report: Near East and South Asia (DR), 1 September 1982. See also *al-Safir*, 15 May 1982.
36. *Al-Watan al-'Arabi*, 9 April 1982; *al-Mustaqbal*, 17 April 1982.
37. The National Charter, which was drafted at the beginning of 1980, was intended to facilitate an extensive national dialogue. It is general enough to accommodate a broad array of political perspectives, thereby making it a useful tool for both building political consensus and deflecting ideological attacks. The amended version was adopted in August 1982 during the GPC session.
38. For more details on the dynamics of oil exploration and policies in the North during the 1980s, see Ian D. Maycock, "Oil Exploration and Development in Marib/Al Jawf Basin, Yemen Arab Republic". *American Association of Petroleum Geologists (AAPG)* 72.2 (1989): 218–219.
39. This assessment was given by 'Abd al-Karim al-Iryani, the Prime Minister of the S. see *Al-Majalla*, No. 334 (23–29 July 1986), p. 25.
40. Gregory F. Gause, *Saudi-Yemeni Relations: Domestic Structures and Foreign Influence.* New York: Columbia University Press, 1990, p. 156.
41. Jaralla 'Umar, memorandum submitted to the YSP Central Committee, 1989, quoted in Dresch, *A History of Modern Yemen*, p. 173. For more details on the Islamists' activities in the South, see Cigar, "Islam and the State in South Yemen: The Uneasy Coexistence", p. 191.
42. Michael C. Hudson, "After the Gulf War: Prospects for Democratization in the Arab World". *Middle East Journal* 45.3 (1991): 407–426 (420).
43. *Al-Nahar*, 19 January 1970.

44. Al-Janahi provides slightly lower assessments. Sa'id Ahmad al-Janahi, *Al-Haraka al-Wataniyya al-Yamaniyya: Min al-Thawra ila al-Wahda*. Aden: Markaz al-'Amal lil-Dirasat wal-Nashr, 1992, p. 517.
45. Many of them, in their bitter disappointment with their home government's policies, settled in Yemen. They were inspired by the famous *hadith*: "If disorder threatens, take refuge in Yemen" (*in hajat al-fitna fa 'alayak al-yaman*). Sa'id 'Abd al-Karim, pp. 78–79, quoted in Dresch, *A History of Modern Yemen*, p. 173.
46. For more details on 'Ali 'Abdallah Salih's tactics in forging the Islamic Front, see Robert D. Burrowes, *The Yemen Arab Republic: The Politics of Development, 1962–1986*. Boulder, CO: Westview Press, 1986, pp. 101–105.
47. Dresch, *A History of Modern Yemen*, p. 173.
48. William A. Rugh, *The Arab Mass Media: Newspapers, Radio and Television in Arab Politics*. Westport: Greenwood Publishing Group, 2004, p. 106.
49. As a leader of the Islamic Front, al-Zindani was said to have chanelled Yemeni volunteers to the Afghan Jihad while enhancing Riyadh's influence in Yemen. For further details see *Terrorism Monitor*, "Yemen's Enduring Challenges: An Interview With Jonathan Winer". 2.7 (2004): n. pag. http://www.jamestown.org/programs/tm/single/?tx_ttnews%5Btt_news%5D=26401&tx_ttnews%5BbackPid%5D=179&no_cache=1#.UjWGZNJkOvI. Last accessed 17 June 2013.
50. *Al-Mustaqbal*, 12 July 1988; *al-Dunya*, 18 August 1988.
51. Muhammad al-Akwa', *Hayat 'Alim wa-Amir*, p. 334, quoted in Dresch, *A History of Modern Yemen*, p. 176.
52. A vivid description of the changing times in North Yemen was provided by Carapico and Myntti who described the upheavals of the time through the experiences of a peripheral family of notables that lived in a traditional house in the old city of Sanaa. The family ran its affairs in the 1970s as it did in the "good old days". The head of the family worked as an employee in the government service in the beginning, and other members of the family engaged in the traditional craft of etching and painting Quranic verses on colourful glass. After forging marriage ties with other families in Sanaa, the family moved outside of the old city in 1989. The move was not easy for all of the family members. The etching handicraft no longer had the same value that it did in the past, and the price increase for the raw materials placed the family business at an unprecedented low point. In the new bureaucratic world and the cosmopolitan atmosphere, the family did not have the ability to integrate. The women of the family, as reported to the authors, regretted their move to Sanaa. Sheila Carapico and Cynthia Myntti, "Change in North Yemen 1977–1989: A Tale of Two Families". *Middle East Report*

170 (1991): pp. 24–29, 47. http://www.jstor.org/stable/pdfplus/3013247.pdf?acceptTC=true. Last accessed 17 June 2013.

Chapter 4. United Yemen

1. Fred Halliday, *Revolution and Foreign Policy: The Case of South Yemen, 1967–1987*. Cambridge: Cambridge University Press, 2002, p. 124.
2. Joseph Kostiner, *South Yemen's Revolutionary Strategy, 1970–1985: From Insurgency to Bloc Politics*. Boulder: Westview Press, 1990, pp. 66–67.
3. *Al-Watan al-'Arabi*, No. 474, 14–20 March 1986.
4. For a detailed analysis of the Soviet policy, see Stephen Page, *The Soviet Union and the Yemens: Influence on Asymmetrical Relationships*. Studies of Influence in International Relations. New York: Praeger, 1985. See also Galia Golan, *Soviet Policies in the Middle East: from World War Two to Gorbachev*. Cambridge: Cambridge University Press, 1990, pp. 228–243.
5. A discussion of the effect of oil on the state system in North Yemen can be found in Robert D. Burrowes, *Historical Dictionary of Yemen*. 2nd ed. Historical Dictionaries of Asia, Oceania, and the Middle East No. 72. Lanham, MD: Scarecrow Press, 2010, pp. 269–272.
6. For further details on the 1988 agreement to establish a joint company for the development and exploitation of minerals see Masahiro Miyoshi, *The Joint Development of Offshore Oil and Gas in Relation to Maritime Boundary Delimitation*. Vol. 2. Durham: International Boundaries Research Unit (IBRU), 1999, pp. 42–43.
7. Marta Colburn, *The Republic of Yemen: Development Challenges in the 21st Century*. London: CIIR, 2002, p. 55.
8. *Al-Wahda*, No. 9, March 1992.
9. Halliday, *Revolution and Foreign Policy: The Case of South Yemen 1967–1987*, p. 136.
10. 'Ali 'Abd al-Qawi al-Ghafari, *al-Wahda al-Yamaniyya: al-Waqi' wal-Mustaqbal*. Sanaa: Kitab al-Thawabit, 1997, pp. 169–170.
11. In May 1984, an American corporation published its findings regarding the oil and natural gas reserves and put it at a commercial level in the provinces of Ma'rib-Shabwa. See *al-Turath*, 17 May and 8 November, 1984.
12. I. William Zartman, *Preventive Negotiation: Avoiding Conflict Escalation*. Oxford: Rowman and Littlefield, 2001, pp. 99–100; L. Carl Brown, *Diplomacy in the Middle East: The International Relations of Regional and Outside Powers*. London: I.B.Tauris, 2004, pp. 44.
13. *Terrorism Monitor*, "Yemen's Enduring Challenges: An Interview with Jonathan Winer". 2.7 (2004): n. pag. http://www.jamestown.org/programs

/tm/single/?tx_ttnews%5Btt_news%5D=26401&tx_ttnews%5Bback Pid%5D=179&no_cache=1#.UjWGZNJkOvI. Last accessed 17 June 2013; Christopher Boucek and Marina Ottaway, Eds. *Yemen on the Brink.* Washington D.C.: Carnegie Endowment, 2010, p. 63.

14. For further discussion on these issues, see Joseph Kostiner, *Yemen: The Tortuous Quest for Unity, 1990–1994.* Chatham House Papers. London: Royal Institute of International Affairs, 1996, pp. 5–12; Sheila Carapico, *Civil Society in Yemen: The Political Economy of Activism in Modern Arabia.* New York: Cambridge University Press, 2007, pp. 48–54.
15. See, for example, Salih's speech marking the May 1990 unification, Radio Sanaa, 22 May 1990, BBC Worldwide Monitoring, 24 May 1990.
16. The US need for Russian support in the Security Council prevented the Americans from responding.
17. Kostiner, Joseph. "Yemen". Middle East Contemporary Survey. Ed. Ami Ayalon, Vol. 14. Boulder, CO: Westview Press, 1990. p. 721.
18. Gwenn Okruhlik and Patrick Conge, "National Autonomy, Labor Migration and Political Crisis: Yemen and Saudi Arabia". *Middle East Journal* 51.4 (1997): 554–565; Mark N. Katz, "Yemeni Unity and Saudi Security". *Middle East Policy* 1.1 (1992): 117–135. http://digilib.gmu.edu/jspui/bitstream/1920/3118/1/yemeni%20unity%20and%20saudi%20security.pdf. Last accessed 13 June 2013.
19. Sheila Carapico, "Yemen: Unification and the Gulf War". *Middle East Report* 21.170 (1991): 26.
20. In his National Day speeches Salih usually depicts unification as a "historical and national accomplishment".
21. Barak A. Salmoni, Bryce Loidolt and Madeleine Wells, *Regime and Periphery in Northern Yemen: The Huthi Phenomenon.* Santa Monica: RAND Corporation, 2010, pp. 76.
22. Shelagh Weir, "A Clash of Fundamentalisms: Wahhabism in Yemen". *Middle East Report* 204 (1997): 22–26 (22). http://www.jstor.org/stable/pdfplus/3013139.pdf?acceptTC=true. Last accessed 17 June 2013.
23. Sarah Phillips, *Yemen's Democracy Experiment in Regional Perspective: Patronage and Pluralized Authoritarianism.* New York: Palgrave Macmillan, 2008, pp. 138–139.
24. *Al-Islah*, 5 January 1993.
25. Sheila Carapico, "Elections and Mass Politics in Yemen". *Middle East Report* 185 (1993): pp. 2–6 (4). http://www.merip.org/mer/mer185/elections-mass-politics-yemen. Last accessed 17 June 2013.
26. *Al-Hayat*, 1, 5, 9 May 1993; *al-Majalla*, 26 May 1993.
27. *Al-Hayat*, 5 May 1993.

28. Nazih N. Ayubi, *Over-Stating the Arab State: Politics and Society in the Middle East*. London: I.B.Tauris, 1995, p. 437, No. 7; *Al-Turath*, 13 July 1995.
29. Carapico, "Elections and Mass Politics in Yemen".
30. Kostiner, *Yemen: The Tortuous Quest for Unity*, p. 68.
31. Ibid., pp. 85–90.
32. Ayubi, *Over-Stating the Arab State*, p. 438.
33. *Al-Watan al-'Arabi*, 18 February 1994.
34. *Al-Turath*, 11 November 1993.
35. *Al-Wasat*, "Interview with al-'Attas". 30 May 1994.
36. Ibid.
37. For a further discussion about the document and its principles, see al-Ghafari, *al-Wahda al-Yamaniyya: al-Waqi' wal-Mustaqbal*, pp. 250–251; *al-Safir*, 12 April 1995.
38. *Yemen Times*, 15 May 1995.
39. Michael C. Hudson, "Bipolarity, Rational Calculation and War in Yemen". *The Arab Studies Journal* 3.1 (1995): 9–19.
40. Simon Edge, "Yemen's Problems and Promise". *MEED (Middle East Economic Digest)* 36.13 (3 April 1992): 4–5.
41. Bashir al-Bakr, *Harb al-Yaman: al-Qabila Tantasir 'ala al-Watan*. Beirut: al-Mu'sasa al-'Arabiya lil-Dirasaat wal-Nashr, 1995, p. 36.
42. The GPC depicted the YSP activists as "secessionists" and declared that al-'Attas "should be removed". See *al-Sharq al-Awsat*, 20 April 1994.
43. *Al-Sharq al-Awsat*, 10 April and 6 June 1994.
44. For a discussion of the war see *al-Majalla*, 27 February 1994; *al-Hayat*, 24 May 1994.
45. Allegedly, Salih even supported attempts on the lives of YSP members and then tried to implicate the al-Islah party. Such arguments were made by the opposition party at the height of the Civil War. For more details, see a comprehensive report on Yemen's civil war, *al-Muraqib al-Arabi*, No. 4, September 2005, pp. 9–47.
46. This dynamic is described by Michael Hudson in his "Obstacles to Democratization in the Middle East". *Contention* 5.2 (1996): 81–105 (90).
47. Phillips, *Yemen's Democracy Experiment in Regional Perspective*, pp. 49, 140–141.
48. *Al-Sharq al-Awsat*, 13 January 1995, 15 September 1995.
49. International Crisis Group (ICG), "Yemen: Coping with Terrorism and Violence in a Fragile State". *Middle East Report* 8 (8 January 2003): 9–13 (9–10). http://www.crisisgroup.org/en/regions/middle-east-north-africa/iraq-iran-gulf/yemen/008-yemen-coping-with-terrorism-and-violence-in-a-fragile-state.aspx. Last accessed 17 June 2013.

50. *Al-Siyasa*, 27 June 1995; *The Independent*, 27 June 1995.
51. *Al-Sharq al-Awsat*, 29 April 1997. The Nasserists and the Ba'thists won five seats, and the remaining 54 were divided between "independent" candidates, most of which gave their support to the General Congress Party.
52. On Salih's policy regarding the al-Islah, see Minister of Justice Isma'il al-Wazir's interview, *al-Wasat*, "Interview with Minister of Justice Isma'il al-Wazir". 28 July 1997.
53. *Middle East International*, 30 May 1997.
54. For a thorough analysis of the parliament's importance in Yemen's political system, see *Yemen Times*, 15 May 1995.
55. Phillips, *Yemen's Democracy Experiment in Regional Perspective*, p. 141.
56. Ibid., p. 139.
57. U.S. Department of State: Bureau of Democracy, Human Rights, and Labor, "Yemen". 4 March 2002. Country Reports on Human Rights Practices (2001). http://www.refworld.org/docid/3e918c3611.html. Last accessed 17 June 2013.
58. *Country Report (CR),* "Yemen". 2 (1997): 34–37.
59. See, for example, President Salih's website, www.presidentsaleh.ye. Last accessed 19 February 2014.
60. Lisa Wedeen, "Seeing Like a Citizen, Acting Like a State: Exemplary Events in Unified Yemen". *Comparative Studies in Society and History* 45.04 (2003): 680–713. http://journals.cambridge.org/download.php?file=%2FCSS%2FCSS45_04%2FS001041750300032Xa.pdf&code=a622dbcf7e710b42799cf8f415584175. Last accessed 17 June 2013.

    This article delves into the complexity of the political system in united Yemen, focusing on three cases that are indicative of the 1999 elections that highlight the anomaly of Yemen.

Chapter 5. Heading Toward a "Failed State"

1. Richard Engel, "Yemen's Weapon Culture". BBC News, 22 January 2002. http://news.bbc.co.uk/2/hi/middle_east/1775938.stm. Last accessed 18 June 2013.
2. Ibid.
3. Hassan al-Zaidi, "Marib Events reflect Crisis between State and Tribe", *Yemen Times*, 14 February 2005, quoted in Sarah Phillips, *Yemen's Democracy Experiment in Regional Perspective: Patronage and Pluralized Authoritarianism*. New York: Palgrave Macmillan, 2008, p. 97.
4. This figure is based on the cautious estimation of 5 million and the exaggerated estimation of 50 million. For an interesting analysis on the weaponry industry in Yemen, see Derek B. Miller, "Demand, Stockpiles, and Social

Controls: Small Arms in Yemen". Occasional Papers. Graduate Institute of International Studies, Geneva 9 (2003): 28.

5. Ahmed Zein, "Armed and Dangerous: Arms Proliferation inside Yemen". *Arab Insight – Emerging Social and Religious Trends* 2.1 (2008): 81–87. World Security Institute, Washington, D.C., 1964.
6. For an interesting analysis of the encounter between tribe and state, see Najib Ghallab, "al-Yaman: al-Bahth 'an Dawla Mu'asira fi Mujtama' Tahkumuhu al-Qabila", *al-Sharq al-Awsat*, 15 December 2007.
7. *Al-Quds al-'Arabi*, 7 June 2000.
8. Warsaw PAP, 3 March 2000; *Middle East International*, 10 March 2000.
9. *Al-Jumhurriya*, "Dr. Hammud al-'Awdi ila al-jumhuriya: thawrat al-mu'asasat ta'bir haqiqi wa-mubashir 'an fashl al-salta hata ma' nafsiha". 5 January 2012. http://www.algomhoriah.net/news_details.php?sid=37521&lng=arabic. Last accessed 19 June 2013.
10. *Al-Arabiyya*/AFP, "Wahdat al-Yaman Tatarajja' bayna al-Qa'ida wal-tamarrud al-Huthi wa-Infisal al-Janub". 13 March 2009.
11. World Bank. "GEM country brief: Yemen 2006", International finance Corporation: Gender Entrepreneurship markets. Washington, DC: World Bank, 2006. http://documents.worldbank.org/curated/en/2006/07, 9543572/gem-country-brief-yemen-2006-gem-country-brief-yemen-2006. Last accessed 9 February 2014.
12. Sheila Carapico, *Civil Society in Yemen: The Political Economy of Activism in Modern Arabia*. New York: Cambridge University Press, 2007, pp. 43, 59.
13. See, for example, *Yemen Post*, Interview with Sa'd al-Din bin Talib. 7 April 2008. Sa'd al-Din bin Talib is a member of the Supreme National Anti Corruption Committee.
14. UNDP Yemen, "How We Work". 28 March 2010. http://www.undp.org.ye/how-do-we-work.php. Last accessed 18 June 2013.
15. BBC News, "Yemen Petrol Riots Leave 12 Dead". 20 July 2005. http://news.bbc.co.uk/2/hi/middle_east/4700813.stm. Last accessed 18 June 2013.
16. Ibid.
17. Alfred B. Prados and Jeremy M. Sharp, "Yemen: Current Conditions and US Relations", CRS Report for Congress, 2007. http://www.fas.org/sgp/crs/mideast/RS21808.pdf. Last accessed 18 June 2013.
18. Richard Fontaine and Andrew Exum, "Yemen's coming disaster". *Los Angeles Times*, 5 January 2010. http://articles.latimes.com/2010/jan/05/opinion/la-oe-fontaineexum5–2010jan05. Last accessed 18 June 2013.
19. Richard Spencer, "Al-Qaeda veterans are flooding into Yemen". *Telegraph.co.uk*, 10 January 2010. http://www.telegraph.co.uk/news/worldnews/middleeast/yemen/6962969/Al-Qaeda-veterans-are-flooding-into-Yemen.html. Last accessed 18 June 2013.

20. *Al-Sharq al-Awsat*, 19 June 2010.
21. See, for example, *al-Majalla*, 18 May 2000.
22. The main tenets of the movement, its essence and its message were explained under the title "Who We Are". *Sawt al-Sha'b*, "Man Nahnu (Who We Are)". 11 February 2010.
23. April Longley Alley, "The Rules of the Game: Unpacking Patronage Politics in Yemen". *The Middle East Journal* 64.3 (2010): 385–409 (406–7).
24. Susanne Dahlgren, "The Southern Movement in Yemen". *ISIM Review* 22 (Autumn 2008): 50–51.
25. Many southerners depicted the regime of Sanaa as the "Sanaa gang" (*'Isabat Sanaa*). See for example, *al-Sharq al-Awsat*, "Interview with 'Abd al-Majid Talib". 19 June 2010.
26. For more on how unification affected the status of women in South Yemen, see: Margot Badran, "Unifying Women: Feminist Pasts and Presents in Yemen". *Gender & History* 10.3 (1998): 498–518. http://onlinelibrary.wiley.com/doi/10.1111/1468–0424.00115/pdf. Last accessed 18 June 2013.
27. *Sawt al-Sha'b*, "Man Nahnu (Who We Are)".
28. Jane Novak, "Yemeni Southern Opposition Leader al Nuba Writes the Brits". *Armies of Liberation*, 20 January 2010. http://armiesofliberation.com/archives/2010/01/20/yemeni-southern-opposition-leader-al-nuba-writes-the-brits/. Last accessed 18 June 2013.
29. *Al-Janub al-Hurr*, No. 6, 1 March 2009, p. 17.
30. Ibid.
31. *Al-Sharq al-Awsat*, 19 June 2010.
32. 'Abd al-Sattar Hatita, "The Battle for Yemen's Unity". *Al-Sharq al-Awsat*, 23 August 2009.
33. *Al-Watan* (Riyadh), 3 July 2008.
34. *Al-Watan* (Riyadh), 1 December 2008.
35. *Al-Janub al-Hurr*, No. 8, 1 May 2009, p. 1.
36. Ibid., pp. 4–5.
37. Abu Muhammad al-Dirjaji, "The South–Identity and History". *Al-Janub al-Hurr*, No. 8, 1 May 2009, p. 30.
38. Ibid.
39. Ibid., pp.27–30.
40. *Al-Janub al-Hurr*, No. 1, 14 October 2008, pp. 9–10.
41. *al-Janub al-Hurr*, 1 May 2009.
42. *Al-Janub al-Hurr*, No. 6, 1 March 2009, p. 17.
43. The Sanaa Declaration intended to bolster the democratic and liberal institutions of the Yemeni state. It was ratified in July 1999. For the text of the

Sanaa Declaration, see *Al-Bab.com,* "The Sanaa Declaration". 1999. http://www.al-bab.com/arab/docs/sanaa.htm. Last accessed 17 May 2013.

44. *Al-Janub al-Hurr,* No. 1, 14 October 2008.
45. Ibid.
46. For further details about the attack on the USS Cole, see Craig Whitlock, "Probe of USS Cole Bombing Unravels". *Washington Post,* 4 May 2008. http://articles.washingtonpost.com/2008–05-04/world/36911922_1_cole-investigation-uss-cole-yemeni-officials. Last accessed 18 June 2013.
47. Khalid Yusuf, "Al-Hall – Dawlatayn". *Al-Janub al-Hurr,* No. 8, 14 October 2008, p.6.
48. *Al-Janub al-Hurr,* No. 6, 1 March 2009, p. 20.
49. *Al-Janub al-Hurr,* No. 8, 1 May 2009, pp. 25–28.
50. Ibid.
51. Ibid. 7 July 1994 is the date that the civil war ended and the north "swallowed up" the south.
52. Ahmad al-Maqrami, "Al-Wahda Awla Min al-Minsab!". *al-Sahwa.net,* 4 April 2009. http://www.alsahwa-yemen.net/view_news.asp?sub_no=2_2009_05_04_70309. Last accessed 18 June 2013.
53. Ibid.
54. *Al-Ayam,* 3 May 2009.
55. *Al-Sahwa.net,* 3 May 2009. http://www.alsahwa-yemen.net/view_news.asp?sub_no=2_2009_05_03_70298
56. Ibid.
57. Ibid.
58. *Al-Watan* (Riyadh), 2 May 2008.
59. *Al-Sharq al-Awsat,* 5 May 2009.
60. *Al-Sharq al-Awsat,* 5 May 2009.
61. Ibid. 14 October signified the beginning of the revolution which led to the evacuation of the British and the creation of South Yemen.
62. *Al-Janub al-Hurr,* No. 8, 1 March 2009, pp. 17–18.
63. *Al-Janub al-Hurr,* No. 2, 1 November 2008.
64. Ibid., pp. 17–18.
65. Ibid.
66. Ibid.
67. *Al-Janub al-Hurr,* No. 8, 1 March 2009, pp. 17–18.
68. It should be noted that among the activists of the Free South, there were also some northerners. Prominent among them was Dr. Muhammad al-Saqqaf, a lawyer and university professor who avocated succession.
69. Sarah Phillips, "Yemen: Economic and Political Deterioration". Ed. M. Dunne and J. Choucair. *Arab Reform Bulletin* 3.7 (2005): n. pag. http://

carnegieendowment.org/2008/08/20/economic-and-political-deterioration-in-yemen/fga5. Last accessed 18 June 2013.

70. For more on sources of tension between the Huthis and the government, see: Barak A. Salmoni, Bryce Loidolt and Madeleine Wells, *Regime and Periphery in Northern Yemen: The Huthi Phenomenon*. Santa Monica: RAND Corporation, 2010, pp. 4–8.
71. Iris Glosemeyer and Don Reneau, "Local Conflict, Global Spin: Uprising in the Yemeni Highlands". *Middle East Report* 232 (2004): 44–46. http://www.jstor.org/stable/pdfplus/1559484.pdf?acceptTC=true. Last accessed 18 June 2013.
72. *Al-Hayat*, 11 July 2008.
73. Yasir al-'Arami, "Tanthim al-Qa'ida fil-Yaman: Min al-Hamish ila al-Matn". *Al-Huthiyyun fil-Yaman*. Dubai: Markaz al-Misbar lil-Dirasat wal-Buhuth, 2010, p. 271.
74. Christopher Boucek, "War in Saada: From Local Insurrection to National Challenge", in Christopher Boucek and Marina Ottaway (Eds.), *Yemen on the Brink*. Washington, DC: Carnegie Endowment for International Peace, 2010, pp. 50–51; Salmoni, Loidolt and Wells, *Regime and Periphery in Northern Yemen: The Huthi Phenomenon*, p. 134.
75. See: Anwar Qasim al-Khidri, "al-Huthi wal-Waraqa al-Ta'ifiya al-Khasira". *Bayyina Institute*, 6 May 2006.
76. *Al-Hayat*, 11 July 2008.
77. *Al-Watan*, 11 June 2007.
78. Barak Barfi, "The Yemenite Imbroglio". *The Jerusalem Report*, 19 March 2007, p. 17.
79. 'Abdallah al-Ahmar estimated that the Jewish community in Yemen numbered 800 in 1992. He provided the estimation in view of the reports from July 1992 that 120 Jews moved from Yemen to Israel. According to other estimations, hundreds of Jews left Yemen during the period 1992–1994, which reduced the community from 1,200 to 400. Barfi, "The Yemenite Imbroglio".
80. Ibid.
81. For further details on the history of the Jews in Yemen, see Dana Adams Schmidt, *Yemen: The Unknown War*. London: Bodley Head, 1968, pp. 102–110.
82. *Al-Watan*, 15 May 2007.
83. *Al-Watan*, 24 July 2007; *al-Hayat*, 11 July 2007.
84. The agreement was confidential at the time of its signing, February 2008. Its articles were published in July 2011. See www.barakish.net/news.aspx?cat=12&sub=11&id=9224. Last accessed 19 February 2014.
85. Salim 'Abd al-Karim, "Fil-Yaman... Irtiyah li-Waqf Harb Sa'da lakin al-Tahaddiyat la Zalat Qa'ima". *Al-Bainah*, 26 March 2007. http://www.albainah.net/ index.aspx?function=Item&id=16632&lang. Last accessed 18 June 2003.

86. *Al-Watan*, 4 January 2008.
87. *Al-Watan*, 19 February 2008.
88. For further explanation about the motivations of Qatar, Saudi Arabia and other Gulf States to pacify events in Yemen, see *Yemen Times*, 19 July 2010.
89. *Al-Watan*, 15 March 2008.
90. *Al-Watan*, 19 April 2008.
91. *Al-Watan*, 4 May 2008.
92. *Al-Watan*, 11 February 2008.
93. *Al-Watan*, 5 May 2008.
94. Ibid.
95. *Al-Watan*, 8 August 2008.
96. Qatar remained active as a mediator, trying to reactivate the Doha Pact, throughout the year 2010. See *al-'Arab*, 14 July 2010 and 14 October 2010.
97. *Al-Watan*, 1 August 2008.
98. Ahmad Muhammad al-Daghshi, "Al-Huthiyyun... 'Indama Yanqalib al-Sahar 'ala al-Sahir". *Majallat al-'Asr*, 7 February 2006, p. 34.
99. Al-'Arami, "Tanthim al-Qa'ida fil-Yaman: Min al-Hamish ila al-Matn", p. 79.
100. Al-Daghshi, "Al-Huthiyyun...'Indama Yanqalib al-Sahar 'ala al-Sahir".
101. Ibid.
102. *Al-Sharq al-Awsat*, 4 April 2009.
103. *Al-Sharq al-Awsat*, 12 April 2009.
104. *Al-Watan*, 20 November 2008.
105. Rasha Muhammad, "Tubul al-Harb Taduqq fi Sa'da". *Al-Fan Online,* 15 December 2008. http://alfanonline.moheet.com/show_news.aspx?nid=79090. Last accessed 18 June 2013.
106. *Al-Watan*, 1 December 2008.
107. *Al-Sharq al-Awsat*, 3 April 2009.
108. *26 Sabtambar*, 1 March 2009.
109. *Al-Sharq al-Awsat*, 30 July 2009.
110. Muhammad, "Tubul al-Harb Taduqq fi Sa'da".
111. Hatita, "The Battle for Yemen's Unity".
112. Ibid.
113. Ibid.
114. *Al-Watan al-'Arabi*, No. 1744, 4 August 2010.
115. Shelagh Weir, "A Clash of Fundamentalisms: Wahhabism in Yemen". *Middle East Report* 204 (1997): 22–26 (22–23, 26). *JSTOR*. http://www.jstor.org/stable/pdfplus/3013139.pdf?acceptTC=true. Last accessed 17 June 2013.

116. *Yemen Post*, 29 March, 2009.
117. *Al-Sharq al-Awsat*, 19 August 2009.
118. Robert Haddick, "This Week at War: The Middle East's Cold War Heats Up", *Small Wars Journal* 28 August 2009. http://www.foreignpolicy.com/articles/2009/08/28/this_week_at_war_the_middle_easts_cold_war_heats_up. Last accessed 18 June 2013.
119. *Al-'Alam*, 23 September 2009.
120. Haddick, "This Week at War: The Middle East's Cold War Heats Up".
121. *Al-Akhbar*, 19 February 2008.
122. *Al-Riyadh*, 8 November 2009.
123. *Al-Watan*, 5 November 2009.
124. *Al-Jazeera*, 8 November 2009.
125. *Al-Watan*, 5 November 2009.
126. Al-Rubaysh was born in 1980 in the ultra-conservative town of Burayda in the al-Qasim region of Saudi Arabia, where he studied until graduating from Imam Muhammad bin Sa'ud University with a BA degree in *sharia*. He then moved to Afghanistan, where he was captured by American troops and shipped to Guantanamo Bay, where he spent five years in prison. In December, 2006, al-Rubaysh and a number of other Saudis were released from Guantanamo and enrolled in the Saudi rehabilitation program. Eventually his name was included in the so-called "85 Most Wanted" list released by Saudi authorities in February 2009. In the meantime, al-Rubaysh left his wife and three children behind to join al-Qa'ida in Yemen in April 2008, along with 11 other Saudi ex-Guantanamo prisoners leaving the Kingdom. *'Ukaz*, 10 October 2009.
127. Ibrahim al-Rubaysh, "Why Muhammad bin Na'if?". Forum post, *Islamic Awakening*. http://forums.islamicawakening.com/f18/why-muhammad-ibn-naif-shaykh-ibrahim-al-28847. Last accessed 27 October 2013.
128. Mark Slackman, "Would-Be Killer Linked to Al Qaeda, Saudis Say". *The New York Times*, 28 August 2009. http://www.nytimes.com/2009/08/29/world/middleeast/29saudi.html?_r=0. Last accessed 18 June 2013.
129. Ghazanfar Ali Khan, "New Measures to Combat Terrorism". *Arab News*, 21 February 2010. http://www.arabnews.com/node/337710. Last accessed 18 June 2013.
130. Saudi Arabia periodically published a list of wanted men. The most recent was that of February 2003, where a list of 85 individuals was published. It was composed of 83 Saudis and two Yemenis. *Arab News*, "Kingdom unveils list of 85 wanted militants abroad". 3 February 2009. http://arabnews.com/node/320619. Last accessed 18 June 2013.
131. For a more illuminating report on the Saudi dealings with terrorism, see Ali Saeed Awadh Asseri, *Combating Terrorism: Saudi Arabia's Role in the War*

on Terror. Oxford: Oxford University Press, 2009. Asseri focuses on the three-pronged Saudi strategy to combat terrorism in its domestic, regional and international dimensions.

132. *Al-Mu'tamar*, 11 May 2007. There were also accusations of Libyan support given to the Huthis' "criminal gang".
133. *Al-Sharq al-Awsat*, 18 June 2009.
134. Hatita, "The Battle for Yemen's Unity".
135. Almotamar.net, 17 August 2009, http://www.almotar.net/en/6571.htm, last accessed 19 February 2014.
136. 'Arafat Madabish, "al-Yaman ... qadiyya ma tahmilha malaf"'. *Al-Muraqib al-'Arabi*, September 2005.
137. Haddick, "This Week at War: The Middle East's Cold War Heats Up".
138. *Al-Watan*, 18 January 2008.
139. Al-Daghshi, "Al-Huthiyyun: 'Indama Yanqalib al-Sahar 'ala al-Sahir".
140. Ian Black, "A New Taliban?". *The Guardian*, 3 September 2008. http://www.guardian.co.uk/world/2008/sep/03/yemen. Last accessed 19 June 2013.
141. *Al-Arabiyya*, 5 July 2008.
142. Some have argued that al-Zindani was very close to Osama bin Laden. Zindani was a major player in Yemeni politics and has likely been as significant a threat as has existed to Salih's control of the country. He was the central figure involved in recruiting, training and sending Yemenis to Afghanistan to fight with the Taliban. Zindani was designated as a global terrorist by the US Treasury, and Yemen was asked to freeze all of his assets. The treasury charged him with actively recruiting for al-Qa'ida training camps and purchasing weapons on behalf of al-Qa'ida and other terrorists.
143. For further details, see Nabil al-Bukairi, "Dr. Aqeel Al-Maqtari Prominent leader in the Yemeni Salafi Movement". *Yemen Post*, 10 April 2010.
144. *Al-Watan al-'Arabi*, 4 August 2010.
145. Tarik al-Homayed, "Disturbing in Yemen". *Al-Sharq al-Awsat*, 30 December 2009.
146. Bruce Riedel, "Al Qaeda's Yemen Connection, America and the Global Islamic Jihad". *The Brookings Institution*, 30 December 2009. http://www.brookings.edu/blogs/up-front/posts/2009/12/30-terrorism-yemen-riedel. Last accessed 19 June 2013.
147. Throughout the 1980s, North Yemen was one of the main providers of volunteers for the Afghani jihad. At this time, Marxist South Yemen sided with the Communist regime in Afghanistan and tried to prevent the movement of volunteers to Afghanistan. More than a few crossed the border to North Yemen and from there went to Peshawar in Afghanistan.

According to estimations from early 2009, 40 per cent of the detainees in Guantanamo were Yemenis. Jaclyn Belczyk, "Yemen Denies Plans to Transfer Guantanamo Detainees to Saudi Arabia". *Jurist*, 15 June 2009. http://jurist.law.pitt.edu/paperchase/2009/06/yemen-denies-plans-to-transfer.php. Last accessed 19 June 2013.

148. Ayman al-Zawahiri. "Risala ila Ahl Al-Yaman (2)". Sada al-Malahim, Issue 9, May 2009, p.26.
149. Ibid.
150. Ibid.
151. At times al-Qa'ida used this title to refer to US President Barak Obama.
152. Abu Hurayra Al-San'ani, "Al-Sumal". *Sada al-Malahim,* No. 4, 2008.
153. 'Adil Amin, "Tanthim al-Qa'ida fil-Yaman". *Ma'rib Press*, 9 July 2007. http://www.marebpress.net/articles.php?id=2121&lng=arabic. Last accessed 19 June 2013.
154. Muhammad Hamdi al-Ahdal was born in Saudi Arabia in 1971. In the mid 1990s al-Ahdal fought in Bosnia and Chechnya where he was wounded. He visited Afghanistan several times in 1998–1999 where he played a role in al-Qa'ida's finances, weapons smuggling and operational planning. In 1999 he was arrested in Saudi Arabia for 14 months because of his illegal activities. When he was released in 2000 Saudi authorities deported him to Yemen, where he quickly associated with al-Harithi and al-Qa'ida activity in Yemen. *Interpol*, "Al-Ahdal, Mohammad Hamdi Mohammad Sadiq". 2 November 2010. http://www.interpol.int/@en/UN/(un_id)/2010–6442. Last accessed 19 June 2013.
155. Jane Novak, "Question on al-Ahdal and the Cole". *Armies of Liberation*, 7 March 2007. http://armiesofliberation.com/archives/2007/03/07/question-on-al-ahdal-and-the-cole/. Last accessed 19 June 2013.
156. In July 2008, for example, al-Qa'ida activists attacked police stations in Sayun in the province of Hadramawt. On 25 July an act of sabotage resulted in the death of four policemen and the injury of 14. See *al-Arabiya.net*, "Two Killed, 20 Injured in Yemen Attack". 25 July 2008. http://www.alarabiya.net/articles/2008/07/25/53700.html. Last accessed 19 June 2013.
157. Al-'Arami, "Tanthim al-Qa'ida fil-Yaman: Min al-Hamish ila al-Matn", p. 271.
158. *Al-Watan*, 15 May 2008.
159. Al-'Arami, "Tanthim al-Qa'ida fil-Yaman: Min al-Hamish ila al-Matn", p. 275.
160. Gregory D. Johnsen, "Al Qaeda's generational split". *The Boston Globe*, 9 November 2007. http://www.boston.com/bostonglobe/editorial_opinion/

oped/articles/2007/11/09/al_qaedas_generational_split/. Last accessed 19 June 2013.

161. Al-'Arami, "Tanthim al-Qa'ida fil-Yaman: Min al-Hamish ila al-Matn", pp. 278–280.
162. "Haqiqat al-Safarat", *Sada al-Malahim*, November 2008.
163. *Sada al-Malahim*, "Kalimat al-Shaykh al-Doktor Ayman al-Zawahiri li-Ahl al-Yaman". January 2009.
164. Al-'Arami, "Tanthim al-Qa'ida fil-Yaman: Min al-Hamish ila al-Matn", pp. 281.
165. *Sada al-Malahim*, No. 7, January 2009.
166. Ibid.
167. *Sada al-Malahim*, March 2008, pp. 5–6.
168. Ibid.
169. BBC News, "Profile: Shoe-throwing Journalist". 15 September 2009. http://news.bbc.co.uk/2/hi/middle_east/7787792.stm. Last accessed 19 June 2013.
170. *Sada al-Malahim*, March 2008, pp. 26–29.
171. Ibid.
172. 'Arafat Madabish, "Al-Qa'ida Tu'lin Da'm al-Infisal fil-Yaman". *Al-Sharq al-Awsat*, 14 May 2009.
173. The government of Sanaa pointed out that cooperation between al-Qai'da and the secessionists did take place. See *Al-Mu'tamar*, 6 September 2010.
174. *Al-Jazeera*, "Al-Qa'idat bil-Jazirat al-'Arab tahaddid bimazid min al-hajamat dad al-gharb". 26 January 2009. http://www.aljazeera.net/News/archive/archive?ArchiveId=1167812. Last accessed 19 June 2013. See also, Thomas Hegghammer, "Saudi and Yemeni Branches of al-Qaida Unite". *Jihadica*, 24 January 2009. http://www.jihadica.com/saudi-and-yemeni-branches-of-al-qaida-unite. Last accessed 19 June 2013.
175. Muhammad Sayf Haydar, "Al-Wajh al-Jadid li-Tanthim al-Qa'ida fil-Yaman: Muhawala lil-Fahm". *Al-Arabiya.net*, 17 September 2008. http://www.alarabiya.net/views/2008/09/17/56762.html.
176. Aqeel al-Halali, "'Unprecedented' Security Alerts to Tighten the Noose around al-Qaeda". *Yemen Times*, 9 February 2009. http://yementimes.com/article.shtml?i=1232&p=local&a=1. Last accessed 19 June 2013.
177. Al-Arabiya.net, "Makhawif min Iktisab Tanthim al-Qa'ida fil-Yaman". 28 July 2009. http://www.alarabiya.net/articles/2009/07/28/80117.html. Last accessed 19 June 2013.
178. *Al-Sharq al-Awsat*, 19 April 2009.
179. Al-'Arami, "Tanthim al-Qa'ida fil-Yaman: Min al-Hamish ila al-Matn", p. 277.
180. *Al-Sharq al-Awsat*, 5 August 2009.

181. *Al-Watan*, 28 March 2009.
182. *Yemen News*, "'Awfi reveals Huthi relationship with al Qaeda and planning attacks in Saudi Arabia from Yemen. Houthi accused Saudi Arabia and Yemen of 'serving the Zionist project in the region'". 28 March 2009. http://web.archive.org/web/20090401154810/http://www.newsyemen.net/view_news.asp?sub_no=1_2009_03_28_26945. Last accessed 19 June 2013.
183. Al-Fadli together with Abu al-Hasan al-Mihdar established what was known as the "Islamic Aden-Abyan Army" (*Jaysh Aden-Abyan al-Islami*) which was responsible for some of the kidnapping incidents. For more details on the army see *Al-Bab*, "Abu al-Hassan and the Islamic Army of Aden-Abyan". January 1999. http://www.al-bab.com/yemen/hamza/hassan.htm. Last accessed 30 September 2013.
184. Madabish, "Al-Qa'ida Tu'lin Da'm al-Infisal fil-Yaman".
185. *Munafiq* is an Islamic term used to describe a religious hypocrite, who outwardly practices Islam, while inwardly concealing his disbelief (*kufr*).
186. *Sada al-Malahim*, March 2008.
187. Nasser Arrabyee, "85 Shops in Yemen to be Closed for Selling Weapons". *Gulf News*, 17 June 2008. http://www.gulfnews.com/News/Gulf/yemen/10221726.html. Last accessed 19 June 2013.
188. "Haqiqat al-Safarat", *Sada al-Malahim*, No. 6, November 2008.
189. Ibid.
190. For more information about interventionist policies of superpowers in failed states see Chen Kertcher, "Same Agenda, Different Results: The UN Interventions in Cambodia and Somalia after the Cold War". *International Intervention in Local Conflicts: Crisis Management and Conflict Resolution since the Cold War*. Ed. Uzi Rabi. London: I.B.Tauris, 2010, pp. 20–33; and Martin Weinbaum, "Lost Faith, Forfeited Trust: Afghan Responses to Post-9/11 International Intervention in State-Building and Insurgency", in *International Intervention in Local Conflicts*, pp. 222–240.
191. Haydar, "Al-Wajh al-Jadid li-Tanthim al-Qa'ida fil-Yaman: Muhawala lil-Fahm, al-'Arabiyya".
192. *26 Sabtambar*, 5 March 2009.
193. Tariq al-Humayd, "al-Yaman ... Shukran lil-Qa'ida!" *Al-Sharq al-Awsat*, 14 May 2009.
194. Ibid.
195. *Al-Watan* (Saudi Arabia), 6 February 2009.
196. *Al-Sharq al-Awsat*, 19 April 2009.
197. *Al-Watan* (Saudi Arabia), 21 January 2009.
198. See, for example, al-'Arami, "Tanthim al-Qa'ida fil-Yaman: Min al-Hamish ila al-Matn", p. 277.

199. *26 Sabtambar*, "Kulluna Yad Wahida Didd al-Irhab", 26 March 2009.
200. Ibid.
201. Ibid.
202. Husayn al-Jarbani, "Na'ib Ra'is al-Wuzara al-Yamani: al-Badil Huwa al-Qa'ida law Hadatha Inhiyar Siasi". *Al-Sharq al-Awsat*, 20 May 2009.
203. Maryam Rubin, "al-Yaman al-Sa'id wal-Irhab". *14 Oktobar*, 5 October 2008.

Chapter 6. The Arab Spring: New Challenges Exacerbate the Old

1. For more analysis on some of the definitions of a failed state, see: Robert I. Rotberg, *When States Fail: Causes and Consequences*. Princeton: Princeton University Press, 2010; and Fund for Peace, "Failed States Index". http://www.fundforpeace.org/global/?q=fsi. Last accessed 20 June 2013.
2. *Al-Sharq al-Awsat*, 8 October 2011.
3. Tawakul Kirman was among those protesting against Salih even before the Arab uprisings. To a large extent, she acted under the auspices of a movement of which she was one of the founders, named *sahafiyyat bila hudud* (Female Journalists with no Boundaries). See also, *Al-Sharq al-Awsat*, 8 October 2011.
4. National Yemen, "US Objects to GPC Constitutional Amendments". 3 January 2011. http://nationalyemen.com/2011/01/03/us-objects-to-gpc-constitutional-amendments/. Last accessed 20 June 2013.
5. Laura Kasinof and Michael Slackman, "In Yemen, protestors face off in peace". *The New York Times*, 3 February 2011. http://www.nytimes.com/2011/02/04/world/middleeast/04yemen.html. Last accessed 20 June 2013.
6. Tom Finn, "Yemeni protestors shot dead at Sana'a University". *The Guardian*, 23 February 2011. http://www.guardian.co.uk/world/2011/feb/23/yemen-protesters-shot-dead-university. Last accessed 20 June 2013.
7. *Al-Sharq al-Awsat*, 8 April 2011.
8. *Al-Sharq al-Awsat*, 1 March 2011.
9. Tom Finn, "45 protestors killed in Yemen". *The Guardian*, 18 March 2011. http://www.guardian.co.uk/world/2011/mar/18/yemen-police-massacre-45-protesters. Last accessed 20 June 2013.
10. Laura Kasinof, "Yemen's President Said to Have Fired Cabinet". *The New York Times*, 20 March 2011. http://www.nytimes.com/2011/03/21/world/middleeast/21yemen.html. Last accessed 20 June 2013.

11. *Al-Sharq al-Awsat*, 23 March 2011.
12. Tom Finn, "Yemen Military Commanders Join Opposition as Tanks Take to the Streets". *The Guardian*, 21 March 2011. http://www.guardian.co.uk/world/2011/mar/21/yemen-military-commanders-opposition-tanks. Last accessed 20 June 2013.
13. April Longley Alley, "The Rules of the Game: Unpacking Patronage Politics in Yemen". *The Middle East Journal* 64.3 (2010): 385–409 (407).
14. Ibid., p. 402.
15. Robert F. Worth and Laura Kasinof, "Evasions by Leader Add Chaos in Yemen". *The New York Times*, 25 May 2011. http://www.nytimes.com/2011/05/26/world/middleeast/26yemen.html. Last accessed 20 June 2013.
16. For more on this, see Alley, "The Rules of the Game: Unpacking Patronage Politics in Yemen".
17. Ibid., p. 407.
18. Laura Kasinof and David E. Sanger, "U.S. Shifts to Seek Removal of Yemen's Leader, An Ally". *The New York Times*, 3 April 2011. http://www.nytimes.com/2011/04/04/world/middleeast/04yemen.html. Last accessed 20 June 2013.
19. For more details, see *al-Sharq al-Awsat*, 25 April 2011.
20. Laura Kasinof, "Gulf Nations Repeat Offer to Mediate Crisis in Yemen". *The New York Times*, 10 April 2011. http://www.nytimes.com/2011/04/11/world/middleeast/11yemen.html. Last accessed 20 June 2013.
21. For more details, see *al-Sharq al-Awsat*, 12 April 2011.
22. Tom Finn, "Yemen Resolution Unlikely as President Dismisses Gulf Plan to End Rule". *The Guardian*, 8 April 2011. http://www.guardian.co.uk/world/2011/apr/08/yemen-president-gulf-saleh. Last accessed 20 June 2013.
23. Quoted in Tom Finn, "Yemen's President Promises to Give Up Power When His Term Ends in 2013". *The Guardian*, 11 April 2011. http://www.guardian.co.uk/world/2011/apr/11/yemen-president-term-2013. Last accessed 20 June 2013.
24. Laura Kasinof, "Yemen's Loyalists Clash With Defiant Troops". *The New York Times*, 13 April 2011. http://www.nytimes.com/2011/04/14/world/middleeast/14yemen.html. Last accessed 20 June 2013.
25. Tom Finn, "Yemeni Forces Kill 18 and Wound Hundreds as Unrest Escalates". *The Guardian*, 12 May 2011. http://www.guardian.co.uk/world/2011/may/12/yemen-protests-republican-guards-troops. Last accessed 20 June 2013.
26. Gregory D. Johnsen, "Yemen's Coming Power Struggle". *The National*, 18 March 2010. http://www.thenational.ae/news/world/yemens-coming-power-struggle?pageCount=0#full. Last accessed 20 June 2013.

27. Gregory D. Johnsen, "The al-Ahmar Family: Who's Who". *Waq al-Waq Big Think*. 3 June 2011. http://bigthink.com/ideas/38715?page=all. Last accessed 20 June 2013.
28. Laura Kasinof and Neil MacFarquhar, "Key Tribal Chief Wants Yemen Leader to Quit". *The New York Times*, 26 February 2011. http://www.nytimes.com/2011/02/27/world/middleeast/27yemen.html. Last accessed 20 June 2013.
29. Al-Jazeera English, "Yemen Transition Deal Collapses". 22 May 2011. http://www.aljazeera.com/news/middleeast/2011/05/201152216373928689.html. Last accessed 20 June 2013.
30. Julian Borger and Tom Finn, "Yemen President's Supporters Trap Diplomats in Embassy". *The Guardian*, 22 May 2011. http://www.guardian.co.uk/world/2011/may/22/yemen-president-supporters-trap-diplomats. Last accessed 20 June 2013.
31. Tom Finn, "Yemen Locked in Power Struggle as Escalation of Fighting Leaves 38 Dead". *The Guardian*, 24 May 2011. http://www.guardian.co.uk/world/2011/may/24/yemen-saleh-ahmar-capital-fighting. Last accessed 20 June 2013.
32. BBC News, "Yemen: Sanaa airport 'shut' as tribes battle Saleh". 26 May 2011. http://www.bbc.co.uk/news/world-middle-east-13544243. Last accessed 20 June 2013.
33. Uri Friedman, "Yemeni tribesmen advance on the capital". *The Atlantic Wire*, 2 June 2011. http://www.theatlanticwire.com/global/2011/06/yemeni-tribesmen-advance-capital/38405/. Last accessed 20 June 2013.
34. Al-Jazeera Blogs – Yemen, "Yemen – July 17, 2011 – 12:11 – Al Jazeera Blogs". http://blogs.aljazeera.net/liveblog/yemen-jul-17–2011-1211. Last accessed 20 June 2013.
35. *National Yemen*, "Houthis Control Sa'da, Help Appoint Governor". 29 March 2011. http://nationalyemen.com/2011/03/29/houthis-control-sa%E2%80%99ada-help-appoint-governor/. Last accessed 20 June 2013.
36. Peter Beaumont, "Yemeni President Arrives in Saudi Arabia as Truce Breaks in Capital". *The Guardian*, 5 June 2011. http://www.guardian.co.uk/world/2011/jun/05/yemeni-president-saudi-arabia. Last accessed 20 June 2013.
37. Robert F. Worth and Laura Kasinof, "Yemeni President Wounded in Palace Attack". *The New York Times*, 3 June 2011. http://www.nytimes.com/2011/06/04/world/middleeast/04yemen.html. Last accessed 20 June 2013.

Conclusion

1. Michael C. Hudson, "Bipolarity, Rational Calculation and War in Yemen". *The Arab Studies Journal* 3.1 (1995): 81–105 (19–20, 36–37).

2. For a detailed report on the challenge posed by tribes to the state, see *Al-Watan al-'Arabi,* "Sira' al-Dawla wal-Qabila ... Lamin al-Nasr?". 21 July 2010.
3. For an analysis of the realities of 9/11, see Faris al-Saqqaf, *al-Yaman wal- Irhab qabla Ahdath 11 Sabtambar wa ma Ba'daha*. Sanaa: Markaz 'Abadi lil-Dirasat wal-Nashr, 2003.

BIBLIOGRAPHY

Arabic

26 Sabtambar. "Kulluna Yad Wahida Didd al-Irhab (All of Us United [One Hand] Against Terrorism)." 26 March 2009.

'Abd al-Fattah, Fathi. *Tajribat al-Thawra fil-Yaman al-Dimuqratiyya (Experiment of Revolution in Democratic Yemen).* Beirut: Dar Ibn Khaldun, 1974.

'Abd al-Karim, Salim. "Fil-Yaman ... Irtiyah li- Waqf Harb Sa'da lakin al-Tahaddiyat la Zalat Qa'ima" (In Yemen ... Ceasefire in Sa'da but Challenges Still Lie Ahead). *Al-Bainah*, 26 March 2007.

'Abd al-Salam, Muhammad. *Al-Jumhuriyya Bayna al-Sultana wal-Kabila fil-Yaman al-Shimaliyya. (The Republic Between the Regime and the Tribe in North Yemen).* Cairo: Sharikat al-Amal lil-Tiba'a wal-Nashr wal-Tawzi', 1988.

Abu Ghanim, Fadhl 'Ali Ahmad. *Al-Buniyya al-Qibliyya fil-Yaman bayn al-'Istimrar wal-Taghayyur (The Tribal Structure of Yemen between Continuity and Change).* Cairo: Dar al-Hikma al-Yamaniyya, 1991.

Ahmad, Ahmad Yusuf. *Al-Dawr al-Masri fil-Yaman, 1962–1967 (The Egyptian Role in Yemen).* Cairo: General Egyptian Book Organization (GEBO), 1981.

Ahmad, Hasan Hudhayri. *Qiyam al-Dawla al-Zaydiyya fil-Yaman (The Establishment of a Zaidi State in Yemen).* Cairo: Madbuli, 1996.

Ahmad, Mahmud 'Adil. *Dhikrayat Harb al-Yaman: 1962–1967 (Memories of the War in Yemen: 1962–1967).* Cairo: Matba'at al-Ukhuwa, 1992.

Al-'Abdali, Samir Muhammad Ahmad. *Al-Wahda al-Yamaniyya wal-Nitham al-Iqlimi al-'Arabi (The Unity of Yemen and the Arab Regional Order).* Cairo: Madbuli, 1997.

Al-Adhal, 'Abdu Husayn Sulayman. *Al-Istiqlal al-Da'i' (The Lost Independence).* Cairo: Dar al-Wazzan lil-Tiba'a wal-Nashr, 1988.

Al-'Arami, Yasir. "Tanthim al-Qa'ida fil-Yaman: Min al-Hamish ila al-Matn (Al-Qa'ida in Yemen: From the Margins to the Mainstream)." *Al-Huthiyyun fil-Yaman (The Huthis in Yemen)*. Dubai, Markaz al-Misbar lil-Dirasat wal-Buhuth, 2010.

Al-Ba'dani, Fu'ad. "Al-Zaydiyyun wal-Thawra al-Yamaniyya (The Zaidis and the Yemeni Revolution)." *Al-Huthiyyun fil-Yaman*. Dubai: Markaz al-Misbar lil-Dirasat wal-Buhuth, 2010.

Al-Bakr, Bashir. *Harb al-Yaman: al-Qabila Tantasir 'ala al-Watan (The Yemen War: The Tribe Prevails over the State)*. Beirut: al-Mu'ssasa al-'Arabiyya lil-Dirasat wal-Nashr, 1995.

Al-Banna, Fu'ad. *Al-Haraka al-Siyasiyya al-Shi'iyya fil-Yaman (The Shi'i Political Movement in Yemen)*. Dubai, 2009.

Al-Daghshi, Ahmad Muhammad. "Al-Huthiyyun ...'Indama Yanqalib al-Sahar 'ala al-Sahir (The Huthis ... When the Tool is Turned Against its Own Maker)." *Majallat Shu'un al-'Asr*, 7 February 2006.

Al-Farah, Muhammad Husayn. *Al-Yaman fi Ta'rikh Ibn Khaldun (Yemen in Ibn Khaldun's History)*. Sanaa: Al-Hay'a al-'Amma lil-Kitab, 2001.

Al-Ghafari, 'Ali 'Abd al-Qawi. *Al-Wahda al-Yamaniyya: al-Waqi' wal-Mustaqbal (The Unity of Yemen: The Present and the Future)*. Sanaa: Kitab al-Thawabit, 1997.

Al-Haddad, Muhammad Yahya. *Ta'rikh al-Yaman al-Siyasi al-Mu'asir (A Political History of Modern Yemen)*. Beirut: Manshurat al-Madina, 1986.

Al-Hariri, Muhammad 'Isa. *Dirasat wa-Buhuth fi Ta'rikh al-Yaman al-Islami (Studies and Research in the Islamic History of Yemen)*. Cairo: 'Alam al-Kutub lil-Tiba'a wal-Nashr wal-Tawzi', 1998.

Al-Humayd, Tariq. "al-Yaman ... Shukran lil-Qa'ida! (Yemen ... Thanks to Al-Qaeda)." *Al-Sharq al-Awsat*, 14 May 2009

Al-Iryani, 'Abd al-Karim. "Tatawwur al-Awda al-Iqtisadiyya fi Shatray al-Yaman wa-Mustaqbal al-Wahda al-Wataniyya (The Economic Developments in the Two Yemens and the Future of Yemen's Unification)." *Dirasat fil-Ta'rikh wal-Siyasa wal-Iqtisad – al-Nadwa al-Diplomasiyya al-Ithna 'Ashariyya*. Ed. 'Ali Humaydan. Abu Dhabi: Foreign Ministry, 1992.

Al-'Izzi, Haydar 'Ali Naji. *Inqilab 'Am 1955 fil-Yaman (1955 Coup in Yemen)*. Aden: Wizarat al-Thaqafah wal-Siyahah, 2004.

Al-Janahi, Sa'id Ahmad. *Al-Haraka al-Wataniyya al-Yamaniyya: Min al-Thawra ila al-Wahda (The Yemeni National Movement: From Revolution to Unity)*. Aden: Markaz al-'Amal lil-Dirasat wal-Nashr, 1992.

Al-Jawhari, Shakir. *Al-Sira' fi Aden (The Conflict in Aden)*. Cairo: Madbuli, 1992.

Al-Juzaylan, 'Abdallah. *Al-Ta'rikh al-Sirri lil-Thawra al-Yamaniyya: 1956–1962 (The Secret History of the Yemeni Revolution: 1956–1962)*. Beirut: Dar al-'Awda, 1977.

Al-Khidri, Anwar Qasim. "al-Huthi wal-Waraqa al-Ta'ifiyya al-Khasira (The Huthis and the Losing Sectarian Card)." *Bayyina Institute*, 6 May 2006.

Al-Masri, Ahmad 'Atiyya. *Tajribat al-Yaman al-Dimuqratiyya (The Experiment of Democratic Yemen)*. Cairo: Dar al-Madani lil-Tiba'a wal-Nashr, 1974.

Al-Nasir, Walid Mahmud 'Abd. "Awwal Tajriba Marksiyya 'Arabiyya (The First Arab Marxist Experience)." *Wujahat Nathar*, May 2010.

Al-Rihani, Amin. *Muluk al-Arab: Rihla fil-Bilad al-'Arabiyya (Kings of Arabia: A Journey to the Lands of Arabia)*. Beirut: Dar al-Jil, 1987.

Al-San'ani, Abu Hurayra. "Al-Sumal ... al-Ard al-Munsiyya (Somalia ... The Forgotten Land)." *Sada al-Malahim*, no. 4, July 2008.

Al-Saqqaf, Ahmad. *Ana 'a'id min al-Yaman (Back from Yemen)*. Cairo: Dar al-Katib al-'Arabi, 1962.

Al-Saqqaf, Faris. *al-Yaman wal-Irhab qabla Ahdath 11 Sabtambar wa ma Ba'daha (Yemen and Terrorism Before and After the Events of September 11)*. Sanaa: Markaz 'Abadi lil-Dirasat wal-Nashr, 2003.

Al-Shahari, Muhammad 'Ali. *Al-Yaman: Al-Thawra fil-Janub wal-Intikasa fil-Shimal (Revolution in the South and Setback in the North)*. Beirut: Dar Ibn Khaldun, 1972.

Al-Shahari, Muhammad 'Ali, and Ibrahim Wahib Fahmi. *Jamal 'Abd al-Nasir wa-Haqa'iq min Harb al-Yaman (Jamal 'Abd al-Nasser and Some Facts of the Yemen War)*. Beirut: Antun Jamil Saba, 1997.

al-Shatiri, Muhammad bin Ahmad. *Adwar al-Tarikh al-Hadrami*. Jeddah: Maktabat al-Irshad, 1962.

Al-Tayyib, 'Abd al-Malik. *Al-Thawra wal-Nafaq al-Muthlim (The Revolution and Its Gloomy Path)*. Sanaa: 'Abd al-Malik bin Muhammad al-Tayyib, 1995.

Al-Thawr, 'Abdallah Ahmad. *Hathihi Hiyya al-Yaman (This is Yemen)*. Beirut: Dar al-Fikr al-'Arabi lil-Tiba'a wal-Nashr, 1976.

Al-Wasi', Husayn bin 'Ali. *Al-Yaman al-Kubra: Kitab Jughrafi Jiuluji Tahrihi (Greater Yemen: Geography, Geology and History)*. Cairo: Matba'at al-Nahdha al-Arabiyya, 1962.

Al-Wasi'i, 'Abd al-Wasi' Ibn Yahya. *Ta'rikh al-Yaman: Al-Musamma Furjat al-Humum wal-Huznfi Hawadith wa-tarikh al-Yaman (The History of Yemen: The Salvation of Interests and Sadness Concerning the Events and History of Yemen)*. Cairo: Al-Matba'ah Salafiyah wa-Maktabatuha, 1927.

Amin, 'Adil. "Tanthim al-Qa'ida fil-Yaman (The Organization of al-Qa'ida in Yemen)." *Ma'rib Press*, 9 July 2007. http://www.marebpress.net/articles.php?id=2121&lng=arabic. Last accessed 19 June 2013.

Hasan, Hasan Ibrahim. *al-Yaman: al-Bilad al-Sa'ida (Yemen: The Joyous Land)*. Cairo: Dar al-Ma'arif, 1958.

Hassan, Shukri. "Al-Ikhwan al-Muslimun fil-Yaman (The Muslim Brotherhood in Yemen)." *Al-Tali'a al-Yamaniyya*, No. 8, 1984.

Haydar, Muhammad Sayf. "Al-Wajh al-Jadid li-Tanthim al-Qa'ida fil-Yaman: Muhawala lil-Fahm (The New Face of al-Qai'da in Yemen)." *Al-Arabiyya.net*, 17 September 2008. http://www.alarabiya.net/views/2008/09/17/56762.html. Last accessed 30 September 2013.

Isma'il, 'Abd al-Fattah. *Al-Turath wal-Thaqafa al-Wataniyya (The Heritage and the National Culture)*. Beirut: Dar Ibn Khaldun, 1986.

—— *Al-Jabha al-Qawmiyya – al-Tanthim al-Siyasi lil-Mu'tamar al-Tawhidi –* October 1975 (The NLF – Political Organization for the Conference on Unity). Beirut: Dar Ibn Khaldoun, 1976.

—— "Makhawif min Iktisab Tanthim al-Qa'ida fil-Yaman (Fears of an al-Qa'ida Victory in Yemen)." *Al-Arabiya.net.* 28 July 2009. http://www.alarabiya.net/articles/2009/07/28/80117.html. Last accessed 30 June 2013.

Muhammad, Rasha. "al-Yaman ... Tabul al-Harb Taduqq fi Sa'da (Yemen ... The Drums of War are Beating in Sa'da)." *al-Fan Online*, 15 December 2008. http://alfanonline.moheet.com/show_news.aspx?nid=79090. Last accessed 18 June 2013.

Muhsin, Muhammad Sa'id 'Abdallah. *Aden: Kifah Sha'bi wa-Hazima Imbaraturiyya (Aden: National Struggle and the Defeat of an Empire).* Beirut: Dar Ibn Khaldun, 1988

Nagi, Sultan. *Al-Ta'rikh al-'Askari lil-Yaman: 1839–1967 (The Military History of Yemen: 1839–1967).* Publisher unknown, 1967.

Nur al-Din, 'Adil. *Al-Yaman, Madiha wa-Hadiruha wa-Mustakbaluha (Yemen: Past, Present, Future).* Cairo: Idarat al-Shu'un al-'Amma wal-Tawzi' al-Ma'nawi, 1964.

Rida, 'Adil. *Muhawala li-Fahm al-Thawra al-Yamaniyya (An Attempt to Understand the Yemeni Revolution).* Cairo: al-Maktab al-Masri al-Hadith, 1974.

Rubin, Maryam. "al-Yaman al-Sa'id wal-Irhab (Happy Yemen [Arabia Felix] and Terrorism)." *14 Oktobar,* 5 October 2008.

Sawt al-Sha'b. "Man Nahnu (Who We Are)." 11 February 2010.

"Sira' al-Dawla wal-Qabila ... Lamin al-Nasr? (The Struggle between the Tribe and the State ... Who Gets the Upper Hand?)". *Al-Watan al-'Arabi,* 21 July 2010.

Tarsisi, 'Adnan. *Bilad Saba wa-Hadarat al-'Arab al-'Ula. (Sheba and the First Arab Civilizations).* Beirut: Dar al-Fikr al-Mu'asir, 1990.

'Umar, Sultan Ahmad. *Nathra fi Tatawwur al-Mujtama' al-Yamani (A look at the Development of Yemeni Society).* Beirut: Dar al-Tali'a lil-Tiba'a wal-Nashr, 1970.

Yusuf Khalid. "Al-Hall – Dawlatayn (The Solution – Two States)." *Al-Janub al-Hurr,* No. 8, 14 October 2008.

al-Zawahiri, Ayman. "Risala ila Ahl Al-Yaman (2)". *Sada al-Malahim*, Issue. 9, May 2009, p. 26.

List of Newspapers and Magazines Cited

26 Sabtambar (Sanaa, daily)
14 Oktobar (Aden, daily)
Al-'Alam (Dubai, daily)
Al-Ahram (Cairo, daily)
Al-Akhbar (Cairo, daily)

Al-'Arab (Doha, daily)
Al-Ayam (Manama, daily)
Al-Bainah (Beirut, daily)
Al-Difa' (Amman, daily)
Al-Dunya (Abu Dhabi)
Al-Dustur (Amman, daily)
Al-Hawadith (London, weekly)
Al-Hayat (London, daily)
Al-Hurriyya (Beirut, weekly)
Al-Islah (Amman, daily)
Al-Janub al-Hurr (Aden, weekly)
Al-Jarida (Kuwait, daily)
Al-Jazeera (Doha)
Al-Jumhuriyya (Cairo, daily)
Al-Madina (sp, Jedda, daily)
Al-Majalla (London, weekly)
Al-Muraqib al-'Arabi (London)
Al-Mustaqbal (Beirut, daily)
Al-Mu'tamar (Sanaa, weekly)
Al-Nahar (Beirut, daily)
Al-Nahar al-'Arabi wal-Duwali
Al-Qabas (Kuwait, daily)
Al-Quds al-'Arabi (London, daily)
Al-Ra'i al-'Amm (Kuwait, daily)
Al-Riyadh (Riyadh, daily)
Al-Safir (Beirut, daily)
Al-Sahwa (Al-Sahwa.net)
Al-Sayyad (Beirut)
Al-Sharq al-Awsat (London, daily)
Al-Siyasa (Kuwait, daily)
Al-Tali'a al-Yamaniyya
Al-Turath (Abu Dhabi, monthly)
Al-Wahda (Abu Dhabi, daily)
Al-Wasat (London, weekly)
Al-Watan (Muscat, daily)
Al-Watan al-'Arabi (Cairo, weekly)
Majallat Shu'un al-'Asr (Sanaa, quarterly)
Radio Aden
Radio Cairo
Radio Sanaa
Ruz al-Yusuf (Cairo, weekly)
Sada al-Malahim (AQAP)
'Ukaz (sp, Jedda, daily)

English and Other

Abdulrab, Habib. *La Reine Étripée*. Paris: L'Harmattan littératures, 1998.

Aboul-Enein, Youssef. "The Egyptian-Yemen War (1962–67): Egyptian Perspectives on Guerrilla Warfare." *Infantry Magazine* 93.1 (2004): 19–23.

Al-Arabiya.net. "Two Killed, 20 Injured in Yemen Attack." 25 July 2008. http://www.alarabiya.net/articles/2008/07/25/53700.html. Last accessed 19 June 2013.

Al-Bab. "The Sanaa Declaration." 1999. http://www.al-bab.com/arab/docs/sanaa.htm. Last accessed 27 October 2013.

——. "Abu al-Hassan and the Islamic Army of Aden-Abyan." January 1999. http://www.al-bab.com/yemen/hamza/hassan.htm. Last accessed 30 September 2013.

Al-Bukairi, Nabil. "Dr. Aqeel Al-Maqtari Prominent leader in the Yemeni Salafi Movement." *Yemen Post*, 10 April 2010.

Al-Halali, Aqeel. "'Unprecedented' Security Alert to Tighten the Noose Around Al-Qaeda". *Yemen Times*, 9 February 2009. http://yementimes.com/article.shtml?i=1232&p=local&a=1.

Al-Madhagi, Ahmad Noman Qasim, *Yemen and the USA: A Super-Power and a Small-state Relationship, 1962–1992*. BAR International. London: I.B.Tauris, 1996.

Al-Rubaysh, Ibrahim. "Why Muhammad bin Na'if?" Forum post, *Islamic Awakening*. http://forums.islamicawakening.com/f18/why-muhammad-ibn-naif-shaykh-ibrahim-al-28847. Last accessed 27 October 2013.

Al-Thawr, 'Abd al-Malik. "YSCC's Upcoming Round Due on Sideline of Riyadh Meeting." *Yemen News Agency (SABA)*, 24 February 2010. http://www.sabanews.net/ar/print206916.htm. Last accessed 19 June 2013.

Alley, April Longley. "The Rules of the Game: Unpacking Patronage Politics in Yemen." *The Middle East Journal* 64.3 (2010): 385–409.

Anderson, Benedict. *Imagined Communities: Reflections on the Origin and Spread of Nationalism*. London; New York: Verso, 1991.

Arab Bulletin. "Idrisi and Imam." 13 (1 August 1916): n. pag.

——. "Yemen: Overtures from the Imam." 58 (5 August 1917): n. pag.

——. "Notes: Yemen News." 60 (20 August 1917): n. pag.

——. "Untitled." 61 (1 September 1917): n. pag.

Arab News. "Kingdom Unveils List of 85 Wanted Militants Abroad." 3 February 2009. http://arabnews.com/node/320619. Last accessed 18 June 2013.

Arendonk, Cornelis van. *Les debuts de l'imamat zaidite au Yemen*. Leyden: E. J. Brill, 1960.

Arrabyee, Nasser. "85 Shops in Yemen to Be Closed for Selling Weapons." *Gulf News*, 17 June 2008. http://www.gulfnews.com/News/Gulf/yemen/10221726.html. Last accessed 19 June 2013.

Asseri, Ali Saeed Awadh. *Combating Terrorism: Saudi Arabia's Role in the War on Terror*. Oxford: Oxford University Press, 2009.

Ayubi, Nazih N. *Over-Stating the Arab State: Politics and Society in the Middle East*. London: I.B.Tauris, 1995.

Badeeb, Saeed M. *The Saudi-Egyptian Conflict Over North Yemen, 1962–1970*. Boulder, CO: Westview Press, 1986.

Badran, Margot. "Unifying Women: Feminist Pasts and Presents in Yemen." *Gender & History* 10.3 (1998): 498–518. http://onlinelibrary.wiley.com/doi/10.1111/1468–0424.00115/pdf. Last accessed 18 June 2013.

Baldry, John. "Al-Yaman and the Turkish Occupation 1849–1914." *Arabica* 23.2 (1976): 156–196.

——. "Anglo-Italian Rivalry in Yemen and ʿAsir 1900–1934." *Die Welt des Islams* 17.1/4 (1976): 155–193.

Barfi, Barak. "The Yemenite Imbroglio." *The Jerusalem Report*, 19 March 2007: 17.

BBC News. "Yemen Petrol Riots Leave 12 Dead." 20 July 2005. http://news.bbc.co.uk/2/hi/middle_east/4700813.stm. Last accessed 18 June 2013.

——. "Profile: Shoe-throwing Journalist." 15 September 2009. http://news.bbc.co.uk/2/hi/middle_east/7787792.stm. Last accessed 19 June 2013.

——. "Yemen: Sanaa airport 'shut' as tribes battle Saleh." 26 May 2011. http://www.bbc.co.uk/news/world-middle-east-13544243. Last accessed 20 June 2013.

Beaumont, Peter. "Yemeni President Arrives in Saudi Arabia as Truce Breaks in Capital." *The Guardian*, 5 June 2011. http://www.guardian.co.uk/world/2011/jun/05/yemeni-president-saudi-arabia. Last accessed 20 June 2013.

Belczyk, Jaclyn. "Yemen Denies Plans to Transfer Guantanamo Detainees to Saudi Arabia." *Jurist*, 15 June 2009. http://jurist.law.pitt.edu/paperchase/2009/06/yemen-denies-plans-to-transfer.php. Last accessed 19 June 2013.

Bidwell, Robin Leonard. *The Two Yemens*. Harlow, Essex; Boulder, Co.: Longman; Westview Press, 1983.

Black, Ian. "A New Taliban?" *The Guardian*, 3 September 2008. http://www.guardian.co.uk/world/2008/sep/03/yemen. Last accessed 19 June 2013.

Borger, Julian, and Tom Finn. "Yemen President's Supporters Trap Diplomats in Embassy." *The Guardian*, 22 May 2011. http://www.guardian.co.uk/world/2011/may/22/yemen-president-supporters-trap-diplomats. Last accessed 20 June 2013.

Boucek, Christopher. "War in Saada: From Local Insurrection to National Challenge." *Yemen on the Brink*. Ed. Marina Ottaway. Washington DC: Carnegie Endowment, 2010. 50–51.

Boucek, Christopher, and Marina Ottaway, eds. *Yemen on the Brink*. Washington DC: Carnegie Endowment, 2010.

Bowen, Donna Lee, and Evelyn A. Early. *Everyday Life in the Muslim Middle East*. Indiana Series in Middle East Studies. Bloomington: Indiana University Press, 2002.

Brown, L. Carl. *Diplomacy in the Middle East: The International Relations of Regional and Outside Powers*. London: I.B.Tauris, 2004.

Burrowes, Robert D. *The Yemen Arab Republic: The Politics of Development, 1962–1986*. Boulder: Westview Press, 1986.

——. *The Yemen Arab Republic: The Politics of Development, 1962–1986*. Boulder: Westview Press, 1987.

——. "Prelude to Unification: The Yemen Arab Republic, 1962–1990." *International Journal of Middle East Studies* 23.4 (1991): 483–506.

——. *Historical Dictionary of Yemen*. 2nd ed. Historical Dictionaries of Asia, Oceania, and the Middle East No. 72. Lanham, MD: Scarecrow Press, 2010.

Carapico, Sheila. "Yemen: Unification and the Gulf War." *Middle East Report* 21.170 (1991): 26.

——. "Elections and Mass Politics in Yemen." *Middle East Report* 185 (1993): 2–6. http://www.merip.org/mer/mer185/elections-mass-politics-yemen. Last accessed 17 June 2013.

——. *Civil Society in Yemen: The Political Economy of Activism in Modern Arabia*. New York: Cambridge University Press, 2007.

—— and Cynthia Myntti. "Change in North Yemen 1977–1989: A Tale of Two Families." *Middle East Report* 170 (1991): 24–29, 47. http://www.jstor.org/stable/pdfplus/3013247.pdf?acceptTC=true. Last accessed 17 June 2013.

Chaudhry, Kiren Aziz. *The Price of Wealth: Economies and Institutions in the Middle East*. Cornell Studies in Political Economy. New York: Cornell University Press, 1997.

Cigar, Norman. "Islam and the State in South Yemen: The Uneasy Coexistence." *Middle Eastern Studies* 26.2 (1990): 185–203. http://www.tandfonline.com/doi/pdf/10.1080/00263209008700814#.UjGRfNJkOvI. Last accessed 17 June 2013.

Colburn, Marta. *The Republic of Yemen: Development Challenges in the 21st Century*. London: CIIR, 2002.

Collard, Elizabeth, ed. *Middle East Economic Digest*. London: Middle East Economic Digest, Ltd., 1981. 68. v. 25.

Country Report (CR). "Yemen." 2 (1997): 34–37.

Crouch, Michael. *An Element of Luck: To South Arabia and Beyond*. London: Radcliffe Press, 1993.

Currivan, Gene. "New Yemen Regime Seizes $40,000,000 Carried Away Just Before Assassination." *The New York Times*, 21 February 1948 : 6.

Dahlgren, Susanne. "The Southern Movement in Yemen." *ISIM Review* 22 (2008): 50–51.

Deeb, Marius. "Radical Political Ideologies and Concepts of Property in Libya and South Yemen." *Middle East Journal* 40.3 (1986): 445–461.

Deffarge, Claude, and Gordian Troeller. *Yemen 62–69: de la révolution "sauvage" à la trêve des guerriers*. L'Histoire que nous vivons. Paris: R. Laffont, 1969.

Douglas, J. Leigh. "The Free Yemeni Movement, 1935–1962." *Contemporary Yemen: Politics and Historical Background.* Ed. B. R. Pridham. London: Croom Helm, 1984. 36–37.

Douglas, J. Leigh and G. Chimienti. *The Free Yemeni Movement, 1935–1962.* Beirut: The American University of Beirut, 1987.

Dresch, Paul. *Tribes, Government, and History in Yemen.* Oxford: Clarendon Press, 1989.

——. "The Tribal Factor in Yemeni Politics." *The Yemeni War of 1994: Causes and Consequences.* Ed. Jamal S. al-Suwaidi. London: Saqi Books, 1995.

——. *A History of Modern Yemen.* Cambridge: Cambridge University Press, 2000.

Edge, Simon. "Yemen's Problems and Promise." *MEED (Middle East Economic Digest)* 36. 13 (3 April 1992): 4–5.

Edwards, Frank. *The Gaysh: A History of the Aden Protectorate Levies 1927–61 and the Federal Regular Army of South Arabia 1961–67.* Solihull: HELION & Company, 2003.

Engel, Richard. "Yemen's Weapon Culture." *BBC*, 22 January 2002. http://news.bbc.co.uk/2/hi/middle_east/1775938.stm. Last accessed 18 June 2013.

Farah, Caesar E. *The Sultan's Yemen: Nineteenth-Century Challenges to Ottoman Rule.* London: I.B.Tauris, 2002.

Field, Michael, Ed. "Saudi Arabia." *Middle East Annual Review.* Ann Arbor: University of Michigan, 1977.

Finn, Tom. "Yemeni Protesters Shot Dead at Sanaa University." *The Guardian*, 23 February 2011. http://www.guardian.co.uk/world/2011/feb/23/yemen-protesters-shot-dead-university. Last accessed 20 June 2013.

——. "45 Protesters Killed in Yemen." *The Guardian*, 18 March 2011. http://www.guardian.co.uk/world/2011/mar/18/yemen-police-massacre-45-protesters. Last accessed 20 June 2013.

——. "Yemen Military Commanders Join Opposition as Tanks Take to the Streets." *The Guardian*, 21 March 2011. http://www.guardian.co.uk/world/2011/mar/21/yemen-military-commanders-opposition-tanks. Last accessed 20 June 2013.

——. "Yemen Resolution Unlikely as President Dismisses Gulf Plan to End Rule." *The Guardian*, 8 April 2011. http://www.guardian.co.uk/world/2011/apr/08/yemen-president-gulf-saleh. Last accessed 20 June 2013.

——. "Yemen's President Promises to Give up Power When His Term Ends in 2013." *The Guardian*, 11 April 2011. http://www.guardian.co.uk/world/2011/apr/11/yemen-president-term-2013. Last accessed 20 June 2013.

——. "Yemeni Forces Kill 18 and Wound Hundreds as Unrest Escalates." *The Guardian*, 12 May 2011. http://www.guardian.co.uk/world/2011/may/12/yemen-protests-republican-guards-troops. Last accessed 20 June 2013.

——. "Yemen Locked in Power Struggle as Escalation of Fighting Leaves 38 Dead." *The Guardian*, 24 May 2011. http://www.guardian.co.uk/world/2011/may/24/yemen-saleh-ahmar-capital-fighting. Last accessed 20 June 2013.

Fontaine, Richard, and Andrew Exum. "Yemen's Coming Disaster." *Los Angeles Times*, 5 January 2010. http://articles.latimes.com/2010/jan/05/opinion/la-oe-fontaineexum5–2010jan05. Last accessed 18 June 2013.

Foster, Donald S. *Landscape with Arabs: Travels in Aden and South Arabia*. Brighton: Clifton Books, 1969.

Friedman, Uri. "Yemeni Tribesmen Advance on the Capital." *The Atlantic Wire*, 2 June 2011. http://www.theatlanticwire.com/global/2011/06/yemeni-tribes-men-advance-capital/38405/. Last accessed 20 June 2013.

Fund for Peace. "Failed States Index." http://www.fundforpeace.org/global/?q=fsi Last accessed 20 June 2013.

Gause, Gregory F. "Yemen." *The Middle East and North Africa: General Surveys*. 43rd ed. London: Emerald Group Publishing Limited, 1977.

——. *Saudi-Yemeni Relations: Domestic Structures and Foreign Influence*. New York: Columbia University Press, 1990.

Glosemeyer, Iris, and Don Reneau. "Local Conflict, Global Spin: An Uprising in the Yemeni Highlands." *Middle East Report* 232 (2004): 44–46. http://www.jstor.org/stable/pdfplus/1559484.pdf?acceptTC=true. Last accessed 18 June 2013.

Gochenour, D. Thomas. "Towards Sociology of the Islamization of Yemen." *Contemporary Yemen: Politics and Historical Background*. Ed. B.R. Pridham. London: Croom Helm, 1984.

Golan. Galia. *Soviet Policies in the Middle East: from World War Two to Gorbachev*. Cambridge: Cambridge University Press, 1990.

Haddick, Robert. "This Week at War: The Middle East's Cold War Heats Up." *Small Wars Journal*, 28 August 2009. http://www.foreignpolicy.com/articles/2009/08/28/this_week_at_war_the_middle_easts_cold_war_heats_up. Last accessed 18 June 2013.

Halliday, Fred. "Yemen's Unfinished Revolution: Socialism in the South." *Middle East Research & Information Project (MERIP)* 81 (1979): 3–20.

——. "The Arabian Peninsula Opposition Movements." *MERIP Reports* 130 (February 1985). *CrossRef*. http://www.jstor.org/stable/pdfplus/3011110.pdf?acceptTC=true. Last accessed 16 June 2013.

——. "The Formation of Yemeni Nationalism: Initial Reflections." *Rethinking Nationalism in the Arab Middle East*. Eds. Israel Gershoni and James Jankowski. New York: Columbia University Press, 1997.

——. *Arabia Without Sultans*. London: Saqi Books, 2002.

——. *Revolution and Foreign Policy: The Case of South Yemen, 1967–1987*. Cambridge: Cambridge University Press, 2002.

Halpern, Manfred. *The Politics of Social Change in the Middle East and North Africa*. A Rand Corporation Research Study Series. Scranton: Princeton University Press, 1963.

Hatita, 'Abd al-Sattar. "The Battle for Yemen's Unity." *al-Sharq al-Awsat*, 23 August 2009.

Hegghammer, Thomas. "Saudi and Yemeni Branches of al-Qaida Unite." *Jihadica*, 24 January 2009. http://www.jihadica.com/saudi-and-yemeni-branches-of-al-qaida-unite. Last accessed 19 June 2013.

Heyworth-Dunne, James. *Al-Yemen: A General Social, Political and Economic Survey*. Cairo: Renaissance Bookshop, 1952.

Hinchcliffe, Peter, John T. Ducker and Maria Holt. *Without Glory in Arabia: The British Retreat from Aden*. International Library of Colonial History. London: I.B.Tauris, 2006.

Hudson, Michael C. *Arab Politics: The Search for Legitimacy*. A Yale Paperbound. New Haven: Yale University Press, 1977.

——. "After the Gulf War: Prospects for Democratization in the Arab World." *Middle East Journal* 45.3 (1991): 407–426.

——. "Bipolarity, Rational Calculation, and War in Yemen." *The Arab Studies Journal* 3.1 (1995): 9–19.

——. "Obstacles to Democratization in the Middle East." *Contention* 5.2 (1996): 81–105.

Ingrams, W. Harold. *The Yemen: Imams, Rulers & Revolutions*. New York and London: Praeger, 1964.

International Crisis Group (ICG). "Yemen: Coping with Terrorism and Violence in a Fragile State." *Middle East Report* 8 (8 January 2003): 9–13. http://www.crisisgroup.org/en/regions/middle-east-north-africa/iraq-iran-gulf/yemen/008-yemen-coping-with-terrorism-and-violence-in-a-fragile-state.aspx. Last accessed 17 June 2013.

Interpol. "Al-Ahdal, Mohammad Hamdi Mohammad Sadiq". 2 November 2010. http://www.interpol.int/@en/UN/(un_id)/2010–6442. Last accessed 19 June 2013.

Johnsen, Gregory D. "Al Qaeda's Generational Split." *Boston Globe*, 9 November 2007. http://www.boston.com/bostonglobe/editorial_opinion/oped/articles/2007/11/09/al_qaedas_generational_split/ Last accessed 19 June 2013.

——. "Yemen's Coming Power Struggle." *The National*, 18 March 2010. http://www.thenational.ae/news/world/yemens-coming-power-struggle?pageCount=0#full. Last accessed 20 June 2013.

——. "The al-Ahmar Family: Who's Who." *Waq al-Waq, Big Think*, 3 June 2011. http://bigthink.com/ideas/38715?page=all. Last accessed 20 June 2013.

Jones, Clive. "Where the State Feared to Tread: Britain, Britons, Covert Action and the Yemen Civil War, 1962–64." *Intelligence and National Security* 21.5 (2006): 717–737. http://www.tandfonline.com/doi/pdf/10.1080/02684520600957688. Last accessed 12 June 2013.

Kasinof, Laura. "Yemen's President Said to Have Fired Cabinet." *The New York Times*, 20 March 2011. http://www.nytimes.com/2011/03/21/world/middleeast/21yemen.html. Last accessed 20 June 2013.

——. "Gulf Nations Repeat Offer to Mediate Crisis in Yemen." *The New York Times*, 10 April 2011. http://www.nytimes.com/2011/04/11/world/middleeast/11yemen.html. Last accessed 20 June 2013.

——. "Yemen's Loyalists Clash With Defiant Troops." *The New York Times*, 13 April 2011. http://www.nytimes.com/2011/04/14/world/middleeast/14yemen.html. Last accessed 20 June 2013.

—— and Michael Slackman. "In Yemen, protestors face off in peace." *The New York Times*, 3 February 2011. http://www.nytimes.com/2011/02/04/world/middleeast/04yemen.html. Last accessed 20 June 2013.

—— and Neil Macfarquhar. "Key Tribal Chief Wants Yemen Leader to Quit." *The New York Times*, 26 February 2011. http://www.nytimes.com/2011/02/27/world/middleeast/27yemen.html. Last accessed 20 June 2013.

—— and David E. Sanger. "U.S. Shifts to Seek Removal of Yemen's Leader, An Ally." *The New York Times*, 3 April 2011. http://www.nytimes.com/2011/04/04/world/middleeast/04yemen.html. Last accessed 20 June 2013.

Katz, Mark N. "Civil Conflict in South Yemen." *Middle East Review* 19.1 (1986): 7–13.

——. "Yemeni Unity and Saudi Security." *Middle East Policy* 1.1 (1992): 117–135. http://digilib.gmu.edu/jspui/bitstream/1920/3118/1/yemeni%20unity%20and%20saudi%20security.pdf. Last accessed 13 June 2013.

Khan, Ghazanfar Ali. "New Measures to Combat Terrorism." *Arab News*, 21 February 2010. http://www.arabnews.com/node/337710. Last accessed 18 June 2013.

Kertcher, Chen. "Same Agenda, Different Results: The UN Interventions in Cambodia and Somalia after the Cold War." *International Intervention in Local Conflicts: Crisis Management and Conflict Resolution Since the Cold War.* Ed. Uzi Rabi. London: I.B.Tauris, 2010. 20–33.

Kostiner, Joseph. *The Struggle for South Yemen*. London: Croom Helm, 1984.

——. "The Yemen Arab Republic." Ed. Ami Ayalon and Haim Shaked. *Middle East Contemporary Survey* 12 (1988): 772.

——. *South Yemen's Revolutionary Strategy, 1970–1985: From Insurgency to Bloc Politics*. Boulder: Westview Press, 1990.

——. *The Making of Saudi Arabia, 1916–1936: From Chieftaincy to Monarchical State*. New York: Oxford University Press, 1993.

——. *Yemen: The Tortuous Quest for Unity, 1990–94*. Chatham House Papers. London: Royal Institute of International Affairs, 1996.

——. Ed. *Middle East Monarchies: The Challenge of Modernity*. Boulder: Lynne Rienner Publishers, 2000.

Kühn, Thomas. "Shaping and Reshaping Colonial Ottomanism: Contesting Boundaries of Difference and Integration in Ottoman Yemen, 1872–1919." *Comparative Studies of South Asia, Africa and the Middle East* 27.2 (2007): 315–331.

Lackner, Helen. *P.D.R. Yemen: Outpost of Socialist Development in Arabia*. Political Science of the Middle East, No. 27. London: Ithaca Press, 1985.

Ledger, David. *Shifting Sands: The British in South Arabia*. London: Peninsular Pub., 1983.

Manea, Elham. *Regional Politics in the Gulf: Saudi Arabia, Oman, Yemen*. London: Saqi Books, 2005.

Mawby, Spencer. "Britain's Last Imperial Frontier: The Aden Protectorates, 1952–59." *The Journal of Imperial and Commonwealth History* 29.2 (2001): 75–100.

——. *British Policy in Aden and the Protectorates 1955–67: Last Outpost of a Middle East Empire*. Vol. 10. London, New York: Routledge, 2004.

Maycock, Ian D. "Oil Exploration and Development in Marib/Al Jawf Basin, Yemen Arab Republic." *American Association of Petroleum Geologists (AAPG)* 72.2 (1989): 218–219.

McGregor, Andrew James. *A Military History of Modern Egypt: From the Ottoman Conquest to the Ramadan War*. Westport: Praeger Security International, 2006.

Miller, Derek B. "Demand, Stockpiles, and Social Controls: Small Arms in Yemen." Occasional Papers. *Small Arms Survey, Graduate Institute of International Studies* 9 (2003).

Miyoshi, Masahiro. *The Joint Development of Offshore Oil and Gas in Relation to Maritime Boundary Delimitation*. Vol. 2. Durham: International Boundaries Research Unit (IBRU), 1999.

Myntti, Cynthia. *Women and Development in Yemen Arab Republic*. Schriftenreihe Der Deutschen Gesellschaft Für Technische Zusammenarbeit. Eschborn: German Agency for Technical Cooperation, 1979.

Nagi, Sultan. "The Genesis of the Call for Yemeni Unity." *Contemporary Yemen: Politics and Historical Background*. Ed. B. R. Pridham. London: Croom Helm, 1984.

Nahrawali, Muhammad ibn Amad, and Clive K. Smith. *Lightning over Yemen: a History of the Ottoman Campaign (1569–71)*. The Library of Ottoman Studies Vol. 3. London, New York: I.B.Tauris, 2002.

National Yemen. "US Objects to GPC Constitutional Amendments." 3 January 2011. http://nationalyemen.com/2011/01/03/us-objects-to-gpc-constitutional-amendments/. Last accessed 20 June 2013.

——. "Houthis Control Sa'ada, Help Appoint Governor." 29 March 2011. http://nationalyemen.com/2011/03/29/houthis-control-sa%E2%80%99ada-help-appoint-governor/. Last accessed 20 June 2013.

Novak, Jane. "Question on al-Ahdal and the Cole." *Armies of Liberation*, 7 March 2007. http://armiesofliberation.com/archives/2007/03/07/question-on-al-ahdal-and-the-cole/. Last accessed 15 May 2014.

——. "Yemeni Southern Opposition Leader Al Nuba Writes the Brits." *Armies of Liberation*, 20 January 2010. http://armiesofliberation.com/archives/2010/01/20/yemeni-southern-opposition-leader-al-nuba-writes-the-brits/. Last accessed 18 June 2013.

Nu'man, Mahmud Ahmad. *Adwa 'ala tariq al-yamaniyyin: al-Atraf al-Ma'niyya fil-Yaman*. Aden: Mu'assasat as-Sabban, 1970.

O'Ballance, Edgar. *The War in the Yemen*. Connecticut: Archon Books, 1971.

Okruhlik, Gwenn, and Patrick Conge. "National Autonomy, Labor Migration and Political Crisis: Yemen and Saudi Arabia." *Middle East Journal* 51.4 (1997): 554–565.

Oron, Yitzhak, Ed. *Middle East Record.* Vol. 2. Tel Aviv: The Moshe Dayan Center, 1961.

Page, Stephen. *The Soviet Union and the Yemens: Influence on Asymmetrical Relationships*. Studies of Influence in International Relations. New York: Praeger, 1985.

Peterson, J. E. *Yemen: The Search for a Modern State.* London: Croom Helm, 1982.

Phillips, Sarah. "Yemen: Economic and Political Deterioration." Ed. M. Dunne and J. Choucair. *Arab Reform Bulletin* 3.7 (2005). http://carnegieendowment.org/2008/08/20/economic-and-political-deterioration-in-yemen/fga5. Last accessed 18 June 2013.

——. *Yemen's Democracy Experiment in Regional Perspective: Patronage and Pluralized Authoritarianism*. New York: Palgrave Macmillan, 2008.

Pieragostini, Karl. "Britain, Aden and South Arabia: Abandoning Empire." *British Policy in Aden and the Protectorates 1955–67: Last Outpost of a Middle East Empire.* Vol. 10. London: Routledge, 2004.

Porter, A.N. and A.J. Stockwell. *British Imperial Policy and Decolonization, 1938–1964.* Vol. 1. 1938–51. Basingstoke: Macmillan, 1987.

Prados, Alfred B., and Jeremy M. Sharp. *Yemen: Current Conditions and US Relations.* CRS Report for Congress, 2007. http://www.fas.org/sgp/crs/mideast/RS21808.pdf. Last accessed 18 June 2013.

Prados, Edward F. *The US and Yemen: A Half-Century of Engagement.* Washington: Center for Contemporary Arab Studies, 2005.

Rabi, Uzi. "Kuwait's Changing Strategic Posture: Historical Patterns." *Journal of South Asian and Middle Eastern Studies* 27.4 (2004): 52–65.

——. *The Emergence of States in a Tribal Society: Oman Under Sa'id bin Taymur, 1932–1970.* Portland: Sussex Academic Press, 2006.

——. "British Possessions in the Persian Gulf and Southwest Arabia: The Last Abandoned in the Middle East." *Britain And the Middle East: From Imperial Power to Junior Partner.* Ed. Zach Levey and Elie Podeh. Portland: Sussex Academic Press, 2008. 264–279.

Rahmy, Ali Abdel Rahman. *The Egyptian Policy in the Arab World: Intervention in Yemen, 1962–1967: Case Study.* Washington D.C.: University Press of America, 1983.

Rashid, Ibrahim. *Yemen under the Rule of Imam Ahmad.* Documents on the History of Arabia. Chapel Hill: Documentary Publications, 1985.

Riedel, Bruce. "Al Qaeda's Yemen Connection, America and the Global Islamic Jihad." *The Brookings Institution*, 30 December 2009. http://www.brookings.edu/blogs/up-front/posts/2009/12/30-terrorism-yemen-riedel. Last accessed 19 June 2013.

Robin, Christian Julien. "Yemen." *Encyclopedia of the Qur'ān.* Ed. Jane Dammen McAuliffe. http://www.paulyonline.brill.nl/entries/encyclopaedia-of-the-quran/yemen-COM_00223. Last accessed 1 May 2013.

Rotberg, Robert I. *When States Fail: Causes and Consequences.* Princeton: Princeton University Press, 2010.

Rouleau, Eric. "L'etoile Rouge sur le Yemen du Sud." *Le Monde*, 27 May 1972.

——. "Le Yemen: Voyage a Travers le Moyen Age." *Le Monde*, 11 May 1967.

Rugh, William A. *The Arab Mass Media: Newspapers, Radio, and Television in Arab Politics*. Westport: Greenwood Publishing Group, 2004.

Sada al-Malahim. "Haqiqat al-Safarat (The Truth about the Embassies)". No. 6, November 2008.

Salmoni, Barak A. Bryce Loidolt, and Madeleine Wells. *Regime and Periphery in Northern Yemen: The Huthi Phenomenon*. Santa Monica: RAND Corporation, 2010.

Sanger, Richard H. *The Arabian Peninsula*. New York: Books for Libraries Press, 1970.

Schmidt, Dana Adams. *Yemen: The Unknown War*. London: Bodley Head, 1968.

Slackman, Michael. "Would-Be Killer Linked to Al Qaeda, Saudis Say." *The New York Times*, 29 August 2009. http://www.nytimes.com/2009/08/29/world/middleeast/29saudi.html?_r=0. Last accessed 18 June 2013.

Spencer, Richard. "Al-Qaeda Veterans 'Are Flooding into Yemen'." *Telegraph.co.uk*, 10 January 2010. http://www.telegraph.co.uk/news/worldnews/middleeast/yemen/6962969/Al-Qaeda-veterans-are-flooding-into-Yemen.html Last accessed 18 June 2013.

Stookey, Robert W. *Yemen: The Politics of the Yemen Arab Republic*. Boulder: Westview Press, 1978.

——. *South Yemen: A Marxist Republic in Arabia*. Boulder: Westview Press, 1982.

Terrorism Monitor. "Yemen's Enduring Challenges: An Interview With Jonathan Winer." 2.7 (2004): n. pag. http://www.jamestown.org/programs/tm/single/?tx_ttnews%5Btt_news%5D=26401&tx_ttnews%5BbackPid%5D=179&no_cache=1#.UjWGZNJkOvI. Last accessed 17 June 2013.

Thesiger, Wilfred. "War in Yemen – 2: Tribesmen Acknowledge the Imam's Rule." *The Times*, 22 December 1966.

Traboulsi, Fawwaz. "Les transformations des structures tribales depuis l'indépendance du Yémen du Sud." *Cahier du Gremamo* 10 (1991): 226.

Trevaskis, Kennedy. *Shades of Amber: A South Arabian Episode*. London: Hutchinson, 1968.

Tritton, A. S. *The Rise of the Imams of Sanaa*. Westport, Conn: Hyperion Press, 1981.

UNDP Yemen. "How We Work." 28 March 2010. http://www.undp.org.ye/how-do-we-work.php. Last accessed 18 June 2013.

U.S. Department of State: Bureau of Democracy, Human Rights, and Labor, "Yemen". 4 March 2002. *Country Reports on Human Rights Practices* (2001). http://www.refworld.org/docid/3e918c3611.html. Last accessed 17 June 2013.

Walker, Jonathan. *Aden Insurgency: The Savage War in South Arabia, 1962–1967*. Kent: Spellmount, 2005.

Wedeen, Lisa. "Seeing Like a Citizen, Acting Like a State: Exemplary Events in Unified Yemen." *Comparative Studies in Society and History* 45.4 (2003): 680–713. http://journals.cambridge.org/download.php?file=%2FCSS%2FCSS45_04%2FS001041750300032Xa.pdf&code=a622dbcf7e710b42799cf8f415584175. Last accessed 17 June 2013.

Weinbaum, Martin. "Lost Faith, Forfeited Trust: Afghan Responses to Post-9/11 International Intervention in State-Building and Insurgency." *International Intervention in Local Conflicts: Crisis Management and Conflict Resolution Since the Cold War*. Ed. Uzi Rabi. London: I.B.Tauris, 2010. 222–240.

Weir, Shelagh. "A Clash of Fundamentalisms: Wahhabism in Yemen." *Middle East Report* 204 (1997): 22–26. http://www.jstor.org/stable/pdfplus/3013139.pdf?acceptTC=true. Last accessed 17 June 2013.

——. *A Tribal Order: Politics and Law in the Mountains of Yemen*. 1st ed. Modern Middle East Series No. 23. Austin: University of Texas Press, 2007.

Wenner, Manfred W. *Modern Yemen, 1918–1966*. Vol. 85, No. 1. Baltimore: Johns Hopkins University Press, 1967.

——. *The Yemen Arab Republic: Development and Change in an Ancient Land*. Boulder: Westview Press, 1991.

Whitlock, Craig. "Probe of USS Cole Bombing Unravels." *Washington Post*, 4 May 2008. http://articles.washingtonpost.com/2008–05-04/world/36911922_1_cole-investigation-uss-cole-yemeni-officials. Last accessed 18 June 2013.

Witty, David M. "A Regular Army in Counterinsurgency Operations: Egypt in North Yemen, 1962–1967." *Journal of Military History* 65.2 (2001): 401–440.

World Bank Group. "Yemen." *Country Brief, Middle East and North Africa Region (MENA)*, 2008.

World Statesmen. "Constitution of the People's Democratic Republic of Yemen." (Aden, amended in 1978). http://www.worldstatesmen.org/YemenPDR1978.pdf. Last accessed 16 June 2013.

Worth, Robert F., and Laura Kasinof. "Evasions by Leader Add Chaos in Yemen." *The New York Times*, 25 May 2011. http://www.nytimes.com/2011/05/26/world/middleeast/26yemen.html. Last accessed 20 June 2013.

——. "Yemeni President Wounded in Palace Attack." *The New York Times*, 3 June 2011. http://www.nytimes.com/2011/06/04/world/middleeast/04yemen.html. Last accessed 20 June 2013.

Yegnes, Tamar. "The Yemeni Arab Republic." *Middle East Contemporary Survey*. Ed. Colin Legum. Vol. 1. New York: Holmes and Meier, 1976. 652–655.

Yemen Post. "Ten People Killed in Conflict in Al-Jawf Governorate." 10 April 2010. http://www.yemenpost.net/Detail123456789.aspx?ID=3&SubID=1072. Last accessed 18 June 2013.

Zartman, I. William. *Preventive Negotiation: Avoiding Conflict Escalation*. Oxford: Rowman and Littlefield, 2001.

Zein, Ahmed. "Armed and Dangerous: Arms Proliferation Inside Yemen." *Arab Insight – Emerging Social and Religious Trends* 2.1 (2008): 81–87. World Security Institute, Washington, DC, 1964.

Archival Documents

Cabinet Papers (CAB) 130	The Yemen: Meetings 1-5
Colonial Office (CO) 1055	Aden Department
Foreign Office (FO) 371	General Correspondence

List of Newspapers and Magazines Cited

Arab News (Saudi Arabia, daily)
Independent (London, daily)
Le Monde (Paris, daily)
Ma'rib Press (Sanaa, daily)
Middle East Economic Digest (London, weekly)
Middle East International (London, bi-weekly)
New York Times (New York, daily)
Polska Agencja Prasowa (Warsaw, daily)
The Times (London, daily)
Washington Post (Washington, DC, daily)
Yemen News (Sanaa, daily)
Yemen Post (Sanaa, daily)
Yemen Times (Sanaa, bi-weekly)

Radio and Television Stations and Monitoring Services

Al-Arabiyya (Dubai)
British Broadcasting Corporation (BBC Monitoring)
Radio Cairo
Radio Sanaa
Summary of World Broadcasts (SWB)
Yemen News Agency (SABA)

INDEX

'Abd al-'Alim, Abdallah, 74
'Abd al-Hakim 'Amir, 42
al-'Abdali, Sultan 'Ali bin 'Abd al-Karim, 31, 35, *see also* Lahaj
'Abdallah, Muhammad "Muhsin" Sa'id, 89
Abu Shawarib, Mujahid, 67, 74, 81, 127
Abyan (province), 84, 89, 103, 141, 180, 186, 202
Aden
  Aden Colony, 11, 12, 13, 16, 29–33, 65, 82
  Aden Free Trade Zone, 131
  Aden Group, 45–47
  Aden Protectorates, 12, 13, 16, 23, 29–35, 47, 59, 65–66
  Aden Trade Union Congress (ATUC), 61–64
Administrative divisions of Yemen, 12, 22, 82, 130
al-Ahdal, Muhammad Hamdi, 177, *see also* al-Qa'ida
Ahmad bin Yahya, Imam, *see* Hamid al-Din family
Ahmad, Muhammad 'Ali, 129
al-Ahmar family, 196–203
  'Abdallah bin Husayn, Shaykh 43, 47, 49, 55, 58, 67, 70, 73, 78–81, 88, 91, 108, 111, 123–124, 129, 132, 134, 159, 162, 200
  'Ali Muhsin, 196–199, 202–203
  'Ali Salih, 108
  Hamid bin 'Abdallah, 49, 162, 196, 200
  Husayn bin Nasir, 28–29, 49
  Muhammad Salih, 122
  Nasir bin Mabkhut, 18
  Sadiq bin 'Abdallah, 197–198, 201
al-Ahnumi, Mahmud, 57
al-Akwa'Muhammad, 113
al-'Alimi, Rashad, 190, 192
'Ali, Salim Rubay', 83–96, 102, 116, 169
Amir al-Mu'minin (title) 5, 15
al-'Amri, Hasan, 50, 57, 67–69, 87–88
al-Anisi, 'Abd al-Wahhab, 123
Ansar al-Shari'a, 202
Antar, 'Ali, 104
Arab Cooperation Council (*Majlis al-Ta'awun al-'Arabi*), 110–111
Arab League, 27, 29, 92, 89, 100, 107, 120–121
Arab Spring in Yemen, 193–208
armed forces in Yemen, 22, 23, 26–27, 74, 85, 122, 130, 151, 197, 199, 201
arms and military aid, 19, 31–32, 45, 47, 52, 74–75, 79, 100–102, 127, 137–138, 147, 153, 157, 161, 164, 168, 171, 187, 189, 201, 205–206

al-'Asa'i, Qa'id Salih, 143, 153
'Asir (region), 9, 16, 19–20, 23, 26, 116
al-Asnaj, Abdallah, 61–64, 70, 82, 101, 129
Assembly of Representatives, 77–78, 81, 133
al-'Attas, Haydar Abu Bakr, 104, 124, 126, 128, 130, 152
al-'Awdi, Hammud, 138
al-'Awfi, Muhammad, 185
'Awlaqi (tribes and region), 31, 35, 65, 85
al-'Ayni, Muhsin, 38, 72, 79, 89–91

Bab al-Mandab, 1, 10, 11, 91, 186, 188
Badawi, Jamal Ahmad, 178, *see also* al-Qa'ida
Ba-Jamal, Abd al-Qadir, 140, 158
Ba-Majbur, Ahmad, 166
Bakil (tribal confederation), 2, 7–8, 14, 18, 23, 26, 28, 39, 43, 58, 80, 91, 123, 129, 131
Bani Hashish (Bakil tribe), 29
Bani Mu'adh (district), 157
Bani Murad (tribe), 29, 43, 68, 71
al-Banna, Jaber, 178, *see also* al-Qa'ida
Ba'th party and Ba'thism, 58, 124
Ba'um, Hasan Ahmad, 143–145
al-Bayd, 'Ali Salim, 104, 117–119, 122, 124–125, 128–130, 134, 151, 153
al-Baydani, 'Abd al-Rahman, 42, 51
Bayhan, 34–35, 46–47, *see also* Sharif Husayn
Bin 'Ali, Zayn al-'Abidin, 194
Bin Farid, Ahmad 'Umar, 145
Bin Ghanim, Faraj, 132–133
Bin Na'if, Mohammad, 169–170
Bin Qa'id, 'Abd al-Latif, 28, 29
Bin Salmon Mosque bombing (2008), 161
Britain's relations with Yemen
  Aden Protectorates, 12–35, 47, 59, 65–66
  British India, 11, 30
  Colony of Aden, 12–33, 82
  Federation, 31–66, 44, 45, 48, 61, 65, 77, 87, 103, 107

Change Square (*maydan al-taghyir*), 194–195, 197
China, China's relations with Yemen, 103, 196
civil war; in North Yemen (1962–1970), 42–69, 81–87
  collective memory and symbolic importance, 48–49, 95, 143, 145–146, 152
  in South Yemen (1963), 62–66
  in United Yemen (1994), 128–129
Committee for the Reconstruction of Yemen, 157
constitution
  the constitution of North Yemen, 47, 70, 73
  the constitution of South Yemen, 62, 97, 99
  the constitution of the unified state, 100, 103, 111, 117, 123, 127, 130–131, 134, 194–195
Consultative Council of North Yemen (*majlis al-shura*), 70, 73, 80, 90–91, 103, 123
Corrective Move (22 June), 85–86
Corrective Movement (*al-Haraka al-Tashihiyya*), 73, 79–80, 85, 89

Da'an Agreement, 15–16
Dahmash, Ahmad Qasim, 76, 79
al-Dali' (town, region and tribes), 31, 35, 46, 59, 143
al-Dali'i, Abd al-'Aziz, 152
Dathina (region and tribes), 34, 60, 85
Dayhan (city), 157, 159
democracy, 95, 117, 122, 124–125, 151, 190, 196
Democratic Popular Union (Marxist party of South Yemen), 76

Demonstrations, protests and riots, 57, 60, 62, 79, 81, 84, 109, 121, 127, 138, 140, 144–145, 151–153, 161–162, 178–196
Dialogue Committee, 126
al-Dirjaji, Abu Muhammad, 146
Djibouti, 147, 192

economy of Yemen, 35, 39–40, 46, 52, 57–58, 65, 68–70, 80–84, 87, 91, 99, 102–106, 109–110, 113, 117–121, 127, 131–132, 136–142, 147–151, 155, 159, 162, 166, 172, 174, 178, 182–183, 187, 190, 195, 205–208
education in Yemen, 37–38, 62, 64, 92–96, 104, 111–112, 131–132, 143, 160–161, 179–180, 187–190, 205
Egypt, Egypt's relations with Yemen: Muhammad 'Ali era, 10–11
  Cairo Agreement (1972), 89, 100
  cultural and educational influences, 24–25, 27, 37, 92–93, 111–112
  Defense Pact (1954), 27
  Egyptian evacuation, 87
  Egyptian intervention (1962–1967), 50–68
  Mubarak era, 110–111, 121, 132 173, 198
  Nasser era, 37–38, 42, 44–49, 94, 120, 124, 205
  Sadat era, 100
  the United Arab Republic, 27, 34, 121
  Yemeni exiles in Egypt, 25, 27, 35, 38, 128
  see also Muslim Brothers
Ethiopia, Ethiopia's relations with Yemen, 92, 147, 153, 173
Extractive Industries Transparency Initiative (EITI), 139–140

Fadli (region), 31, 34–35, 89, 186
al-Fadli, Tariq bin Nasir, 149, 186
Federation of Arab Emirates of the South, 31–36
Federation of South Arabia, 35, 44–66
Feudalism and reaction against, 56, 61, 64, 71, 86, 105, 150
Free South Movement (*al-Janub al-Hurr*; *al-hirak*), 141–154, 197, 203
Free Yemenites movement (*al-Yaman al-Ahrar*), 25–27, 38
Front for the Liberation of Occupied Southern Yemen (FLOSY), 56–57, 64–65, 70, 82

General People's Congress (GPC), 108–109, 112–113, 123–125, 130–134, 155, 194, 197, 200–203
Ghamar (district), 157
al-Ghani, 'Abd al-'Aziz, 74, 129, 133
al-Ghashmi, Ahmad Husayn, 74, 80–82, 96, 98
al-Ghaythi, Naji, 160
Greater Yemen (geographic and political term), 9, 15, 16, 20, 23, 32, 39, 122
Guantanamo, Yemeni prisoners at Guantanamo, 168, 185, 189
Gulf of Aden, 1, 147
Gulf Initiative, 198–203

Hadi, 'Abd Rabbu Mansur
  President of Yemen, 203
  Vice President of Yemen, 131, 152, 171, 198
Al-Hadi Mosque, Sa'da, 163
Hadramawt (region), 2, 9, 16, 30, 64, 66, 84, 89, 94–95, 103, 128, 132, 140, 141, 143–144 148, 180, 189, 190, 206
al-Hadr, Muhammad Saqqaf, 190
Haines, Captain, 11
Hajja (region and province), 2, 26, 28
al-Hajri, 'Abdallah, 72, 77, 79, 91
Hamdan (tribes), 122
al-Hamdani, Abu Muhammad al-Hasan bin Ahmad, 94

al-Hamdi, Ibrahim, 72–81, 91, 94–99, 111, 115–116
Hamid al-Din family, 13, 22, 29, 37, 39, 68, 70
Ahmad bin Yahya, Imam, 3, 18–19, 21, 26, 27–30, 32–40, 43, 49
Amir 'Abbas, 28
Amir 'Abduallah, 28
Amir Hasan, 35, 37, 42–43
Muhammad al-Badr, Imam, 28, 33, 36–39, 43, 53
Muhammad al-Mansur, Imam, 13–14
Yahya bin Muhammad, Imam, 13–40, 71, 113, 148, 158–160, 163
Hamir (region), 78
al-Hamra, 159
al-Haqq party, 124, 132
al-Harad (district), 55
al-Harithi, 'Ali Salim Sinan, 177, 181, *see also* al-Qa'ida
Hasan Tahsin Pasha, 15
al-Hasani, 'Ali Nasir Muhammad, 89, 102, 110, 130
Hashid (tribal confederation) 2, 7–8, 14, 18–19, 23, 26, 28–29, 36–39, 43, 47, 49, 51, 55, 58, 67, 70, 73, 80–81, 91, 98, 108, 123, 128, 131, 164, 196, 200–203, *see also* al-Ahmar family
Hazm, 29
Hickinbotham, Tom, 32–33
High Defense Council (North Yemen), 52
al-Hindi, Salih, 160
Hizballah, Hizballah's interaction with Yemen, 155, 167–169
Hostages and hostage-taking, 20–21, 138, 147, 161
al-Hudayda (city), 2, 4, 6, 10, 16, 19, 20, 48, 52, 81, 88, 91, 173
Hudson, Michael, 126
al-Humayd, Tariq, 189
al-Hurriyya Square, 144
al-Huthi family
'Abd al-Karim, 160
'Abd al-Malik, 157, 159–161, 169
Badr al-Din, 156
Husayn Badr al-Din, 154–172
Yahya, 159–160
Huthi rebellion, 141, 154–172

Iran, Iran's relations with Yemen, 75, 110, 147, 153, 155, 159, 156, 167–171, 179, 185
Iraq, Iraq's relations with Yemen, 25, 61, 67, 100, 110–111, 120–121, 141, 156, 159, 169, 174–175, 180–183, 188
Ibb (city and province), 2, 4, 14, 20, 26, 35, 58
al-Idrisi, 'Ali, 19
al-Idrisi, Muhammad, 16–20
al-Imam, Shaykh Muhammad, 173
al-Iryani, 'Abd al-Karim, 129, 133
al-Iryani, 'Abd al-Rahman, 25, 47, 54, 67–72, 89, 90, 93, 99, 108, 111
al-Iryani, Muhammad 'Abdallah, 77
al-Islah party (*al-tajammu' al-yamani lil-Islah*), 123–126, 131–134, 155, 157, 194, 200
Islamic Front (*al-Jabha al-Islamiyya*), 101–102, 111–112, 123
Islamic Jihad of Yemen, 183
Islamism and Islamic extremism, 24, 111–114, 132, 136, 154, 163, 166, 169, 173–174, 176, 185, 194, 200, 202, 206
Isma'il, 'Abd al-Fattah, 64, 83, 89–90, 94, 97–104, 116
Italy, Italy's relations with Yemen, 19, 20, 28, 36

Jabal Razih, *see* Razih
al-Janub al-Hurr (magazine), 143, 146–149, 153, *see also* Free South Movement
al-Jariri, Sa'id, 190

Jawf (region), 18, 29, 137, 175, 180
al-Jaylani, Husayn, 190
Jibla (town), 2, 3
Jews of Yemen, 157–159, 181
al-Jifri, 'Abd al-Rahman, 130, 144
Jizan (port), 20, 23, 116
Joint Meeting Parties (JMP), 194, 198–199, 203
Joint Political Action Order (*mithaq al-'amal al-siyasi*), 124
Jordon, Jordan's relations with Yemen, 16, 111, 121, 196
Juzaylan 'Abdallah, 50, 57

Kathiri Sultanate, 12, 30, 63–64
Kidnapping of foreign nationals, 183
Kirman, Tawakul, 194
Khalid, Yusuf, 148
Khamir (district), 65, 73
al-Khamis, 'Abd Rabbu Hasan, 145
al-Khawlan, 'Abd al-Latif bin Qayd, 49
Khawlan bin 'Amr (tribal group), 8, 29, 43, 49, 159, 164, 184
Kostiner, Joseph, 124
Kuwait Agreement, 100–101

Lahaj (city, region and Sultanate), 30–35, 64, 84, 103, 141, 145, 165
Lahum, Sinan Abu, 58, 80, 91, 127, *see also* Bakil
al-Lawzi, Hasan, 167
Libya, Libya's relations with Yemen, 89–90, 171
Luce, William, 32–36

al-Madrasa al-Ahliyya, 25
Mahra (province), 31, 141
Makawi, 'Abd al-Qawi, 58, 63
al-Makki, Abu 'Asim, *see* Muhammad Hamdi al-Ahdal
Maqbul, Sayf, *see* Qu'ayti Sultanate
al-Maqtari, Shaykh 'Aqil, 173
Ma'rib (region, province, town and tribes), 20, 117, 119, 137, 175–180, 184, 188
al-Ma'ribi, Abu Hasan, 173
Marxism, Marxist influence in Yemen, 56, 62, 66, 68–69, 75–76, 83, 86, 88, 90, 93–94, 98, 104–107, 119–122, 128, 131, 173, 204, *see also* Democratic Popular Union and National Liberation Front
al-Mashhur, Shaykh al-Habib Abu Bakr, 190
al-Mask, Hamil, 181–182
al-Mazru', 159
Middle East News Agency, 53
Military Council of North Yemen, 73–74, 80–81
Modesty policy in Yemen, 157, 173
Movement for the Liberation of Yemen (*harakat tahrir al-yaman*), 38
Muhammad 'Ali Pasha, *see* Egypt
Mukalla (port), 30, 63, 95, *see also* Qu'ayti Sultanate
Mukha (port), 11, 19
al-Muqbil, Husayn 'Abd al-Salam Muhammad, 76
Muslim Brothers, 24–25, 93–94, 111, 123

Najran (town), 20, 23, 26, 116
National Charter (*al-mithaq al-watani*), 108–109, 112
Nationalism, 16, 27, 30–37, 41, 44–45, 47, 51, 56–58, 61, 64, 67, 71, 89, 93, 97, 99, 101, 103, 105, 107, 109, 111, 113, 120, 138
National Democratic Front (NDF), 76–81, 93–102, 109–116
National Liberation Front (NLF), 47, 55–70, 82–101, 105, 115–116, 120; *see also* Qahtan Muhammad al-Sha'bi
National Resistance Front (*al-jabha al-wataniyya lil-mu'arada*), 130
Nimran, Nagi bin Mansur, 71
al-Nuba, Nasir 'Ali, 143
Nu'man, Ahmad Muhammad, Shaykh, 38, 42, 55, 71

Nu'man, Muhammad Ahmad, 25, 58
Nu'man, Sa'id Yasin, 144

oil in Yemen, 33, 103, 110, 17, 119, 137, 140, 144, 180, 206–207
Oman, Oman's relations with Yemen, 1, 106, 118, 198
Ottoman Empire, Ottoman presence in Yemen, 2, 9–11, 13–19, 23, 54, 137

Pasha, Hasan Tahsin, 15
Perim Island, 91
Phillips, Sarah, 132, 133
Popular Nationalist Congress, 51
Popular Revolutionary Union (*al-Ittihad al-Sha'bi al-Thawri*), 58
population and demographics of Yemen, 70, 84, 93, 99, 113–114, 119, 125, 139, 143, 165
Presidential Committee, 160–161, 163
Presidential Council (*majlis al-ri'asa*), 57, 67, 69, 81, 85, 128, 130

al-Qadi, 'Ali Husayn, 64, 108
al-Qadir, Shaykh Naji, 43
al-Qa'ida, 141, 165, 169, 172–192, 193, 198, 202–203, 206–208
  al-Qa'ida in the Arabian Peninsula (AQAP), 169, 183, 185, 188–189, 193, 198, 203
al-Qa'iti, Hamza, 184, 198
al-Qahtani, Na'if, 189, *see also* al-Qa'ida
al-Qama', Muhammad Ahmad, 146
Qasimi dynasty
  Muhammad bin al-Mansur, Imam, 9
  Qasim bin Muhammad, Imam, 9
Qa'taba, 14, 91
Qatar, Qatar's relations with Yemen, 159–162, 198–199
Qiyari (tribe) 138
al-Qiyari, Khalid, 138
Qu'ayti Sultanate, 12, 30, 46, 63–64
  Sayf Maqbul, 46

Radfan, 46, 129,145
  Radfan revolt (1963) 59–65
al-Rajih, Nu'man bin Qa'id, 49
al-Raymi, Qassim, 178–179, *see also* al-Qa'ida
Razih (district), 52, 157, 159, 167
Red Sea, 2, 10, 19, 176, 186, 192
Reform movements in South Yemen, 47, 61
Representative Council, 78, 81
Revolutionary Democratic Party of Yemen (*al-Hizb al-Dimuqrati al-Thawri al-Yamani*), 76
Revolutionary Resisters (organization), 71
riots, *see* demonstrations
al-Rizami, 'Abdallah, 160
Rouleau, Eric, 57, 86
al-Rubaysh, Ibrahim, 169, *see also* al-Qa'ida

al-Sabihi, 'Idrus Sa'id, 149
Sa'da (city), 2, 4, 52, 74, 78, 141, 154–172, 178, 183–184, 186, 202–203, 206
Sada al-Malahim (magazine), 175–176, 179, 181, 183, 186
Sahar (district), 74, 161
al-Sa'id, 'Abdallah, 196
Sahar (district), 161
al-Sahwa (newspaper), 112, 123, 150
Salafiyya, Salafi movement in Yemen, 155, 157, 163, 166–188, 173–175, 185, *see also* Shaykh Muqbil bin Hadi al-Wadi'i
Salih family,
  Ahmad 'Ali, 135, 194, 196
  'Ali 'Abdallah, President of North Yemen (1978–1990) 97–118
  President of United Yemen (1990–2012) 118–203
  Salim Salih Muhammad, 144
  Tariq Muhammad 'Abdullah, 134

al-Sallal, 'Abdallah, 26, 41–59, 67, 88, 108, 120
Sanaa, 2–4, 9–10, 14, 16, 18–21, 23, 26, 31, 33, 39, 41–43, 44–45, 47–48, 52–56, 67–70, 74, 77–79, 82, 87–88, 91, 95, 98–102, 109–113, 115–118, 120–123, 134, 138, 147, 151–157, 159–166, 170, 175, 180, 182, 184, 187, 192, 194, 195, 197, 199, 200–203, 207
  Sanaa University, 138, 194, 197
Sanaa Agreement, 118
al-San'ani, Abu Hurayra, 176, *see also* al-Qa'ida
Sanhan (tribe and region), 98, 107–108, 122, 196–197, 200, *see also* Hashid
al-Saqqaldi, Salah, 153
Saudi Arabia, Saudi relations with Yemen: 20, 23, 44, 48, 55–57, 64, 68–81, 87–94, 98–103, 107, 110–112, 115–117, 120–123, 131, 136, 167–170, 183–186, 189, 196–199, 204
  Ibn Saud, 20
  King Faisal, 55; King Khalid, 77
  Saudi-Yemeni War (1934), 26
Sawt al-'Arab, 35, 53
Sawt al-Yaman, 38
Sayyid (pl. *sadah*), 5, 13, 21, 23, 25, 29, 50, 52, 163
September 1962 Revolution, 37, 41–50, 83, 89, 92, 135, 137, 146, 155, 204
Seventy Day Siege, 67
al-Sha'bi, Najib Qahtan, 134
al-Sha'bi, Qahtan Muhammad, 47, 58, 64, 76, 82–86, 134
Shabwa, 2, 103, 117, 119, 141, 166, 175, 180
Shafi'is and Shafi'iyya, 4, 6, 10, 14–15, 22–23, 38–39, 42–43, 50–51, 58, 67–68, 75–76, 80, 81, 88, 99, 166
al-Shahari, Sa'id, 189
al-Shanfara, Salih, 182
al-Shami, Ahmad, 132
sharia, 13, 90, 131
Sharif (pl. *ashraf*), 5, 45, 65
Sharif Husayn of Bayhan, 34, 43, 62, 64
al-Sharif, Yahya bin Yahya, 18, *see also* Bakil
al-Sharyan, Da'ud, 150–151
al-Shaybani, Nasir, 152
Shi'a, Shi'i Islam, 4–6, 13, 141, 154–157, 159, 168, 182, 184–186, 206–207
al-Shu'ayb (province), 150
al-Shu'aybi, Salih, 145
al-Siyaghi, Shaykh Ahmad, 49
Somalia, Somalia's relations with Yemen, 92, 147, 176, 181, 186–188, 192, 208
Sons of the Arab South, 144
Sons of the Martyrs for Unity, 165
South Arabian League (*Rabitat al-Janub al-Arabi*), 30–31
Soviet Union, Soviet relations with Yemen, 20, 31, 33, 35–36, 44, 48, 54, 75, 92, 100, 100–119, 122
state-building in Yemen, 18, 20, 23, 58–59, 80, 205
Sudan, Sudan's relations with Yemen, 31, 111–112, 147, 168
Sufyan (tribe), 49, 74, 164, *see also* Bakil
Sunna, Sunni Islam, 4, 6, 10, 39, 155, 157, 159, 166, 168, 185, 207
Supreme National Anti-Corruption Committee (SNACC), 140
al-Suri, Abu Mus'ib, 188

Ta'izz, 2, 3, 4, 6, 10, 15, 20, 26, 48, 51, 52, 56, 71, 74, 81, 82, 88, 93, 98, 123, 146, 195
Tanzimat, 11
al-Thalaya, Ahmad Yahya, 28
The 26th of September (magazine), 156
Thesiger, Wilfred, 54
Tihama (region), 2, 4, 10, 18, 20, 23, 43, 78
Treaty of Sanaa, 20, 23
Treaty of Ta'if, 23, 72, 116
Trevaskis, Kennedy, 45–47, 62

Tribes (theoretical), 7–9, 18, 20–21, 24
tribalism, 41, 55, 76, 85
Tunisia, (Arab Spring), 194

'Ubayda (tribe), 68
'Umar, Jaralla, 111
'Umar, Sultan Ahmad, 99, 101
al-'Umda, Muhammad, 178, *see also* al-Qa'ida
Unification; the idea of unification (1972–1990) 75, 78–83, 87–92, 96, 99–103, 110, 115–118
the act of unification (1990) 118–127
challenges to united Yemen 128–135, 141–154, 165–166, 172, 180, 190, 207
United Arab Emirates (UAE), the UAE's relations with Yemen, 147, 198, 201
United Arab Republic, 27, 34, 121
United Arab States, 34
United Nations, 32, 37, 42, 121
United States, United States' relations with Yemen, 27, 36, 71, 75, 100–103, 107, 118, 120–121, 170–171–179, 182–183, 186–192, 198, 201
USAID, 178, 187, *see also USS Cole* attack
al-'Usaymat (tribe), 164, 196, *see also* Hashid
USS Cole attack (2000), 148–149, 173–174, 177, 188, 206
'Uthman, Muhammad 'Ali, 42, 70–71

al-Wadi'i, Shaykh Muqbil bin Hadi, 173–174
al-Wahayshi, Nasir, 178–184, *see also* al-Qa'ida
Wahhabism in Yemen, 93–94, 155, 167
waqf (religious endowment) system, 105, 132, 152
al-Wartalani, Fudayl, 25
al-Wazir family, 21–22, 26, 29
'Abdallah, 21, 25–26
'Ali bin 'Abdallah, 20
'Ali bin Ahmad, 21
Zayd bin 'Ali, 95
weapons, *see* arms and military aid
Weir, Shelagh, 52, 167
Western Aden Protectorate, 29
women and women's rights in Yemen, 124, 142, 180, 194

Yahya, Yahya bin Ya'ish, *see Jews of Yemen*
Yarim (town), 4, 14
Yasin, 'Abd al-'Aziz, 123, *see also Muslim Brothers*
Yemen Airways, 201
Yemeni-Saudi Coordination Council, 69
Yemeni Socialist Party (YSP), 97–99, 102–106, 111, 115–134, 144, 153, 172
Yemeni Workers Party (*Hizb al-'Amal al-Yamani*), 76
Yemenite Union (*al-Ittihad al-Yamani*), 38
Youth Revolutionary Council, 199
Young Believers Movement, 157–160, 162–163, 155–157
Young Turk Revolution, 15

Zaranik Revolt, 18
al-Zawahiri, Ayman, 179, *see also* al-Qa'ida
Zayd, Muhammad Hasan, 145
Zaydis and Zaydiyya, 4, 5–10, 6, 13–16, 18, 20–22, 24, 27–28, 37, 39, 42–43, 49, 51, 58, 68, 75–76, 78, 80–81, 94, 113, 132, 154–156, 163, 166–167, 185, 206
Zaydi Immamate, 5, 6, 9, 13–40
al-Zindani, Shaykh 'Abd al-Majid, 94, 111, 123, 131–132, 157, 173
Zinjibar, 30, 84, 146
al-Zubayri, Muhammad Mahmud, 25, 27, 38